CompTIA®
DataSys+
Study Guide

CompTIA® DataSys+ Study Guide
Exam DS0-001

Mike Chapple

Sharif Nijim

Published by John Wiley & Sons, Inc., Hoboken, New Jersey.

Published simultaneously in Canada and the United Kingdom.

ISBNs: 9781394180059 (paperback), 9781394180073 (ePDF), 9781394180066 (ePub)

Library of Congress Control Number: 2023944288

Cover image: © Jeremy Woodhouse/Getty Images
Cover design: Wiley

SKY10055399_091823

To Renee. You inspire me to be a better person. Thank you for your love and friendship over the last 25 years. I love you.
—Mike

To Allison, the love of my life. Thank you for accompanying me on life's adventures, for your curious blend of logic and passion, and for your unwavering energy and support. I'm so excited to spend the rest of my life with you.
—Sharif

Acknowledgments

Books like this involve work from many people, and as authors, we truly appreciate the hard work and dedication that the team at Wiley shows. We would especially like to thank senior acquisitions editor Kenyon Brown. We have worked with Ken on multiple projects and consistently enjoy our work with him.

We also greatly appreciated the editing and production team for the book. First and foremost, we'd like to thank our technical editor, John Paul Mueller. John provided us with invaluable insight as we worked our way through the many challenges inherent in putting out a book covering a brand-new certification. We also benefited greatly from the assistance of Shahla Pirnia, whose careful eye helped keep us on track.

We'd also like to thank the many people who helped us make this project successful, including Kathryn Hogan, PhD, our project manager, who brought great talent to the project, and Magesh Elangovan, our content refinement specialist, who guided us through layouts, formatting, and final cleanup to produce a great book. We would also like to thank the many behind-the-scenes contributors, including the graphics, production, and technical teams who make the book and companion materials into a finished product.

Our agent, Carole Jelen of Waterside Productions, continues to provide us with wonderful opportunities, advice, and assistance throughout our writing careers.

Finally, we would like to thank our families who support us through the late evenings, busy weekends, and long hours that a book like this requires to write, edit, and get to press.

About the Authors

Mike Chapple, PhD, Security+, CySA+, CISSP, is author of the best-selling *CISSP (ISC)² Certified Information Systems Security Professional Official Study Guide* (Sybex, 2021) and the *CISSP (ISC)² Official Practice Tests* (Sybex, 2021). He is an information technology professional with more than 25 years of experience in higher education, the private sector, and government.

Mike currently serves as teaching professor in the IT, Analytics, and Operations Department at the University of Notre Dame's Mendoza College of Business, where he teaches undergraduate and graduate courses on cybersecurity, data management, and business analytics.

Before returning to Notre Dame, Mike served as executive vice president and chief information officer of the Brand Institute, a Miami-based marketing consultancy. Mike also spent four years in the information security research group at the National Security Agency and served as an active-duty intelligence officer in the US Air Force.

Mike has written more than 30 books. He earned both his BS and PhD degrees from Notre Dame in computer science and engineering. Mike also holds an MS in computer science from the University of Idaho and an MBA from Auburn University.

Learn more about Mike and his other certification materials at his website, `CertMike.com`.

Sharif Nijim, MS, is an associate teaching professor of IT, Analytics, and Operations in the Mendoza College of Business at the University of Notre Dame, where he teaches undergraduate and graduate courses in business analytics and information technology.

Prior to Notre Dame, Sharif cofounded and served on the board of a customer data-integration company serving the airline industry. Sharif also spent more than a decade building and optimizing enterprise-class transactional and decision support systems for clients in the energy, healthcare, hospitality, insurance, logistics, manufacturing, real estate, telecommunications, and travel and transportation sectors.

Sharif earned both his BBA and his MS from the University of Notre Dame.

About the Technical Editor

John Mueller is a freelance author and technical editor. He has writing in his blood, having produced 124 books and more than 600 articles to date. The topics range from networking to artificial intelligence and from database management to heads-down programming. Some of his current books include discussions of data science, data security, machine learning, and algorithms. His technical editing skills have helped more than 70 authors refine the content of their manuscripts. John has provided technical editing services to various magazines, performed various kinds of consulting, and written certification exams. Be sure to read John's blog at `http://blog.johnmuellerbooks.com`. You can reach John on the Internet at `John@JohnMuellerBooks.com`. John also has a website at `www.johnmuellerbooks.com`. Be sure to follow John on Amazon at `www.amazon.com/John-Mueller/e/B000AQ77KK`.

About the Technical Editor

[illegible]

Contents at a Glance

Contents

Introduction

If you're preparing to take the CompTIA DataSys+ exam, you'll undoubtedly want to find as much information as you can about data and analytics. The more information you have at your disposal and the more hands-on experience you gain, the better off you'll be when attempting the exam. This study guide was written with that in mind. The goal was to provide enough information to prepare you for the test, but not so much that you'll be overloaded with information that's outside the scope of the exam.

We've included review questions at the end of each chapter to give you a taste of what it's like to take the exam. If you're already working in the data field, we recommend that you check out these questions first to gauge your level of expertise. You can then use the book mainly to fill in the gaps in your current knowledge. This study guide will help you round out your knowledge base before tackling the exam.

If you can answer 90 percent or more of the review questions correctly for a given chapter, you can feel safe moving on to the next chapter. If you're unable to answer that many correctly, reread the chapter and try the questions again. Your score should improve.

Don't just study the questions and answers! The questions on the actual exam will be different from the practice questions included in this book. The exam is designed to test your knowledge of a concept or objective, so use this book to learn the objectives behind the questions.

The DataSys+ Exam

The DataSys+ exam is designed to be a vendor-neutral certification for data systems professionals and those seeking to enter the field. CompTIA recommends this certification for those currently working, or aspiring to work, in data systems and database administration roles.

The exam covers five major domains.

1. Database Fundamentals
2. Database Deployment
3. Database Management and Maintenance
4. Data and Database Security
5. Business Continuity

These five areas include a range of topics, from Structured Query Language (SQL) to scripting and from data security to business continuity, while focusing heavily on scenario-based learning. That's why CompTIA recommends that those attempting the exam have 2–3 years of hands-on work experience, although many individuals pass the exam before moving into their first database administration role.

The DataSys+ exam is conducted in a format that CompTIA calls "performance-based assessment." This means the exam combines standard multiple-choice questions with other, interactive question formats. Your exam may include several types of questions such as multiple-choice, fill-in-the-blank, multiple-response, drag-and-drop, and image-based problems.

The exam costs $358 in the United States, with roughly equivalent prices in other locations around the globe. More details about the DataSys+ exam and how to take it can be found here:

`www.comptia.org/certifications/datasys`

You'll have 90 minutes to take the exam and will be asked to answer up to 90 questions during that time period. Your exam will be scored on a scale ranging from 100 to 900, with a passing score of 700.

You should also know that CompTIA is notorious for including vague questions on all of its exams. You might see a question for which two of the possible four answers are correct—but you can choose only one. Use your knowledge, logic, and intuition to choose the best answer and then move on. Sometimes, the questions are worded in ways that would make English majors cringe—a typo here, an incorrect verb there. Don't let this frustrate you; answer the question and move on to the next one.

CompTIA frequently does what is called *item seeding*, which is the practice of including unscored questions on exams. It does so to gather psychometric data, which is then used when developing new versions of the exam. Before you take the exam, you will be told that your exam may include these unscored questions. So, if you come across a question that does not appear to map to any of the exam objectives—or for that matter, does not appear to belong in the exam—it is likely a seeded question. You never really know whether a question is seeded, however, so always make your best effort to answer every question.

Taking the Exam

Once you are fully prepared to take the exam, you can visit the CompTIA website to purchase your exam voucher.

`https://store.comptia.org/Certification-Vouchers/c/11293`

Currently, CompTIA offers two options for taking the exam: an in-person exam at a testing center and an at-home exam that you take on your own computer.

This book includes a coupon that you may use to save 10 percent on your CompTIA exam registration.

In-Person Exams

CompTIA partners with Pearson VUE's testing centers, so your next step will be to locate a testing center near you. In the United States, you can do this based on your address or your ZIP code, while non-U.S. test takers may find it easier to enter their city and country. You can search for a test center near you at the Pearson Vue website, where you will need to navigate to "Find a test center."

`www.pearsonvue.com/comptia`

Now that you know where you'd like to take the exam, simply set up a Pearson VUE testing account and schedule an exam on their site.

On the day of the test, take two forms of identification, and make sure to show up with plenty of time before the exam starts. Remember that you will not be able to take your notes, electronic devices (including smartphones and watches), or other materials in with you.

Be sure to review the Candidate Identification policy at `www.comptia.org/testing/testing-policies-procedures/test-policies/candidate-id-policy` to learn what types of ID are acceptable.

At-Home Exams

CompTIA began offering online exam proctoring in response to the coronavirus pandemic. As of the time this book went to press, the at-home testing option was still available and appears likely to continue. Candidates using this approach will take the exam at their home or office and be proctored over a webcam by a remote proctor.

Because of the rapidly changing nature of the at-home testing experience, candidates who want to pursue this option should check the CompTIA website for the latest details.

After the Data Systems Exam

Once you have taken the exam, you will be notified of your score immediately, so you'll know if you passed the test right away. You should keep track of your score report with your exam registration records and the email address you used to register for the exam.

What Does This Book Cover?

This book covers everything you need to know to pass the Data Systems exam.

Chapter 1: Today's Data Systems Professional

Chapter 2: Database Fundamentals

Chapter 3: SQL and Scripting

Chapter 4: Database Deployment

Chapter 5: Database Management and Maintenance

Chapter 6: Governance, Security, and Compliance

Chapter 7: Database Security

Chapter 8: Business Continuity

Appendix: Answers to Review Questions

Study Guide Elements

This study guide uses a number of common elements to help you prepare. These include the following:

Summaries The summary section of each chapter briefly explains the chapter, allowing you to easily understand what it covers.

Exam Essentials The exam essentials focus on major exam topics and critical knowledge that you should take into the test. The exam essentials focus on the exam objectives provided by CompTIA.

Chapter Review Questions A set of questions at the end of each chapter will help you assess your knowledge and if you are ready to take the exam based on your knowledge of that chapter's topics.

Interactive Online Learning Environment and Test Bank

The authors have worked hard to create some really great tools to help you with your certification process. The interactive online learning environment that accompanies the CompTIA DataSys+ Study Guide: Exam DS0-001 includes a test bank with study tools to help you prepare for the certification exam—and increase your chances of passing it the first time! The test bank includes the following:

Sample tests All the questions in this book are included online, including the assessment test at the end of this Introduction and the review questions at the end of each chapter. In addition, there is a custom practice exam with 90 questions. Use these questions to assess how you're likely to perform on the real exam. The online test bank runs on multiple devices.

Flashcards The online text bank includes more than 100 flashcards specifically written to hit you hard, so don't get discouraged if you don't ace your way through them at first. They're there to ensure that you're really ready for the exam. And no worries—armed with the review questions, practice exams, and flashcards, you'll be more than prepared when exam day comes. Questions are provided in digital flashcard format (a question followed by a single correct answer). You can use the flashcards to reinforce your learning and provide last-minute test prep before the exam.

Glossary A glossary of key terms from this book is available as a fully searchable PDF.

Go to www.wiley.com/go/sybextestprep to register and gain access to this interactive online learning environment and test bank with study tools.

Like all exams, the DataSys+ certification from CompTIA is updated periodically and may eventually be retired or replaced. At some point after CompTIA is no longer offering this exam, the old editions of our books and online tools will be retired. If you have purchased this book after the exam was retired, or are attempting to register in the Sybex online learning environment after the exam was retired, please know that we make no guarantees that this exam's online Sybex tools will be available once the exam is no longer available.

Exam DS0-001 Exam Objectives

CompTIA goes to great lengths to ensure that its certification programs accurately reflect the IT industry's best practices. They do this by establishing committees for each of its exam programs. Each committee comprises a small group of IT professionals, training providers, and publishers who are responsible for establishing the exam's baseline competency level and who determine the appropriate target-audience level.

Once these factors are determined, CompTIA shares this information with a group of hand-selected subject matter experts (SMEs). These folks are the true brainpower behind the certification program. The SMEs review the committee's findings, refine them, and shape them into the objectives that follow this section. CompTIA calls this process a *job-task analysis (JTA)*.

Finally, CompTIA conducts a survey to ensure that the objectives and weightings truly reflect job requirements. Only then can the SMEs go to work writing the hundreds of questions needed for the exam. Even so, they have to go back to the drawing board for further refinements in many cases before the exam is ready to go live in its final state. Rest assured that the content you're about to learn will serve you long after you take the exam.

CompTIA also publishes relative weightings for each of the exam's objectives. The following table lists the five DataSys+ objective domains and the extent to which they are represented on the exam:

Domain	% of Exam
1.0 Database Fundamentals	24%
2.0 Database Deployment	16%
3.0 Database Management and Maintenance	25%
4.0 Data and Database Security	23%
5.0 Business Continuity	12%

DS0-001 Certification Exam Objective Map

Objective	Chapter
1.0 Database Fundamentals	
1.1 Compare and contrast database structure types	Chapter 2
1.2 Given a scenario, develop, modify, and run SQL code	Chapter 3
1.3 Compare and contrast scripting methods and scripting environments	Chapter 3
1.4 Explain the impact of programming on database operations	Chapter 2
2.0 Database Deployment	
2.1 Compare and contrast aspects of database planning and design	Chapter 4
2.2 Explain database implementation, testing, and deployment phases	Chapter 4
3.0 Database Management and Maintenance	
3.1 Explain the purpose of monitoring and reporting for database management and performance	Chapter 5
3.2 Explain common database maintenance processes	Chapter 5
3.3 Given a scenario, produce documentation and use relevant tools	Chapter 5
3.4 Given a scenario, implement data management tasks	Chapter 5
4.0 Data and Database Security	
4.1 Explain data security concepts	Chapter 6
4.2 Explain the purpose of governance and regulatory compliance	Chapter 6
4.3 Given a scenario, implement policies and best practices related to authentication and authorization	Chapter 6
4.4 Explain the purpose of database infrastructure security	Chapter 7
4.5 Describe types of attacks and their effects on data systems	Chapter 7
5.0 Business Continuity	
5.1 Explain the importance of disaster recovery and relevant techniques	Chapter 8
5.2 Explain backup and restore best practices and processes	Chapter 8

Exam objectives are subject to change at any time without prior notice and at CompTIA's discretion. Please visit CompTIA's website (`www.comptia.org`) for the most current listing of exam objectives.

How to Contact the Publisher

If you believe you've found a mistake in this book, please bring it to our attention. At John Wiley & Sons, we understand how important it is to provide our customers with accurate content, but even with our best efforts an error may occur.

To submit your possible errata, please email it to our Customer Service Team at `wileysupport@wiley.com` with the subject line "Possible Book Errata Submission."

Assessment Test

1. Kathleen, a data systems analyst at a midsize tech company, is monitoring and configuring the alerts for the company's cloud-based database. The company wants to manage storage resources effectively to prevent unexpected interruptions. Kathleen wants to set a primary alert related to storage management based on a management-by-exception strategy. Which primary alert should Kathleen set up?
   - A. An alert when the database size reaches 70 percent of the total storage capacity
   - B. An alert when there's an unusual surge in active users
   - C. An alert when the system encounters a sudden increase in error rates
   - D. An alert when the database read/write ratio significantly deviates from the normal range
2. Paige, a database administrator at a multinational company, needs to change the data type of the postal code attribute in the address table to accommodate Canadian addresses, which contain characters and numbers. Which SQL command should she use to achieve this?
   - A. ALTER TABLE
   - B. DROP TABLE
   - C. CREATE TABLE
   - D. SELECT
3. Raseel, a database administrator at a growing company, is responsible for designing and deploying a new database system. She must consider various assets and factors to ensure optimal performance and scalability while adhering to budget constraints. Which of the following factors should Raseel prioritize when acquiring hardware assets for the new database system?
   - A. Storage, network bandwidth, and decorative server cases
   - B. Processing capacity, memory, storage, and network bandwidth
   - C. Number of database administrators, processing capacity, and storage
   - D. Open-source software, processing capacity, and memory
4. Brian is planning to conduct a disaster recovery test. During the test, he will relocate personnel to the hot site, activate the site, and simulate live operations by processing the same data at the hot site as the organization processes at the primary site. The primary site will be taken offline once the test is underway. What type of test is Brian planning?
   - A. Parallel test
   - B. Structured walk-through
   - C. Full-interruption test
   - D. Simulation test
5. Tanika is a data systems analyst at an e-commerce startup working on a class diagram using UML. Which of the following tools best suits her needs?
   - A. Microsoft Word
   - B. erwin
   - C. Google Sheets
   - D. Lucidchart

6. Beth's organization needs to develop policies and procedures to ensure the quality, security, privacy, and regulatory compliance of their data. She would like to identify the appropriate person to lead their data governance activities and work with stakeholders to establish policies and procedures for specific subject area domains. What role in the company would normally be responsible for developing policies and procedures for their data quality, security, privacy, and regulatory compliance and leading their data governance activities?

   A. Data owner

   B. Organizational data steward

   C. Subject area data steward

   D. Data custodian

7. Hassan is a data systems analyst at a midsize e-commerce company. He notices an increasing number of deadlocks in the company's central transaction processing database, impacting the overall performance. Which steps should Hassan take to prevent deadlocks from occurring frequently?

   A. Start and end transactions explicitly and minimize transaction size.

   B. Increase the number of concurrent connections to the database.

   C. Increase the size of the connection pool.

   D. Increase the time period for reaping and refreshing dead connections.

8. Jenn is a software developer working on a new flight booking application. She needs to interact with a relational database storing flight data but wants to focus on the application's business logic rather than dealing with complex SQL queries. Which technique would best suit Jennifer's requirements?

   A. Object-oriented programming (OOP)

   B. User experience (UX)

   C. SQL execution plan optimization

   D. Object-relational mapping (ORM)

9. Hamid is a data systems analyst at an established financial services company. His primary responsibility is to ensure the database system's optimal performance. After observing a constant slowdown in the database's responsiveness, he uses Oracle Enterprise Manager to identify poorly performing queries. Exploring the execution plan for a frequently executed query that supports order processing activities, Hamid sees that the query is doing a full table scan. Hamid realizes that this is causing a bottleneck and decides to take steps to improve this query's performance. Which of the following actions would be most appropriate for Hamid?

   A. Rewrite the query to use joins instead of subselects.

   B. Change the code to use bind variables.

   C. Increase the number of cached sequence values.

   D. Create an index to cover the query.

10. Caroline is a senior network administrator at a logistics company and is configuring an internal firewall to allow web servers in the perimeter network to connect to a PostgreSQL database in a private network using its default port. Which network port must she open to allow traffic to reach the database?

    A. 1521

    B. 1433

C. 5432

D. 50000

11. Samantha is developing an application prototype and needs to store application data in a relational database. Which of the following is the most cost-effective option?

    A. MariaDB

    B. Oracle Enterprise Edition

    C. IBM Db2 Standard

    D. Cassandra

12. John Paul works for a merchant that frequently handles credit card information. She would like to deploy a security control that can detect the presence of credit card records across a variety of systems. What detection technology would be best-suited for this task?

    A. Watermarking

    B. Pattern matching

    C. Host-based

    D. Network-based

13. Omar is selecting a fire-suppression system for his organization's data center. He would like to use a technology that deploys water only at specific sprinkler heads when a fire is detected. He hopes that this approach will limit the damage in the facility when water is deployed. What type of system would best meet his needs?

    A. Wet pipe sprinkler system

    B. Dry pipe sprinkler system

    C. Pre-action sprinkler system

    D. Deluge sprinkler system

14. Omar is a data systems analyst for a large healthcare organization regulated by the Health Insurance Portability and Accountability Act (HIPAA). The vendor has just released a new patch for the company's database software. The patch is not urgent and addresses minor software defects. Omar is wondering when the best time to apply the patch would be. What should Omar do?

    A. Apply the patch immediately in the production environment without testing.

    B. Ignore the patch since it is not urgent and addresses minor software defects.

    C. Test the patch in a nonproduction environment before scheduling a time to apply it in production.

    D. Apply the patch during peak usage hours to ensure maximum user impact.

15. Sarah is a cybersecurity analyst at an online store. She is tasked with ensuring the security of the store's web applications and database server to prevent SQL injection attacks. Which of the following security measures should Sarah prioritize to protect the web applications and database server against these attacks?

    A. Implement browser-based input validation.

    B. Create an input allow list on the server side.

C. Create an input deny list for all user inputs.

D. Deploy a web application firewall only.

16. Gary is designing a multifactor authentication system to protect a database containing highly sensitive information. The database uses a password authentication approach already. What technology could Gary add to best secure the database?

A. PIN

B. Security questions

C. Fingerprint recognition

D. Passphrase

17. Patrizia, a database developer at a midsize company, is in the planning phase of designing a new database. She wants to ensure that the database will meet the needs of its users and applications. Which stakeholders should Patrizia consult to gain insights into business trends and patterns using advanced analytics and predictive models?

A. Executive management

B. Data scientists

C. System administrators

D. Customers

18. The backup administrator configures a system to perform full backups on Sundays at 1 a.m. and incremental backups on Mondays through Saturdays at 1 a.m. The system fails on Wednesday at 4 p.m. What backups must be applied?

A. Sunday only

B. Sunday and Wednesday only

C. Sunday, Monday, and Wednesday only

D. Sunday, Monday, Tuesday, and Wednesday

19. Fayez manages a team of Java developers and wants an object-relational mapping (ORM) tool to insulate his developers from writing database-specific code. What is his best option?

A. Hibernate

B. ActiveRecord

C. RedBean

D. Django

20. Zara is a database administrator at a large corporation. She wants to automate monitoring and maintenance activities on her company's database to improve operational consistency and save time for higher-value tasks. Which type of script would be most suitable for Zara's use case?

A. Client-side script

B. ETL

C. ELT

D. Server-side script

Answers to Assessment Test

1. A. While all of these alerts are relevant to managing a database, this question asks specifically about storage resources, making a surge in active users, an increase in error rates, or a different read/write ratio incorrect. Since database size correlates to storage use, configuring a size-based alert is the best approach, as described in option A.

2. A. CREATE TABLE creates a new table, DROP TABLE permanently removes a table, and SELECT retrieves data from a table. Paige should use the ALTER TABLE command to modify the data type of an existing column in the address table.

3. B. Decorative server cases are irrelevant to the database system's performance, scalability, or reliability. The number of database administrators is not directly related to hardware acquisition. Open-source software is not a hardware asset. The most appropriate choice is to prioritize processing capacity, memory, storage, and network bandwidth when acquiring hardware assets.

4. C. Full-interruption tests activate the alternate processing facility and take the primary site offline. Parallel tests also activate the alternate facility but keep operational responsibility at the primary site. Structured walk-throughs and simulation tests do not activate the alternate site.

5. D. As a diagramming tool that supports UML, Lucidchart is Tanika's best option. erwin is a data modeling tool, Microsoft Word is a word processor, and Google Sheets is for maintaining spreadsheets.

6. B. The organizational data steward is responsible for developing policies and procedures for an organization's data quality, security, privacy, and regulatory compliance. While data owners work with data stewards to establish policies and procedures for their data domain, they are not responsible for developing policies and procedures for an organization's data quality, security, privacy, and regulatory compliance. Subject area data steward is incorrect because while they work on behalf of their data owner to handle daily tasks and are delegated governance activities, their role is specific to their subject area and not responsible for developing policies and procedures for an organization's data quality, security, privacy, and regulatory compliance. Data custodian is incorrect because their role is to implement technical controls that execute data governance policies, such as configuring applications, dashboards, and databases. While important, they are not responsible for developing policies and procedures for an organization's data quality, security, privacy, and regulatory compliance.

7. A. Deadlocks happen when two or more transactions lock a resource the other needs and block each other indefinitely. Starting and ending transactions explicitly and minimizing transaction size are two ways to prevent deadlocks from happening. Since this likely requires code changes, Hassan needs to include developers in this approach. Increasing the size of the connection pool, the time for reaping and refreshing dead connections, or the limit of concurrent connections are ways to address how clients connect to the database and don't directly impact deadlocks.

8. D. Object-oriented programming (OOP) makes software more modular, reusable, and scalable. User experience (UX) design focuses on improving a system's ease of use, efficiency, and usefulness. SQL execution plan optimization refers to understanding and optimizing query performance by examining database engine steps to execute a SQL query. Object-relational mapping (ORM) presents relational data as objects in an object-oriented programming language, allowing developers to work with OOP languages like Java, Python, and C++ without writing the underlying database queries.

9. D. Creating an index is the best option, as full table scans suggest an index does not cover the query. Rewriting the query to use joins instead of subselects is appropriate if the execution plan shows that the query used subselects inefficiently. Changing the code to use bind variables is appropriate if the optimizer needs to parse the query for each execution. Increasing the number of cached sequence values does not impact full table scans.

10. C. The default port for Oracle is 1521, the default for Microsoft SQL Server is 1433, and the default for IBM Db2 is 50000. 5432 is the default port for PostgreSQL.

11. A. You have to pay for both Oracle Enterprise Edition and IBM Db2 Standard. While Cassandra is open-source, it is not a relational database. This makes MariaDB the optimal choice.

12. B. John Paul should select a pattern recognition system because that technology can easily recognize the presence of data with regular patterns, such as credit card numbers. Watermarking technology would require that the organization mark every record that contains credit card data and would be difficult to use in this scenario. The choice of host-based and/or network-based monitoring depends more on where the data exists than what type of data is used. He would likely use a combination of both host-based and network-based DLP but deploy pattern recognition technology on those platforms.

13. C. An appropriate fire suppression system for Omar's needs is a pre-action sprinkler system. This system requires two independent events before water is released, providing an additional layer of protection against accidental water discharge. The first event is the detection of smoke or heat, which opens a valve that fills the pipes with water. The second event occurs when a fire is detected by a separate fire detection system, which opens the sprinkler heads in the affected area to release the water. This approach reduces the risk of water damage caused by accidental sprinkler discharge or leaks. A wet pipe sprinkler system has water constantly in the pipes, which means water will flow from all activated sprinkler heads, potentially causing damage to areas that are not affected by the fire. A dry pipe sprinkler system is similar to a wet pipe system, but with air in the pipes until a fire activates the system. A deluge sprinkler system is designed for high hazard areas, where a large volume of water is needed quickly to suppress fires, and is not suitable for most data center environments.

14. C. Testing the patch in a nonproduction environment is the best option. Even though the patch addresses minor defects and isn't time-sensitive, it's still essential to ensure the patch doesn't interfere with the database configuration or client applications before applying it to the production environment. Ignoring the patch could lead to support issues and is not a good choice. Applying the patch in production without testing it first is similarly unwise, as the impact of the patch is unknown.

15. B. Creating an input allow list on the server side is the most effective measure to prevent SQL injection attacks, as it specifies the exact type of input expected from users and ensures only valid and safe input is accepted. Deploying a web application firewall only, while providing an additional layer of defense, should not be the sole security measure, as input validation remains the primary defense against injection attacks. Creating an input deny list for all user inputs, or input blacklisting, is less effective than input whitelisting, since attackers may still bypass the blacklist. Implementing browser-based input validation should not be relied upon as a security control, as attackers can easily bypass it.

16. C. The system already uses a password, which is a "something you know" factor. Therefore, Gary should add either a "something you have" or "something you are" factor. Fingerprint recognition is a "something you are" (or biometric) authentication factor and would constitute multifactor authenticaiton when combined with a password. The answers to security questions, personal identification numbers (PINs), and passphrases are all "something you know" factors and would not create multifactor authentication when combined with a password.

17. B. Executive management is an important stakeholder group that uses data from the database to track operational performance metrics and inform strategic decisions. However, they typically rely on reporting tools and do not perform advanced analytics and predictive modeling directly.

    System administrators operate the virtual or physical servers where the database runs, handling tasks such as server sizing and disk-space allocation. While they play a crucial role in the database infrastructure, they do not directly analyze the data or work on predictive models.

    Customers typically interact with the database indirectly, using an application to submit orders or retrieve information. They are essential end users of the database but do not perform advanced analytics or develop predictive models.

    Data scientists are essential stakeholders to consult during the planning phase of database design, as they use the database to perform advanced analytics, develop predictive models, and gain insights into business trends and patterns. Their input can help shape the database structure to support their analytical work.

18. D. With incremental backups, you must first restore the most recent full backup and then apply all incremental backups that occurred since that full backup. Therefore, the administrator must restore the backups from Sunday, Monday, Tuesday, and Wednesday.

19. A While all of these are ORM frameworks, Django is for Python, RedBean is for PHP, and ActiveRecord is for Ruby on Rails. Hibernate is an ORM for Java.

20. D. Client-side scripts run on a client machine and are vulnerable to connectivity issues. ETL and ELT scripts move data between databases. Server-side scripts run on the database server and are ideal for administrative tasks.

Today's Data Systems Professional

Data drives the modern business. Virtually every organization collects large quantities of data about its customers, products, employees, and service offerings. Managers naturally seek to analyze that data and harness the information it contains to improve the efficiency, effectiveness, and profitability of their work.

Data systems provide the ability to store, process, and analyze that data in an efficient and effective manner. Teams of dedicated data systems professionals design and manage these systems to improve their organization's ability to compete in today's marketplace. They are able to select appropriate data tools to deploy, manage, and maintain databases. They also understand the importance of maintaining the security of data and databases, as well as the essential nature of ensuring that business continuity programs protect data from loss. These skills allow them to better serve their colleagues throughout the business.

Data Drives the Modern Business

We are fortunate to live in the golden age of analytics. Businesses around the world recognize the vital nature of data to their work and are investing heavily in analytics programs designed to give them a competitive advantage. Organizations have been collecting this data for years, and many of the statistical tools and techniques used in analytics work date back decades. But if that's the case, why are we just now in the early years of this golden age? Figure 1.1 shows the three major pillars that have come together at this moment to allow analytics programs to thrive: data, storage, and computing power.

FIGURE 1.1 Analytics is made possible by modern data, storage, and computing capabilities.

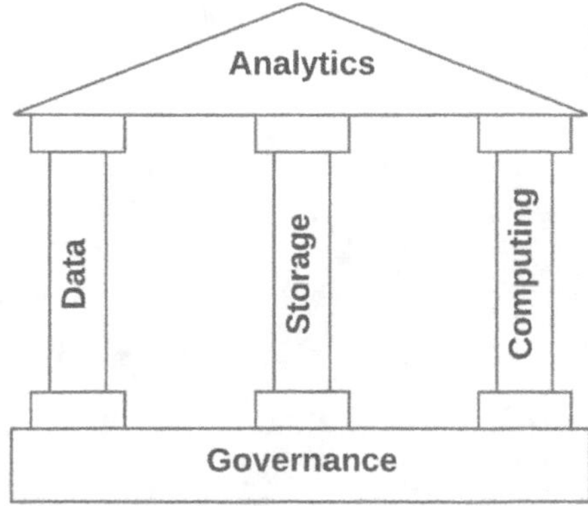

Data

The amount of data the modern world generates on a daily basis is staggering. From the organized tables of spreadsheets to the storage of photos, video, and audio recordings, modern businesses create an almost overwhelming avalanche of data that is ripe for use in analytics programs.

Let's try to quantify the amount of data that exists in the world. We'll begin with an estimate made by Google's then-CEO Eric Schmidt in 2010. At a technology conference, Schmidt estimated that the sum total of all of the stored knowledge created by the world at that point in time was approximately 5 exabytes. To give that a little perspective, the file containing the text of this chapter is around 100 kilobytes. So, Schmidt's estimate is that the world in 2010 had total knowledge that is about the size of 50,000,000,000,000 (that's 50 trillion!) copies of this book chapter. That's a staggering number, but it's only the beginning of our journey.

Now fast-forward just two years to 2012. In that year, researchers estimated that the total amount of stored data in the world had grown to 1,000 exabytes (or one zettabyte). Remember, Schmidt's estimate of 5 exabytes was made only two years earlier. In just two years, the total amount of stored data in the world grew by a factor of 200! But we're still not finished!

In the year 2022, IDC estimates that the world created 94 zettabytes (or 94,000 exabytes) of new information. Compare that to Schmidt's estimate of the world having a total of 5 exabytes of stored information in 2010. If you do the math, you'll discover that on any given day in the modern era, the world generates an amount of brand-new data that is approximately 32 times the sum total of all information created from the dawn of civilization until 2010! Now, *that* is a staggering amount of data!

From an analytics perspective, this trove of data is a gold mine of untapped potential.

Storage

The second key trend driving the growth of analytics programs is the increased availability of storage at rapidly decreasing costs. Table 1.1 shows the cost of storing a gigabyte of data in different years using magnetic hard drives.

TABLE 1.1 Gigabyte Storage Costs over Time

Year	Cost per GB
1985	$169,900
1990	$53,940
1995	$799
2000	$17.50
2005	$0.62

TABLE 1.1 Gigabyte Storage Costs over Time *(continued)*

Year	Cost per GB
2010	$0.19
2015	$0.03
2020	$0.01

Figure 1.2 shows the same data plotted as a line graph on a logarithmic scale. This visualization clearly demonstrates that storage costs have plummeted to the point where storage is almost free, and businesses can afford to retain data for analysis in ways that they never have before.

FIGURE 1.2 Storage costs have decreased over time.

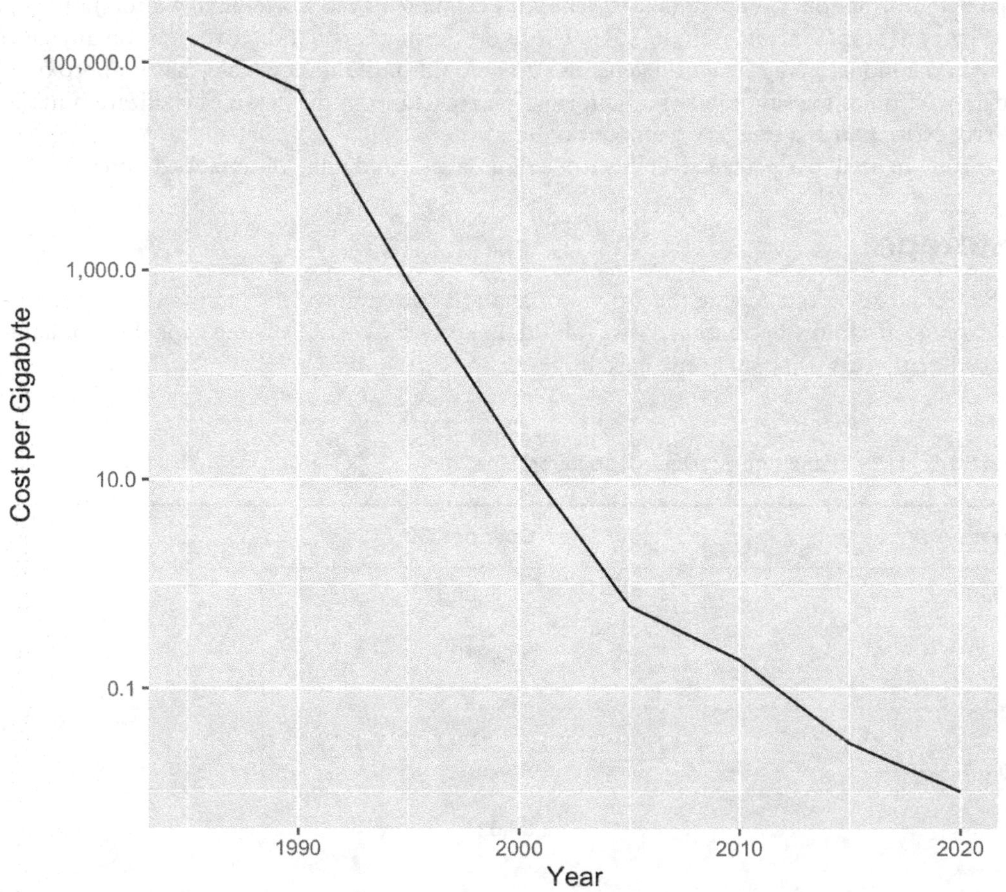

Computing Power

In 1975, Gordon Moore, one of the cofounders of Intel Corporation, made a prediction that computing technology would continue to advance so quickly that manufacturers would be able to double the number of components placed on an integrated circuit every two years.

Commonly referred to as *Moore's law*, this prediction is often loosely interpreted to mean that we will double the amount of computing power on a single device every two years. That trend has benefited many different technology-enabled fields, among them the world of analytics.

In the early days of analytics, computing power was costly and difficult to come by. Organizations with advanced analytics needs purchased massive supercomputers to analyze their data, but those supercomputers were scarce. Analysts fortunate enough to work in an organization that possessed a supercomputer had to justify their requests for small slices of time when they could use the powerful machines.

Today, the effects of Moore's law have democratized computing. Most employees in an organization now have enough computing power sitting on their desks to perform a wide variety of analytic tasks. If they require more powerful computing resources, cloud services allow them to rent massive banks of computers at very low cost. Even better, those resources are charged at hourly rates and analysts pay only for the computing time they actually use.

These three trends—the massive volume of data generated by our businesses on a daily basis, the availability of inexpensive storage to retain that data, and the cloud's promise of virtually infinite computing power—come together to create fertile ground for data analytics.

Data Systems

Let's begin our exploration of data systems by looking at the material covered by each one of the domains on the CompTIA DataSys+ Exam. CompTIA organizes the exam content into five domains, and we have organized this book to follow those domains as well. The five domains and their weights on the exam are as follows:

- Database Fundamentals (24%)
- Database Deployment (16%)
- Database Management and Maintenance (25%)
- Data and Database Security (23%)
- Business Continuity (12%)

You'll find the material for each domain in either one or two chapters of the book. Those chapters are in order, so you will find, for example, complete coverage of the first domain in Chapters 2 and 3, followed by coverage of the second domain in Chapter 4.

The remainder of this chapter will summarize the information covered by each one of these domains and point you to where you will find full coverage.

Database Fundamentals

Databases are the most common way that organizations store their data. *Relational databases* organize data into tables of related information and then maintain relationships between those tables to preserve data integrity. These relational databases are the primary systems used by most organizations to store data, but *nonrelational databases* are growing in popularity. These databases, also called *NoSQL* databases, move beyond the relational model and store data in other formats, such as key-value stores and graphs.

In Chapter 2, "Database Fundamentals," you'll learn how data systems professionals work with databases. That chapter covers two of the major objectives found on the CompTIA DataSys+ Exam.

- 1.1 Compare and Contrast Database Structure Types.
- 1.4 Explain the Impact of Programming on Database Operations.

Chapter 3, "SQL and Scripting," explores the major tools that data systems professionals use to interact with databases. The primary tool is the *Structured Query Language (SQL)*, which provides a way to issue commands to relational databases. SQL includes two major sublanguages: the *Data Definition Language (DDL)* and the *Data Manipulation Language (DML)*. Data systems professionals use DDL to define and alter the structure of databases and then use DML to insert, update, delete, and retrieve data from databases. Figure 1.3 shows an example of a SQL command being executed against a Microsoft SQL Server database using the Azure Data Studio tool. The top portion of the interface shows the SQL query.

```
SELECT FirstName, LastName
FROM Person.Person
WHERE LastName = 'Smith'
```

The bottom portion of the interface shows the data retrieved from the database in response to that query. If you don't understand this syntax yet, don't worry. You'll learn all about it in Chapter 2!

FIGURE 1.3 SQLQuery

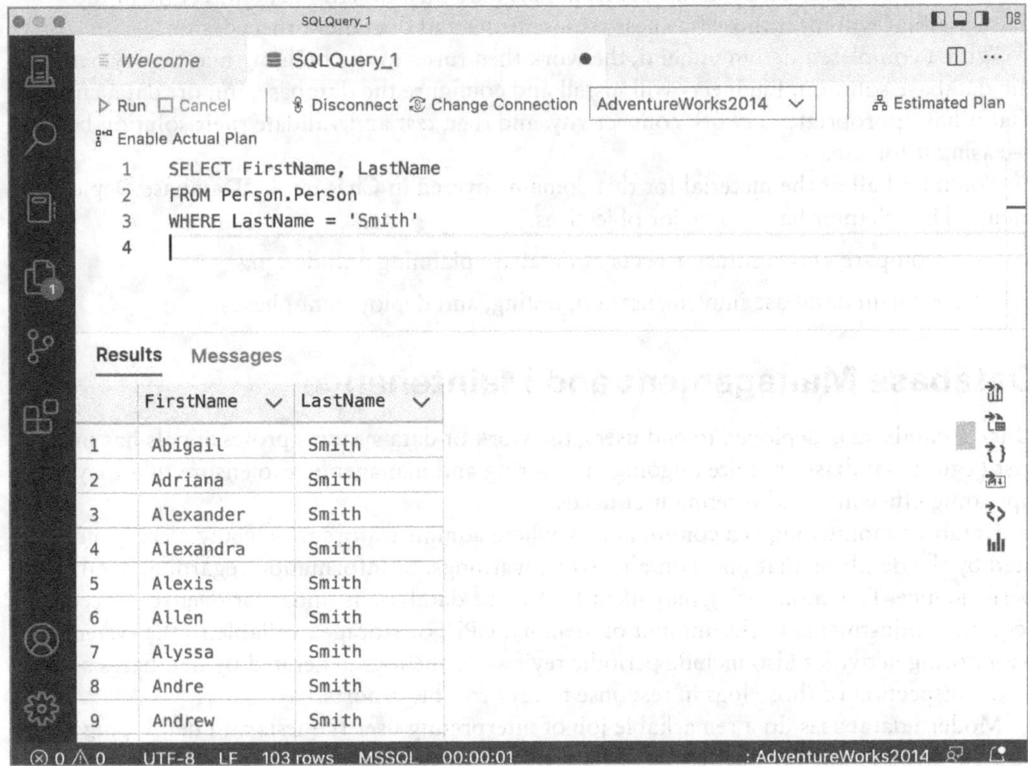

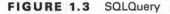

Data systems professionals also use programming and scripting languages to automate their work. You'll learn about the use of PowerShell and Python to create scripts on both Windows and Linux systems. Chapter 3 covers two of the CompTIA DataSys+ Exam objectives.

- 1.2 Given a scenario, develop, modify, and run SQL code.
- 1.3 Compare and contrast scripting methods and scripting environments.

Database Deployment

Data systems professionals must be able to examine a business need, identify the appropriate database tools to use to address that need, and then deploy a solution that fulfills the requirement.

This process begins with requirements gathering, where data professionals collect information from stakeholders to determine the basic parameters of the system. These include details on how many users will access the database, how they will interact with the database, and the type/quantity of storage needed to support the database. With this information in hand, data systems professionals may then design the architecture of the database that will meet those business requirements and document their design.

With a completed design in hand, the work then turns to the building and deployment of the database solution. Engineers will install and configure the database, import data, ensure that it has appropriate network connectivity, and then test and validate their solution before releasing it for use.

You'll find all of the material for this domain covered in Chapter 4, "Database Deployment." That chapter has two major objectives.

- 2.1 Compare and contrast aspects of database planning and design.
- 2.2 Explain database implementation, testing, and deployment phases.

Database Management and Maintenance

Once a database is deployed to end users, the work of data systems professionals has only just begun! Databases require ongoing monitoring and management to ensure that they are operating efficiently and meeting user needs.

Database monitoring is a continual task where administrators review any alerts generated by the database that may contain errors, warnings, or information regarding database performance. This monitoring may identify that the database is under- or over-resourced, requiring adjustments to the amount of memory, CPU, or storage available to the system. Monitoring activities also include periodic reviews of the logs generated by databases as well as the inspection of those logs in response to user trouble reports.

Modern databases do a remarkable job of interpreting user requests and developing efficient ways to answer queries, but data systems professionals have a set of tools at their disposal to improve database performance based upon user needs. For example, the use of *indexes* can dramatically speed up common user queries. Data professionals will also find themselves creating documentation for the database and performing data management tasks to ensure that the database remains useful to the organization.

You'll find all of the material for this domain covered in Chapter 5, "Database Management and Maintenance." That chapter has four major objectives.

- 3.1 Explain the purpose of monitoring and reporting for database management and performance.
- 3.2 Explain common database maintenance processes.
- 3.3 Given a scenario, produce documentation and use relevant tools.
- 3.4 Given a scenario, implement data management tasks.

Data and Database Security

Databases contain extremely sensitive information, including Social Security numbers, credit card numbers, and other personal information. Data systems professionals must be fluent in data security issues to protect their organizations against threats that might disrupt the confidentiality, integrity, or availability of that data.

Fortunately, there are many technical and administrative tools that we can use to protect our data. These include the use of *encryption* and *data masking* to obscure the meaning of sensitive data and secure data destruction techniques to remove data that is no longer needed. Data professionals must be familiar with these techniques and the implementation of auditing practices to ensure that they are properly followed.

Data professionals also play an important role in ensuring that organizations remain compliant with laws and regulations governing the use of personal information. These include the safeguarding of *personally identifiable information (PII)*, *protected health information (PHI)*, and *payment card information (PCI)*.

Chapter 6, "Governance, Security, and Compliance," introduces you to the important security concepts that data systems professionals must understand. It covers three of the objectives from the CompTIA DataSys+ Exam.

- 4.1 Explain data security concepts.
- 4.2 Explain the purpose of governance and regulatory compliance.
- 4.3 Given a scenario, implement policies and best practices related to authentication and authorization.

In addition to understanding the general security concepts described in Chapter 6, data systems professionals must understand the use of specific technologies to protect the data stored in databases. This includes configuring identity and access management systems to ensure appropriate authentication and authorization of user activities. Databases must be protected with logical security controls, including firewalls, perimeter protection, and port security controls. This domain also includes implementing physical security controls, such as surveillance, biometric authentication, fire suppression, and cooling systems.

Finally, data systems professionals must understand the threats posed to their systems by potential attackers in order to better defend against those attacks. This includes understanding SQL injection attacks, denial-of-service (DoS) attacks, on-path attacks, brute-force attacks, phishing attacks, and malware.

Chapter 7, "Database Security," dives into these specifics of securing databases. It covers two of the exam objectives:

- 4.4 Explain the purpose of database infrastructure security.
- 4.5 Describe types of attacks and their effects on data systems.

Business Continuity

Business continuity efforts are a collection of activities designed to keep a business running in the face of adversity. This may come in the form of a small-scale incident, such as a single system failure, or a catastrophic incident, such as an earthquake or a tornado. Business continuity plans may also be activated by human-made disasters, such as a terrorist attack or hacker intrusion.

Disaster recovery is a subset of business continuity activities designed to restore a business to normal operations as quickly as possible following a disruption. The disaster recovery plan may include immediate measures that get operations working again temporarily, but the disaster recovery effort is not finished until the organization is completely back to normal.

Data systems professionals must understand the role of business continuity and disaster recovery plans as well as the technical mechanisms used to achieve these goals in database systems. These include the use of database backups, database replication, and high availability controls to protect database systems.

You'll find all of the material for this domain covered in Chapter 8, "Business Continuity." That chapter has two objectives:

- 5.1 Explain the importance of disaster recovery and relevant techniques.
- 5.2 Explain backup and restore best practices and processes.

Careers in Data Systems

As businesses try to keep up with these trends, hiring managers find themselves struggling to identify, recruit, and retain talented data systems professionals. This presents a supply-and-demand situation that is problematic for businesses but excellent news for job candidates seeking to break into the field.

In a 2023 survey of business leaders, analysts at Gartner found that 84 percent believe that analytics is crucial to achieving their organizational goals. An earlier study from MicroStrategy found that 65 percent of firms planned to increase their analytics investment in the coming year. This will inevitably lead to increased demand for hiring data professionals, a fact that was confirmed by the World Economic Forum in their 2020 Future of Jobs Report. That study listed 10 occupations with the highest demand for professionals. The results, shown in Table 1.2, found that data analysts and data scientists are the most in-demand of any career field, closely followed by several other analytics-related fields.

TABLE 1.2 Highest-Demand Occupations

Rank	Occupation
1	Data analysts and scientists
2	AI and machine learning (ML) specialists
3	Big Data specialists
4	Digital marketing and strategy specialists
5	Process automation specialists

Rank	Occupation
6	Business development professionals
7	Digital transformation specialists
8	Information security analyst
9	Software and applications developers
10	Internet of Things (IoT) specialists

The future is bright. There's no reason to anticipate a reduction in this demand any time soon. It's the right time to enter the exciting field of data systems!

Summary

Analytics programs allow businesses to access the untapped value locked within their data. Today, many organizations recognize the potential value of this work but are still in the early stages of developing their analytics programs. These programs, driven by the unprecedented availability of data, the rapidly decreasing cost of storage, and the maturation of cloud computing, promise to create significant opportunities for businesses and, in turn, for data professionals skilled in the tools and techniques of data systems.

Data systems professionals perform a variety of important tasks within their organizations. These include the design and deployment of new database systems and the ongoing monitoring and management of deployed databases. They must also understand and support their organizations' security and business continuity programs to protect the sensitive and critical information stored within databases.

Database Fundamentals

THE COMPTIA DATASYS+ EXAM TOPICS COVERED IN THIS CHAPTER INCLUDE:

✓ **Domain 1.0: Database Fundamentals**

- 1.1. Compare and Contrast Database Structure Types
- 1.4. Explain the Impact of Programming on Database Operations

Databases are the core technology for storing much of the data we use in our work and personal lives. Whether or not people are aware of it, most people interact with a database daily. At work, you use a database to record sales, manage inventory, process payroll, manage employee performance, and track customer loyalty. At home, you use a database when you check your bank balance or credit card activity, record your latest workout on your favorite fitness tracking application, or create an online photo album. As a data systems analyst, you will help choose a database platform based on an organization's needs.

In the first part of this chapter, you will learn about the different types of databases. Just as organizations and individuals have unique data storage needs, there are different types of databases to choose from that best accommodate these diverse needs. You will explore use cases that lend themselves to choosing a specific kind of database. Once you are familiar with database types and how they differ, the second part of this chapter will explore some particular tools that represent the different types of databases.

Types of Databases

Modern organizations employ various databases to store, manage, and interact with data. An organization's business requirements, availability of a knowledgeable workforce, and ability to integrate with the rest of an organization's technological ecosystem are all factors that influence database selection. There are two broad categories of database engines that an organization can choose from: relational and nonrelational. Let's explore these two types in greater detail.

The Relational Model

Like any piece of software, a database runs on a physical computer. People began using databases in the 1960s when computers and data storage systems were large and expensive. Partially influenced by the hardware constraints of his day, noted computer scientist Edgar F. Codd published a paper called "A Relational Model of Data for Large Shared Data Banks" in 1970. In that paper, Codd describes the *relational model*. The relational model is an approach for structuring and organizing data.

One core concept from Codd's paper is that relations provide the structure for storing data. A *relation*, also known as an *entity* or *table*, is a structure containing a collection of attributes about a data subject. Tables typically store information about people, places, or things. For example, an airline needs a customer table to maintain customer data.

An *attribute* is an individual characteristic of a table. Building on the idea of storing customer information, sample attributes include title, first name, middle name, last name, and date of birth. Consider Figure 2.1, which illustrates a Customer table with these attributes.

FIGURE 2.1 Sample Customer table

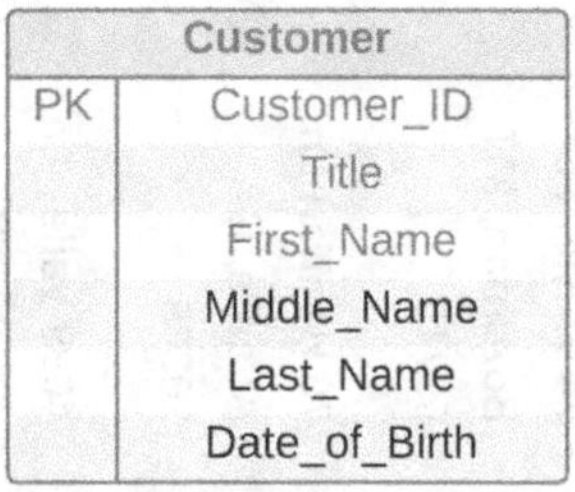

Customer	
PK	Customer_ID
	Title
	First_Name
	Middle_Name
	Last_Name
	Date_of_Birth

Another core concept from Codd's paper is that relations contain tuples. A *tuple*, or *row*, contains specific pieces of data about a single data subject. Each row needs to have an attribute that uniquely identifies the row. This unique identifier is called a *primary key*. A sequential number is frequently used for primary key values, as the purpose of a primary key is to identify individual rows. In Table 2.1, the first row of data has a primary key of 1, with the remaining columns describing a particular customer, Connor Sampson. It is vital to note that data must be consistent in each column to conform with the table's design. For example, the *First_Name* column in Table 2.1 stores first names. Trying to put a date of birth in the *First_Name* column violates this design.

TABLE 2.1 Customer Data

Customer_ID	First_Name	Middle_Name	Last_Name	Date_of_Birth
1	Connor	Andrew	Sampson	March 2, 2001
2	Laurel	Elizabeth	Neuhoff	April 16, 2005
3	Jagadish	Simha	Venkatesan	May 13, 2008

The concept of structuring data in this manner should feel familiar if you've ever worked with a spreadsheet where columns have names and contain consistent values. The relational model extends this spreadsheet-style organizational model by incorporating relationships between tables. For example, it is common for working professionals to have both a work address and a home address. Table 2.2 illustrates what it looks like to append these columns to the customer table.

TABLE 2.2 Customer and Address Data

Customer_ID	First_Name	Middle_Name	Last_Name	Date_of_Birth	Work_Address	Home_Address
1	Connor	Andrew	Sampson	March 2, 2001	24 W Main St Bozeman, MT 59715	213 Masonic Dr Bozeman, MT 59715
2	Laurel	Elizabeth	Neuhoff	April 16, 2005	79 Hanifan Ln Atlanta, GA 30308	3602 Ferry St Atlanta, GA 30308
3	Jagadish	Simha	Venkatesan	May 13, 2008	4098 Valley Ln Austin, TX 78758	2374 Bubby Dr Unit 401 Austin, TX 78758

Looking at the data within the *Work_Address* and *Home_Address* columns in Table 2.2, the value of each column entry is complex. The concept of an address contains multiple attributes, including street name, city, state, and ZIP code. The structure in Table 2.2 makes data manipulation difficult. For example, suppose you want to retrieve all addresses within a specific ZIP code. You must search through each entry in the *Work_Address* and *Home_Address* columns and isolate the ZIP code.

You can break the address data into a separate table to facilitate data manipulation. While Figure 2.1 illustrates attributes associated with people, Figure 2.2 shows a table design for storing address information.

FIGURE 2.2 Sample Address table

	Address
PK	Address_ID
	Street_Line_1
	Street_Line_2
	City
	State
	Zip_Code
	Address_Type

Table 2.3 illustrates what the address data from Table 2.2 looks like when using the Address table pictured in Figure 2.2. Note that the values for *Address_ID*, the table's primary key, are arbitrary. The *Address_ID* column could contain any value as long as it is unique per row.

TABLE 2.3 Address Data

Address_ID	Street_Line_1	Street_Line_2	City	State	Zip_Code	Address_Type
100	24 W Main St		Bozeman	MT	59715	Work
101	213 Masonic Dr		Bozeman	MT	59715	Home
102	79 Hanifan Ln		Atlanta	GA	30308	Work
103	3602 Ferry St		Atlanta	GA	30308	Home
104	4098 Valley Ln		Austin	TX	78758	Work
105	2374 Bubby Dr	Unit 401	Austin	TX	78758	Home

The beauty of the relational model comes from connecting tables that contain related information. Table 2.2 has customer information, including addresses. Table 2.3 fixes the structural issue of storing address information in a single column. However, looking at the data in Table 2.1 and Table 2.3, there is no way to associate a specific customer and their addresses.

A *foreign key* creates a link between two tables by adding an attribute to one table that references the primary key of another table. In Figure 2.3, adding the *Customer_ID* attribute to the Address table associates a specific address to a particular customer. Figure 2.3 is technically an *entity-relationship diagram (ERD)*, as it illustrates the relationship between the Customer and Address tables. You will learn more about ERDs in Chapter 5, "Database Management and Maintenance."

FIGURE 2.3 Customer and Address tables

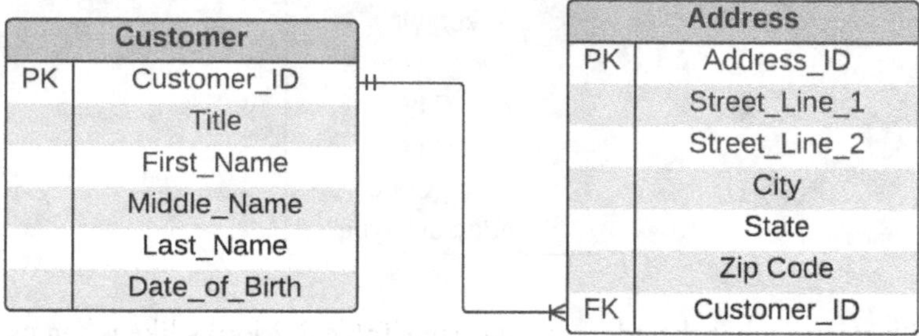

Suppose you are working with the data from Table 2.1 and need to retrieve the address information for Laurel Neuhoff. You first need the value for Laurel's primary key from Table 2.1. Once you have the primary key, you can look for matches in the *Customer_ID* column in Table 2.4, where the *Customer_ID* column is a foreign key referring to the *Customer_ID* column in Table 2.1.

Relational Databases

Based on the relational model from Codd's paper, a *relational database* organizes and stores data. A *relational database management system (RDBMS)* is a complex piece of software that lets people create, maintain, and operate relational databases. In 1979, *Oracle* became the first commercially available RDBMS. Oracle remains one of the most popular database platforms to this day. In 1983, International Business Machines (IBM) launched a relational database called DB2, rebranded as Db2 in 2017.

The 1980s and 1990s saw continued growth in the number of available RDBMS platforms. Additional proprietary offerings, including *Microsoft SQL Server*, *Informix*, and *Teradata*, became available. The open-source community created database platforms such as *PostgreSQL* and *MariaDB*.

TABLE 2.4 Address Data with Foreign Key

Address_ID	Street_Line_1	Street_Line_2	City	State	Zip_Code	Address_Type	Customer_ID
100	24 W Main St		Bozeman	MT	59715	Work	1
101	213 Masonic Dr		Bozeman	MT	59715	Home	1
102	79 Hanifan Ln		Atlanta	GA	30308	Work	2
103	3602 Ferry St		Atlanta	GA	30308	Home	2
104	4098 Valley Ln		Austin	TX	78758	Work	3
105	2374 Bubby Dr	Unit 401	Austin	TX	78758	Home	3

The nature of computing shifted dramatically with the rise of cloud computing in the 2010s. Cloud computing providers like *Amazon Web Services (AWS)*, *Google Cloud Platform (GCP)*, and *Microsoft Azure (Azure)* have their own relational database offerings. *Aurora* is AWS's primary relational database offering, GCP offers Google *BigQuery*, and Azure has *Azure SQL Database*. *Relational Database Service (RDS)* is another managed relational database offering from AWS that lets you run alternative relational database engines beyond *Aurora*, including *MariaDB*, *PostgreSQL*, *Oracle*, and *Microsoft SQL Server*. As cloud providers, Google and Microsoft have similar offerings that let you choose an open-source database, leaving the administration of the database platform to the cloud provider.

Today, there are many relational database management systems from which to choose. Selecting a platform depends on many considerations, including the complexity of your requirements, your technical ecosystem, and the human and capital resources you devote to maintenance and operational tasks. There are many considerations when selecting a relational database management system, including licensing model, scaling, and storage and hosting needs. Let's explore each criterion in greater detail.

Licensing Model

One of the first considerations facing an organization is whether it is worth paying a licensing fee to use a relational database. Oracle, Db2, and SQL Server are all capable RDBMS platforms supported by established companies. The companies that provide these database platforms have teams of people who fix software defects, improve performance, and add features to enhance the platform's capabilities. These companies also have dedicated organizations to support you if you need platform help. Providing these services is expensive, and you need to pay license fees if you want to use these platforms.

There are open-source database platforms alternatives if an organization wants to avoid expensive licensing fees. The most popular open-source platforms include PostgreSQL and MariaDB. Anyone with an Internet connection can freely download and install either of these databases. Keep in mind that if you select an open-source database, there is no formal support structure. Instead, you will have to rely on the community for bug fixes and feature enhancements. If being entirely responsible for database operations is troubling, rest assured that some companies offer support and hosting options for open-source database platforms.

Open-core is similar to open-source in that the core database technology remains freely available for people to use. MySQL is a popular open-core database that Oracle owns. While Oracle offers the Community Edition of MySQL for free, other versions are available for purchase, including a Standard, Enterprise, and Cluster Carrier Grade Edition. The paid versions of MySQL offer advanced scaling, backup, and monitoring capabilities.

Scale

Another consideration is your expected operational scaling requirements. Suppose you have relatively simple needs and use the Microsoft productivity ecosystem, which includes Microsoft Windows and Microsoft 365 (Microsoft Office). Microsoft Access (Access) is an approachable starter database that integrates nicely with the rest of the Microsoft ecosystem.

However, Microsoft Access has limitations that exclude it from consideration for larger organizations. For example, Access was initially designed to support one person at a time.

As a legacy of that original design, database performance starts to degrade when more than one person uses an Access database simultaneously. Another limitation is that Access stores all of its data in a single file, with a size limit of 2 gigabytes (GB). While these limits may be sufficient for individual use, they are not suitable for tasks like keeping track of the location of each package sent by a logistics company such as FedEx, UPS, or DHL.

Suppose you operate a database that supports a hotel. Hotels have a fixed number of rooms, so the number of possible reservations for any given date has a known limit. A reservation can come from the hotel's branded website or online travel shopping sites. Regardless of where a reservation comes from, the maximum number of daily reservations is known. The database would not need to scale beyond this maximum unless the hotel added rooms or opened another property in a different location. With known scaling targets, you can choose from open-source and proprietary RDBMS options.

For example, Microsoft SQL Server is available if you want to stay within the Microsoft technology ecosystem. As a product, SQL Server is designed to support more than 32,000 concurrent connections and can handle databases that exceed one petabyte (PB) of data. If your technology stack uses an operating system other than Microsoft Windows, platforms including PostgreSQL, Oracle, Db2, and Teradata support thousands of concurrent connections and petabyte-scale databases.

Hosting

Another crucial operational consideration is whether you want to host an RDBMS platform yourself or rely on a platform running in the public cloud. This decision ultimately comes down to the location of other systems that interact with your database and your overall technology strategy.

Suppose you have servers in a data center you own or a colocation facility where you rent space. In that case, you host the database platform yourself. When you host, you are responsible for the installation, maintenance, and operations of the database platform and any databases running on that platform. When hosting, you control when to take patches and when to upgrade the database software version.

It is possible to outsource the operational aspects of an RDBMS platform to a public cloud provider. For example, AWS offers Aurora, an RDBMS that supports open-source database engines, including MySQL and PostgreSQL. You don't have to worry about installing and configuring the database software when using Aurora. With the hosted model, you also avoid concerning yourself with the underlying hardware. The trade-off is that you must use a version of the database platform supported by the cloud provider.

Structured Query Language (SQL)

You may have noticed that the names of more than one relational database platform contain the letters "SQL." SQL stands for Structured Query Language, the programming language that allows you to define tables and other objects within a database. SQL also allows you to manipulate data. You will explore SQL in greater detail in Chapter 3, "SQL and Scripting."

Nonrelational Databases

A nonrelational database is any type that doesn't conform to the predefined tabular structure in relational databases. This approach results in a highly flexible manner of organizing and storing data. However, this unstructured approach means that consuming applications need to know more about the data than in a relational environment.

From a licensing standpoint, there are proprietary, open-source, and open-core nonrelational options. When selecting a nonrelational basis, you must consider the same operational, maintenance, and support considerations as when choosing a relational database.

One of the most significant benefits of a nonrelational database is that, as a category, they are easier to distribute across multiple servers than their relational counterparts. As a result of this design, scaling nonrelational databases is less complicated than scaling a relational database.

Nonrelational databases enjoy similar hosting options as relational databases. If you have the servers and the knowledge, you can operate a nonrelational database. Hosting companies exist that handle operational tasks, and there are proprietary offerings from public cloud vendors, including AWS and GCP.

Since nonrelational databases don't have defined table structures, using SQL isn't possible. As a result, people refer to any nonrelational database as a *NoSQL database*. There is a lack of consensus as to the definition of NoSQL. One perspective defines NoSQL as "non-SQL" since you don't use SQL to interact with a nonrelational database. Another view is that since a NoSQL database can exist adjacent to a relational database, NoSQL stands for "not only SQL." Regardless of how you define it, *key-value*, *document*, *column-oriented*, and *graph* are all examples of NoSQL types of databases.

Key-Value

Of the NoSQL options, a key-value database takes the most simplistic approach to storing data. A key-value database stores data as a collection of keys and their corresponding values. Each key is a unique index pointing to its associated value. Therefore, each key must be globally unique across the entire database. This definition of a key is different from a relational database. In a relational database, a primary key identifies an individual row in a specific table and is not guaranteed to be unique across all tables in the database. With a key-value database, there are no structural limitations to a key's values. A key can be a sequence of numbers, alphanumeric strings, or anything else, as long as it is globally unique.

The value, or data, that keys reference includes text, images, and videos. Figure 2.4 provides an example of an identifying key and its associated value. Since there are no underlying table structures and few data storage limitations, operating a key-value database is much simpler than a relational database. Another potential advantage to a key-value database is the ability to scale to accommodate many simultaneous requests with a minimal performance impact. However, since the values can contain multiple data types, the only way to find a specific record is by using the key.

FIGURE 2.4 Key-value sample data

Key	Value
jkKJF399zjfjkl300qearfj	
b173c84a-1f40-4063	
UPWT24XEEFSWYMc0	

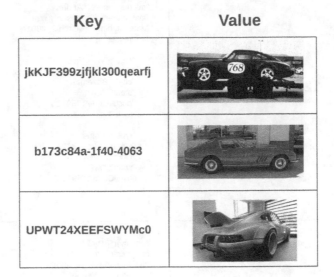

One reason for choosing a key-value database is that you have a lot of data and can search by a key's value. Imagine an online music streaming service that uses a song's name as a key and the corresponding digital audio file as the value. When subscribers want to listen to music, they search for the song's name. With a known key, the application can quickly retrieve and stream the song to the user.

Document

A document database extends the key-value concept by adding restrictions on the stored values. The value in a key value database can contain virtually anything. On the other hand, the value in a document database must conform to a specific structured format. For example, Figure 2.5 shows the data for the first two people from Table 2.2 using JSON as the document format.

FIGURE 2.5 JSON document sample data

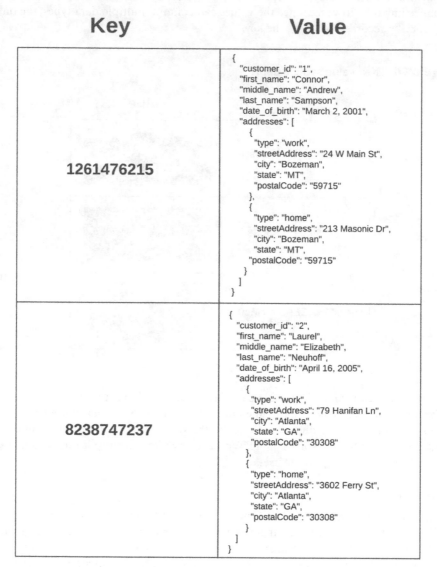

Key	Value
1261476215	{ "customer_id": "1", "first_name": "Connor", "middle_name": "Andrew", "last_name": "Sampson", "date_of_birth": "March 2, 2001", "addresses": [{ "type": "work", "streetAddress": "24 W Main St", "city": "Bozeman", "state": "MT", "postalCode": "59715" }, { "type": "home", "streetAddress": "213 Masonic Dr", "city": "Bozeman", "state": "MT", "postalCode": "59715" }] }
8238747237	{ "customer_id": "2", "first_name": "Laurel", "middle_name": "Elizabeth", "last_name": "Neuhoff", "date_of_birth": "April 16, 2005", "addresses": [{ "type": "work", "streetAddress": "79 Hanifan Ln", "city": "Atlanta", "state": "GA", "postalCode": "30308" }, { "type": "home", "streetAddress": "3602 Ferry St", "city": "Atlanta", "state": "GA", "postalCode": "30308" }] }

With a known, structured format, document databases have additional flexibility beyond what is possible with key-value. While searching by document key yields the fastest results, it is possible to search on a field within the document. Suppose you store social network profiles using an arbitrary numeric value as the document key. Meanwhile, the document is a JSON object containing details about the person, as shown in Figure 2.5. With a document database, it is possible to retrieve all profiles that match a specific ZIP code. The potential to search in this manner is possible because the database understands the document's structure. Therefore, the contents of a document are available for search.

JavaScript Object Notation

JavaScript Object Notation (JSON) is a lightweight data-interchange format. It is a text-based format used to represent and store data in a structured manner. Exchanging data on the web is commonly done with JSON. It is a language-independent format that many different programming languages can manipulate. Each entry in the *Value* column in Figure 2.5 is an example of a JSON document.

Column-Oriented

A column-oriented database uses an index to identify data in groups of related columns. A relational database stores the data in Table 2.1 in a single table, where each row contains a value for each of the *Customer_ID*, *First_Name*, *Middle_Name*, *Last_Name*, and *Date_of_Birth* columns. The *Customer_ID* becomes the index in a column-family database, with the other columns stored independently. This design makes it easy to distribute data across multiple machines. This ability to scale enables the handling of massive amounts of data. Handling large data volumes is possible because of the technical implementation details of how column-oriented databases organize and store data. Data warehousing and business intelligence applications use this design pattern, aggregating and summarizing the contents of a column across many rows.

One reason for selecting a column-family database is its ability to scale. For instance, imagine you need to build a data warehouse to analyze US stock transactions over three decades. Since daily trade volumes exceed 6 billion records, processing that data on a single database server is not practical. A column-family database is an excellent choice for this type of situation.

Graph

Graph databases specialize in exploring relationships between pieces of data. While relational models focus on mapping the relationships between abstract entities, graphs map relationships between actual pieces of data. For instance, Figure 2.3 shows the tables that store the relationship between people and addresses.

Figure 2.6 illustrates how you could model data from Tables 2.1 and 2.4 as a graph. Each person and address represents a *node* in the graph. Each node can have multiple *properties*. Properties store specific attributes for an individual node. The arrow that links nodes together represents a *relationship*. Note that relationships are directional. For instance, Connor works at 24 W Main St in Bozeman. However, an address doesn't "work" on a person. Relationships can also have properties.

FIGURE 2.6 Data in a graph

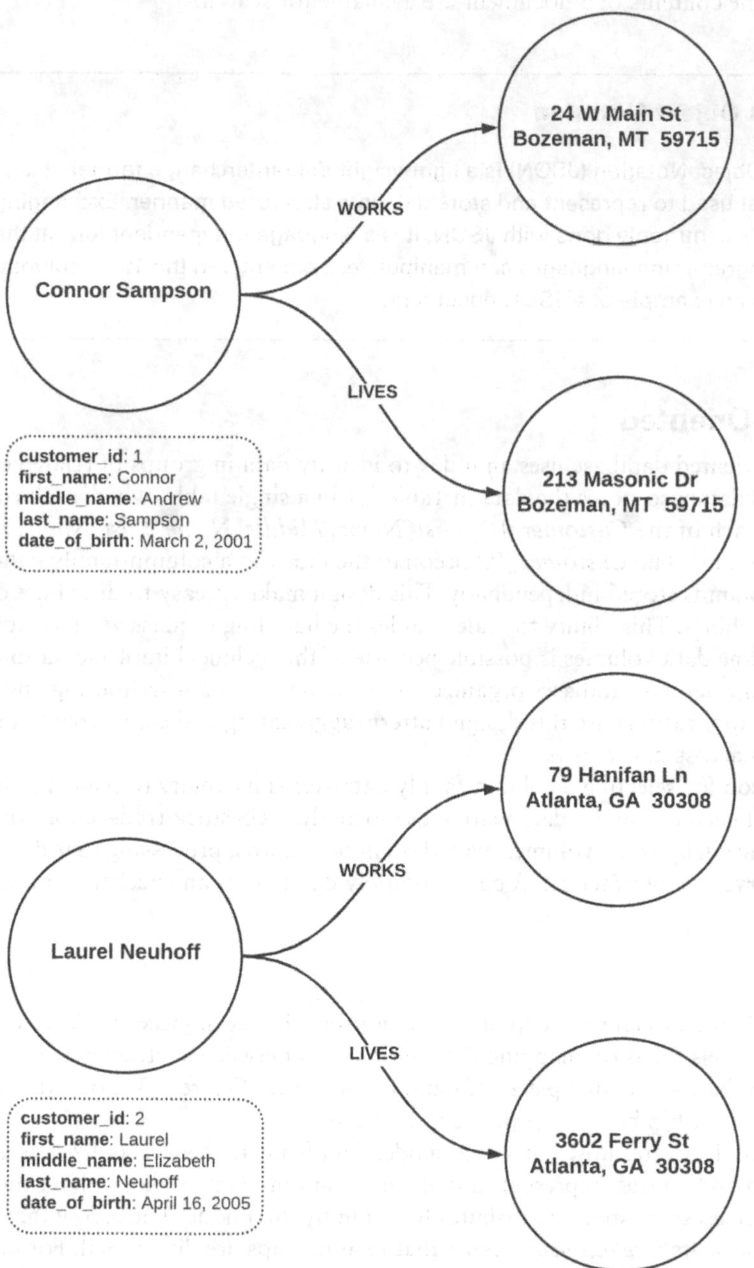

Graphs are optimal if you need to create a recommendation engine, as graphs explore relationships between individual pieces of data. For example, consider a recommendation system where the nodes in the graph represent users and items and the relationships between them. With this design, you can see which people have purchased similar items. This approach allows for the generation of personalized recommendations based on the user's past behavior and the behavior of other users in the graph.

Linear vs. Nonlinear Format

With a linear data format, you organize data into a sequence of records where each record has a fixed number of fields. Tables in relational databases are examples of a linear data format, as each row represents the values for each column. From a text file standpoint, a comma-separated values (CSV) file represents data linearly. Linear data formats are often used for storing and exchanging simple data and are well-suited for applications requiring efficient sequential data access.

Comma-Separated Values

A CSV file is a text file that uses a simple format for storing data in a tabular form. In a CSV file, each line of text represents a record. A comma separates the record's values for each field. Figure 2.7 illustrates the data from Table 2.1 in CSV form. This simple format makes CSV files easy to create, read, and write. As a result, people frequently use CSV files to exchange data between systems and relational databases.

FIGURE 2.7 Sample data in CSV form

```
customer_id,first_name,middle_name,last_name,date_of_birth
1,Connor,Andrew,Sampson,March 2 2001
2,Laurel,Elizabeth,Neuhoff,April 16 2005
3,Jagadish,Simha,Venkatesan,May 13 2008
```

Nonlinear data formats are those in which data is organized in a hierarchical or nested structure, allowing for complex relationships between data entities. JSON is an example of a nonlinear data format. Another example is Extensible Markup Language (XML), which represents data in a tree-like structure of nested objects and elements. Nonlinear data formats are well-suited for describing complex data structures.

You typically use a relational database to store linear data. Meanwhile, NoSQL databases are better suited to handling nonlinear data. When choosing between a relational and nonrelational database, you need to consider the structural nature of the data you are storing. Data in a linear format lends itself to a relational database, while data in a nonlinear format tends to be more suited to a nonrelational database.

Exam Tip

Organizational needs change over time. Suppose you traditionally work with linear data in a relational database and have a new requirement to incorporate nonlinear data. Think carefully before trying to wedge nonlinear data into a relational database. While it is possible, remember that relational databases are optimal for linear data when selecting a database model. When you need to store nonlinear data, a NoSQL database is a better choice.

NoSQL Database Tools

A popular key-value database is *Amazon DynamoDB (DynamoDB)*, available from AWS. DynamoDB is a highly available NoSQL database that supports the document data model and key-value pairs. Knowing that DynamoDB is available only as a fully managed service from AWS is vital. With the underlying hardware abstracted, DynamoDB scales automatically and supports thousands of read-and-write transactions per second. DynamoDB is globally known for its ability to handle large amounts of data. Other key-value options include *Redis* and *Memcached*.

MongoDB is a popular document database you can run on servers you manage. MongoDB can scale across multiple servers and handle high volumes and velocities of data. Suppose you prefer to use MongoDB without operating the underlying hardware. In that case, *MongoDB Atlas* is a fully managed service that supports three of the leading global public cloud providers: AWS, Azure, and GCP. If you are looking for document database alternatives to MongoDB and DynamoDB, GCP offers both *Realtime Database* and *Cloud Firestore* as hosted offerings.

Cassandra is one of the most broadly adopted column-oriented databases. Cassandra is an open-source, highly scalable, column-oriented database system that runs on hardware that you manage. Distributed by design, Cassandra can handle large amounts of data and can scale across many commodity servers. Cassandra's defining characteristics include its ability to handle large amounts of data while being highly available. *Bigtable* from GCP is another offering that supports both key-value and column-oriented data. *Hbase* and *Microsoft Azure Table Storage* are additional offerings in the column-oriented space.

Neo4j is one of the leading graph database management systems. Like all graph databases, Neo4j stores and manages data in the form of nodes and relationships. It is well-suited for highly interconnected data, including social network and product recommendation data. Similar to MongoDB, you can install Neo4j on servers that you manage. If you prefer to use Neo4j as a service, *AuraDB* is a fully managed Neo4j database available in both AWS and GCP. As in any quickly growing segment, alternative graph databases exist. *JanusGraph* and *TigerGraph* are available if you prefer to operate a graph database on your hardware. Meanwhile, AWS offers *Neptune* if you're looking for an alternative graph database as a service.

Database creators offer multiple database engine types within a single, multimodel platform. Available solely as a hosted offering from Azure, *Microsoft Azure Cosmos DB (Cosmos)* is a multimodel database that supports key-value, document, column-oriented, and graph workloads. This multimodel approach lets you choose the best data model for your application. At the same time, its distributed design ensures the ability of Cosmos to support large data volumes and high-throughput workloads.

> **The Database Landscape**
>
> Relational databases are more mature pieces of technology than their nonrelational counterparts. According to `DB-Engines.com`, a website that tracks trends in the database space, relational databases are by far the most popular database platform. Thousands of organizations rely on relational databases to manipulate and store data.
>
> However, nonrelational databases, particularly the graph category, are experiencing the most significant growth in new implementations. That said, relational databases are the dominant database type and will likely remain so for years to come.

Programming and Database Operations

While databases are lovely tools for storing and manipulating data, they are not for use directly by an end user. Imagine trying to book a flight by directly interacting with an airline's flight database. You would have to know which database the airline uses and have the necessary software to connect to that database. You would also have to understand the structure of the database and how to interact with the database programmatically. As this situation is impractical, organizations develop applications to serve their customers. These applications, not the users themselves, interact with databases.

> **User Experience**
>
> *User experience (UX)* is a discipline that focuses on how people feel when they interact with a system. Career paths exist that focus solely on improving the user experience. Ease of use, efficiency, and usefulness are among the attributes that UX designers focus on as they strive to improve the customer experience.

One of the things applications do is abstract the structure of a database from an end user. Once again, consider booking a flight. You provide data to the application, including departure airport, arrival airport, date of travel, the number of travelers, and the travel class. The application takes those inputs and retrieves flights that satisfy those parameters. With this approach, you can focus on your desired outcome, which is booking a flight. You don't need any database knowledge to book travel, much less understand the structure of the database.

Programming and database operations are closely related since applications interact with databases. Software developers use programming languages, including *Java*, *Python*, and C++, to write code that manipulates data in a database. Fortunately, several frameworks exist that make it easier for software developers to work with databases and improve developer productivity.

Object-Oriented Programming

Object-oriented programming (OOP) is a software development paradigm that uses the concept of "objects." With a traditional, procedural approach to writing software, code follows logical steps to achieve a business requirement. In OOP, the software consists of objects that interact with other objects. The focus is on creating objects with specific properties and behaviors and then writing code that uses these objects to encapsulate business logic. Taking an OOP approach can make software more modular, reusable, and scalable, which makes it easier to develop and maintain.

Object-Relational Mapping

Object-relational mapping (ORM) is a technique that presents relational data as objects in an object-oriented programming language. ORM lets developers work with data stored in relational databases using object-oriented programming languages, including Java, Python, and C++. An ORM framework provides a layer of abstraction between the programming objects and the data in the database, making it easier for developers to work with the data more intuitively and naturally.

In practical terms, developers can write code that uses objects and classes to represent data rather than writing complex SQL queries that directly manipulate the data. The ORM framework translates the operations performed on these objects into the appropriate SQL commands. This abstraction frees developers from needing to understand the organization or structure of data in the database.

One of the main benefits of using an ORM framework is that it allows developers to write more reusable and maintainable code. Since ORM frameworks abstract away the data's structural details, the generated code can work with different proprietary and open-source relational databases. The flexibility that ORM frameworks provide lets developers write portable code that can easily migrate to new database platforms. ORMs allow developers to maximize the percentage of their time toward feature creation instead of worrying about the underlying database structures.

Overall, ORM frameworks are tools that improve the productivity of modern software development. ORM frameworks allow developers to focus on the business logic of their applications rather than the details of how data is stored and retrieved. By using ORM, developers can create more robust, scalable, and maintainable applications to meet their users' needs better.

There are a variety of ORM frameworks from which to choose. *Hibernate* and *Ebean* are both open-source ORM frameworks for the Java programming language. As ORM frameworks, Hibernate and Ebean let developers use Java objects directly to manipulate data without writing SQL queries. Ebean is the less complex of the two frameworks, prioritizing ease of use. In addition to abstracting a database's structure, Hibernate provides additional features, including caching and transaction management. With caching, it is possible to improve the performance of an application. However, if the database gets directly modified by a SQL statement and not through the ORM framework, the Hibernate cache could contain stale data.

The *Entity Framework* is an open-source ORM framework for the .NET programming language. As with all ORM frameworks, it provides a layer of abstraction over a relational database. One unique feature of the Entity Framework is that it supports Language Integrated Query (LINQ). LINQ lets .NET developers write queries using a syntax similar to the syntax used in the C# programming language.

There is at least one ORM framework for every object-oriented programming language. *ActiveRecord* is an ORM framework built into *Ruby on Rails*. *Doctrine* and *RedBean* are among the ORM frameworks for the *PHP* programming language. *SQLAlchemy*, *Django*, and *Storm* are among the most broadly adopted options for Python developers.

Process to Gauge Impact

As with any tool, you need a process to gauge the impact of using an ORM framework on a relational database. ORMs generate SQL code as part of abstracting the database to the programmer. One step that can help you assess impact is to review the SQL code generated by the ORM. Specifically, you can compare the SQL code generated by the ORM with the SQL you would write manually for the same operations. Comparing the generated and manual code can help you understand how the ORM translates your code into SQL. In addition, this manual comparison lets you understand whether the ORM generates efficient and effective SQL.

To help confirm the validity of the generated SQL code, you can start by setting up a test environment with a sample database and some test data. Then you can write some code using the ORM to perform database operations consistent with those needed by your application, such as querying, inserting, updating, and deleting data. Once you have the ORM-generated SQL, you can compare it to the SQL code you would write manually to perform the same operations.

To determine the ORM's impact on the database server, you can use database performance tools to examine the efficiency of the ORM-generated SQL. One thing to pay close attention to is SQL's explain plan, also known as an *execution plan*. A SQL explain plan represents a database engine's steps to execute a SQL query. It provides information about the operations performed, the order in which they occur, and the database objects used to store and access data. This information can help developers and database administrators understand how a SQL query is executed, which aids in troubleshooting performance issues and optimizing query performance. Figure 2.8 shows the difference between two SQL statements that return the same data. Note that the query on top spends 17 percent of its time sorting data, while the query on the bottom spends only 8 percent. For optimizing queries to minimize sort time, the query corresponding to the bottom explain plan is the better choice.

FIGURE 2.8 Comparing SQL execution plans

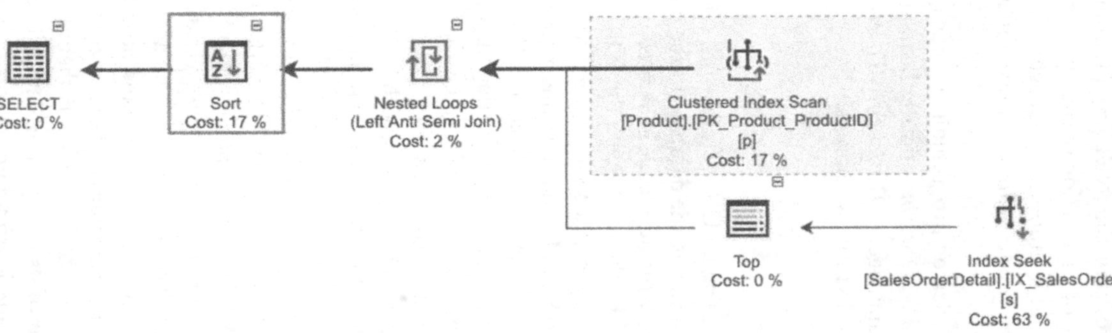

entify all finished products available for sale SELECT DISTINCT Name, p.ProductID FROM Production.Product p WHERE FinishedGoodsFlag = 1 AND SellEn

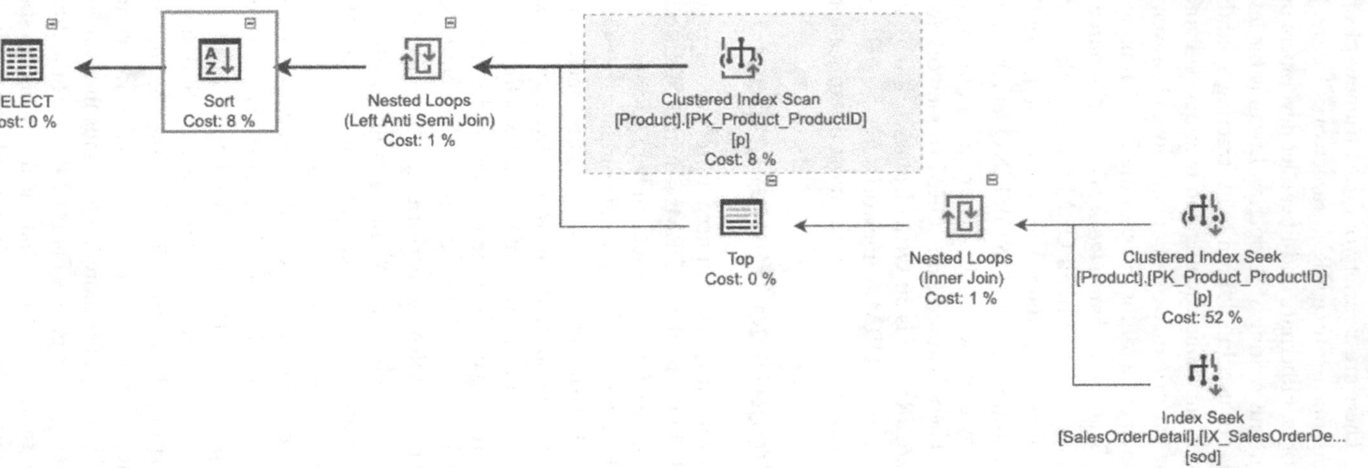

Once you have a representative sample of how the ORM-generated SQL compares with queries you write manually, you can assess the ORM's viability for your needs. You can choose your ORM framework if its generated queries provide solutions to your data interaction use cases.

Some situations will cause you to pursue an alternate approach. For example, the complexity of your decision increases if you are developing a new application against a database that is in use by existing applications. In that case, you might get data inconsistency in the ORM's caching layer because of an update that doesn't go through the ORM. As a result, you might opt against using an ORM for this specific use case.

Summary

A database is a structured collection of data stored and accessed electronically. Databases store and manage large amounts of data and allow for easy access, organization, and manipulation of that data. Database management systems are platforms where you create databases. You interact with databases when you do things online, including buying something from a retailer, managing your finances, or making a service appointment for your car.

There are two main database categories. The most dominant type of database is the relational database. A relational database is rooted in Codd's 1970 paper that describes the relational model. The relational model is a way of organizing data in a database.

In the relational model, you organize data into tables with well-defined relationships between them. You use primary and foreign keys to establish these relationships. A primary key is a field in a table that uniquely identifies each record in the table. A foreign key is a field in one table that refers to the primary key in another table.

Relational database management systems let you create relational databases. Based on the relational model, relational databases easily manipulate and query data and are widely used in various applications. Relational databases are powerful and flexible ways of organizing and storing linear data. Proprietary databases include Oracle, SQL Server, and Db2. PostgreSQL and MariaDB are among the open-source options, while MySQL is one of the most popular open-core databases.

NoSQL is another database category. While not as prevalent as the relational database, NoSQL's popularity is rising. NoSQL databases don't use a traditional relational model and handle large amounts of nonlinear data by design. Key-value, document, column-oriented, and graph are all NoSQL databases.

The key-value database is the most basic of the NoSQL options. In a key-value database, a globally unique key identifies a specific value. That value can contain virtually anything, including text, a file, an image, or a video. DynamoDB is one of the leading key-value database options.

Document databases are conceptually similar to the key-value database. A document database uses globally unique keys while enforcing some structure on the values. For example, MongoDB is a document database based on the JSON structure.

Column-oriented databases store data in a column-based format, differing from the row-based approach of a relational database. Suppose you have millions of financial transactions you need to aggregate. A column-oriented database, like Cassandra, is well-suited to that task.

Graph databases excel at exploring connected data, storing data as individual nodes, and connecting them with relationships. Graph databases, like Neo4j, are ideal choices when creating recommendation engines.

When building applications, it is possible to use an object-relational mapping framework to let software developers manipulate data in their preferred programming language instead of directly in SQL. ORMs translate data manipulations from object-oriented programming languages such as C++, Python, and Java into SQL.

There are several things to keep in mind when deciding whether to use an ORM. You need to confirm that the SQL code the ORM generates is valid for your use case. You also need to consider the efficiency of the SQL queries that the ORM generates, as poorly performing queries negatively impact overall database performance. You also need to consider the complexities of caching within the ORM, primarily if multiple applications use the same database.

Exam Essentials

Describe the difference between relational and nonrelational databases. Relational and nonrelational, or NoSQL, are two different types of databases used to store and manage data. Relational databases use a structured data model, which organizes data into tables with rows and columns. Nonrelational databases use a variety of data models, including key-value, document, column-oriented, and graph. With relational databases, you need to define data structures before using the database. Nonrelational databases often have a more flexible data structure, allowing them to store data in various formats. From an operational standpoint, nonrelational databases are easier to scale than their relational counterparts.

Describe the difference between linear and nonlinear data. Linear and nonlinear data formats are two different ways of organizing and storing data. Linear data formats are relatively straightforward to work with, given that the data is in a linear, sequential format. A CSV file is an example of a linear data format. Since relational databases are highly structured, they are well-suited to storing linear data.

Nonlinear data formats store data in a more complex, interconnected manner. Nonlinear data are more complicated to work with than linear data and allow for multiple connections and relationships between different pieces of data. Among the NoSQL database options, graph databases are particularly well-suited for storing and manipulating nonlinear data.

Describe common NoSQL database categories. Key-value, document databases, column-oriented, and graph are four categories of NoSQL databases that store and manage data differently. Key-value databases store data in key-value pairs and are ideal for storing audio, image, and video data. Document databases are similar to key-value, restricting the values in a known, JSON-like document format. Column-oriented databases store data in columns rather than rows, making them suitable for the aggregations associated with data warehousing and business intelligence applications. Graph databases store data in nodes and edges, representing the entities and relationships in a data set. Graph use cases include real-time recommendation engines, fraud detection, and identity and access management.

Describe object-relational mapping. Object-relational mapping is a technique that allows developers to work with databases using object-oriented programming languages rather than writing SQL statements. Available for many object-oriented programming languages, ORM frameworks provide a layer of abstraction between a relational database and an application, allowing developers to work with objects in their code. Meanwhile, the ORM handles the translation of these objects into SQL statements.

ORM frameworks make it easier for developers to work with databases, allowing them to use familiar object-oriented concepts and syntax rather than learning the details of SQL. It can also improve the maintainability and flexibility of an application as it decouples the application's data access logic from the underlying database structure.

Describe the impact of using an object-relational mapping framework. To gauge the impact of using an object-relational mapping framework, you first need to decide how to assess the ORM's impact. You need to select a performance measure, such as response time, throughput, or resource utilization, as the basis for comparison. You can then compare database performance between the ORM's SQL and the SQL a human writes. If you have multiple applications using the same database, be sure to include the effect of the ORM's caching layer in your evaluation, as stale data in the cache can cause inconsistent application behavior. You can also incorporate other factors, including code maintainability, in your assessment. If you determine the ORM is having an outsized impact on performance, you decide whether it is viable to evaluate a different ORM framework or use human-generated SQL.

Review Questions

1. Lionel is creating a financial data warehouse. Which type of database should he consider?
   A. Key-value
   B. Document
   C. Column-oriented
   D. Graph

2. Inaya wants to use a graph database to build an identity and access management system. Which of the following is a viable option?
   A. Cassandra
   B. Neo4j
   C. MongoDB
   D. DynamoDB

3. Monique is a database administrator for a company managing customer information. She is optimizing the existing database structure to make it easier to retrieve customer addresses. Which database concept should she use to associate customer information with their addresses while maintaining data integrity?
   A. Primary Key
   B. Tuple
   C. Foreign Key
   D. Relation

4. Howard is a database designer for an e-commerce website working on creating a table to store customer information. He wants to ensure that each customer can be uniquely identified within the table. Which database concept should Jack use to accomplish this goal?
   A. Primary Key
   B. Tuple
   C. Foreign Key
   D. Relation

5. Lisa is a database administrator for a growing online retail company that requires a relational database management system to handle hundreds of concurrent connections. Lisa's company makes extensive use of Linux. Which RDBMS platform should Lisa consider for her company's needs?
   A. Access
   B. PostgreSQL
   C. SQL Server
   D. Aurora

6. Miguel is responsible for database strategy for a growing online retail company that requires a relational database to handle what will eventually be a petabyte-scale database. Most of the company's infrastructure runs Linux in the cloud, and Miguel prefers a cloud-based solution that minimizes administrative overhead. Which RDBMS platform should Miguel consider for his company's needs?
   - **A.** Access
   - **B.** PostgreSQL
   - **C.** SQL Server
   - **D.** Aurora
7. Allison is working on building a database for a new online store. She is developing a feature to recommend products based on similar purchases and search history. Which type of database would be best suited for Allison's needs?
   - **A.** Key-value
   - **B.** Document
   - **C.** Column-oriented
   - **D.** Graph
8. Katie works for a social network startup and needs a database to store social network profiles. While profiles are all JSON documents, each profile may contain different fields. Which type of NoSQL database would be Katie's best choice?
   - **A.** Key-value
   - **B.** Column-oriented
   - **C.** Graph
   - **D.** Document
9. Andy is building an environment to analyze five decades worth of financial transactions. If Andy uses commodity servers and a column-oriented design, which of the following databases best fits Andy's needs?
   - **A.** MySQL
   - **B.** MongoDB
   - **C.** Cassandra
   - **D.** SQLite
10. Sameer is a software developer working on a project that requires storing and managing JSON data. He is considering different approaches to storing the data. Which of the following best describes what Sameer should choose for this project.
    - **A.** Relational database with linear data format
    - **B.** NoSQL database with nonlinear data format
    - **C.** Relational database with nonlinear data format
    - **D.** NoSQL database with linear data format

11. Luca is a software developer working on an application that requires interaction with a relational database. He is considering using an ORM framework to simplify his work. What is the primary benefit of using an ORM framework in this context?
    A. Reduces the size of the database
    B. Allows developers to work with data using object-oriented programming languages
    C. Increases the number of supported database platforms
    D. Makes the database more secure

12. Enzo is a software developer working on a project incorporating nonlinear data to support a new initiative at his company. Which type of database would be the most appropriate choice for this situation?
    A. Relational database
    B. NoSQL database
    C. Flat-file database
    D. Spreadsheet

13. Gina is a developer in a growing organization that uses a relational database for its linear data. They have recently identified the need to store and manage highly interconnected data for product recommendations. Which type of database would be the most appropriate choice for this situation?
    A. Relational
    B. Graph
    C. Key-value
    D. Column-oriented

14. Jane is a software developer working on a file-based interface sending employee data to her company's insurance provider. She needs a format that is easy to create, read, and write. Which file format should she choose?
    A. JSON
    B. XML
    C. CSV
    D. BSON

15. Ron is developing an application that requires storing complex data structures with hierarchical relationships. He needs a file format that can effectively represent these relationships and be easily readable. Which file format should he choose? Select the best answer.
    A. CSV
    B. DOCX
    C. JSON
    D. XML

16. Katie is designing a web application requiring an efficient approach for exchanging structured data between clients and the server. The application must easily parse and generate data in this format. Which file format should she choose? Select the best option.

A. XML

B. CSV

C. JSON

D. TSV

17. Christa is working on an application that requires storing and managing a list of customer records, each with a fixed number of fields, such as name, email address, and phone number. The data will be used for simple data analysis and primarily accessed sequentially. Which type of data format should Christa choose for this task?

A. Linear data format

B. Nonlinear data format

C. Graph data format

D. Tree data format

18. Swan is a software developer working on a project to improve his company's application. He is enhancing the overall user interaction and ensuring that the application is intuitive and user-friendly. Which aspect of the application should Swan focus on?

A. UX

B. Database optimization

C. APIs

D. Load balancing

19. Sven is a development manager at a financial services firm. He wants to create a software system that is easy to maintain, scale, and modify. He's considering using a design principle focusing on object interaction and encapsulating data and behavior. What design principle should Sven use for his application?

A. Functional programming

B. Object-oriented programming

C. Procedural programming

D. Logic programming

20. Monique is a development manager for a group of Java programmers. Which of the following ORM frameworks should she evaluate to abstract away the structural details of a relational database and facilitate more reusable and maintainable code?

A. ActiveRecord

B. Django

C. Hibernate

D. LINQ

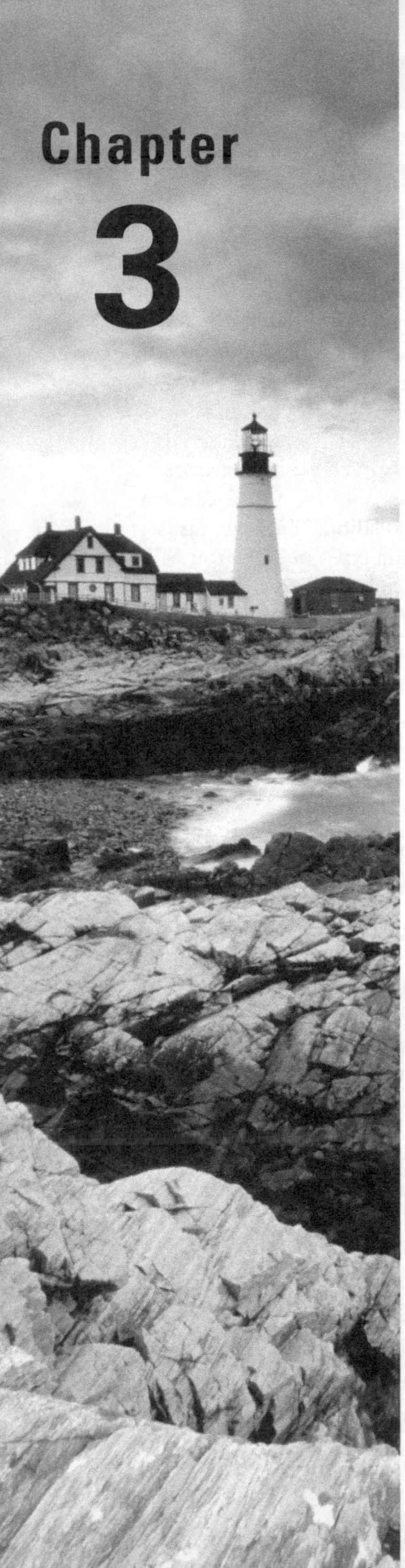

SQL and Scripting

THE COMPTIA DATASYS+ EXAM TOPICS COVERED IN THIS CHAPTER INCLUDE:

✓ **Domain 1.0: Database Fundamentals**

- 1.2. Given a Scenario, Develop, Modify, and Run SQL Code
- 1.3. Compare and Contrast Scripting Methods and Scripting Environments

Structured Query Language is the standard programming language for managing and manipulating data stored in relational databases. It is used by organizations of all sizes and in various industries to store, retrieve, and analyze data. SQL is essential for working with relational databases because it allows developers and database administrators to create data structures and manipulate data. Scripting is the process of automating a series of tasks. As you can imagine, a data systems analyst frequently needs to automate routine relational database tasks.

In the first part of this chapter, you will learn about the two main types of SQL. You will explore the theory that makes SQL so powerful and the four principles behind a SQL transaction. You will then learn about different ways you can program with SQL. In the latter part of this chapter, you will delve into the nuances of various scripting languages, locations, and approaches.

Flavors of SQL

Structured Query Language (SQL) is the standard programming language for interacting with a relational database. Recognizing the need for standardization, the *American National Standards Institute (ANSI)* adopted SQL as a standard in 1986. The *International Organization for Standards (ISO)* followed suit in 1987, establishing SQL as a worldwide standard for interacting with relational databases. Relational databases support SQL, making it easy for developers, analysts, and administrators to use the same language to work with various relational databases, from PostgreSQL to Oracle.

SQL has gone through several significant revisions over the years. The first version defined the basic syntax and data types for SQL and the structure and syntax of SQL statements. The 1992 revision introduced several new features and improvements, including support for *views*, *triggers*, and *stored procedures*. This revision also included enhancements to SQL's data types and syntax. In 1999, ANSI updated the standard to include support for recursive queries, common table expressions, and embedding SQL in Java. Subsequent releases in 2003, 2006, 2008, 2011, and, most recently, 2016, continued to further enhance and improve the language. As it continues to evolve, SQL remains an essential tool for working with relational databases, playing a critical role in managing and analyzing data in many organizations. While the 2016 revision is the most recent version of ANSI SQL as of this writing, database platforms do not uniformly support every feature of ANSI SQL.

In addition to evolving, SQL has a distinguishing characteristic in that you can use it to define data structures within a database and manipulate data within those structures. It is vital to understand these two flavors of SQL.

Data Definition Language

Data Definition Language (DDL) is the flavor of SQL that defines the structure and organization within a relational database. Think of DDL as an architectural blueprint for a building. Similar to how a blueprint outlines the layout of a building, DDL defines the internal structures in a database. You use DDL for creating, changing, or removing database structures, including tables, fields, relationships between tables, indexes, views, and more. Common examples of DDL statements include CREATE, ALTER, and DROP. *CREATE* creates a new database object, *ALTER* modifies an existing database object, and *DROP* permanently removes a database object.

For example, Figure 3.1 shows the CREATE TABLE DDL command to build the customer table you first saw in Chapter 2, "Database Fundamentals." Note that the CREATE TABLE statement takes the table's name as a parameter, while the code block within the parentheses specifies the column names and associated data types.

A *data type* defines what kind of values each column can contain. Every column in a table must have a specific data type. Table 3.1 illustrates some common SQL data types.

TABLE 3.1 Common Data Types

Data Type	Definition	Sample Data
DATE	A date value	2023-04-22
FLOAT	A floating-point number	3.14159265359
INTEGER	A whole number	911
VARCHAR	A variable-length character string	Gleeful

A new, empty customer table results from executing the DDL command in Figure 3.1.

FIGURE 3.1 DDL for sample Customer table

	Customer
PK	Customer_ID
	Title
	First_Name
	Middle_Name
	Last_Name
	Date_of_Birth

```
CREATE TABLE CUSTOMER
(
    CUSTOMER_ID   INTEGER,
    TITLE         VARCHAR(50),
    FIRST_NAME    VARCHAR(200),
    MIDDLE_NAME   VARCHAR(200),
    LAST_NAME     VARCHAR(200),
    DATE_OF_BIRTH DATE
);
```

Note that the DDL in Figure 3.1 merely creates the table. There are additional components to consider before the table is ready for use.

Primary and foreign keys are essential concepts in relational databases that establish relationships between tables. A *primary key* is a unique identifier for a record in a table and cannot contain duplicate or null values. A *foreign key* is a field in a table that refers to the primary key of another table. By linking tables through these keys, databases can join two tables together in an efficient manner.

You must follow a few more steps to make *Customer_ID* the primary key for the Customer table. The first step is to update the table's definition using the ALTER TABLE statement. By definition, a primary key cannot be NULL, meaning it must contain a value. The syntax for ALTER TABLE differs slightly across relational database management platforms. The following ALTER TABLE command is compatible with Microsoft SQL Server 2014 and newer. This statement modifies the structure of the customer table so that when you add data to the table, there must be a valid value for *Customer_ID* for each row you enter.

```
ALTER TABLE customer ALTER COLUMN customer_id INTEGER NOT NULL;
```

After altering the table to require data for the *Customer_ID* column, you can specify that column as the primary key with another ALTER TABLE statement.

```
ALTER TABLE customer
ADD CONSTRAINT customer_pk PRIMARY KEY (customer_id);
```

In the interest of efficiency, you can consolidate the creation of the customer table instead, including the primary key on the *Customer_ID* column, in a single CREATE statement.

```
CREATE TABLE CUSTOMER (
   CUSTOMER_ID INTEGER NOT NULL,
   TITLE         VARCHAR(50) NULL,
   FIRST_NAME    VARCHAR(200) NULL,
   MIDDLE_NAME   VARCHAR(200) NULL,
   LAST_NAME     VARCHAR(200) NULL,
   DATE_OF_BIRTH DATE NULL,
   CONSTRAINT CUSTOMER_PK PRIMARY KEY (
      CUSTOMER_ID
   )
);
```

Note that the previous statement specifies whether each column has to contain a value. The CONSTRAINT section of the command creates the primary key constraint on the *Customer_ID* column.

NULL Values

NULL is a special value in SQL, as it represents the absence of a value. NULLs differ from an empty string or a zero value, as they represent the absence of any data. When you define a column as NOT NULL, every row in the table must contain a valid value for that column. However, if a column is nullable, that column is optional.

To permanently remove a table, you use the DROP TABLE command. Note that the data is lost when you drop a table containing data. Before dropping a table, you must be entirely sure that any data in the table is no longer required. It is vital to consider the operational consequences of dropping a table. You most commonly need a database backup to restore it if you need data from a table you dropped. The following DDL command destroys the customer table from Figure 3.1:

```
DROP TABLE customer;
```

As Figure 3.1 shows, you use DDL to create a database ready for use from an initial design document. You need to complete initial DDL operations before proceeding to manipulate data. Operationally, you want to minimize the number of DDL operations, as each DDL command modifies the structure of the database.

Adding or removing tables comes with its own set of complexities. For instance, adding a table increases the overall storage requirements for the database. Meanwhile, dropping a table removes all of that table's data, directly impacting applications that rely on that data.

Suppose you need to add or remove columns from an existing table. Adding a column to a table increases the storage space required for that table. Adding a column can also impact the performance of queries that retrieve data from that table. Like removing an entire table, dropping a column from an existing table removes all the stored data in that column. Removing data can cause data integrity issues within the database and for any applications that use that data.

Consider the address table in Figure 3.2. This table design specifies a numeric data type for postal code. A numeric data type accommodates addresses in the United States. For example, Cedar Falls, Iowa, has a postal code of 50613.

FIGURE 3.2 Sample Address table

Address		
PK	Address_ID	INTEGER
	Street_Line_1	CHAR(200)
	Street_Line_2	CHAR(200)
	City	CHAR(200)
	State	CHAR(50)
	Postal_Code	INTEGER

However, postal codes in Canada contain characters and numbers. For example, the postal code for the township of Cavendish on Prince Edward Island is C0A 1N0. To handle Canadian addresses, you need to alter the data type for the postal code attribute from numeric to alphanumeric. Since programming languages deal with numbers and character strings differently, you must consider the implications of this change before modifying the postal code's data type.

Once you conclude that a DDL operation is necessary, testing the changes in a nonproduction environment is essential. Testing will help you identify any unforeseen issues. Before modifying your production database, you want to be confident that your DDL will have only the impact you intend.

Data Manipulation Language

Data Manipulation Language (DML) is the flavor of SQL that lets you manipulate data within a database. While DDL creates database objects, DML modifies the data those objects contain. You can think of DML as the tools used to move things around inside a building once the building is complete. Just as a person uses tools to move furniture or hang artwork on a wall, you use DML to create, modify, or delete data within the tables defined by DDL.

Create, read, update, and delete are the primary DML operations. As a result, you may see DML referred to as CRUD operations: Create, Read, Update, and Delete. Table 3.2 illustrates each operation and its corresponding SQL verb. INSERT, UPDATE, and DELETE all change data at rest in a table. SELECT is a read-only operation that retrieves data from a table.

TABLE 3.2 Data Manipulation Language Operations

DML Operation	SQL Verb
Create	INSERT
Read	SELECT
Update	UPDATE
Delete	DELETE

INSERT

The *INSERT* command creates new rows in a table. INSERT requires that you specify a target table and the values you want to place into each column. Optionally, you can specify the columns within the table for each value you want to insert. Figure 3.3 shows the syntax of the INSERT statement.

FIGURE 3.3 SQL INSERT syntax

```
INSERT INTO <table_name>
      (<col_1>, <col_2>, ... <col_n>
VALUES
      (<value_1>, <value_2>, ... <value_n>);
```

The following INSERT statement adds Connor Sampson's information from Table 2.1 into the Customer table from Figure 3.1.

```
INSERT INTO customer
  (customer_id, title, first_name, middle_name, last_name,
   date_of_birth)
VALUES
  (1, 'Mr', 'Connor', 'Andrew', 'Sampson', '2001-03-02');
```

You do not need to specify the column parameters when inserting a row that contains data for every column. However, identifying columns is a good practice. When inserting data into a subset of columns, it is easiest to identify the target columns. Suppose you have a customer named Anitej Gupta with no middle name. The following INSERT statement adds Anitej to the Customer table from Figure 3.1:

```
INSERT INTO customer
  (customer_id, title, first_name, last_name, date_of_birth)
VALUES
  (2, 'Mr', 'Anitej', 'Gupta', '2004-05-22');
```

To accomplish the same insert without specifying the columns, you need to add a null string as the value for the middle initial, as follows:

```
INSERT INTO customer
  (customer_id, title, first_name, middle_initial last_name,
   date_of_birth)
VALUES
  (2, 'Mr', 'Anitej', '', 'Gupta', '2004-05-22');
```

SELECT

The *SELECT* command retrieves data from one or more tables in a database. SELECT statements cannot alter data at rest in the underlying table. Figure 3.4 shows the basic syntax of the SELECT command.

FIGURE 3.4 SQL SELECT syntax

```
SELECT <col_1>, <col_2>, ... <col_n>
FROM <table_name>
WHERE <optional filter_conditions>;
```

The SELECT keyword indicates that the statement is a query to retrieve data. The column parameters after SELECT identify the names of the columns you want to retrieve. If you're going to retrieve all columns, you can use the * wildcard character instead of naming each column. The FROM keyword indicates the table from which you want to obtain data. You can use the optional WHERE clause to specify filter conditions that reduce the number of returned rows.

For example, the following SELECT query retrieves all rows from the customer table, returning only the first and last names:

```
SELECT first_name, last_name
FROM customer;
```

Now suppose you want to retrieve all of the data for a specific customer. Since the *Customer_ID* column is the primary key, each value in that column uniquely identifies a row. You can use that unique identifier to retrieve data about a specific customer. For example, the following query returns all of Connor Sampson's data:

```
SELECT *
FROM customer
WHERE customer_id = 1;
```

If there was no WHERE clause in the previous SQL statement, all the customer data is retrieved.

The SELECT command is one of the most commonly used SQL commands and is the foundation of many database applications. You use SELECT statements to extract data from a database and display it to users, generate reports, or feed data to other systems.

UPDATE

The *UPDATE* command changes existing values in a table. Similar to the SELECT statement, there is an optional WHERE clause that impacts the values that are updated. Figure 3.5 shows the syntax of the UPDATE statement.

FIGURE 3.5 SQL UPDATE syntax

```
UPDATE <table_name>
SET <col_1> = <value_1>,
    <col_2> = <value_2, ...
    <col_n> = <value_n>
WHERE <optional conditions>;
```

The UPDATE keyword indicates that the statement is an update operation, which will change the values at rest in the underlying table. The *table_name* is the name of the table that you want to update. The SET keyword identifies the columns you want to update and their new values. Note that you can modify one or more columns at the same time.

The optional WHERE clause identifies the rows that will get updated. Similar to the SELECT statement, you will update all rows in the table if you don't have a WHERE clause.

For example, suppose Connor Sampson finishes medical school and becomes a doctor, and you need to change his title accordingly. With an UPDATE statement, you don't have to know or specify the current value you want to replace. The following UPDATE statement changes Connor's title:

```
UPDATE customer
SET title = 'Dr'
WHERE customer_id = 1;
```

Suppose you omit the WHERE clause in the previous SQL statement. In that case, all customers will have a new title of "Dr." Even though it is possible to revert changes, you have to be very careful. Using the UPDATE clause appropriately ensures you change only the intended rows, avoiding unwanted updates and potential data loss.

DELETE

The *DELETE* command removes rows from a table. While the UPDATE statement operates at the column level, DELETE operates at the row level. Similar to the UPDATE statement, an optional WHERE clause impacts the values removed by the DELETE. Figure 3.6 shows the syntax of the DELETE statement.

FIGURE 3.6 SQL DELETE syntax

```
DELETE FROM <table_name>
WHERE <optional conditions>;
```

The DELETE keyword indicates a delete operation, which will remove rows from the underlying table. The FROM keyword identifies the table from which you will remove data. The optional WHERE clause lets you specify conditions that affect the scope of the delete operation.

Suppose Connor is no longer a customer, and you want to remove all of his data from the customer table. The following statement removes all the data about Connor from the Customer table:

```
DELETE FROM customer
WHERE customer_id = 1;
```

Using the WHERE clause appropriately with the DELETE statement is even more crucial, as you remove all rows in the table if you omit or forget the WHERE clause.

Remember the Difference Between DDL and DML

One of SQL's defining features is that you can use it to both create structure and manipulate data. Remember that the Data Definition Language creates database objects, while the Data Manipulation Language modifies the contents of those objects.

Set-Based Logic

Set-based logic is a way of thinking about and working with data emphasizing the manipulation of data sets rather than individual rows. This approach uses the mathematical concept of sets and set theory, where a set is a collection of unique elements. In relational databases, you use set-based logic to retrieve, update, and manipulate data in tables by working with sets of rows rather than individual rows. This approach is more efficient and easier to work with than procedural logic, which works on data one row at a time. Consider Figure 3.7, which illustrates two independent sets. Each set consists of elements, in this case, automotive brands.

FIGURE 3.7 Two independent sets

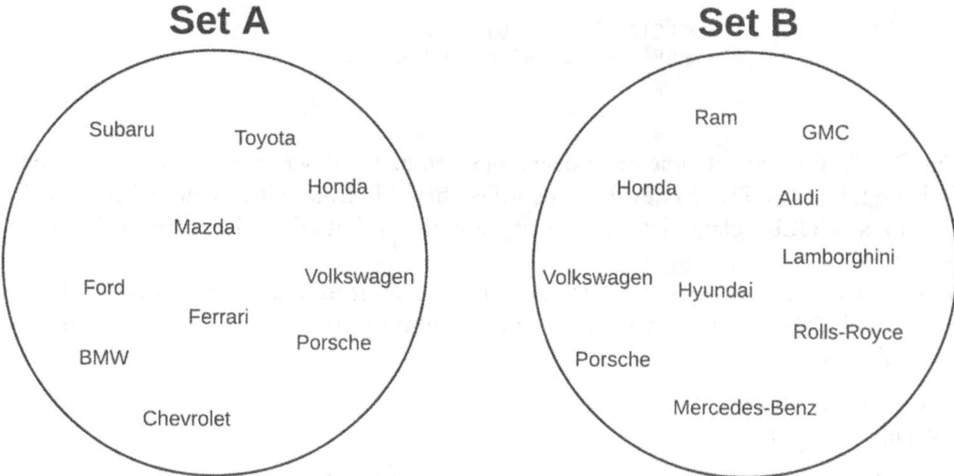

Three primary set operations let you manipulate data sets, including finding the union, intersection, and difference of two or more sets.

UNION

The *union* of two sets, A and B, is the set of all elements in A, B, or both A and B. Put another way, the union of two sets results in a single set containing all elements from both sets. If you want to retrieve all members from two independent sets, you take the union of those sets. The shaded area in Figure 3.8 illustrates the union of the sets shown in Figure 3.7.

FIGURE 3.8 Union of two sets

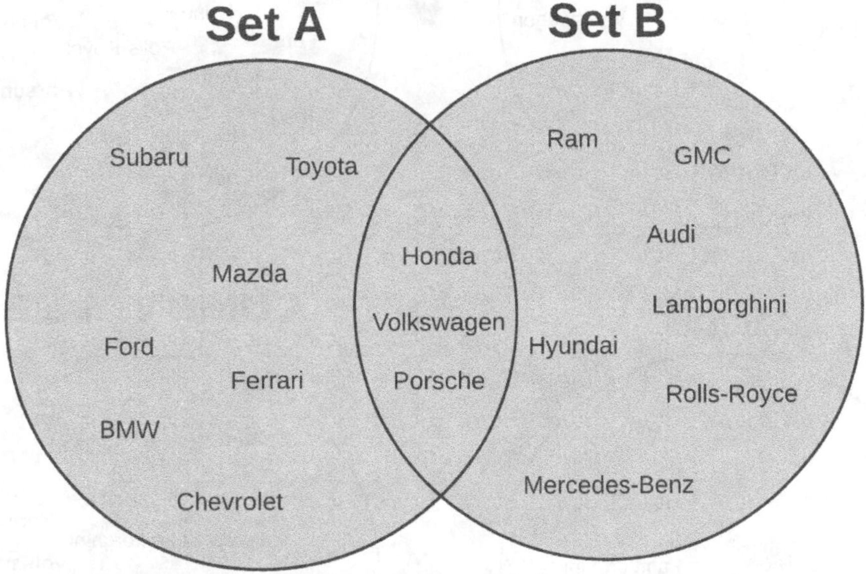

In SQL, the UNION operator will retrieve the distinct values from the sets on which it operates. For example, both set A and set B in Figure 3.8 contain Honda, Volkswagen, and Porsche as elements. A SQL UNION would return a single entry for these three brands. To count the total number of elements in both sets, including duplicates, you need to use the UNION ALL command. If you use a UNION ALL, then Honda, Volkswagen, and Porsche are each included twice in the result set. Figure 3.9 illustrates the difference between a UNION and UNION ALL in SQL, with the duplicates bolded for emphasis.

FIGURE 3.9 Comparing UNION and UNION ALL result sets

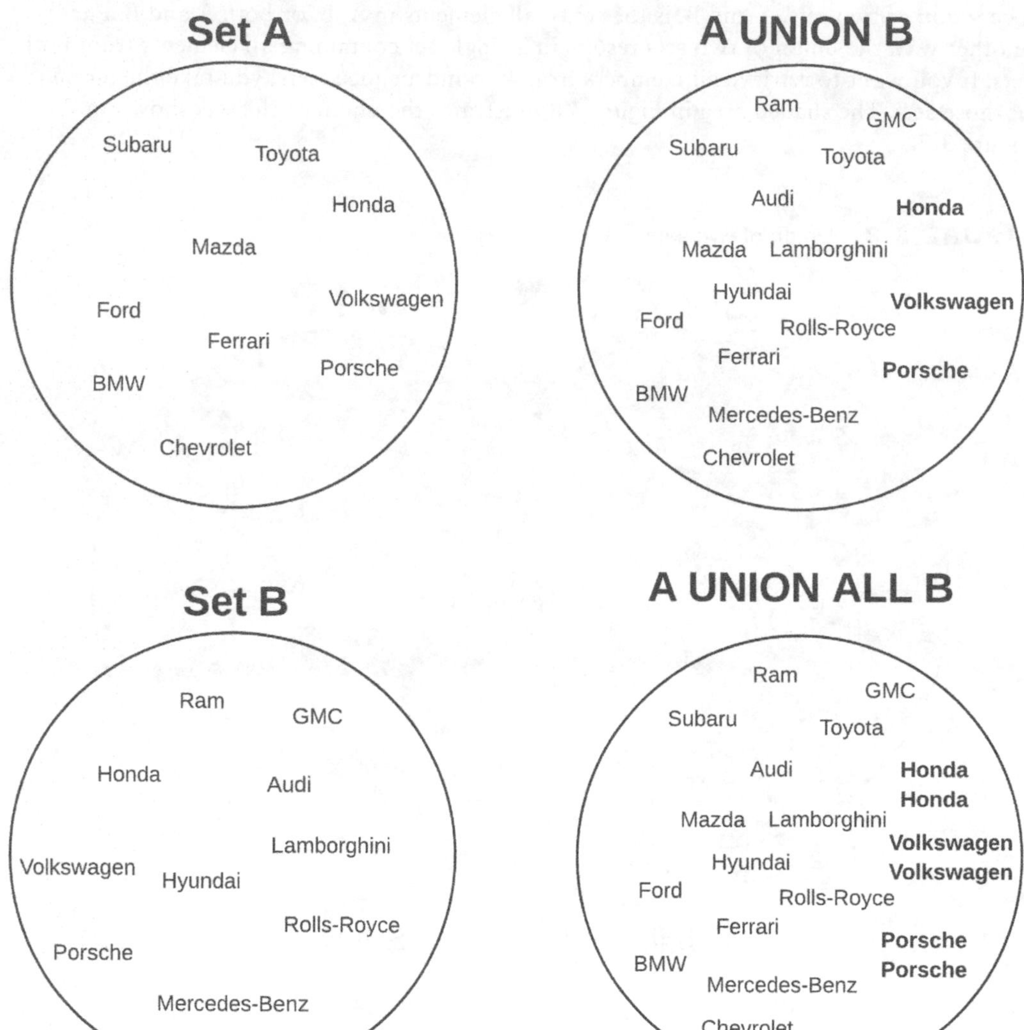

INTERSECTION

The *intersection* of two sets, A and B, is the subset of elements in both A and B. Put another way, the intersection contains only the common, unique elements from both sets. Figure 3.10 illustrates the intersection of the two sets shown in Figure 3.7.

FIGURE 3.10 Intersection of two sets

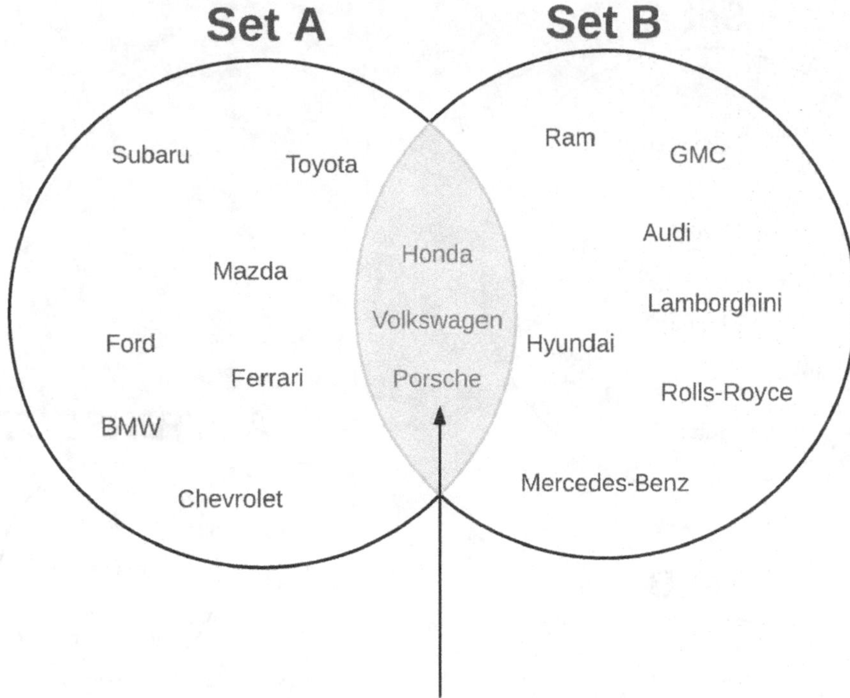

In SQL, the INTERSECT operator retrieves the intersection of the sets on which it operates. The resulting set excludes duplicates by definition. Figure 3.11 shows the new set resulting from the intersection of two sets.

DIFFERENCE

The *difference* between two sets, A and B, is the set of all elements that exist only in A and are not in B. The difference contains only the members from A that are not in the intersection between A and B. Figure 3.12 illustrates the difference between sets A and B from Figure 3.7. Note that the difference excludes Honda, Volkswagen, and Porsche.

The SQL keyword for taking the difference between sets depends on the platform. In Oracle, the MINUS keyword takes the difference between sets, while SQL Server uses EXCEPT. Unlike with the union and intersection, it is vital to note that order matters when taking the difference between sets. Figure 3.13 illustrates how the difference between A and B is not equal to the difference between B and A.

FIGURE 3.11 INTERSECT result set

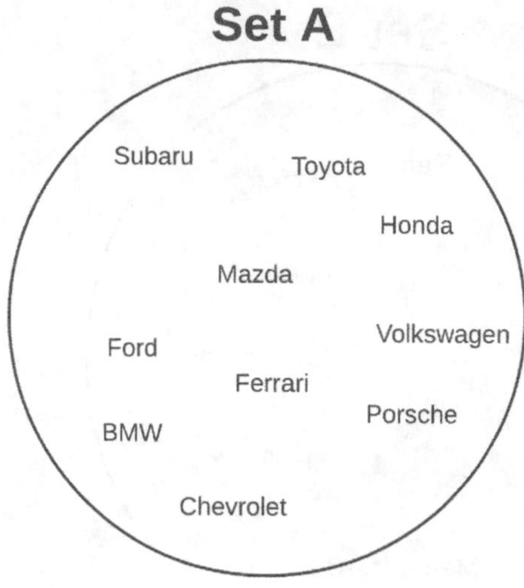

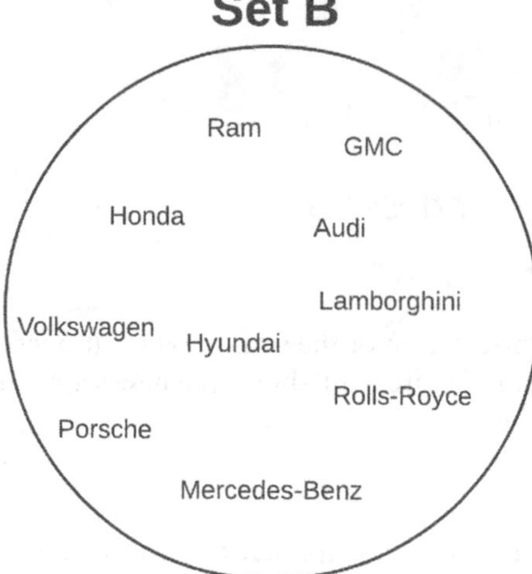

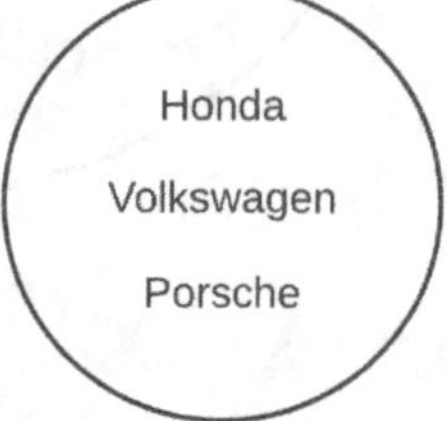

Transaction Control Languages

Transaction control languages (TCLs) manage multiple database changes as a single unit of work called a *transaction*. A transaction is a sequence of one or more SQL statements that need to execute together as a single atomic unit. Every SQL statement must succeed within a transaction, or the entire transaction fails. If any statement within a transaction fails, the entire transaction is reverted, or rolled back, to its original state. Rolling a transaction back means that the database undoes any changes made by the SQL statements within the transaction. These are some of the most commonly used TCL commands:

- *BEGIN TRANSACTION*: This command starts a new transaction.
- *COMMIT*: This command saves the changes made by the statements in the current transaction and ends the transaction.
- *ROLLBACK*: This command undoes the changes made by the statements in the current transaction and ends the transaction.
- *SAVEPOINT*: This command establishes a marker within an ongoing transaction, allowing for a partial rollback to this marker instead of rolling back the entire transaction.

FIGURE 3.12 Difference between two sets

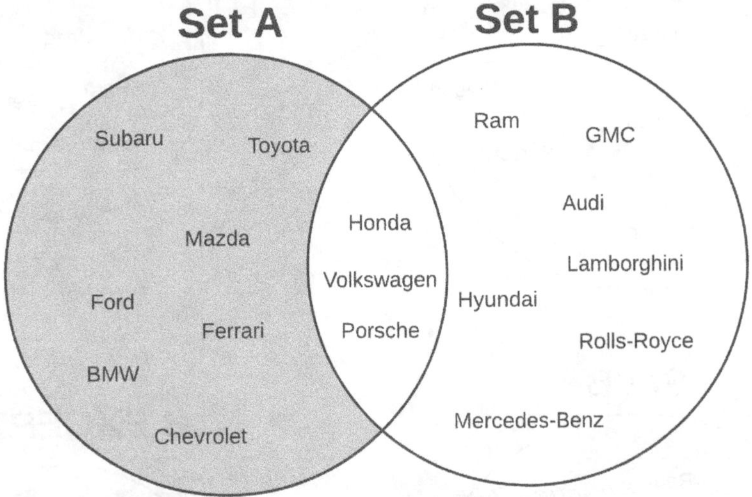

For example, Figure 3.14 illustrates how TCL makes moving $1,000 from a checking account to a savings account a single logical unit of work. Using a transaction ensures that removing $1,000 from the checking account and adding $1,000 to savings happens as a single atomic action.

If the update that removes funds from checking or adds funds to savings fails, the entire operation fails, and the transaction gets rolled back. Using TCL ensures that the $1,000 returns to the checking account if the second update fails. If this transaction rolls back, both checking and savings end up in their original states.

Transaction length is another essential factor when designing transactions in a multiuser environment. Transaction length is critical because transactions lock tables on which they operate. Not only are the tables reserved for use by the transaction, but any changes made until either a commit or rollback happens are not visible to other people using the database.

FIGURE 3.13 Differences between sets

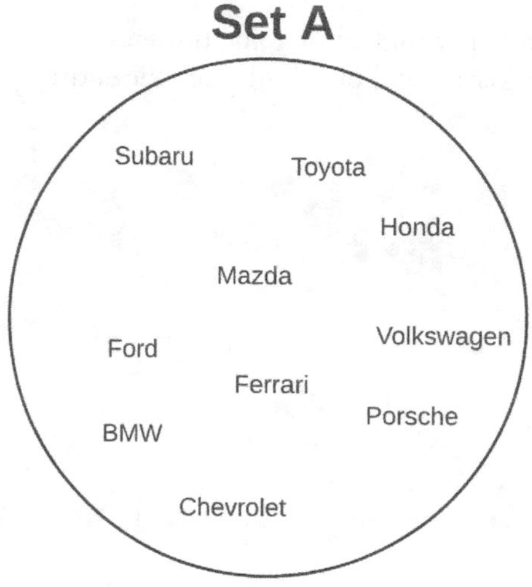

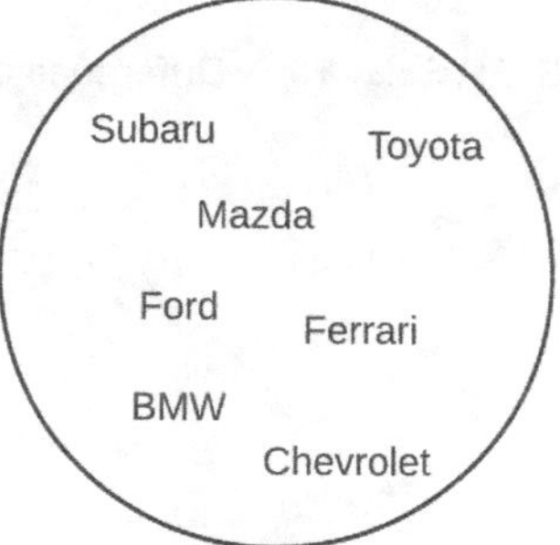

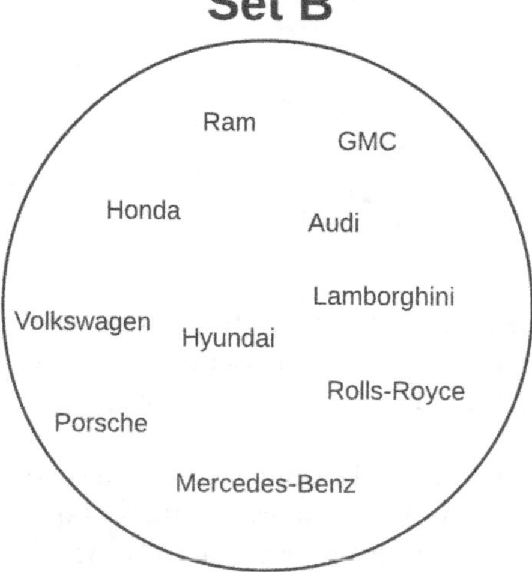

B EXCEPT A

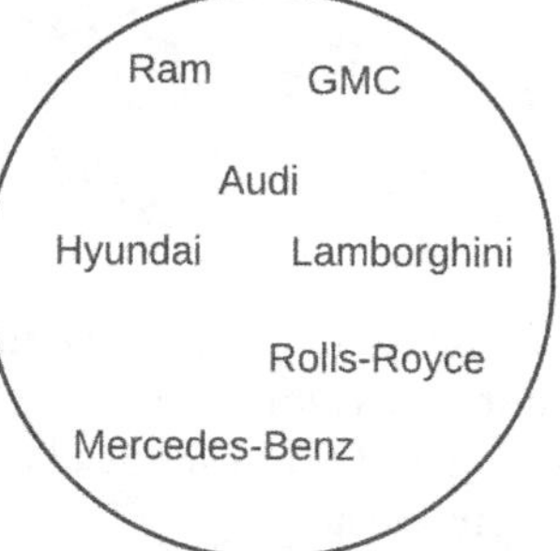

FIGURE 3.14 TCL example

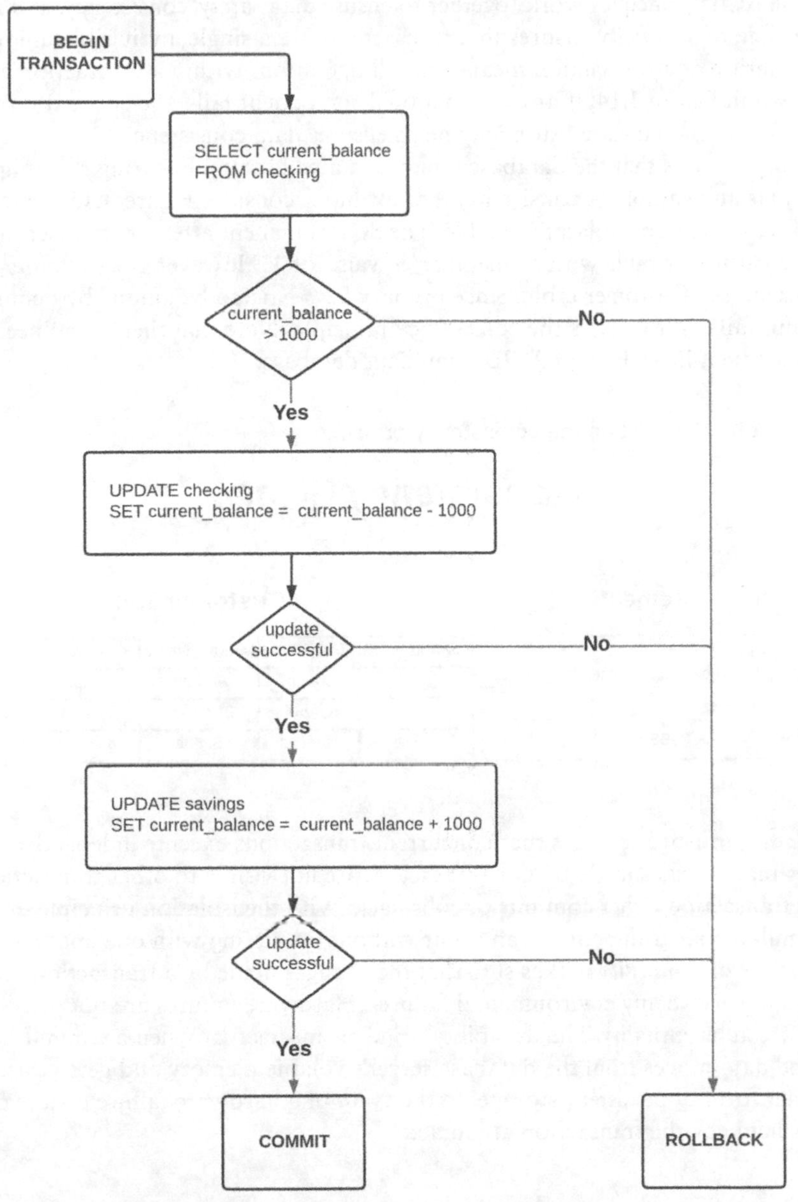

ACID Principles

ACID is an acronym that stands for Atomicity, Consistency, Isolation, and Durability. These four principles ensure data reliability and consistency when processing database transactions. Databases that are ACID-compliant maintain data consistency even when the unexpected happens. The ACID principles work together to ensure data safety, consistency, and reliability.

The principle of *atomicity* ensures that transactions are a single, indivisible unit of work. The atomic nature of a transaction means that all operations within a transaction execute as one. As shown in Figure 3.14, if any transactional component fails, the entire transaction is rolled back to its original state. Atomicity helps ensures data consistency.

Consistency ensures that the database remains in a valid state. Ensuring the uniqueness of primary keys is an example of consistency. For example, consider Figure 3.15, which shows an INSERT statement and a database table. The SQL statement attempts to insert a new row into the Customer table with a *customer_id* value of 1. However, the *customer_id* of 1 already exists in the Customer table. Since primary keys have to be unique by definition, this insert attempt fails as it violates the consistency principle. Note that there is no need to wrap the insert statement in TCL in an ACID-compliant database.

FIGURE 3.15 Illustrating the consistency principle

Consistency Error

Insert Statement

```
INSERT INTO customer
  (customer_id, first_name, middle_name, last_name,
  date_of_birth)
VALUES
  (1, 'Tom', 'David', 'Vicari', '2008-04-12')
```

Customer Table

Customer_ID	First_Name	Middle_Name	Last_Name	Date_of_Birth
1	Connor	Andrew	Sampson	2001-03-02
2	Laurel	Elizabeth	Neuhoff	2005-04-16
3	Jagadish	Simha	Venkatesan	2008-05-13

The *isolation* principle ensures that concurrent transactions execute independently. Isolation ensures that changes made by one transaction are not visible to other transactions until the current transaction either commits or rolls back. With the isolation principle in place, multiple simultaneous transactions can occur without interfering with one another.

The principle of *durability* makes sure that the changes made by a transaction are permanent and survive any environmental failures. Hardware failures are not just a possibility; they are an eventuality. The durability principle means that when a commit happens, any modified data moves from the database server's volatile memory and gets written to disk or some other form of persistent storage. In the event of a hardware failure or loss of power, the changes made by the transaction are intact.

SQL

SQL is the language of choice for creating objects and manipulating data within a relational database. American National Standards Institute Structured Query Language (ANSI SQL) is a standard version of SQL that conforms to standards set by the American National Standards Institute. One of the great benefits of ANSI SQL is that it is portable across different relational database management system platforms. This portability means that ANSI SQL code written on an Oracle database will run on an ANSI SQL–compliant database, like MySQL, PostgreSQL, or SQL Server.

ANSI SQL defines basic SQL commands, including SELECT, INSERT, UPDATE, and DELETE. ANSI SQL also establishes a set of standard data types. For example, as shown in Figure 3.4, the SELECT statement must have a FROM clause specifying the table or tables from which to retrieve data, while the WHERE clause is optional. As shown in Figure 3.3, the INSERT statement must have an INTO clause specifying the destination table for the insert.

While standardization is generally a good thing, there are varying degrees to which each database platform complies with ANSI standards. As a result, each platform supports its own set of non-ANSI-compliant SQL that extends the platform's capabilities. These non-ANSI SQL statements are unique to each platform. For example, Oracle's DATE data type supports date and time data, ranging from January 1, 4712 BCE to December 31, 4712 CE. Meanwhile, SQL Server offers DATE, DATETIME2, and DATETIME for handling dates and times. SQL Server's DATE data type supports dates between January 1, 0001 CE through December 31, 9999 CE. The inconsistent handling of dates and times is one of the most significant considerations when porting applications between database platforms.

The degree to which you use non-ANSI-SQL should be a deliberate decision. If you limit yourself to only ANSI SQL, you are not taking advantage of the full capabilities of your chosen database platform. If you develop software that needs to support multiple database platforms, use ANSI SQL as much as possible. If you are strongly committed to your existing database, using the platform's proprietary SQL components lets you take advantage of some of the features that differentiate that database from its competitors.

Programmatic SQL

While writing individual SQL statements allows you to manipulate data, programming with SQL lets you perform bulk administrative tasks as well as encapsulate business logic. SQL has various features that let you interact programmatically with a database or automate actions within the database based on a series of events.

Triggers

A *trigger* is a database object that executes SQL automatically when an event happens. You typically use triggers to react to changes to data within the database, such as inserting, updating, or deleting data in a table. Triggers are a great way to enforce business rules and can execute before or after a pending data change.

Before-update triggers take action before the intended data modification. For example, a bank may want to prevent customers from withdrawing more money than they have in their account. Figure 3.16 shows how a before-update trigger can prevent negative account balances.

Suppose customer 834 attempts to withdraw $100. Before updating the account table to reflect the withdrawal amount, the before-update trigger fires. The trigger checks to ensure that the amount available exceeds the withdrawal amount. Since the available account balance exceeds $100, this transaction decreases customer 834's balance by $100. If the customer attempts to withdraw $500, the trigger recognizes that the requested amount exceeds the existing account balance, causing the transaction to fail. In the failure scenario, customer 834's account balance does not change.

FIGURE 3.16 Before-update trigger example

Before-Update Trigger

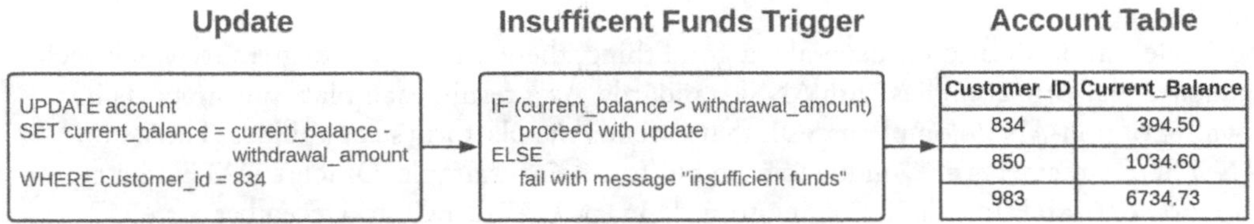
Update
Insufficent Funds Trigger
Account Table
UPDATE account
SET current_balance = current_balance -
withdrawal_amount
WHERE customer_id = 834
IF (current_balance > withdrawal_amount)
proceed with update
ELSE
fail with message "insufficient funds"
Customer_ID
Current_Balance
834
394.50
850
1034.60
983
6734.73

After-update triggers execute after a data modification. For instance, a bank lets customers configure low-balance alert notifications. Figure 3.17 shows how you can use an after-update trigger to implement low-balance alerts.

FIGURE 3.17 After-update trigger example

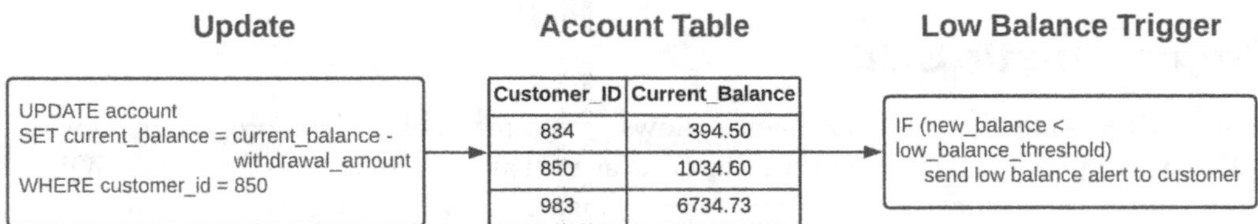
After-Update Trigger
Update
Account Table
Low Balance Trigger
UPDATE account
SET current_balance = current_balance -
withdrawal_amount
WHERE customer_id = 850
Customer_ID
Current_Balance
834
394.50
850
1034.60
983
6734.73
IF (new_balance <
low_balance_threshold)
send low balance alert to customer

Suppose customer 850 has a low-balance alert threshold of $1,000 and withdraws $100. As part of the withdrawal transaction, the update in Figure 3.17 executes successfully and reduces the account's current balance from $1,034.60 to $934.60. Since the new balance is less than $1,000, the low balance trigger will notify customer 850. However, if customer 983 withdrew $100, the low balance trigger still fires. However, the trigger doesn't output a message for customer 983 because the updated account balance exceeds the threshold amount.

It is possible to use before-change and after-change triggers on the same table. When incorporating triggers into your application design, it is vital to consider the performance implications, as triggers execute every time the underlying data changes. If you have a specific table that changes frequently, the overhead of having many triggers on that table can negatively impact performance.

Stored Procedures

A *stored procedure* is a database object containing a precompiled set of SQL statements stored within the database. Stored procedures are subroutines, or blocks of SQL code, and can include variables. One of the primary reasons for using stored procedures is their ability to implement flow control logic. The ability to write programmatic SQL allows you to combine flow control and set-based operations, making stored procedures an attractive option for implementing business logic within the database.

Since stored procedures are precompiled and stored in the database, they have a performance advantage. This performance advantage is because the database engine does not have to compile the SQL code every time you call the stored procedure. Stored procedures make it easy to reuse the code they contain, improving consistency and reducing variability.

It is common for customers to withdraw funds from an automated teller machine. Figure 3.18 shows that you can encapsulate the multiple SQL statements for withdrawing funds into a single Withdraw_Funds stored procedure. Instead of knowing how to write individual SQL statements against the tables that are part of this transaction, you need to supply the customer's ID, the account number, and the requested withdrawal amount.

The first thing the Withdraw_Funds procedure does is validate the input parameters. If the customer ID or account numbers are invalid or if the withdrawal amount is not a positive number, the procedure immediately fails. After beginning a transaction, the procedure checks to see if the specified customer's account has sufficient funds to support the withdrawal. If the funds are available, the procedure updates the account table to reflect the withdrawal and creates a transaction history record. The entire transaction is reverted if the balance verification, account update, or transaction history SQL statements fail.

Using a stored procedure abstracts the complexity of the business logic. With this configuration, you can call the procedure from an automated teller machine, a web application, or an application used by tellers at a physical bank branch. If the business logic for withdrawing funds changes, only the stored procedure needs modification. However, if the inputs to the stored procedure change, then the calling applications need updating.

Functions

A *function* is a precompiled set of SQL statements that perform a specific task or computation, commonly returning a single value. One distinguishing characteristic of a function is that you can use one in a SELECT statement, with its output available as a column in the result set of the SELECT. You can also use functions in a WHERE clause to filter results. Most relational database management systems incorporate commonly used aggregation functions such as the following:

- *COUNT(expression)*: Counts the number of rows matching the expression. For example, COUNT(*) returns a count of all rows, including null values, while COUNT(column_name) excludes any row with a null value in that column.

FIGURE 3.18 Stored procedure example

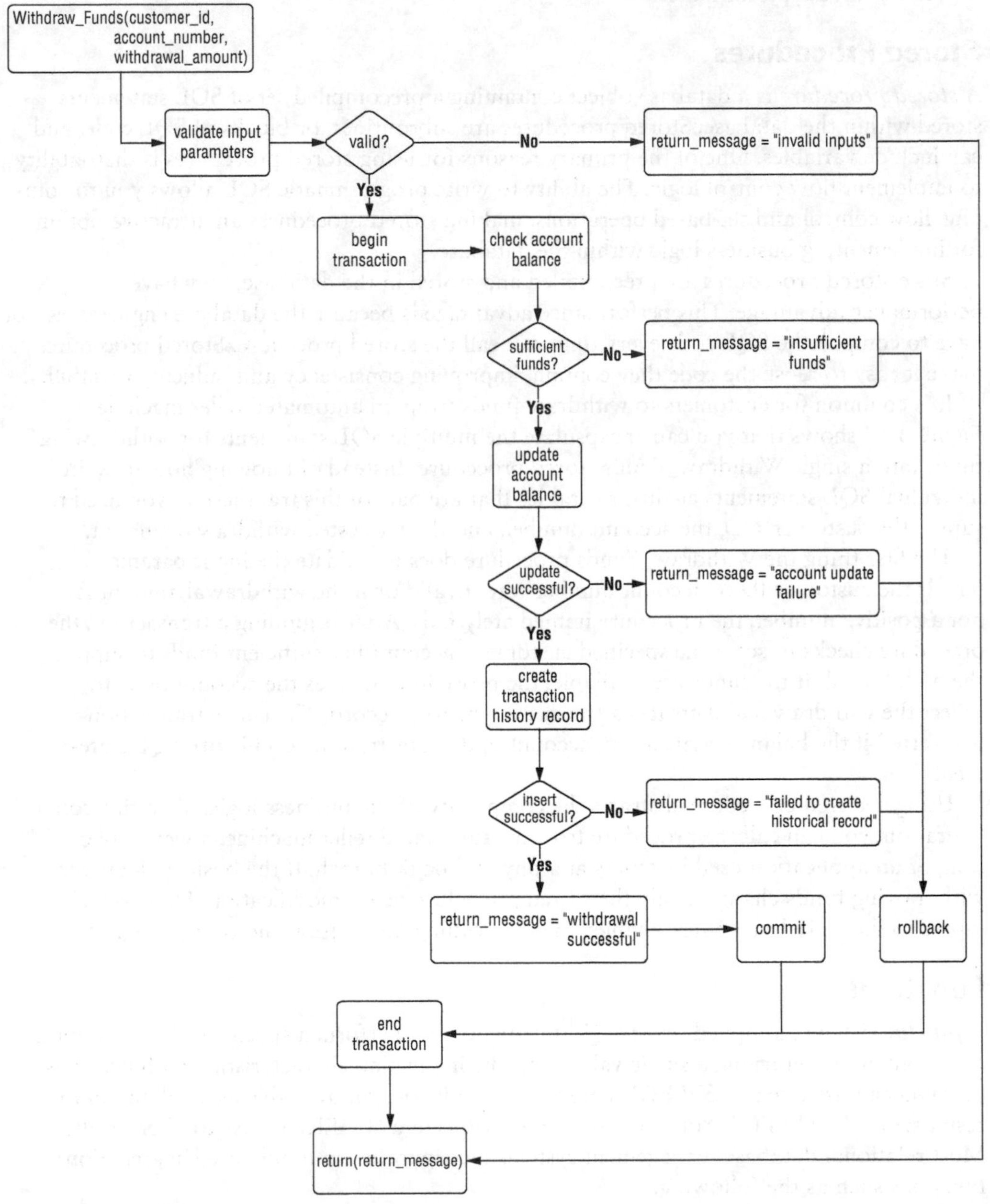

- *SUM(expression)*: Adds together the values in the expression. For example, if you have a numeric column, the SUM of that column returns all numbers added together.
- *MIN(expression)*: Finds the minimum value in the expression. You can use the MIN function on many data types, including dates, characters, and numbers.
- *MAX(column_name)*: Finds the maximum value in the expression. MAX applies across multiple data types, including dates, characters, and numbers, like the MIN function.

Aggregation functions are helpful when you need to identify a single value. Consider the Customer table in Figure 3.19.

FIGURE 3.19 Customer data

Customer Table

Customer_ID	First_Name	Middle_Name	Last_Name	Date_of_Birth	Loyalty_ID
1	Connor	Andrew	Sampson	2001-03-02	934
2	Laurel	Elizabeth	Neuhoff	2005-04-16	902
3	Jagadish	Simha	Venkatesan	2008-05-13	672
4	Sarah	Ann	O'Brien	1998-09-12	367
5	Karl	Ryan	Babcock	2000-07-01	984
6	Aleac	Marie	DeLillo	1994-08-18	814
7	Colin	Elliot	Coats	2003-03-28	315
8	Ramana	Kawnain	Bhatia	2008-05-30	747

To identify the first and last names of the youngest person from the table in Figure 3.19, you can use the MIN function on the Date_of_Birth function as follows:

```
SELECT First_Name, Last_Name
FROM  customer
WHERE Date_of_Birth = MIN(Date_of_Birth);
```

Other functions are available to facilitate data manipulation. For example, there are a variety of functions that help you work with character data. Functions exist to remove leading or trailing white space, extract a subset of characters, convert to uppercase or lowercase, and retrieve the number of characters for a given character value.

It is also possible to write custom functions. For example, suppose you frequently need to retrieve a customer's Loyalty_ID in Figure 3.19 using the Customer_ID. While the SQL to retrieve Loyalty_ID from Customer_ID is straightforward, you could develop the function shown in Figure 3.20 to centralize business logic, maximize code reuse, and make it easier for multiple programmers in your organization to work with Loyalty_IDs.

FIGURE 3.20 Custom function

Custom Function Example

```
CREATE FUNCTION getLoyaltyID (custID IN INTEGER)
  RETURN INTEGER
  IS loyaltyID INT;
  BEGIN
     SELECT Loyalty_ID
     INTO   loyaltyID
     FROM   customer
     WHERE  Customer_ID = custID
     RETURN(loyaltyID);
  END;
```


The function in Figure 3.20 is named getLoyaltyID and expects the customer ID number as a parameter. After the name and input parameters, there is a local variable called loyaltyID for storing the customer's loyalty ID. The function proceeds to select the Loyalty_ID value from the Customer table and place it in the local loyaltyID variable; then it returns that value to the caller.

Summarizing Data Across Subsets

Aggregation functions like SUM return a single value. You will frequently use aggregation functions across subsets of data, which you can accomplish by using the GROUP BY clause. The GROUP BY clause allows you to organize and condense the data in your result set by grouping rows that share the same values in the specified columns.

Suppose you have a sales table with region, product, and revenue columns. Suppose you want to calculate the total revenue for each product in each region. In that case, you need to use the GROUP BY clause in combination with an aggregation function that calculates a total. You specify the aggregation function in the SELECT clause and then add a GROUP BY as follows:

```
SELECT region
              ,product
              ,SUM(revenue) AS total_revenue
FROM sales
GROUP BY region, product
```

This query groups the rows by region and product and then calculates the sum of the revenue column for each group. The result set displays the total revenue for each product in each region.

When using the GROUP BY clause, you must include it after FROM and JOIN. The GROUP BY clause requires a comma-separated list of column names to indicate the criteria for grouping the rows.

Note that any nonaggregated columns in the SELECT clause must also appear in the GROUP BY clause. If you don't include all nonaggregated columns, the SQL statement fails since the query is trying to return one row for each group.

The GROUP BY clause is a crucial aspect of SQL that helps you aggregate and analyze data more effectively, providing valuable insights into your data. Properly using the GROUP BY clause is essential as you prepare for the exam.

Views

A *view* presents the result set of a SELECT statement as a virtual table. Most database engines implement views as read-only, so you cannot update any data using a view. Since a view contains only the columns in its defining SELECT statement, you can use a view to suppress sensitive information. This approach helps enforce data access restrictions and improve data security. Figure 3.21 illustrates how a view can obscure a column containing restricted data.

Note that the original Person table in Figure 3.21 contains Social Security numbers. While storing Social Security numbers is necessary, only a restricted set of people in an organization requires access. The view definition does not contain the Social_Security_Number column as part of the SELECT statement. Therefore, that column is not available in the view.

Once you create a view, it is available for querying, just like a regular table. The main difference is that the SQL that defines the view executes before your query. Suppose you wrote the following query on the Customer_Clean view from Figure 3.21:

```
SELECT First_Name, Last_Name
FROM  customer_clean
WHERE Customer_ID = 7;
```

Behind the scenes and transparent to the user, the database begins by running the SELECT statement that defines the customer_clean view. Upon generating the result set, the database executes the customer_clean query on the result set. Since the database runs the SELECT portion of the view whenever you query the view, the view contains any changes to the underlying table. As a result, you don't have to worry about synchronizing data between views and the tables they reference.

The SELECT statement that powers a view can source data from more than one table, making views a powerful tool for simplifying complex queries that join multiple tables. For example, suppose you have one table containing data on people, a second table with address data, and a third table with telephone numbers. Figure 3.22 illustrates how to create a view that combines data from three tables into a view. The new view is easy for people to query since it abstracts the underlying tables.

FIGURE 3.21 Using a view to restrict access

Customer Table

Customer_ID	First_Name	Middle_Name	Last_Name	Date_of_Birth	Social_Security_Number
1	Connor	Andrew	Sampson	2001-03-02	039-48-7997
2	Laurel	Elizabeth	Neuhoff	2005-04-16	038-22-0170
3	Jagadish	Simha	Venkatesan	2008-05-13	413-07-1441
4	Sarah	Ann	O'Brien	1998-09-12	221-88-2724
5	Karl	Ryan	Babcock	2000-07-01	527-67-2874
6	Aleac	Marie	DeLillo	1994-08-18	635-12-2323
7	Colin	Elliot	Coats	2003-03-28	300-02-0723
8	Ramana	Kawnain	Bhatia	2008-05-30	009-58-6515

Create View

```
CREATE  VIEW customer_clean
AS
SELECT Customer_ID,
       First_Name,
       Middle_Name,
       Last_Name,
       Date_of_Birth
FROM person;
```

Customer_Clean view

Customer_ID	First_Name	Middle_Name	Last_Name	Date_of_Birth
1	Connor	Andrew	Sampson	2001-03-02
2	Laurel	Elizabeth	Neuhoff	2005-04-16
3	Jagadish	Simha	Venkatesan	2008-05-13
4	Sarah	Ann	O'Brien	1998-09-12
5	Karl	Ryan	Babcock	2000-07-01
6	Aleac	Marie	DeLillo	1994-08-18
7	Colin	Elliot	Coats	2003-03-28
8	Ramana	Kawnain	Bhatia	2008-05-30

Recall that when queried, views execute the SQL SELECT that defines them. This characteristic can lead to performance problems as data volumes in the underlying tables grow. Performance can also degrade if the view's query is exceptionally complex. One way of mitigating performance problems is with a materialized view.

A materialized view stores the result of the SELECT statement in a physical table instead of returning the result set each time you query the view. Materializing a view improves query performance since the data is not retrieved from the underlying tables when the query executes. However, since the data in a materialized view is static, changes to the underlying table are not included. The absence of data changes results in a data freshness issue.

FIGURE 3.22 Using a view to combine data from multiple tables

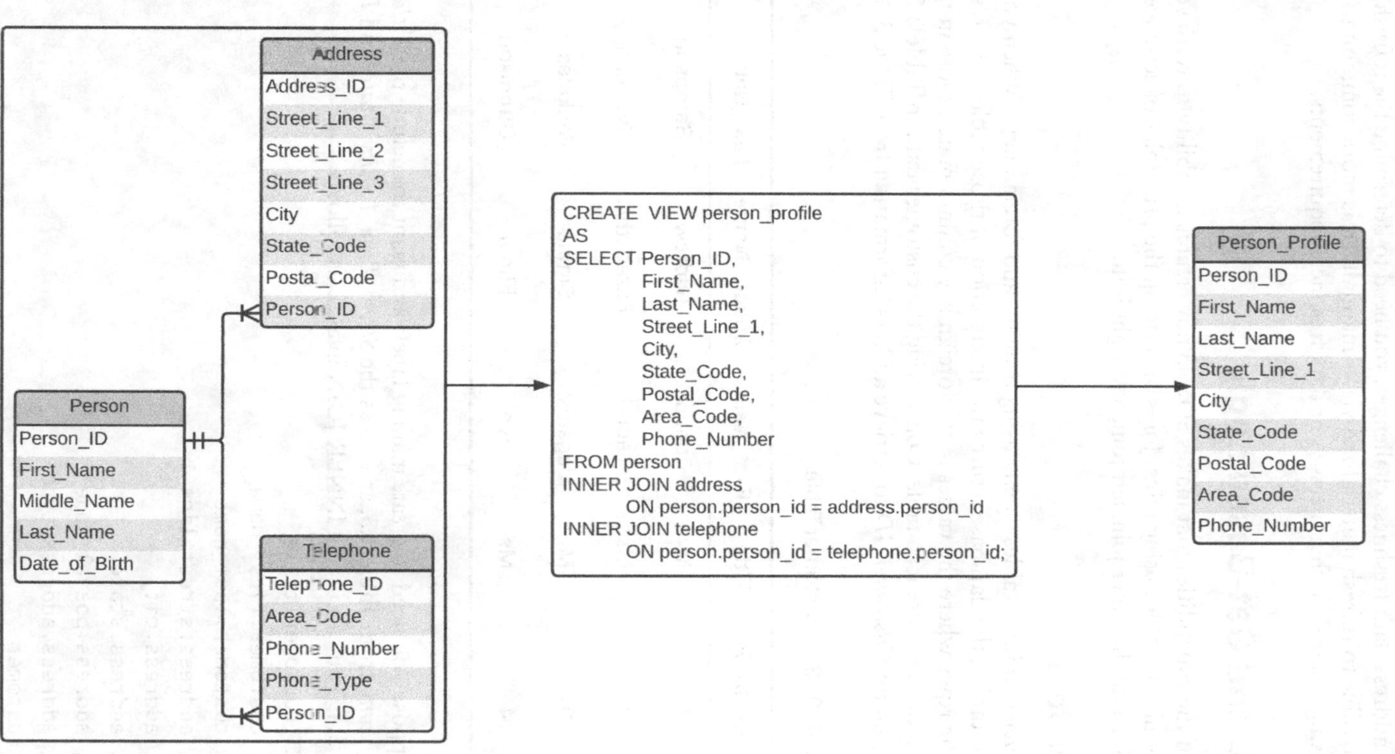

To address data freshness challenges, you need to determine the refresh frequency. While it is possible to refresh materialized views manually, it is more common to automate the process using a schedule that meets your data freshness requirements.

SQL and Set-Based Logic

One of the capabilities that makes SQL so powerful is its ability to retrieve associated data from multiple tables using joins. Joins operate on the principles of set-based logic. Types of joins include the inner join, left join, and right join.

Inner Join

An *inner join* joins tables chiefly using primary and foreign keys. When you use an inner join on two tables, the database returns the intersection of those tables. The result set includes only the rows where the values in the foreign key column match those in the primary key column of the referenced table. Considering the customer data in Table 3.3, you can use an inner join on *Customer_ID* to retrieve address information from Table 3.4.

TABLE 3.3 Customer Table

Customer_ID (PK)	Title	First_Name	Middle_Name	Last_Name	Date_of_Birth
1	Mr	Connor	Andrew	Sampson	March 2, 2001
2	Ms	Laurel	Elizabeth	Neuhoff	April 16, 2005
3	Mr	Jagadish	Simha	Venkatesan	May 13, 2008
4	Ms	Eve	Elinor	Gunnison	July 13, 1998

Suppose you need to create mailing labels and want to include the *Title*, *First_Name*, and *Last_Name* from Table 3.3, as well as the *Street_Line_1*, *City*, *State*, and *Postal_Code* from Table 3.4. You can use an INNER JOIN in SQL as follows:

```
SELECT customer.title
    , customer.first_name
    , customer.last_name
    , address.street_line_1
    , address.city
    , address.state
    , address.postal_code
    , address.address_type
FROM customer
INNER JOIN address
ON customer.Customer_ID = address.Customer_ID;
```

TABLE 3.4 Address Data

Address_ID (PK)	Street_Line_1	Street_Line_2	City	State	Postal_Code	Address_Type	Customer_ID (FK)
100	25 W Main St		Bozeman	MT	59715	Work	1
101	213 Masonic Dr		Bozeman	MT	59715	Home	1
102	79 Hanifan Ln		Atlanta	GA	30308	Work	2
103	3602 Ferry St		Atlanta	GA	30308	Home	2
104	4098 Valley Ln		Austin	TX	78758	Work	3
105	2374 Bubby Dr	Unit 401	Austin	TX	78758	Home	3

Examining the previous SQL statement, it starts with a SELECT statement, specifying the Customer table in the FROM clause. The SQL statement then extends the FROM clause by adding an INNER JOIN, which identifies the table to include in the inner join. The ON keyword specifies the customer and address table columns to use in the join operation. Finally, the WHERE clause filters the data to only addresses with an *address_type* of "Work." Table 3.5 depicts the result set for this query.

TABLE 3.5 Name and Work Address Result Set

Title	First_ Name	Last_Name	Street_Line_1	City	State	Postal_ Code	Address_ Type
Mr	Connor	Sampson	25 W Main St	Bozeman	MT	59715	Work
Mr	Connor	Sampson	213 Masonic Dr	Bozeman	MT	59715	Home
Ms	Laurel	Neuhoff	79 Hanifan Ln	Atlanta	GA	30308	Work
Ms	Laurel	Neuhoff	3602 Ferry St	Atlanta	GA	30308	Home
Mr	Jagadish	Venkatesan	4098 Valley Ln	Austin	TX	78758	Work
Mr	Jagadish	Venkatesan	2374 Bubby Dr	Austin	TX	78758	Home

Left/Right Join

A *left join*, or *left outer join*, returns every row from the left table and the matching rows from the right table. If there are no matching rows in the right table, the result set includes NULLs for those columns. Looking at the data in Table 3.3 and 3.4, Eve Gunnison exists in Table 3.3 but not in Table 3.4. Consider the following query, which performs a left join between the Customer and Address tables:

```
    SELECT customer.title
    , customer.first_name
    , customer.last_name
    , address.street_line_1
    , address.city
    , address.state
    , address.postal_code
    , address.address_type
FROM customer
LEFT JOIN address
ON customer.Customer_ID = address.Customer_ID;
```

You can see that syntactically, this query resembles an inner join, replacing the word *inner* with the word *left*. Since the Customer table precedes the join statement, it is the left table in the join operation. Table 3.6 shows the result set of that SQL statement, including a row for Eve Gunnison with NULL values for her address information.

TABLE 3.6 LEFT JOIN Name and Address Result Set

Title	First_ Name	Last_Name	Street_Line_1	City	State	Postal_ Code	Address_ Type
Mr	Connor	Sampson	25 W Main St	Bozeman	MT	59715	Work
Mr	Connor	Sampson	213 Masonic Dr	Bozeman	MT	59715	Home
Ms	Laurel	Neuhoff	79 Hanifan Ln	Atlanta	GA	30308	Work
Ms	Laurel	Neuhoff	3602 Ferry St	Atlanta	GA	30308	Home
Mr	Jagadish	Venkatesan	4098 Valley Ln	Austin	TX	78758	Work
Mr	Jagadish	Venkatesan	2374 Bubby Dr	Austin	TX	78758	Home
Ms	Eve	Gunnison	*NULL*	*NULL*	*NULL*	*NULL*	*NULL*

By understanding how left joins work, you can use this knowledge to identify only people who do not have an address by adding a filter condition in the WHERE clause. Consider the following SQL statement, which checks to see if the customer_id in the address table is null:

```
    SELECT customer.title
  , customer.first_name
  , customer.last_name
  , address.street_line_1
  , address.city
  , address.state
  , address.postal_code
  , address.address_type
FROM customer
LEFT JOIN address
ON customer.Customer_ID = address.Customer_ID
WHERE address.customer_id IS NULL;
```

This query's result set only contains a row for Eve because she has an entry in the Customer table and no corresponding data in the Address table.

A *right join*, or *right outer join*, returns all rows from the table on the right side of the join condition while only including the matching rows from the left table. A right join is similar in concept but opposite in execution to a left join.

Full Join

A *full join*, or *full outer join*, combines the results of a left outer join and a right outer join. A full join returns all rows from both tables and includes NULL values for columns that do not match the join condition. Suppose you work in an environment with poor relational discipline and lacking primary and foreign keys. The full join statement can help you identify data inconsistencies. Consider the Employee and Order tables in Figure 3.23.

Suppose the Employee table in Figure 3.23 has a primary key of Employee_ID, while the Order table has a primary key of *Order_ID*. However, no foreign key connects the order table's *Employee_ID* column to the Employee table. Without a foreign key, orders can exist without an associated employee. Similarly, you can have employees who have no orders. Looking at the result set, it is plausible that Rakesh Gupta has no orders, which is possible if Rakesh is a new employee and has yet to make a sale. However, looking at the row for order 69, there is no corresponding row for employee 103. Possible explanations include that the employee's record no longer exists or someone is committing fraud by entering orders for fake employees. Either way, the result of the full join identifies both employees without orders as well as orders without employees.

Automating Operations

Databases are complex and require a significant amount of operational care and feeding. To ensure that queries perform efficiently, you must ensure indexes are up-to-date. If you have large tables with billions of rows, you might consider partitioning them. To protect the data within a database, you need a plan for backing that data up. Taking backups helps you mitigate the risk of media failures and other catastrophic events. Testing the recovery of those backups is equally important, because the backups have value only if you can recover your data from those backups.

Additional crucial operational tasks include monitoring and maintaining the database. From a monitoring standpoint, you need to ensure that the database's allocated storage, memory, and compute resources have enough capacity to tolerate activity spikes. You must also maintain the database software, applying the inevitable security, performance, and new feature patches. Considering all of these operational activities, it is easy to see why database administration requires a lot of people and takes a lot of time.

Fortunately, you can use automation to increase the impact of an individual database administrator. Database administrators can create time for higher-value projects and tasks by developing scripts to automate routine tasks. In addition to making time for other activities, automating maintenance tasks improves consistency since scripts ensure that the tasks they perform happen the same way every time.

FIGURE 3.23 Employee and Order tables

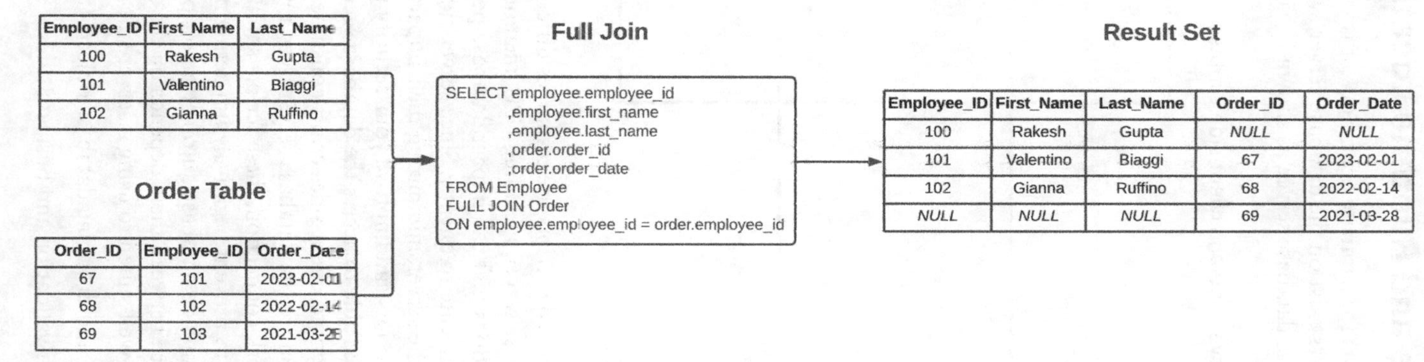

Employee Table
Employee_ID First_Name Last_Name
100 Rakesh Gupta
101 Valentino Biaggi
102 Gianna Ruffino
Order Table
Order_ID Employee_ID Order_Date
67 101 2023-02-01
68 102 2022-02-14
69 103 2021-03-28
Full Join
SELECT employee.employee_id
,employee.first_name
,employee.last_name
,order.order_id
,order.order_date
FROM Employee
FULL JOIN Order
ON employee.employee_id = order.employee_id
Result Set
Employee_ID First_Name Last_Name Order_ID Order_Date
100 Rakesh Gupta NULL NULL
101 Valentino Biaggi 67 2023-02-01
102 Gianna Ruffino 68 2022-02-14
NULL NULL NULL 69 2021-03-28

Script Purpose and Runtime Location

When developing scripts for database operations, it is vital to consider where those scripts reside. *Server-side scripts* exist on the database server, while *client-side scripts* run from a computer other than the database server, as shown in Figure 3.24.

FIGURE 3.24 Server-side and client-side scripts

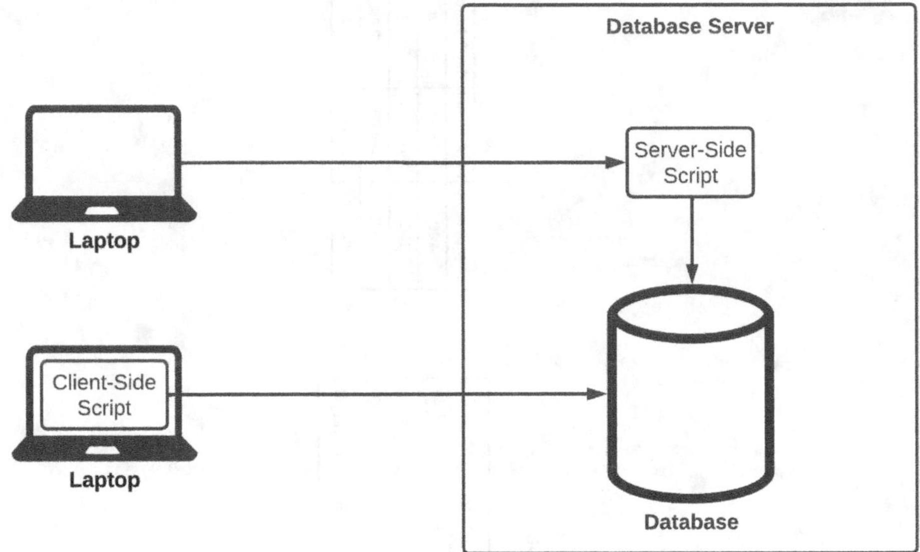

Server-side and client-side scripts use resources differently. Server-side scripts consume resources on the database server, including CPU, memory, and disk space. Scripts also generate database transactions that can impact database performance, mainly if the scripts are resource-intensive or execute frequently. Since server-side scripts can compete with the database for resources on the server, minimizing their impact on the database is vital. Additionally, using server-side scripts can improve your security posture since the only people who can access them must be able to access the database server.

Unlike server-side scripts, client-side scripts consume resources on the client machine, only sending instructions to the database server over a network connection. Since client-side scripts rely on a network connection, these scripts should avoid generating or manipulating large amounts of data to prevent negatively impacting network performance.

Server-side and client-side database automation scripts both have advantages and disadvantages, and the choice between them depends on the specific needs and requirements of a project. Tasks that are well-suited to using a server-side script include the following:

- Creating, altering, and dropping database objects (tables, views, indexes, etc.)
- Implementing data validation and business rules

- Implementing security and access controls
- Running complex data transformations and aggregations

Since client-side scripts offload resources from the database server, they are better suited for tasks such as the following:

- Extracting data from the database for reporting and analysis
- Presenting data to users in web or mobile applications
- Performing ad hoc data analysis and manipulation tasks

Transforming Data: ETL or ELT?

It is common for data to move from transactional databases to databases designed for analytics through an *extract, transform, and load* (*ETL*) process. In the extract phase, you export data from a database. During the transform phase, you convert and restructure the data so it is ready to import into the analytical database. The import phase loads data into the destination database.

With the ETL approach to data migration, minimizing the load on the source and destination database servers is a common practice. In this scenario, a general-purpose programming language handles the compute-intensive data transformation step on a separate server.

Extract, load, and transform (*ELT*) is an alternative to ETL. With this approach, you load the raw transactional data directly into your analytical database. You leverage the power of the analytical database to do the necessary data transformations. With the transform step happening within the analytical database, this approach puts more load on the database server.

Both ETL and ELT approaches are valid. Choosing between ETL and ELT comes down to several factors, including organizational preference, alignment with team skills, and available server resources.

Languages

You can choose from various programming languages when automating database operations. Suppose you want to use the power of the database to transform data before sending it to a different environment for analysis. In this case, running a server-side script is a good approach. When running server-side scripts, it is common to use database-specific scripting languages, such as *Procedural Language for SQL (PL/SQL)* for Oracle or *Transact-SQL (T-SQL)* for Microsoft SQL Server. Both PL/SQL and T-SQL are proprietary languages that run within their respective database engines and let you control the flow of a program, declare variables, and implement exception handling. You might also use a more general-purpose programming language to perform maintenance tasks on the database server.

Client-side scripts typically use a more general-purpose programming language, such as *Java*, *JavaScript*, *PowerShell*, or *Python*. Since these languages do not depend on a specific database, it is easier to use these languages to automate everyday tasks across multiple database platforms. These languages are also typically easier to integrate with other applications.

Command-Line Scripting

When automating database operations, you will invariably need to create command-line scripts. A command-line script is a series of commands executed in sequence from a command-line interface. While it can be easier for people to perform administrative tasks through a web or graphical interface, the path to automating and scaling repetitive or complex tasks belongs in the world of command-line scripting. Frequently, the operating system you use influences your choice of scripting language.

Linux

Linux is a free and open-source operating system that is one of the world's most widely used operating systems, powering everything from smartphones and servers to supercomputers and embedded devices. One reason you find Linux in so many places is that the operating system requires relatively few resources from the computer where it runs. Administrators typically use a command-line interface when configuring, maintaining, and automating tasks on the Linux operating system. Many database platforms, including Oracle, MySQL, and PostgreSQL, run efficiently on Linux.

There are a wide variety of scripting languages to choose from on Linux, including the following:

- *Bash*: Bash (Bourne-Again SHell) is the default shell for most Linux distributions. As the default, Bash is a popular option for scripting on Linux. Since Bash scripts are simple text files, you can use any text editor to modify them. You can use Bash scripts to automate everyday administrative tasks such as backing up a database or scheduling the execution of a batch process.
- *Python*: Initially released in 1991, Python is an effective general-purpose programming language. Python is very efficient for automating system tasks as well as transforming data. One of the reasons Python is so popular is that many libraries and modules are available that simplify tasks such as text manipulation.
- *Perl*: Perl is a general-purpose programming language widely used for scripting on Linux. Initially released in 1987, Perl is a relatively dated scripting language. Perl is a good option for text processing and data manipulation. You will likely find Perl scripts in established environments as organizations migrate from Perl toward more modern scripting languages like Python.

In addition to Bash, Python, and Perl, there are many other scripting languages on Linux. You might also encounter more specialized languages like Sed and Awk when processing text.

Windows

Microsoft Windows is a proprietary operating system developed and sold by Microsoft Corporation. Unlike Linux, Windows is a graphical user interface (GUI) operating system. First released in 1985, you will find Windows on personal computers, laptops, and servers. With roughly 70 percent market share, Windows powers most of the world's personal computers. Windows Server hit the market in 2003, becoming increasingly capable with each new release. While there is no doubt that Windows dominates the endpoint computing market, Linux is the operating system of choice for more than 90 percent of the top 1 million websites in the world.

Similar to Linux, there are several common scripting languages used for Microsoft Windows, including the following:

- *Batch* scripts: Batch scripts are simple text files that execute a series of commands using Windows' command-line interface, the Windows command prompt. Like Bash scripts on Linux, you can edit Batch scripts in any simple text editor like Notepad. While it is possible to create Batch scripts, most modern Windows-centric organizations take advantage of the additional features of PowerShell for automating administrative tasks.
- *PowerShell* scripts: PowerShell is a powerful and flexible scripting language that provides a feature-rich, advanced environment for automating tasks in Windows. Numerous modules are available for PowerShell that let you efficiently accomplish administrative tasks like managing processes, services, or file systems. You can even invoke existing Batch scripts from PowerShell, and installing the PowerShell interpreter on Linux is possible.
- *VBScript*: VBScript is a scripting language based on the Visual Basic programming language that predates PowerShell. Like Perl on Linux, you might encounter VBScript in mature Windows-centric organizations, with most ongoing development happening in PowerShell.
- *Python*: One of the benefits of Python is that it runs on both Linux and Windows. Many Python libraries are available to make the automation of tasks on Windows easier to accomplish.

Many scripting languages are available for automating database and operating system–related administrative tasks regardless of the operating system.

Summary

Relational databases are the most common type of databases. Structured Query Language is the language that lets you interact programmatically with relational databases. There are two flavors of SQL: Data Definition Language and Data Manipulation Language.

DDL is a set of SQL commands used to define the structure of a database, including creating, altering, and deleting tables, indexes, constraints, and other database objects. Administrators use DDL statements to design and maintain the structure of a database. However, DDL statements do not modify the data stored within the database.

DML is the set of SQL commands for manipulating data in a database. Commonly used DML statements include INSERT, SELECT, UPDATE, and DELETE. These statements let you add, retrieve, modify, and delete data in a database. Data analysts, web applications, and reporting tools use DML statements to interact directly with the data stored in the database. Administrators use DML to monitor the database and to migrate data between databases.

Set-based logic is a way of processing data in relational databases by treating it as sets of rows rather than individual rows. This approach enables the efficient use of powerful DML statements to perform operations such as finding the intersection, union, or difference between sets of data. The result is a more optimized and scalable approach to processing data in a relational database.

Transaction control languages (TCL) are used to manage multiple database changes as a single unit of work, called a transaction. A transaction consists of one or more SQL statements that must execute together as an atomic unit. If any SQL statement within the transaction fails, the entire transaction reverts to its original state. TCL commands include BEGIN TRANSACTION, COMMIT, and ROLLBACK. In a multi-user environment, the length of transactions is an essential consideration, as transactions lock tables during the operation, which can impact other users.

ACID stands for Atomicity, Consistency, Isolation, and Durability. It is a set of principles that ensure the reliability and consistency of data in database transactions. Atomicity ensures that transactions are a single, indivisible unit of work. Transactions exhibit the principle of atomicity since all operations within a transaction execute as one. Consistency ensures that the database remains in a valid state, and any violation of constraints will result in transaction failure. Isolation ensures that concurrent transactions execute independently and changes made by one transaction are not visible to other database users until committed or rolled back. Durability ensures that a transaction's changes are permanent and survive environmental failures.

SQL is a standard programming language for managing and manipulating relational databases. American National Standards Institute Structured Query Language is the standardized version of SQL. ANSI SQL specifies standard SQL commands and syntax that database management systems must follow to comply, ensuring compatibility and portability across different platforms and systems. ANSI SQL provides a consistent framework for working with relational databases, regardless of the underlying technology. Most relational database platforms comply with a subset of ANSI SQL standards and add adjacent features that help make each platform unique.

Programmatic SQL refers to using SQL programming constructs like triggers, stored procedures, functions, and views to encapsulate business logic, abstract complex queries, foster code reuse, and improve the reliability of your SQL. Triggers are SQL statements that automatically execute in response to a triggering event, such as data modification. Stored procedures let you define variables and implement flow control, allowing the combination of set-based and programmatic logic with database transactions. Stored procedures can optionally take inputs and return results. Functions are similar to stored procedures, typically returning a single value. Unlike stored procedures, functions are callable within the SELECT component of a SQL statement. Views use a SELECT statement to create a virtual table. You can use views to simplify data access, enforce security, and improve performance.

Databases require ongoing maintenance to ensure efficient operational performance and data protection. Maintenance tasks include regularly updating indexes, partitioning large tables, taking backups, testing backup recovery, monitoring resource usage, and applying software updates. While database administration is complex and time-consuming, using scripts to automate routine tasks frees up time for other activities and improves consistency in maintenance processes.

When developing scripts for database operations, it is vital to consider the location of the scripts server-side or client-side. Server-side scripts run on the database server and consume its resources. Client-side scripts run on a separate computer and send instructions to the database server only over a network connection. Tasks that benefit from a server-side approach include creating and altering database objects, implementing security and data validation, and running complex data transformations. Examples favoring a client-side approach include data extraction for reporting and analysis, data presentation to users, and ad hoc data manipulation. The choice between server-side and client-side scripts depends on a project's specific needs and requirements.

You typically use command-line scripts to automate database operations. You will find command-line scripts useful on both Linux and Windows operating systems. Many scripting languages are available, including Bash, Perl, and Python on Linux and Batch, PowerShell, and VBScript for Windows. Some scripting languages, including Python and PowerShell, work on both Linux and Windows servers.

Exam Essentials

Describe the difference between DML and DDL. Data Definition Language creates, modifies, and removes database objects, including tables, views, and indexes. Data Manipulation Language creates, reads, updates, and deletes data. With a few exceptions, like dropping a table, DDL statements do not change data within the database. You use DML statements to interact with data, while you use DDL when you need to alter the structure of the database.

Describe the importance of set-based logic. Set-based logic manipulates sets of data as a whole rather than as individual records. This approach is vital in database development and management because it is typically more efficient and scalable than a procedural approach. Manifesting the set principles of intersection, union, and difference, SQL implements set-based logic, allowing administrators and developers to create fast, concise, and maintainable code.

Describe the importance of transaction control languages. TCLs represent a framework for incorporating one or more SQL statements into a single unit of work. If any subcomponent of a transaction fails, the entire transaction fails, reverting any changes made during the transaction. A commit statement saves and ends a transaction, while a rollback undoes any work and ends the transaction.

Describe the ACID principles. ACID refers to Atomicity, Consistency, Isolation, and Durability. TCLs enable atomicity by letting you treat more than one SQL statement as a single unit of work. A primary key constraint enforces consistency by ensuring that every value for the primary key is unique. Isolation keeps transactions separate from one another, allowing simultaneous concurrent transactions without corrupting the data. Durability ensures data safety, so data is not lost during a database crash or hardware failure.

Describe the importance of scripting and runtime location. Scripting is essential for efficient database operations. Scripting lets you programmatically maintain, patch, upgrade, back up, and restore databases. Server-side scripts run on the database server, while client-side scripts run on a network-adjacent server. Long-running scripts that rely on a persistent database connection are usually server-side, while client-side activity tends to be shorter in duration and less crucial to database operations.

Review Questions

1. Eve needs to change the value of an existing customer's address in the database. What DML command should she use?
   - A. INSERT
   - B. SELECT
   - C. UPDATE
   - D. DELETE
2. Satish is working on automating the deployment of database software patches in a Linux environment. Which of the following approaches describes his optimal choice?
   - A. Implement a client-side script using Python.
   - B. Implement a server-side script using Bash.
   - C. Implement a client-side script using PowerShell.
   - D. Implement a server-side script using Batch.
3. Monica is a database administrator at a midsize company. She wants to create a new table named Employees and ensure that every row has a unique identifier in the *employee_id* column, which cannot be NULL. She also wants to specify data types for each column. Which SQL flavor and commands should Susan use to achieve this?
   - A. Data Definition Language (DDL); CREATE TABLE, ALTER TABLE
   - B. Data Definition Language (DDL); INSERT, SELECT
   - C. Data Manipulation Language (DML); CREATE TABLE, ALTER TABLE
   - D. Data Manipulation Language (DML); INSERT, SELECT
4. Jenny is a data analyst at a midsize company. She needs to retrieve data on specific clients from a table and update their contact information based on the latest data provided. Which flavor of SQL should Jenny use to perform these tasks?
   - A. Data Definition Language (DDL)
   - B. Data Control Language (DCL)
   - C. Transaction control language (TCL)
   - D. Data Manipulation Language (DML)

5. In a company database, there are two tables: Employees and Salaries. The Employees table has the following columns: *EmployeeID*, *FirstName*, *LastName*, and *Department*. The Salaries table has the following columns: *EmployeeID*, *Salary*, and *Bonus*. Bob, the HR manager, wants to see a list of employees who work in the IT department, along with their total annual income (Salary + Bonus). Which SQL query should Bob use to retrieve this information?

   A. SELECT Employees.FirstName, Employees.LastName, (Salaries .Salary + Salaries.Bonus) AS TotalAnnualIncome

   FROM Employees

   INNER JOIN Salaries ON Employees.EmployeeID = Salaries.EmployeeID

   B. SELECT Employees.FirstName, Employees.LastName, (Salaries .Salary + Salaries.Bonus) AS TotalAnnualIncome

   FROM Employees

   INNER JOIN Salaries ON Employees.EmployeeID = Salaries.EmployeeID

   WHERE Employees.Department = 'HR'

   C. SELECT Employees.FirstName, Employees.LastName, Salaries .Salary, Salaries.Bonus

   FROM Employees

   JOIN Salaries ON Employees.EmployeeID = Salaries.EmployeeID

   WHERE Employees.Department = 'IT'

   D. SELECT Employees.FirstName, Employees.LastName, (Salaries .Salary + Salaries.Bonus) AS TotalAnnualIncome

   FROM Employees

   JOIN Salaries ON Employees.EmployeeID = Salaries.EmployeeID

   WHERE Employees.Department = 'IT'

6. The following SQL query should retrieve a list of products, prices, and categories from a database for all products that cost more than $50. However, the SQL statement does not work as written:

   SELECT ProductName, Price, Category

   FROM Products

   INNER JOIN Categories ON Products.CategoryID Categories.CategoryID

   WHERE Price > 50;

   Which of the following options should be applied to correct the SQL query?

   A. Replace the INNER JOIN with a LEFT JOIN.

   B. Set Products.CategoryID = Categories.CategoryID in the ON clause.

   C. Change the WHERE clause to look for Price >= 50.

   D. Set Products.CategoryID - Categories.CategoryID in the ON clause.

7. Alex is a data analyst at an online retail company. He needs to determine the total revenue generated for each product category in each country. The company's database has a table called orders with the following columns: *country*, *product_category*, and *revenue*. Which of the following SQL queries should Alex use to achieve his goal?

A.
```
SELECT country
    ,product_category
    ,SUM(revenue) AS total_revenue
FROM orders
```

B.
```
SELECT country
    ,product_category
    ,SUM(revenue) AS total_revenue
FROM orders
GROUP BY country
```

C.
```
SELECT country
    ,product_category
    ,SUM(revenue) AS total_revenue
FROM orders
GROUP BY country, product_category
```

D.
```
SELECT SUM(revenue) AS total_revenue
FROM orders
GROUP BY country, product_category
```

8. Xavier is a data analyst at a medium-sized company. He is working on a report and needs customers' full names and work addresses. The customer information exists in two related tables: Customer, containing name data, and Address, containing work address data. Xavier needs to join these tables together to create the desired report. Which type of join should he use to retrieve the required information?

   A. INNER JOIN
   B. LEFT JOIN
   C. RIGHT JOIN
   D. FULL JOIN

9. Andy is a systems analyst at a growing e-commerce company. He needs to create a report that includes all customers, their full names, and their shipping addresses, if available. The customer information exists in two related tables: Customer, containing name data, and Address, containing address data. Andy must join these tables together to get the data he needs. Which type of join should Andy use to retrieve the required information?

   A. INNER JOIN
   B. LEFT JOIN
   C. RIGHT JOIN
   D. FULL JOIN

10. Sherry is a database administrator at a regional bank. She needs to create a mechanism that automatically sends low-balance alert notifications to customers whenever their account balance falls below a certain threshold. Which database object should Sherry use to accomplish this task?
   A. Stored procedure
   B. Function
   C. Before-update trigger
   D. After-update trigger

11. Gina is a data analyst for a large e-commerce organization. She wants to understand sales volume over the past three hours, getting the required data from the database. Which type of script should she use to minimize the impact on the database server?
   A. Server-side script
   B. Client-side script
   C. ETL script
   D. ELT script

12. Bushra, a database administrator, must apply a security patch to the database software for her company's financial system. Which type of script would be best suited for this task?
   A. Server-side script
   B. Client-side script
   C. ETL script
   D. ELT script

13. Peter, a database administrator, is working on a project where he needs to perform maintenance tasks within a Microsoft SQL Server database. Which scripting language would be most appropriate for Peter?
   A. JavaScript
   B. Python
   C. T-SQL
   D. Bash

14. Sandy, a database developer, wants to automate extracting transactional data from a Linux-based PostgreSQL database and reshaping it for analytical purposes. Which scripting language would be the most appropriate choice for her to use for client-side automation tasks?
   A. Bash
   B. T-SQL
   C. PL/SQL
   D. Python

15. Tracey is a database administrator who needs to automate a set of administrative tasks on a Windows Server. She wants a modern scripting language that provides a feature-rich, advanced environment for automating tasks in Windows. Which scripting language should Tracey choose?
    A. Batch scripts
    B. PowerShell
    C. VBScript
    D. Java
16. As a Linux DevOps engineer, Joe needs to automate a series of administrative tasks on a Linux server. He wants to use a native scripting language so the scripts he develops will run on virtually any Linux machine. Which language should Joe use for his automation needs?
    A. Python
    B. PowerShell
    C. Batch
    D. Bash
17. Elinor is a business intelligence manager at a medium-sized company. Her team is responsible for migrating data from the company's transactional databases to a data warehouse. Given her team's existing Python expertise, she wants to choose the best data migration approach. Which approach should Elinor consider for this data migration?
    A. ETL
    B. ELT
    C. FTP
    D. API
18. Maggie is a database administrator at a software development company. She needs to implement a database object that automatically enforces a business rule whenever a user's email address changes. Which database object should Maggie create?
    A. Stored procedure
    B. View
    C. Trigger
    D. Function
19. Julia is a database developer at an e-commerce company. She needs to implement a reusable and precompiled set of SQL statements to handle order processing, which involves updating inventory, creating an order record, and recording the transaction history. Which database object should Julia create to achieve this?
    A. Trigger
    B. Stored procedure
    C. View
    D. Function

20. Allison is a database developer at a software company. She needs to ensure that a series of SQL statements execute as a single atomic unit, and if any statement within this group fails, the entire group of statements reverts to its original state. Which transaction control language (TCL) command should Allison use to accomplish this task?

    A. BEGIN TRANSACTION

    B. COMMIT

    C. ROLLBACK

    D. SAVEPOINT

Database Deployment

THE COMPTIA DATASYS+ EXAM TOPICS COVERED IN THIS CHAPTER INCLUDE:

✓ **Domain 2.0: Database Deployment**

- 2.1. Compare and Contrast Aspects of Database Planning and Design
- 2.2. Explain Database Implementation, Testing, and Deployment Phases

Relational databases are complex pieces of software that process and store vast amounts of data. Careful planning is needed to ensure that a database meets the needs of the people who use it and the applications that use it for storing and retrieving data. The ultimate objective is to create a database that satisfies users, meets operational demands, and requires minimal maintenance. As a data systems analyst, you will be a crucial perspective as part of the team that brings a new database to life.

In this chapter, we will first explore considerations for database implementation planning. We will then examine some fundamental questions influencing database design, ensuring that the database fits into an organization's strategic architectural direction, and then delve into the artifacts essential for a well-understood database design.

With an understanding of how to plan and design a database, we will examine the implementation, testing, and deployment phases that take a database from concept to reality.

Planning and Design

The planning and design phases are vital to creating a dependable, reliable, and operationally viable relational database. Proper planning and design can ensure the database is scalable and secure, in addition to performing well while reducing the risk of data corruption and loss. The planning and design process is iterative, as you might surface a new requirement during planning that influences design.

The goal of this phase is a database design consistent with an organization's strategic architectural goals. The design should also align with the organization's overall technology strategy. This phase produces several artifacts, including requirements specifications, a conceptual data model, a logical data model, a physical data model, a data dictionary, and other design documents. These artifacts are vital for database administrators, application developers, and other stakeholders who will end up using the database.

Requirements Gathering

Requirements gathering is a critical step in the database design process, as it ensures that the database meets the needs of its users and applications. As you start to gather requirements, you first need to identify the stakeholders who will end up using the database. Many parties may be interested in the database you are creating. As you identify stakeholders, you will want to consider the following:

- *End users*: End users directly input or retrieve data from the database.
- *Executive management*: Executives use data from the database to track operational performance metrics and inform strategic decisions. Executives most frequently use a reporting tool like *Tableau*, *Qlik*, or *Power BI* instead of interacting directly with the database.
- *Data analysts*: Data analysts use the database to perform complex queries, generate reports, and perform other data-related tasks. Data analysts may write SQL directly against the database or use reporting tools.
- *Data scientists*: Data scientists use the database to perform advanced analytics, develop predictive models, and gain insights into business trends and patterns.
- *Application developers*: Application developers write applications that interact with the database. Application developers use generalized programming languages like JavaScript, Java, C#, and Swift to create APIs, mobile applications, or web applications that store data in the database.
- *Database developers*: Database developers write SQL to create tables, views, stored procedures, and other database objects. Occasionally, database developers may be involved in maintaining or upgrading the database.
- *Database administrators*: Database administrators (DBAs) are responsible for the ongoing maintenance and management of the database. DBAs are responsible for many tasks, including backups, performance tuning, security, and database upgrades.
- *System administrators*: System administrators operate the virtual or physical servers where the database runs. Typical system administration tasks include sizing servers, allocating and configuring disk space, and operating system upgrades and maintenance.
- *Customers*: Customers usually interact with the database indirectly, using an application to submit orders or retrieve information. For example, when you look at the location history of a FedEx package on the web, you are using FedEx's web application to retrieve the package location history from a database.
- *Vendors*: Vendors may use the database to manage inventory, track shipments, or perform other business functions related to their products or services. While vendors can interact directly with a database, it is more common for vendors to use an application.
- *Regulators*: Regulators may require access to the database to ensure compliance with industry or government regulations, such as the Health Insurance Portability and Accountability Act (HIPAA) for healthcare databases or Payment Card Industry Data Security Standard (PCI DSS) for payment card databases. You will explore these in detail in Chapter 6, "Governance, Security, and Compliance."

- *Auditors*: Auditors may review the database to ensure it meets internal or external audit standards, such as Sarbanes-Oxley compliance for financial databases. You will learn more about other compliance obligations in Chapter 6.
- *Legal team*: Legal teams may review the database to ensure compliance with legal requirements or to prepare for litigation.

Once you have identified the relevant stakeholders, you can ask them questions during the planning phase to inform the database design. You can also use these conversations to determine the total number of users who will ultimately use the database.

Database Objectives

An excellent place to start is by gathering requirements that define database needs. Identifying business problems the database will address is crucial to planning and designing a database. Once you understand the database's purpose, you can implement appropriate design considerations. The business problem is that the database addresses will depend on an organization's specific needs. For example, a company may need a database to store customer information, inventory data, or financial records. The database might need to generate reports, analyze trends, and make predictions to help the company improve its operations. A common way to describe database objectives is in the form of use cases.

A *use case* is a document that identifies a business objective and the actions that accomplish it. For example, a global logistics company might write a use case stating that senders and recipients have current information about the location of a package. Considering this use case, storing information about packages at each waypoint in their journey is necessary. This use case also lets you know that operational reporting on package location needs to be visible to users in as close to real time as possible.

It is vital to group use cases into transactional and analytical categories, as that will inform the type of database you are designing. You will develop a transactional database if you need to process transactions. You will likely create a data warehouse if your use cases are primarily analytical. A *data warehouse* is a centralized repository that facilitates reports, business intelligence, and other analytical activities. Suppose your use cases encompass both transactional and analytical needs. In that case, you may need to plan for a transactional database to support your operational use cases and an analytical database for reporting purposes.

As you proceed with planning and design, it is helpful to incorporate functional objectives and have a framework for categorizing use cases by functional objective. Let's take a closer look at some representative categories.

Data Capture

The data capture use case category focuses on collecting, validating, and cleaning data in pursuit of accuracy and completeness. Data capture use cases identify where data originates and how it flows into a database. With transactional databases, people typically use applications to input data into a database, as shown in Figure 4.1. Both the application and the database can check for accuracy and completeness.

FIGURE 4.1 Transactional data sources

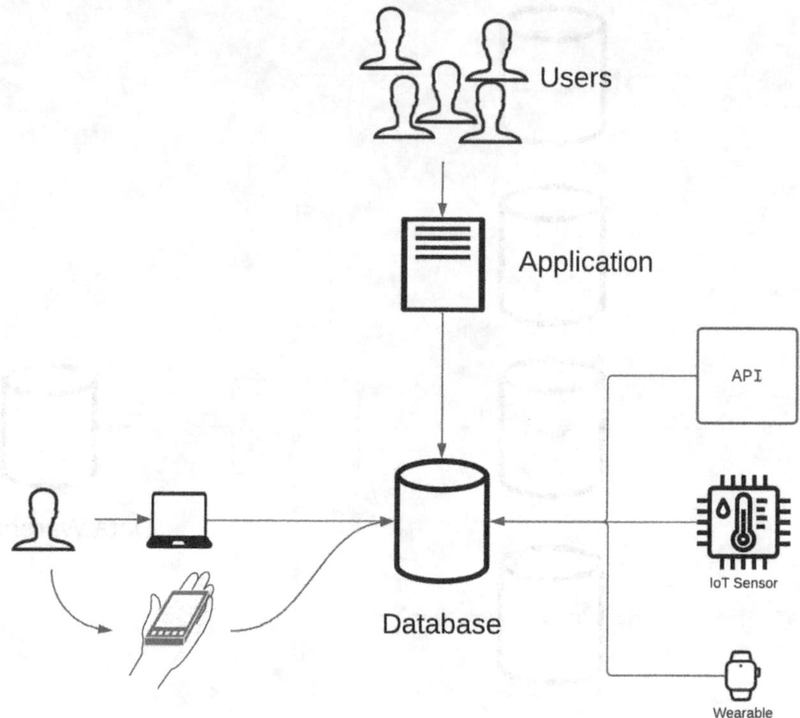

Data may also come from *application programming interfaces (APIs)*, *Internet of Things (IoT)* sensors, wearable devices, and mobile applications. While unlikely, it is also possible for end users to input data into the database directly.

Consider data capture in the context of our logistics company scenario. For a sender or recipient to get detailed tracking information, a change in package location generates a scan. Each scan sends data to the database, including the package tracking number, location, date, and time.

Data warehouses get their data from various upstream systems instead of directly from users. User-facing applications do not typically write directly into a data warehouse. Instead, extract, transform, and load (ETL) processes move data from the source system database into the data warehouse, as Figure 4.2 illustrates.

FIGURE 4.2 Analytical data sources

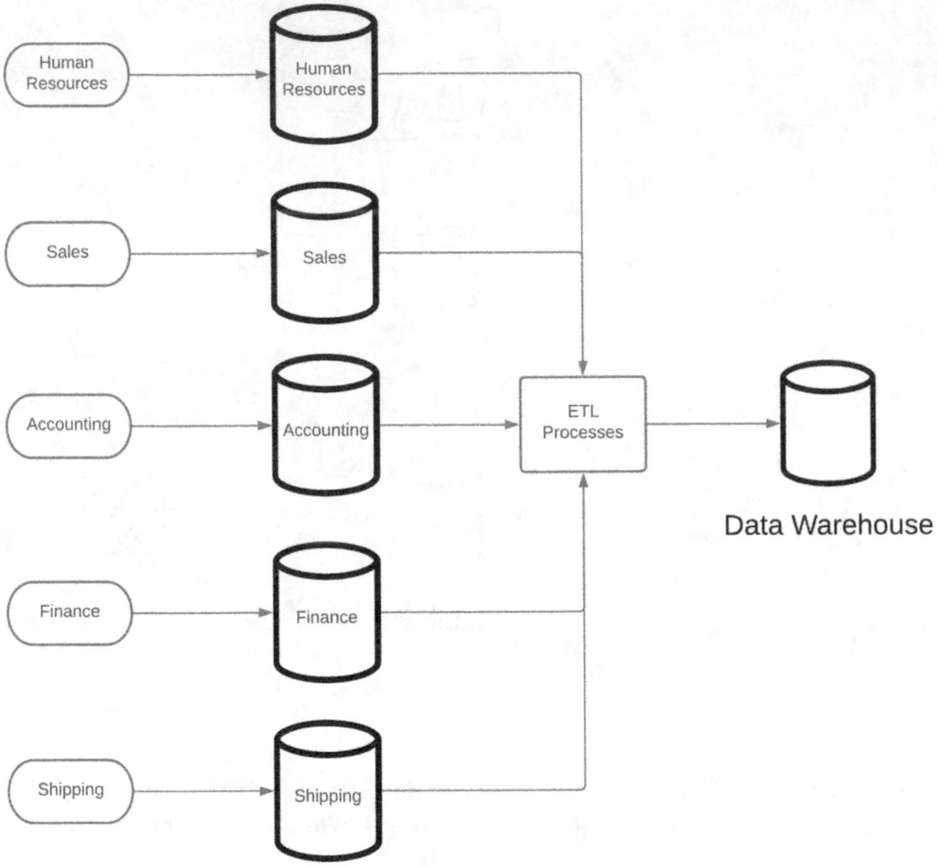

Data Storage

The data storage category impacts the type of storage you need, informed by size and speed requirements. To develop a capacity estimate, focus on the volume and velocity of your data. *Volume* refers to how much data you store, and *velocity* describes how quickly data changes. Examining volume and velocity together helps inform your storage needs. For example, a reference table storing each state in the United States has a low volume and low velocity. While the number of states can change, it is unlikely, as Congress would need to approve such a change. However, the volume and velocity of data for a global logistics company are high, as every waypoint in every package's journey creates data. Defining the volume and velocity requirements help you determine the size of the database and how much storage capacity it will need. Establishing the database's expected maximum capacity during planning is imperative, as the maximum capacity informs your overall storage capacity needs.

Following our logistics example, here is a sample volume and velocity estimate for the main package scan database table. First, you determine how many years of data reside in the transactional system before being archived and sent to the data warehouse. With that time frame in mind, you can build your estimate by identifying the expected daily package volume, incorporating trend analysis, anticipated growth, and historical data. You then multiply the daily package volume by the number of scans per package to approximate the total daily scans. Once you have the total daily scan number, you multiply the number of scans by the record size of each scan to come up with an overall sizing estimate for the package scan table.

With a complete package scan table estimate, repeat the volume and velocity analysis for other large tables in the database, like those that store customer and address data. While this may seem like a lot of work, this type of analysis is crucial for identifying your database storage needs.

Combining total data velocity with users' performance expectations helps you decide the type of storage the database requires. The two primary types of storage are *solid-state drives (SSDs)* and *hard disk drives (HDDs)*. In general, SSDs are more expensive and reliable than HDDs. SSDs have no moving parts, consume little power, and have fast access times. This combination of attributes makes SSDs ideal for large, high-velocity tables. You can find SSDs in smartphones and most modern laptop computers.

HDDs store data on rotating platters of magnetic media. Platter rotation speeds range from 1,200 to 15,000 revolutions per minute (rpm) and directly impact cost and performance. The faster an HDD rotates, the more expensive it is and the better it performs. Because HDDs have moving parts, they consume more power and make more noise than SSDs. Their lower cost makes HDDs an attractive option for storing low-velocity or sequentially written data. When designing an expansive, complex database, the best way to satisfy your storage requirements might be a combination of SSDs and HDDs. In this scenario, you put your high-velocity tables on the faster, more expensive SSDs while using slower, cheaper HDDs for the rest of your storage needs.

Cloud providers offer another category known as object storage. AWS offers *Simple Storage Service (S3)*, Microsoft has *Azure Blob Storage*, and Google provides *Cloud Storage*. While object storage offers low pricing, it is not an option for relational databases since it can't attach directly to operating systems like SSDs or HDDs. If you build virtual machines in the cloud to host your relational databases, you need to use your cloud provider's version of attached storage. In AWS, attached storage is called *Elastic Block Storage (EBS)*, Microsoft has *Azure Managed Disks*, while Google calls its offering *Persistent Disk*.

Techniques for Improving Storage Availability and Performance

Large databases have storage performance needs beyond the capabilities of a single SSD or HDD. Striping and mirroring are two common techniques used in data storage management, particularly in *Redundant Array of Independent Disks* (*RAID*) configurations. They each serve different purposes and offer unique performance and data protection advantages.

Striping refers to dividing data into blocks and then distributing these blocks across multiple storage devices. This process improves performance by allowing multiple drives to read and write data simultaneously rather than relying on a single drive to perform all the operations. In a *RAID 0* configuration, data is split evenly across two or more disks. The main disadvantage of striping is that it doesn't provide any redundancy. If one drive fails, all data in the striped set is lost.

Mirroring duplicates the same data on two or more drives. By storing data on multiple drives, mirroring improves redundancy and availability. If one drive fails, the system can continue operating by using the data on the other drives. A *RAID 1* configuration mirrors data across two disks. While mirroring provides robust data protection, it does so at the cost of storage efficiency, as it requires doubling the storage capacity to store the same amount of data.

A common strategy combines striping and mirroring for both performance and redundancy. For example, a *RAID 10* (or *RAID 1+0*) configuration stripes data across multiple drives for performance, then mirrors the drives for redundancy. This setup can handle numerous drive failures if no mirrored pair fails simultaneously.

Other RAID configurations incorporate *parity*, a calculated value used to reconstruct data if a drive fails. Combining striping with parity information allows for data reconstruction when a disk fails.

Choosing the appropriate RAID configuration depends on what's more important for your database: performance, data protection, or a balance of both. These configurations can significantly enhance the performance and reliability of storage systems, making them crucial for high-availability and high-performance databases.

Data Retrieval

The data retrieval category focuses on how users access the data they need from the database. Specifying what users want to see is essential to use-case development. Database and application developers are vital constituents when designing retrieval-related transactional use cases, as end users typically interact with the database indirectly with an application.

Following our logistics example, a transactional use case can specify that the sender and recipient want transparency about what is happening during the shipping process. Specifically, a user may want to search for a package using a tracking number. Figure 4.3 shows a web page that, given a tracking number, displays the delivery journey details of a package:

FIGURE 4.3 Travel history data

Travel history

SORT BY DATE/TIME: Ascending | TIME ZONE: Local Scan Time

Date	Time	Event	Location
Thursday, 9/15/2022	2:38 PM	Shipment information sent to FedEx	
	6:07 PM	Picked up	CARSON, CA
	8:56 PM	Arrived at FedEx location	CARSON, CA
Friday, 9/16/2022	6:15 AM	Left FedEx origin facility	CARSON, CA
	6:22 PM	In transit	MOAPA, NV
Saturday, 9/17/2022	7:25 AM	In transit	THOMPSON, UT
	8:26 PM	In transit	DONIPHAN, NE
Sunday, 9/18/2022	6:09 PM	In transit	CHICAGO, IL
Monday, 9/19/2022	11:26 AM	In transit	CHICAGO, IL
Tuesday, 9/20/2022	1:13 AM	In transit	CHICAGO, IL
	10:56 AM	Arrived at FedEx location	CHICAGO, IL
	11:09 AM	Shipment arriving On-Time	CHICAGO, IL
	8:42 PM	Departed FedEx location	CHICAGO, IL
Wednesday, 9/21/2022	4:46 AM	At local FedEx facility	SOUTH BEND, IN
	4:48 AM	Arrived at FedEx location	SOUTH BEND, IN
	4:50 AM	On FedEx vehicle for delivery	SOUTH BEND, IN
	10:49 AM	Delivered Left at front door. Signature Service not requested.	Granger, IN

Meanwhile, the management team likely tracks corporate performance using *key performance indicators (KPIs)*. KPIs are quantitative measures that provide organizational targets and facilitate executive decision-making. Common logistics-related KPIs include shipping time, order accuracy, number of shipments, delivery time, and average days late. As executive management identifies the KPIs they want to see, data analysts, data scientists, and database developers work together to design how data will flow from the database into a visualization tool, ultimately presented as a management-facing dashboard.

Data Processing

The data processing category focuses on manipulating data within the database, including data aggregation, calculations, and transformations. Use cases frequently span the data processing and data retrieval categories. Consider a use case that specifies an average-days-late KPI. You must calculate the average number of days packages are late for a given period to satisfy that use case successfully. For KPIs, it is common for users to adjust the time scale. For instance, management may want to see average-days-late by day, day of week, week, month, quarter, and year. Each change in the time scale requires a recalculation of the average.

Considering the data processing aspects of transactional and analytical use cases will influence whether you use specific components within the database. For example, you can centralize aggregation logic within the database using stored procedures, triggers, or functions. Alternatively, you can place aggregation logic in applications, data visualization tools, and integration platforms.

Data Analysis

The data analysis category focuses on using data from the database to develop insights for making data informed decisions. Directed by organizational leadership, data scientists are the primary constituents in this use case category. When data scientists mine data to pursue insight, they extract and integrate data from multiple sources. Data scientists also use data to create predictive models.

For example, suppose data scientists within our logistics organization want to determine whether rising fuel costs will affect the average-days-late KPI. To achieve their goal, the data scientists incorporate data from transactional, analytical, and external sources. To inform how much processing power and memory the database will need, work with the data scientists to clarify how they will use the database and external programming languages to gather, reduce, transform, and analyze data. Ensure that you define how long the data scientists will need their environment. Some efforts are tactical and complete within a month or two, while ongoing analysis typically requires a dedicated environment.

Data Integration

This category focuses on sharing data between the database, the applications it supports, and other systems that consume data from the database. This category overlaps with the data capture and data retrieval categories. The key objective of the integration category is to reduce the number of unique integrations with the database. Instead of direct connections to the database, the goal is to reuse and centralize logic through APIs and data exchange protocols.

Following our logistics example, many different constituencies interact with the database. Figure 4.4 illustrates a design where the end users, delivery personnel, management, and external commercial customers directly connect to the database. With this approach, if code changes for one commercial customer, you need to make the equivalent change for your other commercial customer, leaving you open to data quality issues.

FIGURE 4.4 Direct database integration

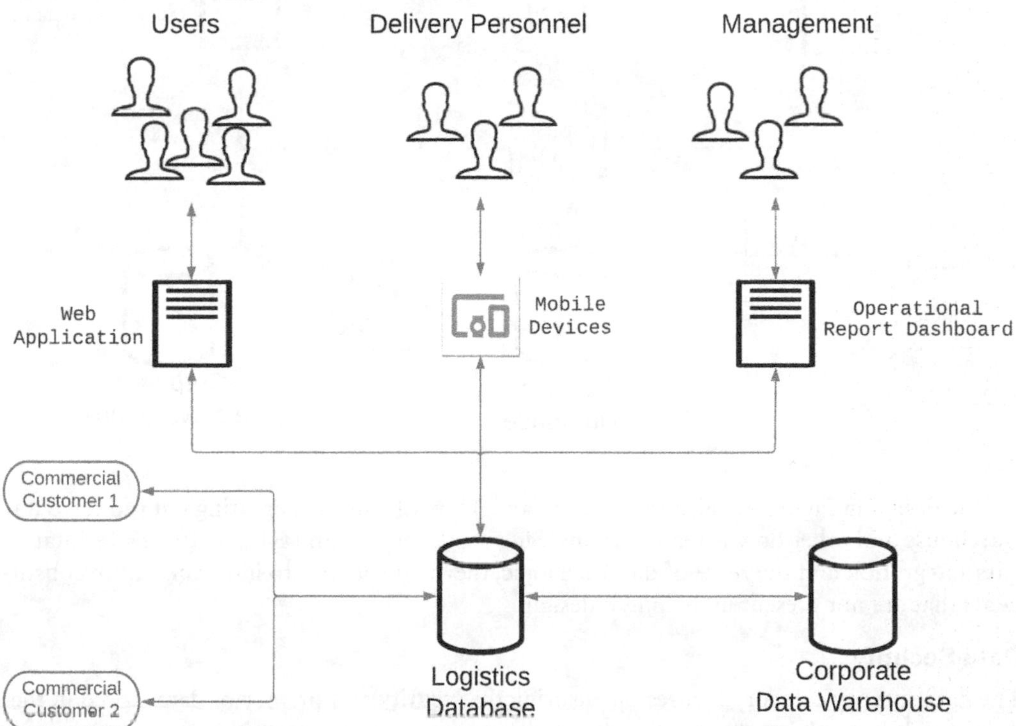

To address the potential for data quality issues and to advance data integration goals, implement an API platform, as Figure 4.5 illustrates. With this approach, you centralize data manipulation logic, which improves data quality. For example, suppose the delivery personnel and end users need to retrieve package-related data. The same database code can satisfy both constituencies with this API-centric approach.

FIGURE 4.5 Centralized database integration

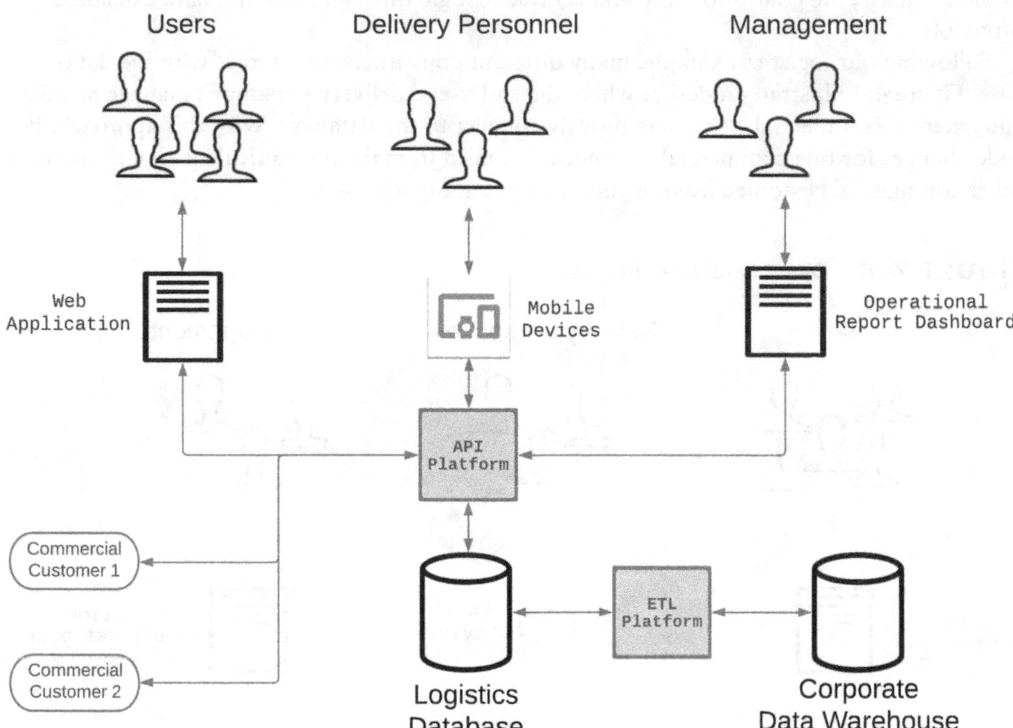

The design in Figure 4.5 also implements an ETL platform for migrating data to the data warehouse and other downstream systems. Since both the API and ETL platforms facilitate data integration and the reuse of database logic, they make it easy to integrate future constituents that are not present in the initial design.

Data Security

The data security category focuses on ensuring the security and privacy of data stored in the database. It is helpful to develop a data classification system to inform this use case category while gathering requirements. A data classification system aims to group individual data elements into categories.

Consider the data our example logistics company uses. You can group white papers, blog posts, and web pages into a publicly accessible data category. While you want to manage who creates or updates publicly accessible data, you don't have to worry about who can read it since the general public is the intended consumer.

However, payment-related data belongs to a more restrictive data classification category. For example, the general public should not see an individual's payment-related details. Instead, you restrict access to payment data to individual customers. There are also legislative and compliance-related standards that inform data classification categories. You may need to incorporate encryption into your design for specific types of sensitive data. For a deeper exploration of data classification, see Chapter 6.

Once you have a data classification framework, you can develop designs for assigning and enforcing permissions. Instead of granting permissions to individuals, it is a best practice to set permissions based on job roles. For example, all customer service representatives should have the same data access level, since each individual performs the same job. With the combination of a data classification framework and data access roles, you can create an effective permissions management design.

Data retention also informs data security use cases. To determine data retention requirements, consider organizational needs and compliance obligations. For example, in the United States, a company must retain payroll records for at least three years under the Fair Labor Standards Act (FLSA). You can develop data retention policies to automate archiving data from a transactional database into a data warehouse.

Database Architecture

Once you have clarity on the purpose of the database and the use cases it will support, you can assess how the database fits into your overall IT portfolio. Starting with your existing infrastructure, you can conduct a gap analysis to develop an inventory of needed assets to fulfill your defined requirements. Before completing the plan for your new database, you must understand the technical direction of your organization, any relevant existing assets, and any technical or operational constraints.

Infrastructure Location

One of the fundamental operational factors influencing where your new database will live is where your organization hosts any existing applications and databases. Organizations typically operate infrastructure on premises or cloud-based. It is also common to use a hybrid cloud approach that integrates on-premises and cloud components.

The *on-premises* approach means you have to manage the physicality of your infrastructure by having a data center. A data center is a space that is purpose-built for housing computer equipment. Suppose your organization fulfills its IT needs with an on-premises approach. In that case, you will want to determine whether or not your database can fit on existing servers or if you will need to purchase additional equipment. If you need to buy additional equipment, consider whether the data center has sufficient power, cooling, and space to accommodate the new hardware.

A *cloud-based* approach means that an organization is outsourcing its physical infrastructure to a cloud provider like *Amazon Web Services (AWS)*, *Microsoft Azure (Azure)*, or *Google Cloud Platform (GCP)*. A cloud-based approach allows for greater organizational agility than an on-premises approach. For example, if you need new servers for your database, you can provision virtual servers in the cloud quickly and easily. In an on-premises environment, if you need additional physical servers, you must place an order with a hardware vendor and wait for the servers to arrive. When the servers come, you unbox them, mount them in racks in your data center, power them up, attach them to the network, and install any relevant software before you can use them.

With a cloud-based or hybrid approach, there are three types of cloud-hosted environments to consider: infrastructure as a service, platform as a service, and software as a service.

Infrastructure as a Service

Infrastructure as a service (IaaS) is a tier of cloud computing that provides access to virtualized computing resources over the Internet. IaaS allows organizations to rent and use computing infrastructure on-demand without purchasing and maintaining physical hardware and data centers. IaaS is the most similar to having an on-premises environment on the spectrum of cloud computing services.

While IaaS abstracts away the physical hardware, you need engineers to build, operate, and maintain servers. If you already have database administrators (DBAs) on staff, their job is essentially the same in an on-premises and IaaS environment. DBAs still need to install database software, monitor database performance, and implement data protection strategies.

IaaS allows you to customize and configure virtual servers to meet your needs. Depending on what your chosen IaaS vendor offers, you have the flexibility to create a tiny 1-CPU cloud server, a massive 128-CPU server, or anything in between. Naturally, the more computing power a virtual server has, the more it costs. IaaS also accommodates specific operating system, software, or database version dependencies. If you need to maximize flexibility and control while outsourcing the physical infrastructure, IaaS is a sound choice.

Platform as a Service

Platform as a service (PaaS) is a cloud computing tier that provides a platform for users to develop, deploy, and manage applications without worrying about the underlying infrastructure. PaaS goes further than IaaS by abstracting the management of virtual servers and database software. With PaaS, you specify the database engine and configuration settings, while the provider builds the virtual servers, installs the database software, and creates the database. Your interaction with the database software is limited to connecting to it over the network. AWS, Azure, and GCP all have database PaaS offerings. AWS's Relational Database Service (RDS) is the most comprehensive in terms of choice and includes MySQL, PostgreSQL, MariaDB, Oracle, and Microsoft SQL Server in addition to its proprietary Aurora offering.

Database PaaS providers offer a range of database management tools and services, reducing the effort to administer, operate, monitor, backup, and recover the database. For example, suppose you need to apply a minor database patch. PaaS lets you select the database patch and schedule when to apply it. Implementing a database protection scheme by configuring scheduled backups is also straightforward.

With PaaS, you trade flexibility and features for ease of administration. For example, PaaS providers only support some database platforms. For instance, while you can run IBM Db2 in an IaaS environment, AWS, Azure, and GCP don't have it as a PaaS offering. PaaS database options are limited to a subset of available software versions and may provide limited or no access to advanced features of specific database engines.

Software as a Service

Software as a service (SaaS) is a cloud computing tier that delivers functioning software applications over the Internet. A user only needs an internet connection and a web browser to access a SaaS application. With SaaS, the hardware, database version, and application software are opaque to the user. SaaS further reduces the administrative burden as there is no software to install or maintain.

SaaS solutions exist for various use cases. For example, Salesforce is a SaaS offering for customer relationship management (CRM). Google Workspace allows for personal productivity and team collaboration, and Workday offers human resources functionality as a SaaS offering.

Suppose you are building an analytics database and must retrieve data from a SaaS application. SaaS providers typically provide access to data through APIs. As part of the planning and design process, you must clearly identify the data elements from the SaaS provider and the data processing pipeline that will copy the data into your database.

Cost

Developing an overall budget is foundational when planning your database. Infrastructure location, hardware, software, database licensing, maintenance, and personnel all impact the overall cost of your database. For example, you may plan for a small database that fits your existing infrastructure and operational environment. On the other hand, you may need to hire more people for a database that will serve as the foundation for an extensive application.

As you develop the budget for the database, consider how availability, scalability, and performance targets can significantly impact the cost of implementing and operating a database.

Availability

Availability refers to the ability of a database to remain accessible and usable to users without interruption or downtime. Availability measures how often the database is available and how quickly you can recover the database after the inevitable outage or failure.

Your requirements may dictate that you create a highly available database to reduce the risk of downtime. The goal of high availability is to remove single points of failure. Table 4.1 illustrates how long a database can be down based on availability requirements.

TABLE 4.1 Availability Targets

Availability %	Yearly Downtime	Daily Downtime
90%	36.5 days	2.4 hours
95%	18.3 days	1.2 hours
99%	3.7 days	14.4 minutes
99.9%	8.7 hours	1.4 minutes
99.99%	52.6 minutes	8.6 seconds
99.999%	5.3 minutes	864 milliseconds

The cost of achieving an availability target is proportionally greater the closer you get to 100 percent. A small business can tolerate multiple hours of daily downtime since it is unlikely to be open every hour of the day. However, a global logistics copy cannot afford to be down for multiple hours per day and has the budget to invest in solutions with higher availability capabilities. You can improve availability using techniques like clustering, replication, and failover.

Clustering is a technique that improves the availability of a database system by combining multiple database servers into a cluster, which appears to the user as a single database system. Figure 4.6 illustrates a single-server database approach. In this figure, the application attaches directly to the single database on the database server. With a single-server approach, the application cannot access the data it needs if the database or the server fails.

FIGURE 4.6 Single database server

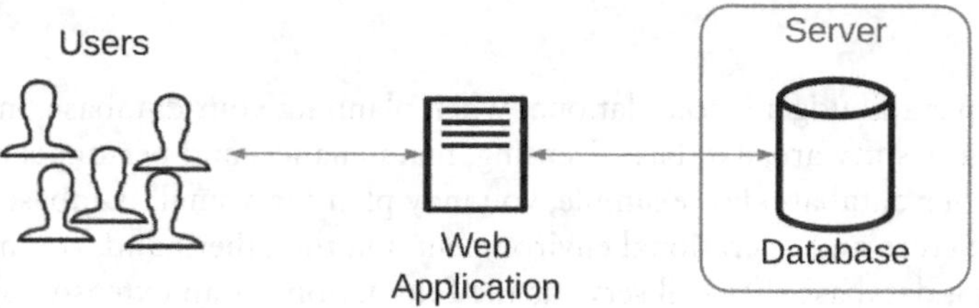

In a clustered database environment, each server in the cluster connects to a shared storage system, which provides a common data repository for all the servers. The servers work together to distribute processing and data storage tasks, improving the database's availability. Figure 4.7 illustrates how clustering improves database availability. If Cluster Server A or Cluster Database A fails, Cluster Server B and Cluster Database B still exist and can handle the query activity coming from the web application.

FIGURE 4.7 Active-active database cluster

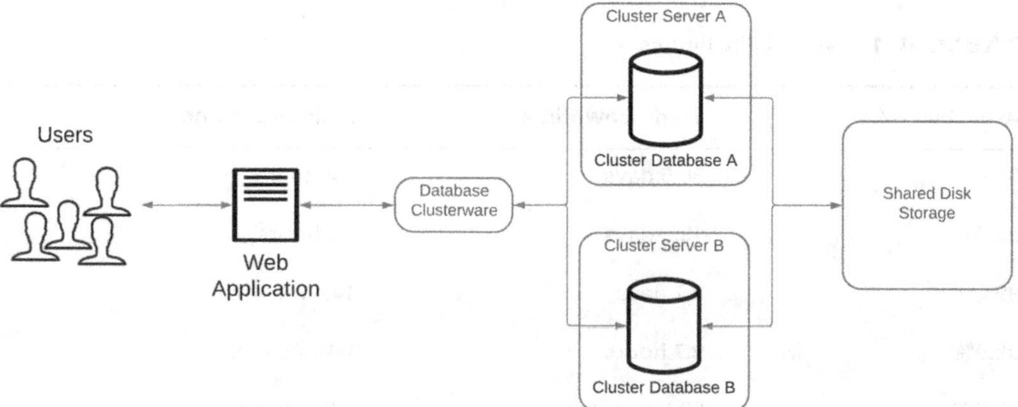

There are two main types of database clustering: active-active and active-passive. With *active-active clustering*, all the nodes in the cluster are active and share the processing load. If one node fails, the others transparently take over its workload. Figure 4.7 illustrates an active-active configuration. While this approach provides high availability, it is complex to set up, operate, and maintain. While you can have more than two database nodes, each additional node increases cost and complexity.

With *active-passive clustering*, only one node is active at a time, while the others are passive and ready to take over if the active node fails. Figure 4.8 illustrates an active-passive configuration.

FIGURE 4.8 Active-passive database cluster

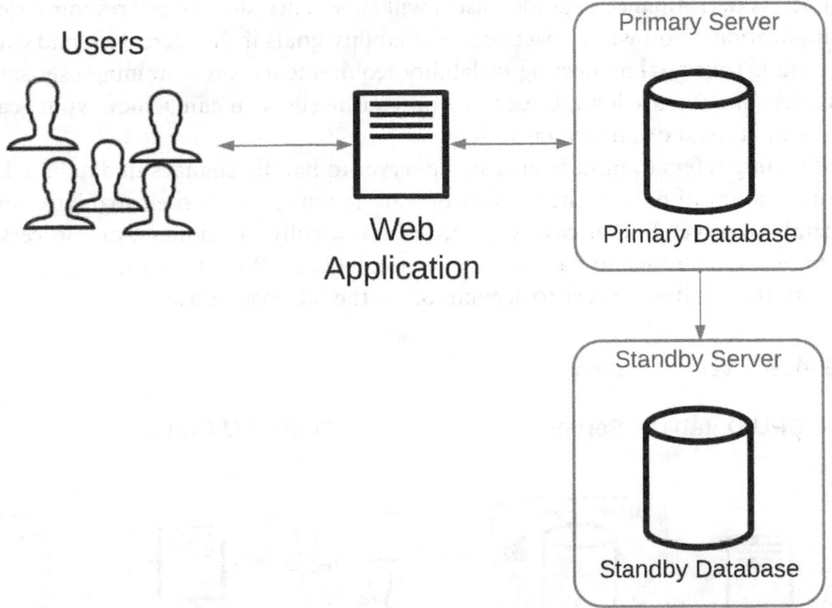

An active-passive approach is simpler to configure, operate, and maintain than an active-active approach. The most impactful difference between active-passive and active-active is what happens in a failure scenario. A node failure is transparent to the calling application in an active-active environment. With the active-passive approach, you must promote the standby database to primary status when the primary database fails. During the promotion process, applications cannot interact with the database, negatively impacting availability.

When making implementation plans, you need to consider your existing infrastructure and availability capabilities. For example, suppose you are designing a database to support a few users who work similar hours. In that case, you could meet your availability requirement by creating a new database on one of your existing database servers. However, suppose you are planning a database to power a globally accessible application that must be available at any hour of the day. In that case, you likely need to budget for database-specific infrastructure to meet your availability requirements.

Scalability

Scalability is the ability of a database to handle increasing amounts of data, users, and workload without sacrificing performance or availability. When considering scalability, you want to understand the minimum, average, and peak workload the database needs to handle. You should also prepare for the possibility that the peak workload exceeds your original requirements.

Clear scalability requirements are vital because as the amount of data or the number of users and transactions increase, performance degrades if the database cannot keep up with the demands. As performance degrades, users will experience slow query response times and sluggish applications. You will impact your availability goals if the increased load causes the database to fail. Your goal in meeting scalability requirements is maintaining user satisfaction, regardless of database load. Depending on your needs, you can achieve your scalability objectives with vertical or horizontal scaling.

Vertical scaling refers to modifying a single server to handle changes in database load. Suppose the amount of data or the number of transactions exceeds the capabilities of the existing database server. In that case, you can scale vertically by adding more processing power, memory, and storage to handle the increase. Figure 4.9 illustrates adding an additional CPU to the database server to accommodate the increase in users.

FIGURE 4.9 Vertical scaling

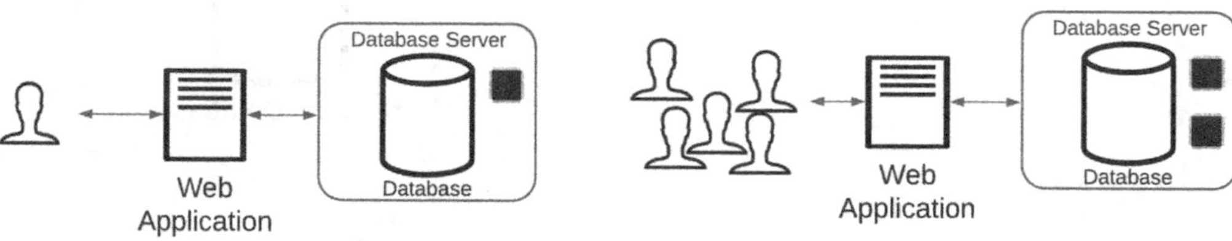

While vertical scaling is effective and relatively easy to accomplish, the approach has some limitations. The most impactful limitation is that vertical scaling incurs downtime. For example, to achieve the scaling illustration in Figure 4.9, you have to shut down the database, shut down the server, add the CPU, start the server, and finally start the database. While this approach may be sufficient for a small-scale database, the downtime required may be unacceptable for a mission-critical service. For large, global applications, the load requirements may exceed the capabilities of a single database server.

Horizontal scaling refers to adding or removing nodes in a server cluster to respond to changes in database load. Horizontal scaling is more operationally complex than vertical scaling, as the horizontal approach requires sophisticated clustering software to manage the addition and removal of database nodes. Despite the increase in complexity, a significant advantage of horizontal scaling is that it allows for greater flexibility than vertical scaling.

For example, suppose the two-node database cluster in Figure 4.7 is sufficient to meet the average load coming from your application. However, you need to augment the combined capacity of the two servers to handle peak demand. Figure 4.10 illustrates how adding a node to the cluster can accommodate the increase in demand.

FIGURE 4.10 Horizontal scaling

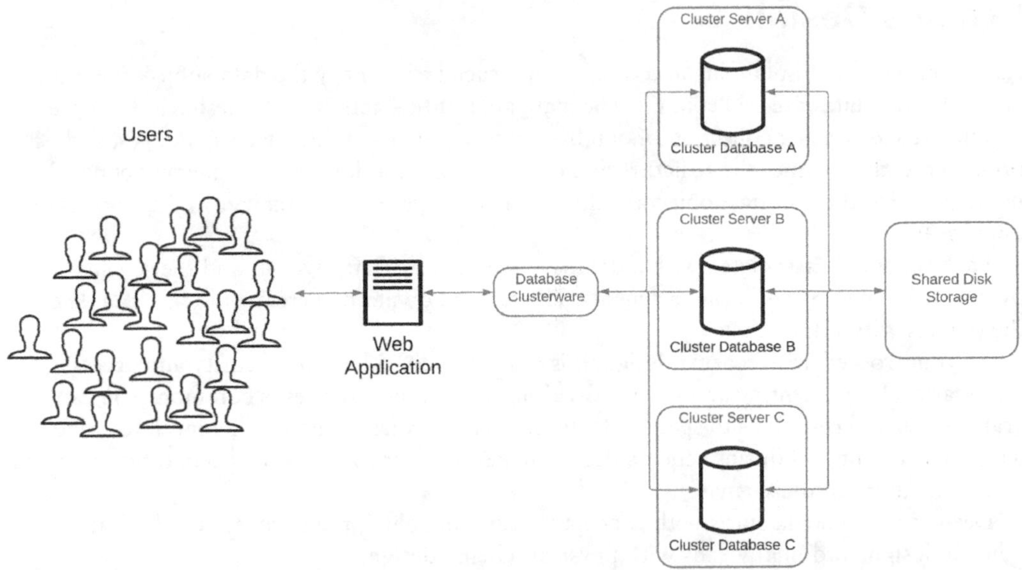

The most significant advantage of horizontal scaling is adding or removing capacity without impacting users. Horizontal scaling also improves availability, as the database remains accessible when one cluster node fails. While the cost and complexity are too high for a small database, it is the most viable design option if your availability targets exceed 99.9 percent.

It is common to develop scalability objectives together with availability goals, as the two disciplines are interrelated. Combining these goals leads to a database that is there when you need it and supports the workloads you place on it. As you evaluate your objectives, you want to ensure the database can handle any anticipated growth in data volume and user traffic.

Performance

When designing your database, it is imperative to establish performance targets. The ultimate performance goal is to ensure fast response times and efficient data retrieval while minimizing cost. Crucial considerations when setting performance goals include the number of total users, the number of concurrent users, and the most frequently executed queries. Creating load estimates with these factors will help you understand if your existing infrastructure is sufficient or whether you need to augment it to handle your new database.

Your performance objectives can also impact your scalability and availability. For instance, if an application using the database must process transactions in less than one second at any time of day, you may need a clustered, high-availability design. On the other hand, if you only need to process 10 subsecond requests per hour during business hours, a single database server will meet your needs.

Schema Design

As you proceed with planning and design, it is crucial to identify the data subject areas and attributes the database will contain. The main goal of this activity is to design a database schema. A *schema* is a collection of database objects, such as tables, views, indexes, and procedures, that defines the structure and organization of a database. A schema defines the namespace for the database objects within it, providing a way to organize and group related objects.

Each schema is associated with a database user or role that owns it, and the schema owner owns the objects within a schema. The schema owner can create, modify, and delete the objects within the schema.

As you proceed with schema design, it is crucial to consider data security and access boundaries. Implementing access controls along schema boundaries is common. You can grant or deny permissions to specific database users or roles at the schema level. Keeping data security in mind during schema design makes it easier to implement separation of access in a multi-user database environment.

Designing a schema starts with conceptual data modeling, then proceeds to logical schema design, and finally ends with physical schema design.

Conceptual Data Modeling

A *conceptual data model* is a high-level representation of an organization's data that defines the relationships between entities without including implementation details such as data types or database structures. Conceptual data modeling aims to provide a clear understanding of an organization's business requirements and facilitate communication and collaboration between stakeholders such as business analysts, developers, and end users.

A conceptual data model captures essential elements of the database structure and can include entities, attributes, and relationships. Recall from Chapter 2, "Database Fundamentals," that an entity is a structure that contains a collection of related characteristics, or attributes, about a data subject. An entity typically stores information about a noun, such as people, locations, and objects. When developing a conceptual data model, you first identify the entities that are in scope, then define the relationships between those entities.

For example, some of the core entities for our global logistics company include customer, package, and address. With the entities in place, you can define the relationships between them. For example, a customer can send multiple packages. A customer can have multiple addresses. A package has an origin and destination address. Figure 4.11 shows a conceptual data model for this scenario.

FIGURE 4.11 Conceptual data model

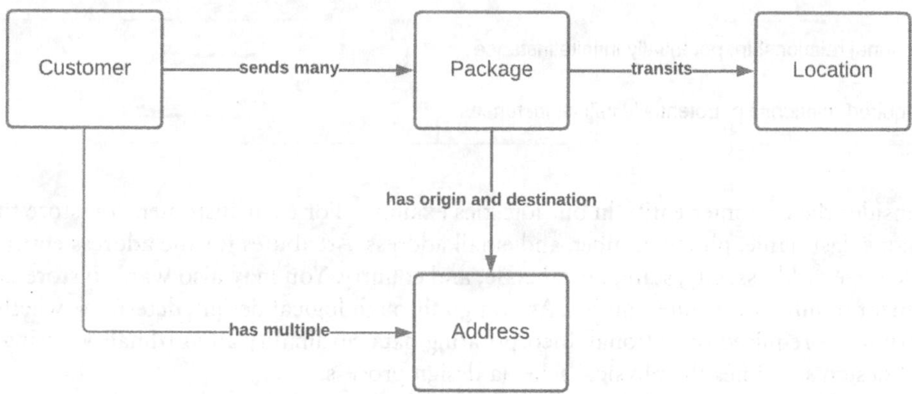

Conceptual data modeling is an iterative process. For example, you may learn about a new requirement that adds a new entity to the data model. Once you understand the core data entities, you are ready to proceed with logical schema design.

Logical Schema Design

A *logical schema* depicts database entities and their relationships without implementation details. The goal of logical schema design is to refine the data model, identify the attributes of each entity, and normalize the structure of the entities. The logical schema design process results in a logical model that provides a blueprint of the database structure without specifying any implementation details. This logical model delivers a high-level view of the database structure.

It is vital to consider data cardinality and ordinality during the design process. *Data cardinality* refers to the relationship between two entities, showing how many instances of one entity relate to instances in another entity. *Data ordinality* is the minimum number of times a specific instance in one entity associates with an instance in the related entity. You specify cardinality in an ERD with various line endings. While there are multiple approaches to depicting cardinality, one of the most common is the "crow's foot notation," which uses two symbols at each line terminator. The first symbol shows ordinality, indicating whether the relationship between two entities is optional or required. The second symbol describes cardinality, indicating whether an entity instance in the first table is associated with a single entity instance in the related table or if an association can exist with multiple entity instances. Figure 4.12 illustrates the possible combinations for representing relationships.

FIGURE 4.12 Entity-relationship diagram line terminators

Relationship Description	Ordinality and Cardinality Symbols
Optional relationship, at most one instance	
Required relationship, at most one instance	
Optional relationship, potentially infinite instances	
Required relationship, potentially infinite instances	

Consider the customer entity in our logistics example. For each customer, you store their first name, last name, phone number, and email address. Attributes for the address entity include street address, city, state, postal code, and country. You may also want to store an apartment number or a suite number. As you go through logical design, determine whether an attribute is required or optional. Incorporating data cardinality and ordinality during logical design simplifies the physical schema design process.

Figure 4.13 shows a sample logical data model for our logistics company, documenting the attributes of each entity. Your logical model should be as flexible as possible to minimize future changes to the schema because, operationally, it is more complex to change the structure of a database than it is to modify data within the database.

FIGURE 4.13 Logical data model

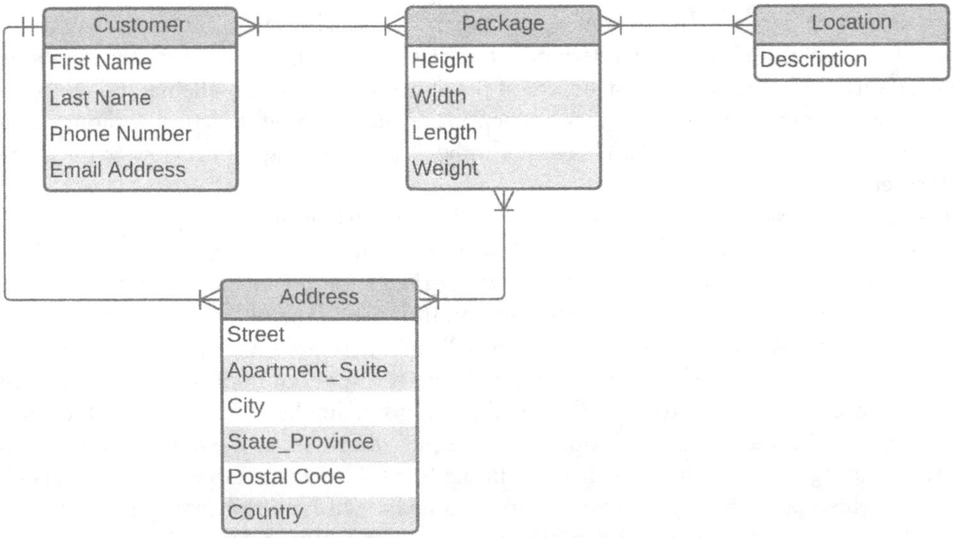

Customer
First Name
Last Name
Phone Number
Email Address

Package
Height
Width
Length
Weight

Location
Description

Address
Street
Apartment_Suite
City
State_Province
Postal Code
Country

Once logical design is complete, you are ready to take on physical design details.

Normalization

Normalization is a process for structuring a database to minimize duplication of data. One of the principles is that a given piece of data is stored once and only once. As a result, a normalized database is ideal for processing transactions.

First normal form (1NF) is when every row in a table is unique, and every column contains a unique value. Consider Figure 4.14, where there are separate rows for Ella and Valentino.

FIGURE 4.14 Data in first normal form

Person_ID	First_Name	Last_Name	Address_Type	Street	City	State_Province	Country_Code	Country
834	Ella	Rossi	Work	Vicolo S. Giovanni Battista, 3	Caiazzo	CE	IT	Italy
834	Ella	Rossi	Home	Via San Francesco, 14	Caiazzo	CE	IT	Italy
835	Valentino	Marini	Work	Vicolo S. Giovanni Battista, 3	Caiazzo	CE	IT	Italy

While Ella and Valentino share the same work address, Adding Valentino's name to the *First_Name* and *Last_Name* columns of Ella's row would violate 1NF. However, since each row is unique, Figure 4.14 is in 1NF.

Second normal form (2NF) picks up where 1NF leaves off. In addition to each row being unique, 2NF applies an additional rule stating that all nonprimary key values must depend on the entire primary key. To get to 2NF, the table from Figure 4.14 evolves into the tables in Figure 4.15. Note that the table containing address information has a composite primary key composed of *Address_ID* and *Person_ID*. All other columns in the address table are associated with the composite primary key.

FIGURE 4.15 Data in second normal form

Person_ID	First_Name	Last_Name	Address_ID
834	Ella	Rossi	9312
834	Ella	Rossi	9313
835	Valentino	Marini	9314

Address_ID	Person_ID	Address_Type	Street	City	State_Province	Country_Code	Country
9312	834	Work	Vicolo S. Giovanni Battista, 3	Caiazzo	CE	IT	Italy
9313	834	Home	Via San Francesco, 14	Caiazzo	CE	IT	Italy
9314	835	Work	Vicolo S. Giovanni Battista, 3	Caiazzo	CE	IT	Italy

In the table that contains address information, the country's name does not depend on the composite primary key of *Address_ID* and *Person_ID*. However, you can identify the name of the country given a *Country_Code*. Suppose you want to change the country's name from "Italy" to the "Republic of Italy." The way the address table currently exists, you have to update three rows to reflect this one change. You can normalize the data to third normal form to resolve this duplicate update problem.

Third normal form (3NF) builds upon 2NF by adding a rule stating all columns must depend on only the primary key. Normalizing Figure 4.15 into 3NF results in Figure 4.16, where we have country information in a separate table.

FIGURE 4.16 Data in third normal form

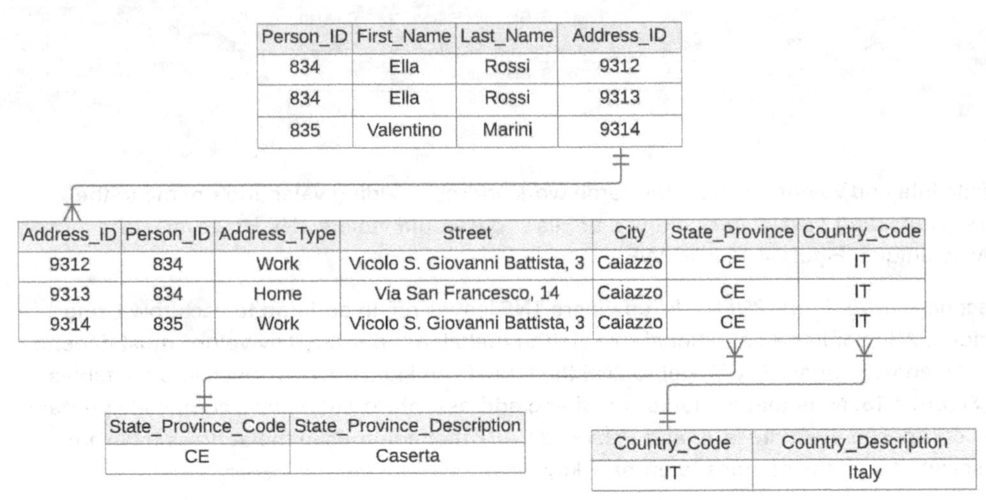

Person_ID	First_Name	Last_Name	Address_ID
834	Ella	Rossi	9312
834	Ella	Rossi	9313
835	Valentino	Marini	9314

Address_ID	Person_ID	Address_Type	Street	City	State_Province	Country_Code
9312	834	Work	Vicolo S. Giovanni Battista, 3	Caiazzo	CE	IT
9313	834	Home	Via San Francesco, 14	Caiazzo	CE	IT
9314	835	Work	Vicolo S. Giovanni Battista, 3	Caiazzo	CE	IT

State_Province_Code	State_Province_Description
CE	Caserta

Country_Code	Country_Description
IT	Italy

Separating country information from the address table eliminates data duplication and solves the duplicate update problem. With this table structure, changing the name of "Italy" to the "Republic of Italy" updates a single row. Despite the update happening in one place, all addresses with the IT country code reflect that change due to the relationship between address and country tables. Databases in third normal form are said to be highly normalized.

While many transactional databases are at least in 3NF, additional normalization levels exist. If you want to learn more, `https://en.wikipedia.org/wiki/Database_normalization` is a good place to start.

Physical Schema Design

A *physical schema* is a detailed, low-level representation of the database structure that includes all the technical details necessary for the physical implementation of the database. The physical schema design process aims to produce a physical schema that defines each attribute's data types, sizes, and constraints for every entity. The physical schema can also include the indexes, keys, and other database objects required to enforce data integrity and ensure efficient query performance. Figure 4.17 extends our logistics example by illustrating a potential physical schema.

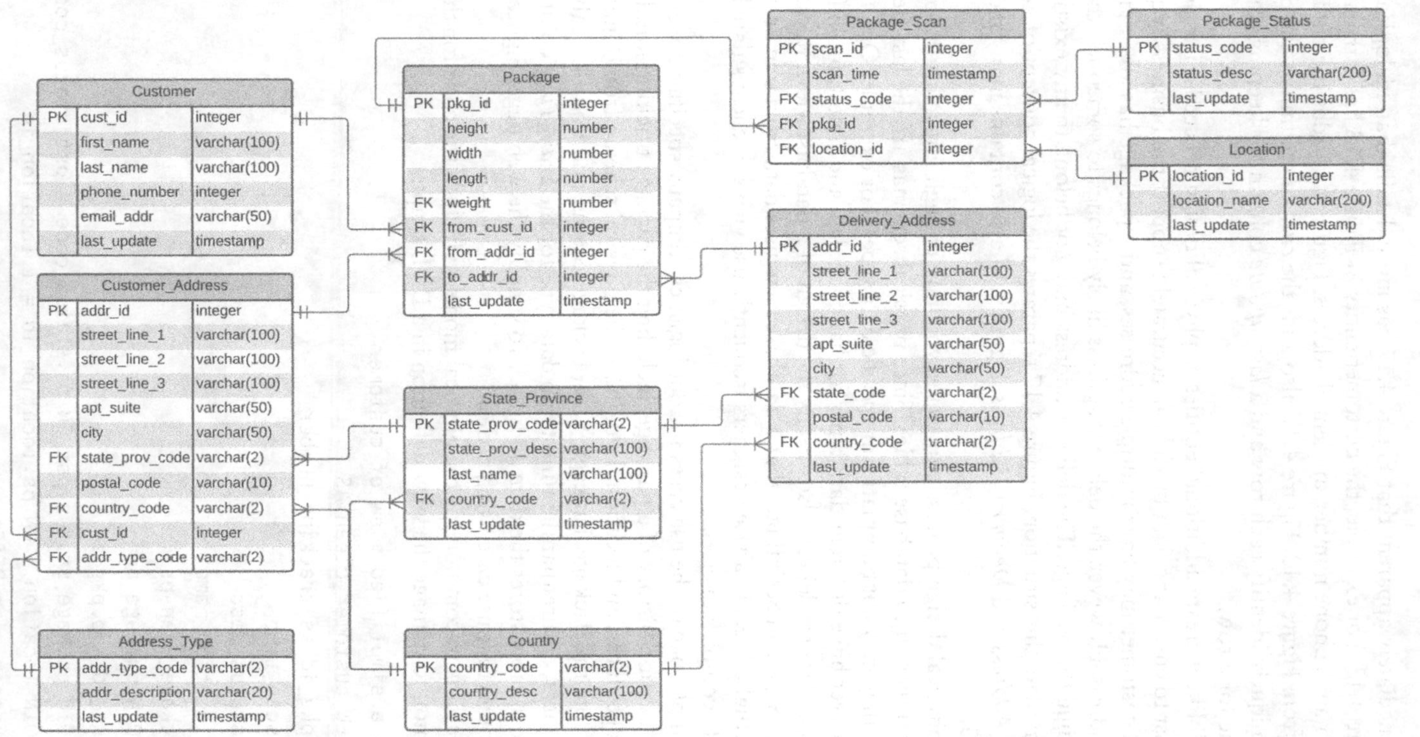

FIGURE 4.17 Physical data model

It is immediately apparent that Figure 4.17 has more details than its logical counterpart from Figure 4.13. For example, the customer entity in Figure 4.13 has attributes for first name, last name, phone number, and email address. Figure 4.17 adds the data types to the attributes from Figure 4.13. Figure 4.17 also adds the *cust_id* column as the primary key that will uniquely identify each row and a *last_update* column for keeping track of the last update time for a row.

You will likely create additional entities as physical design proceeds. The additional entities exist to ensure the data model can accurately support the business requirements. For example, a customer may have multiple addresses, and a package has an origination and delivery address. However, the delivery address likely belongs to someone other than the customer sending the package. The delivery address may not belong to any existing customer. To accommodate this situation, Figure 4.17 separates the logical concept of address into *Customer_Address* and *Delivery_Address*. Figure 4.17 also contains many more entities than Figure 4.13.

As the physical design process completes, you have enough information about each entity to transform them into database tables. Since physical schemas are the last step before implementation, they may contain platform-specific data types. For example, Oracle and Microsoft SQL Server have different data types for handling date and timestamp information.

A physical data model can also specify the design of a database view. Recall from Chapter 3, "SQL and Scripting," that a database view uses data from one or more tables to create a virtual table. Database designers frequently use views to encapsulate business logic and simplify complex queries.

For example, one of the use cases for our logistics company specifies a web page that details the location history of a package, including the package tracking number, date and time, package status, and location. Looking at the physical schema from Figure 4.17, you need data from the Package, Package_Scan, Package_Status, and Location tables. To meet the requirement, ensure that the timestamp data type for the *Scan_Time* column in the Package_Scan table stores the date and time. To simplify the web page, Figure 4.18 illustrates how to address that use case using a view.

Note that it is uncommon for the physical model to include the code for the view. It is more common to manage the view definition in a DDL script:

```
-- Create a simplified view of customer
CREATE VIEW customer_clean AS
  SELECT pkg_id as tracking_number
        ,scan_time
        ,status_desc
        ,location_name
  FROM package_scan ps
  INNER JOIN package pon
  ON ps.pkg_id = p.pkg_id
  INNER JOIN package_status pst ON ps.status_code = pst.status_code
  INNER JOIN location l ON ps.location_id = l.location_id
  ORDER BY scan_time DESC;
```

FIGURE 4.18 Package history view

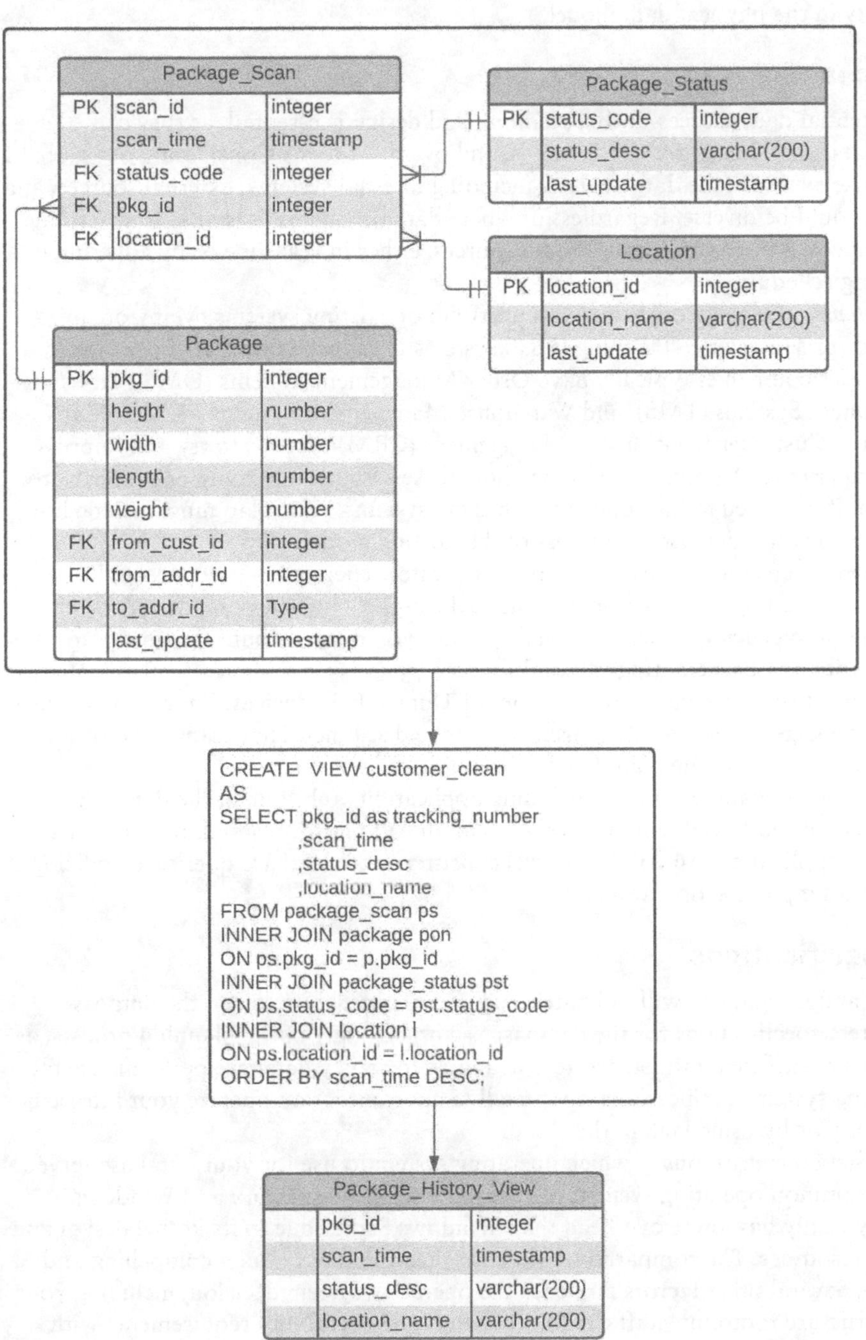

Figure 4.19 illustrates a more typical ERD approach, where the view appears as an individual entity in the physical data model.

Data Sources

Identifying potential data sources during planning and design is essential, as they can influence the database's structure, relationships, and overall success. Considering our global logistics database example, the data sources, including internal systems, external sources, and real-time data, could be diverse. Regardless of where data originates, it is vital to determine how the database will interact with these data sources, either in real time or by adhering to a batch-processing schedule.

Internal systems refer to an organization's portfolio of existing systems. Many organizations use Enterprise Resource Planning (ERP) systems to manage disparate operational divisions. Logistics companies typically have Order Management Systems (OMS), Transportation Management Systems (TMS), and Warehouse Management Systems (WMS). Many organizations use Customer Relationship Management (CRM) systems to try and improve the customer experience. An organization may host these systems internally or subscribe to a SaaS solution. If you need to interoperate with these systems, your plan must include how the data will get to your database, regardless of the hosting model.

External sources refer to systems a third party operates. There are many potential external sources, including systems from suppliers, third-party logistics providers, and customs and regulatory agencies. As with internal systems, you must account for how you exchange data with any participating external source.

You may also get real-time data from Internet of Things (IoT) devices. For example, when drivers deliver packages, they scan them using a handheld scanner. That scanner needs a network connection to transmit the scan data to the database.

Regardless of where data originates, including application architects in the database design process is crucial. Recall from Figure 4.5 that an API platform standardizes inputs from any calling application. An API layer adds consistency to database queries, stabilizing performance and simplifying operations.

System Specifications

After planning and design, you will ultimately require infrastructure to run the database. Identifying system specifications for the database is a crucial part of the planning process, as you want to ensure sufficient infrastructure is available to satisfy database performance targets. Determining system specifications is especially important if you operate your infrastructure, either locally or by using IaaS in the cloud.

One of the first considerations is which operating system to use for your database server. The two most common operating systems for database servers are Linux and Windows Server. Linux typically has lower overhead than Windows Server due to its kernel design and efficient use of resources. The comparatively low overhead makes Linux a compelling and popular option. Several other factors influence the operating system decision, including your existing infrastructure footprint, staff capabilities, and interoperability requirements with other applications.

FIGURE 4.19 Physical data model with package history view

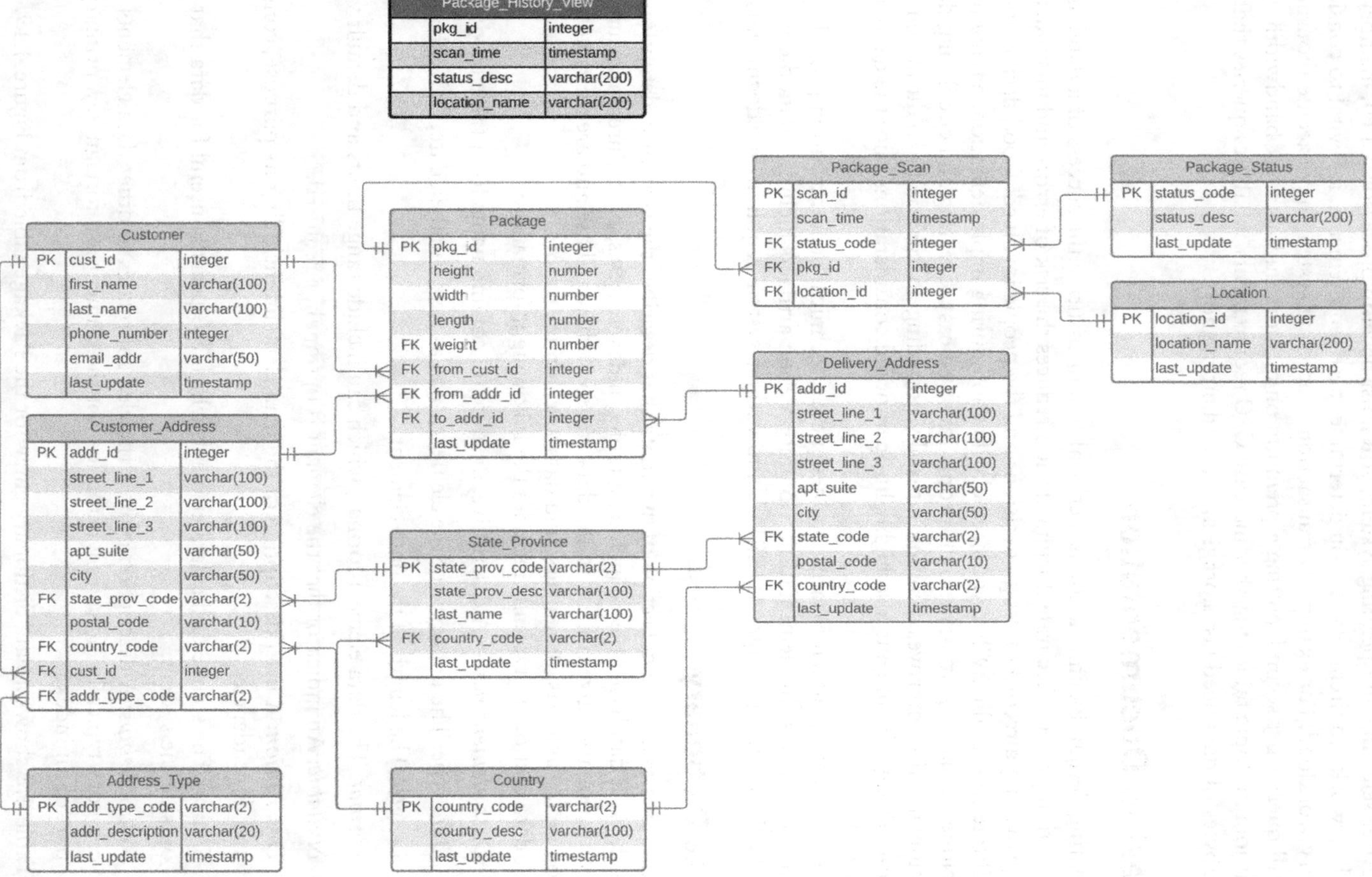

After selecting an operating system, you must develop processor (CPU), memory, storage, and network requirements. As you determine these requirements, it is vital to consider the query workload. For example, a transaction processing system may execute thousands of small queries per second, putting a premium on memory and network bandwidth. Queries that join multiple tables together increase CPU requirements. Analytics queries that scan terabytes of data need fast storage and abundant memory.

Design Documentation

Creating design documentation is a critical step in ensuring the success of a database implementation project. Accurate documentation reduces the risk of errors and misunderstandings by providing a record of design decisions and the people involved. Good design documents facilitate traceability. When you need clarification during implementation, having up-to-date documents makes getting the right people involved easy. Creating and circulating design documents also improves communication by providing a clear roadmap during implementation. Design documents also highlight operational considerations once the database is in production.

As use-case documents clarify business needs, technical documentation provides a blueprint for database implementation. Common design artifacts include a data dictionary, Entity Relationship Diagrams (ERDs), and various system requirements documents.

Data Dictionary

A *data dictionary* is a collection of metadata that describes the structure, definition, and relationships of database objects, including tables, indexes, views, procedures, and functions. Data dictionaries give context to the data stored in the database and are an essential resource for analysts, developers, and database administrators.

A data dictionary typically includes the following information:

- *Data element name*: A descriptive, meaningful column name for a table or view.
- *Data type*: The data type of the element, such as text, number, date, or Boolean.
- *Length*: The length of the data element.
- *Format*: The data element format, which can include range limits and default values.
- *Nullable*: An indicator that the element is optional or required.
- *Description*: A brief description of the data element, including its purpose, constraints, and dependencies.
- *Source*: The source of the data element, which is especially useful for data that originates outside the system.
- *Relationships*: A description of how the element relates to other data elements. This category typically indicates whether or not the element is a foreign key, primary key, or part of an index.

Table 4.2 shows a data dictionary entry for the Package table from Figure 4.19.

TABLE 4.2 Default Database Ports

Relationships	Name	Data Type	Format	Nullable	Description	Source
Primary Key	pkg_id	integer		No	Unique identifier for a package, commonly known as the tracking number	Values come from the pkg_ id_seq sequence number
	height	number	2 digits of pre-cision	Yes	Length of a package in centimeters	Entered upon creation for non-envelope items
	width	number	2 digits of pre-cision	Yes	Width of a package in centimeters	Entered upon creation for non-envelope items
	length	number	2 digits of pre-cision	Yes	Length of a package in centimeters	Entered upon creation for non-envelope items
	weight	number	2 digits of pre-cision	Yes	Weight of package in grams	Entered upon creation for non-envelope items
Foreign Key	from_ cust_id	integer		No	Unique identifier for the customer sending the package	Primary Key on the Customer table
Foreign Key	from_ addr_id	integer		No	Unique identifier for the custom-er's originating shipping address	Primary Key on the Customer_ Address table
Foreign Key	to_addr_ id	integer		No	Unique identifier for the ship-to address	Primary Key on the Delivery_ Address table
	last_ update_	time-stamp		No	Creation date and timestamp for the row	Populated when a package is first entered into the database

Data dictionary entries serve many constituents. For example, a database administrator can refer to Table 4.2 when creating the Package table, a developer can look at the Source column when troubleshooting data errors in production, and an analyst can get additional context about the units of measure for a package's dimensions.

Entity Relationship Diagram

An *Entity Relationship Diagram* (*ERD*) is one of the data modeling process's most frequently referenced visual artifacts, depicting entities and their relationships. In an ERD, boxes represent entities, which become database tables. The lines that connect the entities represent their relationship. A relationship is a connection between entities. Figure 4.13 illustrates a logical ERD, while Figure 4.19 depicts a physical ERD. Administrators, developers, and analysts all use ERDs to understand the structure of a database.

Understanding line terminators from Figure 4.12 and the ordinality and cardinality they represent is vital to interpreting an ERD. Consider Figure 4.20, which shows the Package and Package_Scan entities. The line between the entities illustrates their relationship. The symbols at the end of each relationship line describe the ordinality and cardinality of the relationship.

FIGURE 4.20 Excerpt of an entity relationship diagram

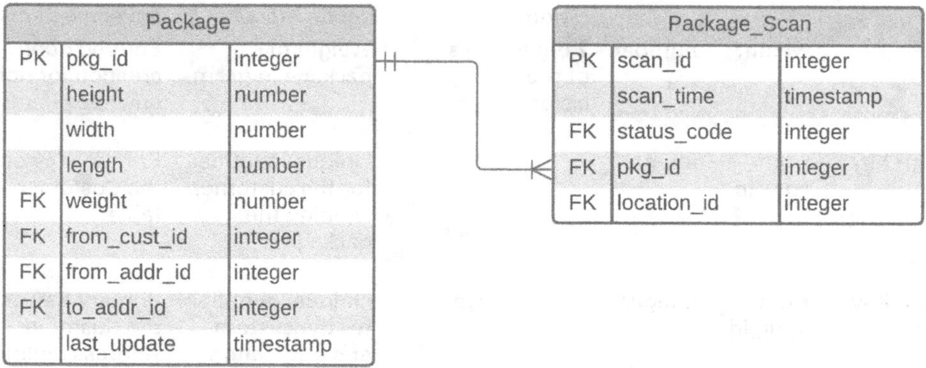

With an understanding of cardinality and ERD line terminators, let's apply it to Figure 4.20. Reading the diagram aloud from left to right, you say, "An individual package must have at least one and possibly many package scans." Reading from right to left, you say, "A specific package scan must belong to one and only one package."

There are three cardinality types: one-to-one, one-to-many, and many-to-many. When the cardinality is *one-to-one* (*1:1*), each instance of one entity is related to only one instance of another entity. Suppose you want to illustrate the relationship between employees and private offices. Figure 4.21 shows how each employee can optionally have at most one office, while each office can be assigned to at most one employee.

FIGURE 4.21 One-to-one cardinality

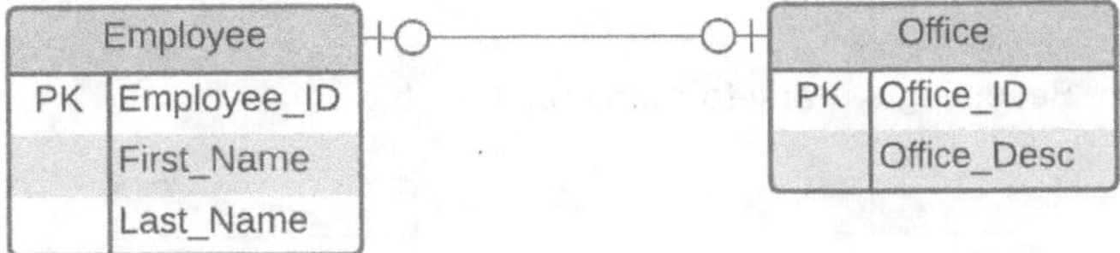

In a *one-to-many (1:N)* relationship, each instance of one entity is related to multiple instances of another entity. For example, Figure 4.20 shows how a package can have multiple scans, but a specific scan belongs to a single package.

In a *many-to-many* (*N:N*) relationship, multiple instances of one entity are related to multiple instances of another entity. Figure 4.22 shows how a package passes through many locations, and a single location can contain multiple packages.

FIGURE 4.22 Many-to-many cardinality

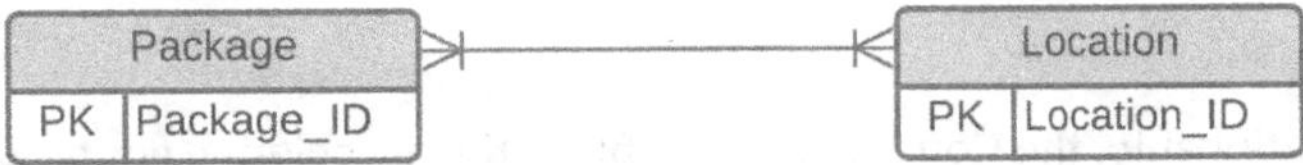

Understanding data cardinality is essential for designing a well-structured and efficient database system. By correctly identifying the cardinality of the relationships between entities, developers can ensure that the database schema is normalized.

Cardinality, Logical ERDs, and Physical ERDs

When modeling complex business scenarios, using many-to-many relationships is common during the logical design phase. Many-to-many relationships make sense during logical design because they accurately reflect the real-world relationships between entities. For example, consider a university database that tracks courses and students. A student can enroll in multiple courses, and a course typically has multiple students enrolled. A many-to-many relationship makes sense in this scenario because it accurately reflects the relationship between students and courses. However, it is impossible to identify the specific students enrolled in a particular course.

To resolve many-to-many relationships during physical design, you need an associative entity. An *associative entity* is both an entity and a relationship. An associative entity typically contains the foreign keys from the entities it connects, establishing one-to-many relationships between the entities and the associative table. The first diagram in Figure 4.23

shows the logical relationship between students and courses, while the second illustrates the physical relationship.

FIGURE 4.23 Resolving a many-to-many relationship

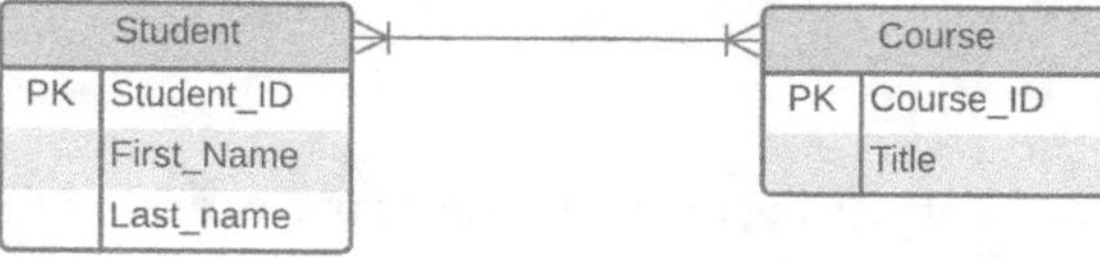

Physical:

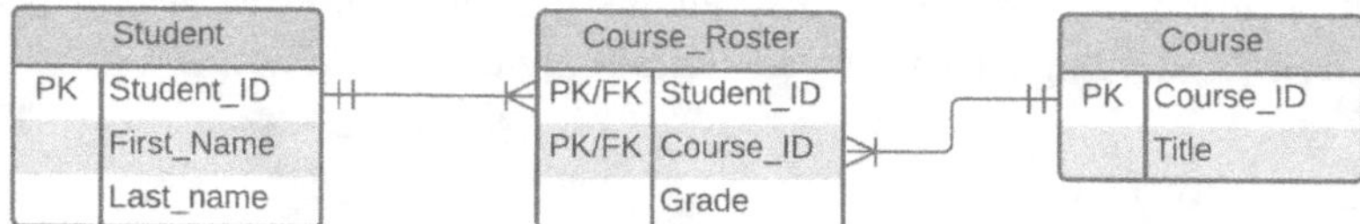

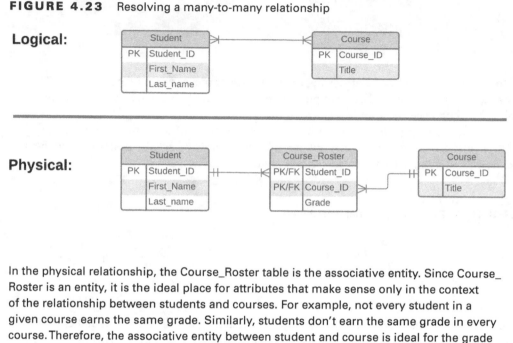

In the physical relationship, the Course_Roster table is the associative entity. Since Course_Roster is an entity, it is the ideal place for attributes that make sense only in the context of the relationship between students and courses. For example, not every student in a given course earns the same grade. Similarly, students don't earn the same grade in every course. Therefore, the associative entity between student and course is ideal for the grade attribute.

System Requirements Documentation

In addition to the entity relationship diagram and accompanying data dictionary, the planning and design process typically produces several additional system requirements documents. The *Business Requirements Document* (*BRD*) describes the high-level business objectives and requirements. It includes information such as the business goals, scope, constraints, and success criteria. Business stakeholders and their technical counterparts typically collaborate on the BRD to ensure the database system aligns with the overall business strategy.

A *Functional Requirements Document* (*FRD*) describes the functional requirements for the database. The FRD typically includes use cases, user roles, and other details relating to expected functionality. It is typical to find input requirements, output requirements, data processing rules, and system performance requirements in an FRD.

A *Technical Requirements Document* (*TRD*) details the technical requirements for the database. The TRD includes hardware and software requirements, database size, capacity, and performance metrics. The TRD may also specify additional details about the development environment, the number of testing environments, data refresh and obfuscation policies, and deployment procedures.

Implementation, Testing, and Deployment

Implementation, testing, and deployment are critical stages in developing a robust, efficient, and reliable database system. These stages encompass a range of activities, including asset acquisition, software configuration, and building the actual database. As the database becomes available, you load any initial data and validate database connectivity. After confirming connectivity, you validate data quality and verify database functionality before establishing performance capabilities. As you prepare to deploy the database into a production environment, you plan for initial operational considerations.

Acquisition of Assets

The acquisition of assets plays a crucial role in successfully developing and deploying a database system. You need hardware, software, data, and people to build, maintain, and operate a database. During asset acquisition, you must account for one-time needs that occur during creation, testing, and validation. You also want to identify recurring assets for ongoing management, maintenance, and operations.

The choice of appropriate hardware is vital to ensure optimal performance, scalability, and reliability of the database system. From a hardware standpoint, you need servers, storage devices, and networking equipment to satisfy the database's physical infrastructure needs. Including networking equipment is especially vital when deciding between an on-premises and cloud-deployment environment. A comprehensive approach to the required hardware assets helps ensure you are accounting for the total cost of operating the database.

When acquiring hardware assets, you must carefully consider processing capacity, memory, storage, and network bandwidth to ensure the database can handle the anticipated workload. You also want to acquire sufficient resources to account for growth projections while abiding by budget constraints.

The two primary considerations in acquiring software assets are the operating system and database platform. You must decide whether your organization is embracing open-source or proprietary platforms. You must negotiate software licensing and vendor support costs if you select a proprietary platform. If you choose an open-source platform, consider whether or not to engage a vendor to provide support.

Your plan must include the acquisition of data assets. Data may come from internal databases, external data providers, and organizations you interoperate with. As part of acquiring data, ensure you have the necessary tools for loading that data into the database.

A skilled and knowledgeable team is indispensable for developing and operating a database. Various roles make up the team, including database administrators, data analysts, and developers. Acquiring human resources entails identifying the required skill sets. Assessing any hiring or training needs is vital, particularly if you are implementing a new platform for your organization.

Phases of Deployment

Database deployment is when you transform the database design from concept to reality. Before proceeding with software installation and configuration, you must identify and resolve any database prerequisites. A *database prerequisite* is a system requirement that must be satisfied before installing the database. For example, your chosen database platform may require specific hardware for compatibility reasons. You must also consider the operating system version and any required software libraries. Any dependencies or integrations with other systems or applications should be on your prerequisite checklist to ensure they are compatible with the new database.

Once you resolve any prerequisites, you can proceed with infrastructure provisioning. Provisioning includes setting up storage arrays, database servers, and networking equipment, as well as verifying communication between the components. In addition to sufficient storage space, ensure that you provision enough memory and processing power to meet the needs of the database.

With infrastructure provisioning complete, it is time to install the database software. Download the appropriate software package from its open-source community page if you are using open-source software. If you are going with packaged software, obtain the software from the vendor. Once you have the software, install it onto the database server.

If you build a new database in an established environment, you may need to upgrade the operating system or database software to a more current version. There are many reasons for upgrading components, including applying patches to address security vulnerabilities or performance issues. When upgrading components currently supporting production applications, ensure the upgrades are compatible with existing applications.

If the database you are deploying consists of additional features in an existing application, you may modify an existing database. Modifying a database involves changing the schema, data structures, or configuration settings. Typically, accommodating new requirements results in database modifications. You may also modify a database to enhance performance or improve maintainability.

Database Connectivity

Database connectivity establishes a connection between a client application or system and a database server to facilitate data exchange, retrieval, and manipulation. It is a critical aspect of database management, enabling applications and users to interact with the database. From a security standpoint, it is a best practice for the database server location to be in a private network. Figure 4.24 illustrates the importance of isolating the database server.

In Figure 4.24, incoming user connections pass through the firewall and connect to the web application. The web application connects to the database server. The issue with this approach is that both the web application server and the database server are in a publicly accessible network. If an intruder can see the database server on the network, the dashed line shows how it is possible to try and compromise the database directly. Isolating the database server in a private network, as Figure 4.25 shows, resolves this design flaw.

FIGURE 4.24 Flat network

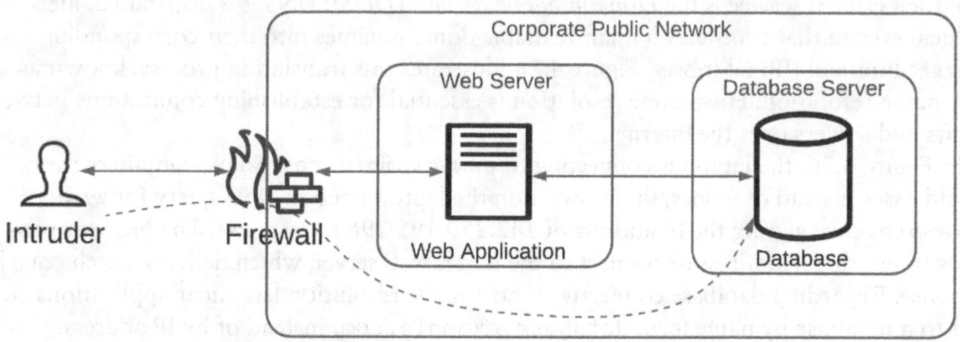

Figure 4.25 shows how to divide the corporate network into publicly and privately accessible segments, or subnets. A *subnet* is an isolated network segment within a more extensive network. In this approach, the public network only houses servers that provide user-facing applications. However, the database server exists on a private network inaccessible from the public Internet. With this design, the only way for an intruder to see the database server is to compromise the application server.

FIGURE 4.25 Network with public and private subnets

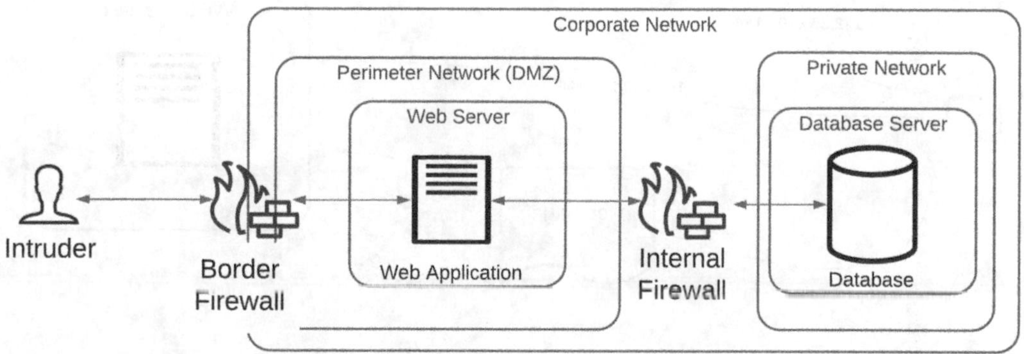

Networking Concepts

Database connectivity also relies on various networking concepts and services to facilitate seamless communication between client applications and database servers. Beyond understanding where in the network to place a database server, data systems analysts must also understand some additional networking concepts and services.

Doman Name Service (DNS)

One such critical service is the *Domain Name Service* (*DNS*). DNS is a distributed, hierarchical system that translates human-readable domain names into their corresponding Internet Protocol (IP) addresses. Figure 4.26 illustrates this translation process, known as host-name resolution. Host-name resolution is essential for establishing connections between clients and servers over the Internet.

In Figure 4.26, the laptop is connecting to `www.example.com`. Since computers use IP addresses instead of names, the browser on the laptop issues a DNS query for `www.example.com`, getting the IP address of 142.250.191.196 in response. The browser proceeds to use this IP address to connect to the target web server, which delivers a web page in response. Regarding database connectivity, host-name resolution lets client applications connect to a database by name (e.g., `database.example.com`) instead of by IP address.

FIGURE 4.26 DNS host-name resolution

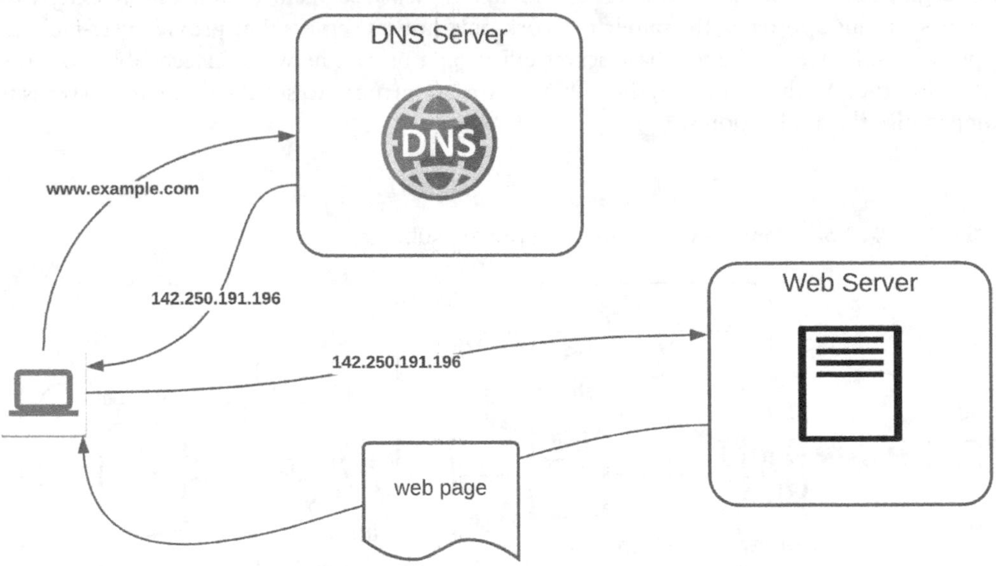

DNS is also useful for load balancing in distributed or high-availability database architectures where multiple database servers or replicas handle client requests. DNS can distribute the load among these servers by resolving the domain name to different IP addresses, effectively balancing the traffic and improving the overall performance and reliability of the system.

The ability to map a domain name to an IP address facilitates failover, improving availability in the event of a failure. When a database server fails, DNS can redirect traffic to an alternative server, minimizing downtime and ensuring continuous availability of the database service. It can take some time for DNS to recognize an underlying database failure. To further reduce downtime, client applications should reconnect to the database automatically when the inevitable disruption occurs.

Using a domain name instead of an IP address also improves the security of database connections. Using domain names instead of IP addresses can make it more difficult for attackers to identify and target specific servers while enabling secure DNS services (e.g., DNSSEC) to protect against DNS-related attacks and spoofing attempts.

Client/Server Architecture

A client/server architecture divides the database system into two main components: the client and the server. Examples of clients include applications, application servers, and API endpoints. The server is where the database management system resides. Database clients send requests to the server to perform actions such as querying, inserting, updating, or deleting data. The server processes these requests, interacts with the database, and returns the results to the clients. Beyond centralizing data onto a server, this architecture improves security.

Properly configuring network devices is one way to enhance security using a client/server architecture. Specifically, you can use firewalls to protect the database server from unauthorized access. A *firewall* is a security device that monitors and controls incoming and outgoing network traffic using predetermined security rules. As barriers between trusted internal networks (e.g., a corporate network) and untrusted external networks (e.g., the Internet), firewalls prevent unauthorized access while protecting internal resources from potential security threats. In a client-server architecture, firewall configurations control and monitor the traffic between clients and the database server, allowing only legitimate requests and blocking potential threats.

There are also perimeter network considerations when designing a network to enable database connectivity. A *perimeter network*, also known as a *demilitarized zone* or *DMZ*, is an additional layer of security that separates the database server from the public Internet, offering further protection against attacks. The perimeter network typically consists of a separate subnet, with additional firewalls or security appliances to control access to the database server. Figure 4.27 incorporates sound network design and firewall implementation, with a border firewall protecting the publicly accessible perimeter network and an internal firewall with additional network restrictions.

FIGURE 4.27 Border and internal firewalls

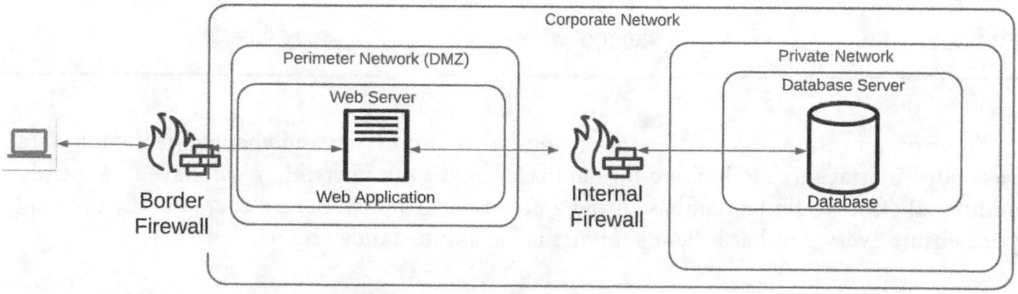

Considering static and dynamic IP addressing is crucial when enabling database connectivity. Static IP addresses are fixed and manually assigned to a specific device, ensuring the device's address remains constant. Historically, setting a static IP address for database servers was common practice. Currently, the best approach is to connect to a database using its DNS name. In the event of a failure, modifying DNS to resolve to a different database adds flexibility without reconfiguring database clients.

A Dynamic Host Configuration Protocol (DHCP) server assigns dynamic IP addresses to clients. As the name implies, clients are not guaranteed the same IP address whenever they connect to a network. It is vital to design firewall rules to accommodate IP address ranges, as inbound connections to the database server can come from multiple clients.

Ports and Protocols

Planning for the relevant networking ports and protocols as you design for database connectivity is vital. *Ports* are unique numerical identifiers that distinguish different services or processes on a single device. People are typically familiar with the ports used by web applications: port 80 for unencrypted traffic and port 443 for encrypted traffic.

Connection protocols provide standardized methods of communication between a client application and the database server. Most modern networks run the standard Transmission Control Protocol (TCP) and the Internet Protocol (IP), commonly known as TCP/IP, for communicating between machines. Table 4.3 lists popular relational database engines, their default port, and the supported protocols.

TABLE 4.3 Default Database Ports

Relational Database	Default Network Port	Network Protocol
MySQL	3306	TCP/IP
PostgreSQL	5432	TCP/IP
Microsoft SQL Server	1433	TCP/IP
Oracle	1521	TCP/IP
MariaDB	3306	TCP/IP
IBM Db2	50000	TCP/IP

Some organizations take a "security by obscurity" approach and change the default database port. If attackers are looking for databases on default ports, they will have to expend additional effort to find a database using a non-standard port. Before changing the default port, ensure every database client supports using a non-standard port.

Firewall rules specify an action, source, destination, port, and protocol. The action parameter is binary, either allowing or denying traffic. The source parameter sets a range of IP addresses where network traffic comes from, while the destination parameter is where traffic goes. The port parameter is the network port the rule applies to, while the protocol specifies the networking protocol. Figure 4.28 summarizes the network considerations to facilitate database connectivity. The web server has a public IP address for handling external requests and an internal, private IP address for communicating within the corporate network.

FIGURE 4.28 Firewall rules for web and database traffic

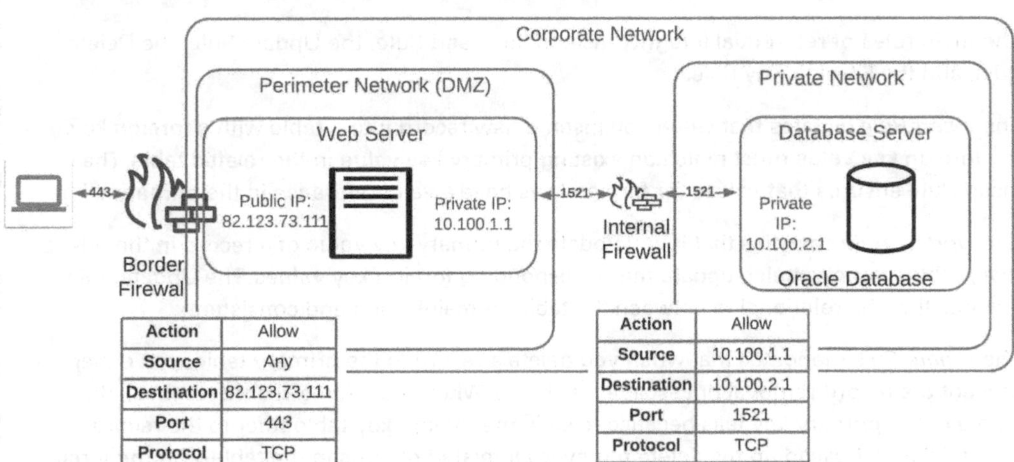

The border firewall rule in Figure 4.28 allows traffic from any source to access the web server on port 443. Since this diagram uses an Oracle database, the internal firewall rule must allow traffic on port 1521, per Table 4.3. Examining the internal firewall rule, it only allows traffic on port 1521 from the web server's private IP address to the private IP address of the database server. With this configuration, the internal firewall denies any attempt to directly access the database server on a port other than 1521 from any location other than the private IP of the web server. You would need additional firewall rules to facilitate operational duties like maintaining operating system and database software.

Testing

Testing is a critical aspect of the database implementation process, as it helps to ensure the database system's correctness, performance, security, and overall quality. Including database-specific tests to detect and address potential issues, validate functionality, and ensure the database meets its intended requirements is vital.

Referential Integrity

Referential Integrity is a fundamental concept in relational database management systems that ensures the consistency and accuracy of relationships between tables. It enforces the proper maintenance of these relationships by ensuring that changes made to the data in one table do not cause invalid or orphaned records in another table. You achieve referential integrity by using primary keys and foreign keys. Recall from Chapter 3, "SQL and Scripting," that a primary key uniquely identifies a row in a table, while a foreign key is a field in another table that refers to the primary key in the first table. The foreign key links the two tables, establishing a relationship between the corresponding records.

The main rules of referential integrity include the Insert Rule, the Update Rule, the Delete Rule, and the Foreign Key Rule.

The *Insert Rule* dictates that when you insert a new record into a table with a foreign key, the foreign key value must match an existing primary key value in the related table. The Insert Rule ensures that values for foreign keys have a valid reference in the primary table.

The *Update Rule* specifies that if you update the primary key value of a record in the primary table, you must also update the corresponding foreign key values. The Update Rule ensures that the relationship between the tables remains valid and consistent.

The *Delete Rule* mandates that when you delete a record in the primary table, you either prevent the record removal or cascade the delete. When preventing record removal, the delete of the primary key fails because rows in the foreign key table refer to the record being deleted. Cascading the delete removes all related records in the table with the foreign key. Determining how your organization wants to maintain referential integrity when removing records is vital, as cascading a delete can have unintended consequences. For example, a cascading delete of a customer can remove that customer's purchase history, creating historical reporting problems.

The *Foreign Key Rule* stipulates that you cannot modify a foreign key value if it results in an orphaned record, as an orphaned record would no longer have reference to a valid primary key in the related table.

By enforcing referential integrity, relational databases ensure that relationships between tables remain consistent and that data is not inadvertently lost or corrupted. Referential integrity is crucial for maintaining a database's quality, accuracy, and reliability.

Database Quality Checks

Database quality checks are validation procedures that help ensure the database's correctness, consistency, and overall quality. Some of these checks are structural, focusing on columns, tables, and fields. Validating the schema, data types, and data values are among the checks that are vital to ensuring quality.

Schema validation validates that the implementation conforms to the original requirements. Structurally, verify that each table matches the design and that no columns are missing. To ensure the integrity of each column, check for data type consistency. Verifying data type consistency ensures that each column uses an appropriate data type for its content. For example, a column that stores quantity should use a numeric data type instead of text to facilitate aggregation. During schema validation, you also confirm that data types for primary and foreign keys are consistent across tables to ensure referential integrity.

Nullability checks and default value validation are additional methods of ensuring data integrity. *Nullability checks* validate that optional columns are nullable and required columns are not. *Default value constraints* supply a default value for a column. For example, suppose a table containing data about people has a *Living* column to indicate whether the person is alive. As inserts add data to the table, a default value constraint can set the *Living* column to Yes.

To limit values in a given column to a specific range of values, you can use either referential integrity or check constraints. Figure 4.29a shows how the foreign key on the Customer Address uses the primary key of the State_Province table to enforce range control. Meanwhile, Figure 4.29b shows how to implement range control using a check constraint.

FIGURE 4.29a Range control with referential integrity

Customer_Address		
PK	addr_id	integer
	street_line_1	varchar(100)
	street_line_2	varchar(100)
	street_line_3	varchar(100)
	apt_suite	varchar(50)
	city	varchar(50)
FK	state_prov_code	varchar(2)
	postal_code	varchar(10)
	country_code	varchar(2)
	last_update	timestamp

State_Province		
PK	state_prov_code	varchar(2)
	state_prov_desc	varchar(100)
	last_name	varchar(100)
FK	country_code	varchar(2)
	last_update	timestamp

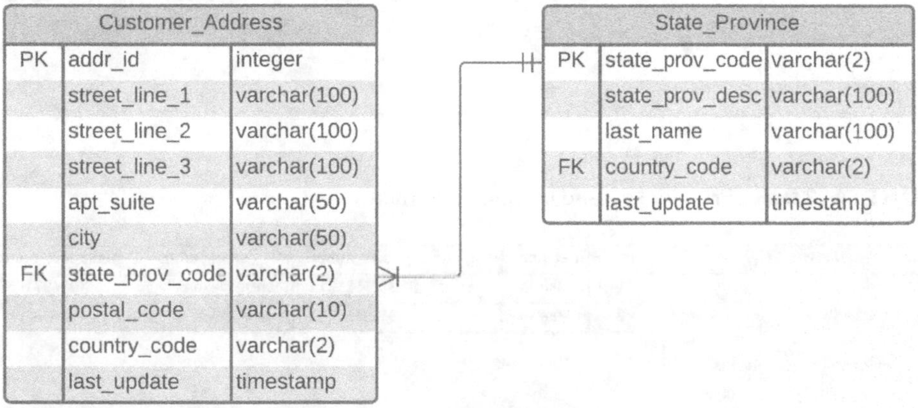

FIGURE 4.29b Range control with a check constraint

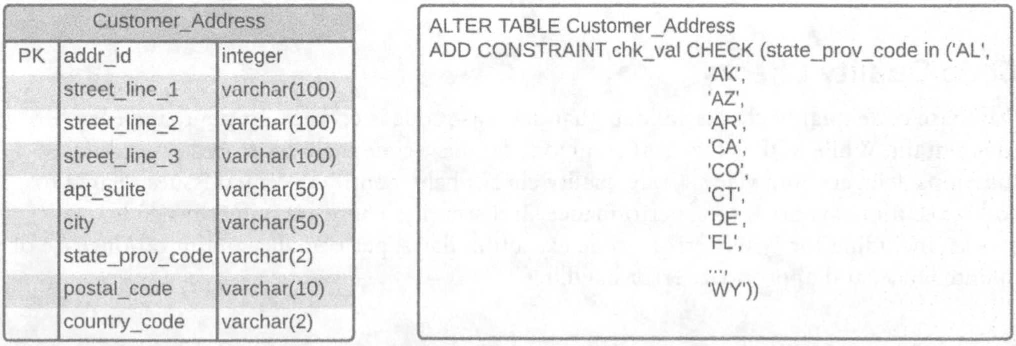

Customer_Address		
PK	addr_id	integer
	street_line_1	varchar(100)
	street_line_2	varchar(100)
	street_line_3	varchar(100)
	apt_suite	varchar(50)
	city	varchar(50)
	state_prov_code	varchar(2)
	postal_code	varchar(10)
	country_code	varchar(2)

```
ALTER TABLE Customer_Address
ADD CONSTRAINT chk_val CHECK (state_prov_code in ('AL',
                                                   'AK',
                                                   'AZ',
                                                   'AR',
                                                   'CA',
                                                   'CO',
                                                   'CT',
                                                   'DE',
                                                   'FL',
                                                   ...,
                                                   'WY'))
```

Selecting between referential integrity and check constraints depends on operational preference and how quickly data will change. Some organizations find adding data to a table simpler than altering a check constraint.

Another way to improve data quality is to use database features to limit the possibility of duplicate data. It is common for primary keys to be unique values whose sole purpose is uniquely identifying a row. While this is useful, it does not prevent the creation of duplicate records. The Customer table in Figure 4.30a has a primary key of *cust_id*. A sequence number within the database generates unique values for *cust_id*. While the primary key enforces the uniqueness of the row, this configuration allows for duplicating Manish Harris's information since the database generates the values for the primary key. Using a unique key constraint on customer-supplied data prevents this duplication from happening.

A *unique key constraint* ensures that each value in a column is unique. Figure 4.30b adds a unique key constraint to the *passport_number* column. Since this constraint enforces uniqueness, the second insert for Manish Harris's data fails, preventing a duplicate insert.

FIGURE 4.30a Primary key

	Customer	
PK	cust_id	integer
	first_name	varchar(100)
	last_name	varchar(100)
	phone_number	integer
	email_addr	varchar(50)
	passport_number	varchar(10)
	last_update	timestamp

cust_id	first_name	last_name	phone_number	email_addr	passport_number
1	Manish	Harris	3125551212	manish@example.com	X93497106
2	Manish	Harris	3125551212	manish@example.com	X93497106

FIGURE 4.30b Primary key and unique constraint

	Customer	
PK	cust_id	integer
	first_name	varchar(100)
	last_name	varchar(100)
	phone_number	integer
	email_addr	varchar(50)
UC	passport_number	varchar(10)
	last_update	timestamp

cust_id	first_name	last_name	phone_number	email_addr	passport_number
1	Manish	Harris	3125551212	manish@example.com	X93497106
~~2~~	~~Manish~~	~~Harris~~	~~3125551212~~	~~manish@example.com~~	~~X93497106~~

Code Quality Checks

Database code quality checks validate that database code is correct, efficient, and easy to maintain. While SQL is the most common, database code includes stored procedures, functions, triggers, and views. Code quality checks help identify potential issues related to code execution, syntax errors, performance, and security. There are numerous code quality checks, including for syntax errors, code execution flaws, performance optimization, ease of maintenance, and appropriate error handling.

A *syntax error* is a coding flaw that prevents correct execution. Common syntax errors result from incorrect keyword use, missing or mismatched parentheses, and improper use of operators. For example, consider the table in Figure 4.30b. The following query is missing a comma between the column names in the select clause, resulting in a syntax error:

```
   SELECT first_name last_name
FROM Customer
```

When validating code execution, you verify that the code runs successfully and produces the expected results. When validating code, including various input parameters and edge cases is crucial, checking for any runtime errors or unexpected behavior. For example, suppose a stored procedure inserts new records into the Customer table in Figure 4.30b. The code that inserts a new record into a table should be validated to confirm that it correctly obtains a unique value for the primary key, inserts the data, and handles any constraint violations on *passport_number*.

It is crucial to include performance optimization during testing to have an operationally viable database. Analyzing code for potential performance bottlenecks, such as inefficient queries, improper use of indexes, or excessive use of cursors and loops, is part of optimizing for performance. For example, when retrieving data from multiple tables, joining the tables together is generally faster than using a nested subquery. For example, consider the package and package_scan tables from Figure 4.20. The following code block illustrates two valid approaches to retrieving the same information:

```
   -- Original query: functional
SELECT package.pkg_id
       ,package_scan.scan_time
       ,package_scan.location_id
FROM   package
WHERE  package.pkg_id IN (SELECT pkg_id
                          FROM   package_scan)
-- Rewritten as a join, which is more efficient:
SELECT package.pkg_id
       ,package_scan.scan_time
       ,package_scan.location_id
FROM   package
INNER JOIN package_scan
ON     package.pkg_id = package_scan.pkg_id
```

Note that performance optimization should be an ongoing process. Once the database is operational, new use cases crop up, workloads shift, and unexpected spikes all impact performance.

Considering readability is essential in evaluating how easy it is to maintain code. Validate that code complies with any organizational standards for formatting or organizing code. While code formatting standards vary by organization, they commonly include naming conventions, comment placement and style, and appropriate indentation and spacing.

By maintaining high-quality code, developers can make it easier to maintain, troubleshoot, and modify the database system in the future. While the following code is functionally equivalent to the previous query, it is hard to read, making it more challenging to maintain:

```
   -- Hard to read query, please reformat!
select package.pkg_id, package_scan.scan_time ,package_scan.location_id from
package inner join package_scan on package.pkg_id = package_scan.pkg_id
```

Appropriate error handling makes troubleshooting and debugging easier when problems inevitably happen. Consistency in where to log and how to surface errors is vital to operational stability. For example, a stored procedure should include error handling using try/catch blocks in SQL Server:

```
   CREATE PROCEDURE SampleProcedure
AS
BEGIN
   BEGIN TRY
     -- Code that might result in an error
   END TRY
      BEGIN CATCH
      -- Handle the error
      -- Option 1: write details to a log
      -- Option 2: write details to an error table
      -- Option 3: return a custom error message
   END CATCH
END;
```

The frequency and reason for notifications are crucial to ensuring code quality and operational stability. When testing procedures, triggers, and the alerts they generate, take a manage-by-exception approach. Managing by exception focuses on addressing anomalies in a database instead of receiving alerts for expected events. For example, inserting a row should not trigger an alert. However, a query failure due to an accidentally dropped table warrants a notification.

Version Control Checks

Version control software tracks and manages changes to the source code, database scripts, and configuration files. Version control enables developers to collaborate more effectively, maintain a history of changes, and revert to previous versions if necessary. Among version control systems, Git enjoys broad adoption. Defining processes for implementing change in your database is as important as selecting version control software.

Version control testing validates how you use version control software in your environment. Version control is not limited to managing SQL and stored procedures. Any file that impacts the database should be under version control, including database code, ETL code, database configuration files, and operating system configuration files. You can be confident that your version control software and processes function well when developers collaborate without overwriting each other's code. Other signs of success include understanding what components change, when those changes happen, and how to revert them.

Stress Testing

Stress testing evaluates a database's performance, stability, and reliability under extreme conditions. The primary goal of stress testing is to identify when and how the system fails in its current configuration. To find the breaking point, you intentionally exceed the target-operating capacity of the database. The four most common bottlenecks are as follows:

- Saturating the database server's available CPU
- Consuming all of the RAM on the database server
- Consuming all available storage
- Saturating the available network or storage network bandwidth

Once you identify what ultimately governs database performance, you can combine that knowledge with any growth objectives to plan future resource acquisitions.

It is crucial to identify load sources when designing a stress test. Database load comes from various sources, including stored procedures, applications, API platforms, and ETL jobs. Stress testing these load sources identifies the maximum sustainable transaction volume and the maximum number of concurrent users the database can support without compromising the overall system performance or experiencing failures.

The key to successful stress testing is test-scenario design. Design realistic test scenarios that simulate high-stress conditions, such as many concurrent users, a high volume of transactions, or intensive data processing tasks. For instance, you should understand the database's ability to handle an ETL job and a high transaction volume simultaneously. The scenarios you design should represent the real-world use cases and challenges the system might face.

To successfully perform a stress test, ensure you have sufficient budget and resources for a dedicated test environment. The test environment must closely resemble the final production environment, including load sources, database, requisite hardware, and network configurations. Stress testing in an environment that mimics production gives you a more accurate understanding of how the production system will perform.

A crucial part of stress testing is data preparation. Suppose one of the use cases an application supports is retrieving customer profile information. Suppose you only have ten test customers in the database and are simulating thousands of profile retrievals. In that case, the database will quickly cache the 10 test customers' data in RAM instead of retrieved from disk. As retrieving from RAM is much faster than from disk, the lack of representative test data may lull you into a false sense of security. To ensure your stress testing is accurate, you will likely have to generate large amounts of synthetic data to stress test effectively. If you are working with a database already in production, you can use a copy of the production data as an alternative to generating synthetic data. Be aware if you take this approach, you may need to mask sensitive data elements like Social Security numbers, bank account numbers, and other personally identifiable information.

Once you have an environment and sufficient test data, it's time to execute the stress test. Ensure you have the necessary tools for monitoring the database's performance, infrastructure resource usage, and rate of errors. Once the initial test is complete, analyze the results to identify performance bottlenecks, resource constraints, or stability issues.

Suppose bottlenecks arise at a threshold that does not surpass your performance objectives. In that case, you need to fix the root cause. Fixes can take many forms, including refactoring stored procedures, changing application code, and adjusting configurations in the database software.

Stress testing is an iterative process. Repeat the test, and then analyze and fix the cycle as often as necessary to ensure the database doesn't fail when it reaches production. Identify and include the most likely source of excessive resource consumption in your operational monitoring plan.

Regression Testing

Regression testing re-executes tests for existing use cases to ensure that changes like bug fixes or feature enhancements don't have unintended negative consequences. For example, some use cases for a package-tracking database include customer creation, package creation, and package tracking. Suppose you need to deploy a critical security patch. Regression testing ensures those use cases continue functioning after you apply the patch.

It is worth building a suite of regression tests that grows over time. Your regression test library will fluctuate as you implement new use cases. Changing or removing existing use cases also affects the test library.

For stable use cases, consider automating the regression tests. Automated regression testing enhances the overall effectiveness and efficiency of the testing processes by improving the consistency, accuracy, and reusability of tests. It is common for organizations to use a combination of manual tests for rapidly evolving use cases and automated tests for stable core business functionality.

Many organizations use a *continuous integration and continuous delivery (CI/CD)* approach to developing systems. Automated regression tests easily integrate into CI/CD pipelines, allowing continuous testing and issue identification and resolution during development.

Negative Testing

Negative testing provides invalid, unexpected, or incorrect inputs to ensure the database can gracefully handle such situations without crashing, producing inaccurate results, or compromising data integrity. Negative testing identifies and addresses potential issues when the database encounters unexpected data or user activity. Using invalid SQL queries, checking for data type mismatches and constraint violations, exceeding data limits, and using invalid database credentials are all valid negative test conditions.

Invalid SQL queries test the database system's ability to handle SQL queries with syntax errors. For example, try executing an SQL query with a missing keyword or a misspelled table name to ensure the system returns an appropriate error message.

To check for data type mismatches, provide input data that does not match the expected data type for a particular column or field. For example, insert a text string into a numeric field or a date into a Boolean field to confirm the database doesn't accept the incorrect data.

Design tests that ensure your check constraints function as intended. For example, try inserting a duplicate value in a column with a unique constraint to verify that the system rejects the invalid data.

Exceeding data limits is a negative test that supplies data outside a column's allowed size or range. For example, try inserting a text string longer than the maximum allowed length for a varchar column to ensure the database appropriately handles the overrun.

Checking for invalid credentials is another example of negative testing. To test for invalid credentials, reconfigure an application with an invalid user ID or database password and then verify that it can't interact with the database.

Database Validation

As you conclude functional and performance testing, validating the overall database configuration is essential to ensure operational stability. Data mapping, data values, query performance, index analysis, referential integrity, and scalability are among the configuration items needing validation.

Data Mapping

Data mapping ensures that data elements consistently map to similar data types as data flows between the database and the systems it interacts with. Databases are both sources of and destinations for data, and no database exists in isolation. It is essential to map data correctly when integrating multiple systems. Data mapping is also vital when migrating data from an existing database to a new one. For example, suppose you have an address table that stores postal codes as numeric. If you discover addresses from a legacy system have alphanumeric postal codes, validating the mapping of postal codes would cause you to change the data type of the postal code column from numeric to alphanumeric. By appropriately mapping the data, you ensure that data from the source system will transfer successfully to the database without loss or corruption.

Data Values

Validating data values involves ensuring the accuracy, consistency, and completeness of data stored in the database. Checking for missing values and verifying data accuracy based on business rules are among the tasks to perform. Suppose you need to migrate data about people from a legacy system, and a change in business rules makes the title a required field for each person. While loading the data, some records fail because the title for that record is missing in the original database. You need to resolve these missing values to finish migrating the data successfully.

Queries

Query validation tests the correctness and performance of SQL queries, stored procedures, and views within the database and connected applications. Validating queries includes testing for correct results, optimizing execution time, and verifying error handling. For example, if a stored procedure retrieves details about a particular shipment, ensure that it returns the correct data, performs efficiently, and handles cases where the requested shipment is missing.

One way to facilitate efficiency is to reduce the database's need to parse queries. *Parsing* a query is when a database's optimizer determines the optimal execution plan for a

SQL statement. As you validate queries, ensure that calling applications and stored procedures use bind variables instead of hard-coding parameters in SQL queries.

A *bind variable* dynamically substitutes parameter values at runtime. When you use bind variables in a query, you replace literal values with placeholders, followed by a parameter name. Database engines use different characters for the placeholder. For example, Oracle uses a colon (:), Microsoft SQL Server uses the at sign (@), and MySQL uses a question mark (?). These placeholders are then bound to actual values at runtime.

In Figure 4.31, the database sees each query without bind variables as individual queries. Therefore, the database treats the queries independently and parses each one individually. This parsing creates a unique execution plan for each query.

FIGURE 4.31 Queries with and without bind variables

Customer		
PK	cust_id	integer
	first_name	varchar(100)
	last_name	varchar(100)
	phone_number	integer
	email_addr	varchar(50)
UC	passport_number	varchar(10)
	last_update	timestamp

cust_id	first_name	last_name	phone_number	email_addr	passport_number
1	Manish	Harris	3125551212	manish@example.com	X93497106
2	Chris	Tandy	3125551213	chris@example.com	F34483482
3	Adhira	Patel	3125551214	adhira@example.com	M83490243
4	Ehsan	Aamer	3125551215	ehsan@example.com	P94359277
5	Renna	Abboud	3125551216	renna@example.com	L93284853

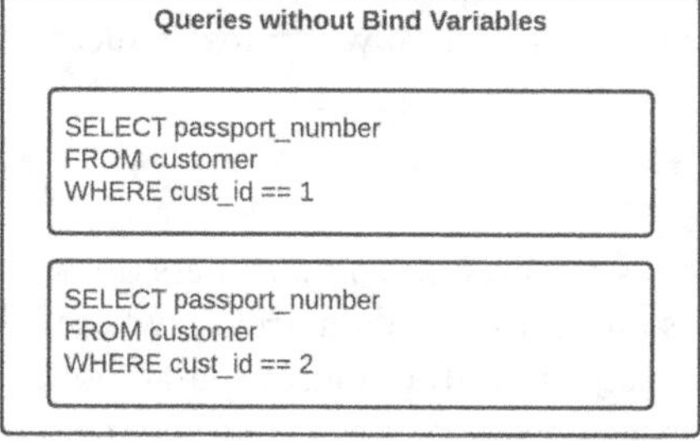

Queries without Bind Variables
SELECT passport_number
FROM customer
WHERE cust_id == 1
SELECT passport_number
FROM customer
WHERE cust_id == 2

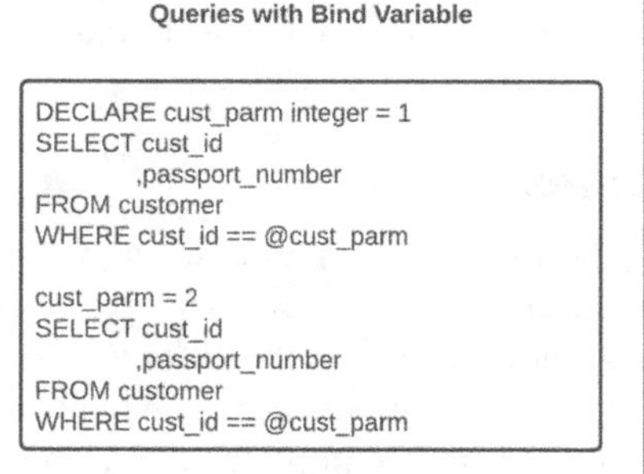

Queries with Bind Variable
DECLARE cust_parm integer = 1
SELECT cust_id
,passport_number
FROM customer
WHERE cust_id == @cust_parm
cust_parm = 2
SELECT cust_id
,passport_number
FROM customer
WHERE cust_id == @cust_parm

Figure 4.31 also illustrates defining a bind variable in Microsoft SQL Server. With the bind-variable approach, the database parses the queries using the bind variable only once. Updating the *cust_parm* variable to match a different *cust_id* changes only the value of the bind variable and bypasses the parsing stage. At scale, eliminating the parsing stage reduces the work the database does, improving performance. Ensure that calling applications and internal stored procedures use bind variables when assembling query strings to improve query consistency and performance.

Index Analysis

Index analysis focuses on analyzing and optimizing database indexes to improve query performance. Since indexes store the data for their columns, look for and consider removing redundant indexes. Index analysis and query performance are closely related, as identifying missing indexes improves query performance. In addition, you want to ensure that you cover frequently executed queries with indexes.

A *covered query* is a database query where all the required data for the query is retrieved directly from an index without accessing the actual table data. In other words, the index "covers" all the columns needed for the query execution. Covered queries significantly improve query performance, as reading data from an index is typically faster than reading it from the table. Ensuring that queries are covered is increasingly important as data volumes grow.

In Figure 4.32a, the query retrieves the *cust_id* and the *passport_number* from the Customer table. In this example, the index does not cover the query because the index only includes the *cust_id* column, while the query also requires the *passport_number*. Thus, the database system must access the underlying table to retrieve the additional column data. Accessing the base table results in a less efficient query.

FIGURE 4.32a Uncovered query

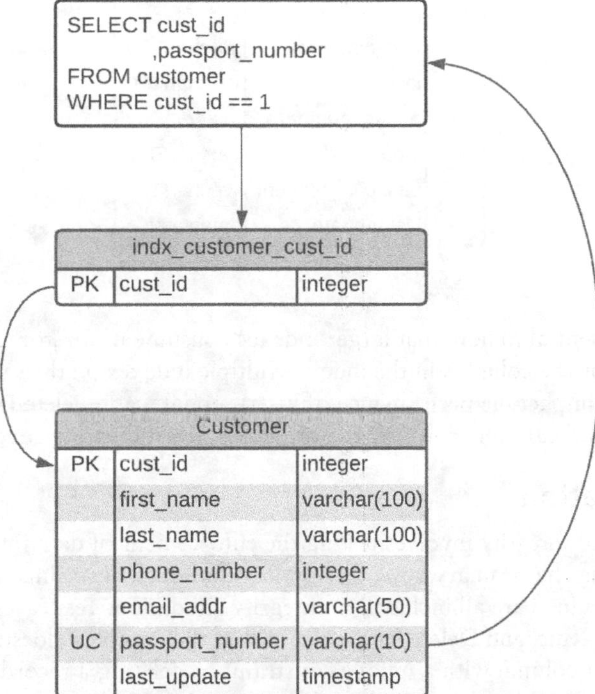

The index in Figure 4.32b includes both columns the query requires. As a result, the database retrieves all the necessary data directly from the index without accessing the Customer table. The index covers the query, improving its performance.

FIGURE 4.32b Covered query

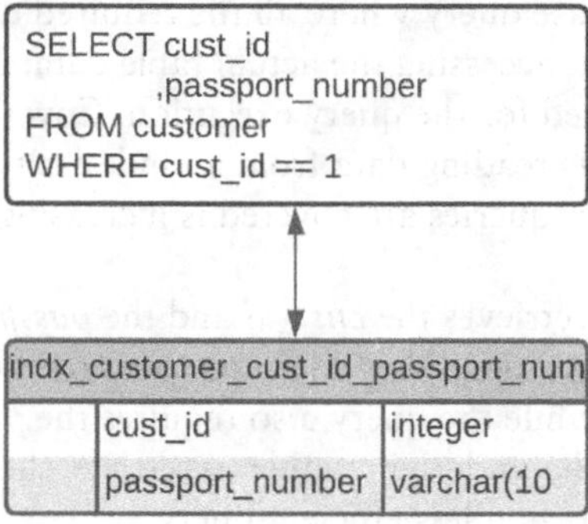

Customer		
PK	cust_id	integer
	first_name	varchar(100)
	last_name	varchar(100)
	phone_number	integer
	email_addr	varchar(50)
UC	passport_number	varchar(10)
	last_update	timestamp

That said, it's essential to note that larger indexes consume more storage since the index contains the data for the columns in the index. Multiple indexes on the same columns can also negatively impact the performance of insert, update, and delete DML operations. Therefore, you should carefully consider the trade-offs when creating covering indexes.

Integrity Validation

Validating referential integrity involves testing the enforcement of data integrity rules and constraints. Ensuring that primary keys, foreign keys, unique constraints, and check constraints work as designed are all included in integrity validation. Test cases encompassing the Insert Rule, Update Rule, and Delete Rule ensures that the database doesn't allow inserting duplicate values in a column with a unique constraint or deleting a record referenced by a foreign key in another table.

Scalability Validation

Scalability validation focuses on assessing the database system's ability to handle increased loads. The additional load can come from a user, transaction, or data volume growth. Validating scalability is closely associated with stress testing. Where stress testing identifies bottlenecks, validating scalability ensures the database can meet the business's scalability goals.

Summary

Precise requirements are crucial when planning and designing a database. As you gather requirements, identify the total number of users, the total amount of anticipated storage, and any other hardware and software requirements. Be sure to keep the database objective in mind, as transactional databases have different needs than databases that support analytics. Transactional databases are highly normalized, balancing read and write performance. Databases for reporting and analytics are denormalized, focusing on read performance.

Include database architecture factors as you develop your design. You can begin by documenting an inventory of the assets required and conduct a gap analysis against the assets that already exist in your environment. Evaluating the overall database architecture, you want to consider how cloud-hosted SaaS and PaaS applications will integrate with the database. You also want to determine if you will host the database on-premises or in an IaaS environment.

Developing logical and physical schemas is an integral part of designing a database. Recall that designing schemas is an iterative process, as you may need to make changes as you gather additional requirements. Ideally, you finalize the logical schema before proceeding with the physical schema. Finalizing the logical schema before proceeding with the physical schema minimizes rework.

The planning and design process results in a comprehensive set of design documents. This documentation includes a data dictionary, entity-relationship diagrams, and system requirements documents. The data dictionary describes tables, views, and other database objects. These details help the reader understand the purpose behind each table and the data type of each column. The data dictionary also includes nuances about individual columns, such as describing a range of valid values.

Once the planning and design phases are complete, you proceed with implementation, testing, and deployment. These phases involve acquiring assets, including people, infrastructure, software, and data.

Database deployment transforms a database design into an operational system. Before starting, database prerequisites, such as hardware compatibility, operating system versions, software libraries, and dependencies, must be resolved. After addressing prerequisites, infrastructure provisioning occurs, involving setting up storage arrays, database servers, and networking equipment. Once provisioning is complete, you install the database software on the server.

If you deploy the database in an existing environment, you may need to upgrade the operating system or database software. Reasons for upgrading include applying software patches to improve performance or security. If you need to update the environment to accommodate the new database, it is vital to ensure that the updates don't cause compatibility issues with existing applications.

Considering where the database is from a networking perspective is crucial to ensuring client connectivity. Ideally, place databases in private network segments inaccessible to the public internet. Configure database clients to refer to the database by its DNS name instead of its IP address. Using DNS names maximizes operational flexibility if you need to replace a failed database server or use a clustered database.

After verifying database connectivity, you must test the database and validate that the implementation matches the original design and satisfies the business requirements. From a micro level, validate database quality by checking for poorly formed queries or mismatched table definitions. Verify that the database appropriately handles malformed requests and properly logs exception conditions.

Considering the database system in its entirety, conduct stress tests against the database to identify bottlenecks. As you identify bottlenecks, note the threshold at which they occur and formulate a plan to alleviate them. Building out a regression test suite gives you a foundation for ensuring quality in the future as bug fixes and feature enhancements impact the database.

To validate that the database is ready for operational workloads, perform final quality checks on data mapping, data values, queries, indexes, and referential integrity. Data mapping ensures consistent data types across systems, while validating data values focuses on accuracy, consistency, and completeness. Query validation verifies the correctness, performance, and error handling of SQL queries, stored procedures, and views. Index analysis optimizes database indexes to improve query performance, with covered queries significantly boosting efficiency. Integrity validation tests the enforcement of data integrity rules and constraints, such as primary and foreign keys, unique constraints, and check constraints.

Exam Essentials

Distinguish between IaaS, PaaS, and SaaS. IaaS provides virtualized computing resources over the Internet. Users manage the infrastructure while the provider maintains the physical hardware, making IaaS similar to an on-premises environment. With PaaS, the provider also operates the database software. In a SaaS environment, the end user lacks visibility into the hardware, database, or application software.

Describe data cardinality. Data cardinality represents the relationship between two tables, indicating the number of rows in one table that relate to rows in another table. ERDs illustrate cardinality with different line terminators. These terminators can show if the relationship between tables is optional or required and whether a row in the first table refers to one or more than one row in the related table.

Describe referential integrity. Referential integrity is a fundamental concept that improves data quality by ensuring that data is consistent and accurate across tables in relational databases. Referential integrity uses primary and foreign keys to enforce these relationships. A design must comply with the Insert Rule, the Update Rule, the Delete Rule, and the Foreign Key rule to achieve referential integrity.

Explain why databases should be a private network. By isolating a database in a private network, you can restrict access to specific users and applications, minimizing the risk of data breaches. Having the database in a private network also enables organizations to implement additional security measures, with firewalls and intrusion-detection systems furthering safeguarding the database.

Explain the importance of stress testing. Stress testing a database is essential for ensuring its performance, reliability, and stability under heavy workloads. Stress testing helps identify bottlenecks, optimize resource allocation, and validate system resilience during peak workload conditions.

Review Questions

1. Samia is a database developer tasked with designing a new database system for a retail company. Before she proceeds with the design, she needs to gather requirements from stakeholders. Which stakeholders should Samia primarily consult with during the planning phase to inform the database design?
   - **A.** End users
   - **B.** Executive management
   - **C.** Regulators
   - **D.** Legal team

2. Bassim, a database administrator at a large organization, is working on the database design for a new project. To ensure the database meets the needs of its users and applications, he must gather requirements from stakeholders. Which of the following stakeholders is most likely to be responsible for operating the virtual or physical servers where the database runs?
   - **A.** Data analysts
   - **B.** Application developers
   - **C.** Database developers
   - **D.** System administrators

3. Giacomo is a database developer for a growing e-commerce company. The company wants to enhance the storage and retrieval of its customer and order data. Giacomo's supervisor asks Giacomo to analyze the current database setup to identify improvements to the system. Which of the following factors should Giacomo consider in order to determine the appropriate storage type for the company's database?
   - **A.** Data capture requirements
   - **B.** Volume and velocity of data
   - **C.** Data processing techniques
   - **D.** Data security classifications

4. Leila is a database administrator at a large healthcare organization. She is designing a database that will provide real-time access to patient information for medical staff, as well as historical reporting for the organization's management. Which of the following database designs would best meet these requirements?
   - **A.** Implement a transactional database only.
   - **B.** Implement a data warehouse only.
   - **C.** Implement a transactional database and an analytical database.
   - **D.** Implement a database with a single use case.

5. Coleman is the lead database designer for an e-commerce company that requires a database to store and manage customer information, product inventory, and financial transactions. The company also wants to analyze historical sales data and predict future trends. Coleman has identified several use cases and grouped them into categories. Which use case category should Coleman focus on for designing the company's database to facilitate predictions and trend analysis?

   A. Data capture
   B. Data storage
   C. Data retrieval
   D. Data analysis

6. Diane is a database administrator at a rapidly growing company. Her organization wants to move its database to the cloud to keep up with increasing data and users without sacrificing performance and with minimal overhead. Which cloud-hosted environment should Diane recommend?

   A. Infrastructure as a service (IaaS)
   B. Platform as a service (PaaS)
   C. Software as a service (SaaS)
   D. On-premises data center

7. Jenna, the lead IT engineer at a midsize company, is selecting the appropriate cloud environment for its new database. She aims to maintain flexibility and control over the server configuration while outsourcing the physical infrastructure. She needs to determine which cloud environment is most suitable for her needs. Which of the following should Jenna choose?

   A. Infrastructure as a service (IaaS)
   B. Platform as a service (PaaS)
   C. Software as a service (SaaS)
   D. On-premises data center

8. Karen is a database designer for a logistics company. She is designing a new database for the company to store and manage customer and package information. Which of the following design steps should Karen perform first to establish a clear understanding of the organization's business requirements? Choose the best answer.

   A. Physical schema design
   B. Logical schema design
   C. Conceptual data modeling
   D. Implementing access controls

9. Jennifer is a database administrator tasked with improving the structure of her company's database to minimize data duplication. She decides to apply normalization principles to the existing database. Which of the following normal forms is the first to define that all nonprimary key values must depend on the entire primary key?

   A. First normal form (1NF)
   B. Second normal form (2NF)
   C. Third normal form (3NF)
   D. Prime normal form (PNF)

10. Sofia is a database administrator for a logistics company and is designing a new database for the organization. She needs to visually represent the database structure, depicting entities and their relationships. Which of the following artifacts should she create to achieve this goal?
   A. Data dictionary
   B. Entity-relationship diagram (ERD)
   C. Business requirements document (BRD)
   D. Functional requirements document (FRD)

11. Asad is a network administrator at a midsize company that plans to deploy a new database server. His primary concern is securing the database server while allowing access from authorized applications. Which of the following approaches should Asad implement to enhance the security of the database server?
   A. Configure the database server to use a static IP address.
   B. Place the database server in a private network and implement a perimeter network.
   C. Disable the firewall on the database server to allow unrestricted access.
   D. Store the database server and web application server on the same public network.

12. Housni, a network administrator at a midsize company, is working on improving the database connectivity of a client/server architecture. He wants to ensure the security of the connections and prevent unauthorized access to the database server. Which of the following network components should Housni configure to achieve this objective?
   A. Domain Name System (DNS)
   B. Firewall
   C. Database schema
   D. Dynamic Host Configuration Protocol (DHCP) server

13. Suneel is a senior network administrator at a financial services firm that recently acquired a Qlik server for generating reports. He needs to update the configuration for the firewall that protects his Microsoft SQL Server database to allow access from the Qlik server using the default database port. What port does he need to ensure is open between the two servers?
   A. 1521
   B. 5432
   C. 1433
   D. 50000

14. Samar is a database administrator who maintains multiple relational databases in her organization and must understand referential integrity. Which rule requires that when a new record is inserted into a table with a foreign key, the foreign key value must match an existing primary key value in the related table?
   A. The Insert Rule
   B. The Update Rule
   C. The Delete Rule
   D. The Foreign Key Rule

15. Gerald is a database developer working on a new project. He is responsible for maintaining the quality of the database and ensuring that the data stays consistent. Gerald wants to limit the possibility of duplicate data in a particular column. Which constraint should he apply to the column to achieve this?

    A. Primary key constraint

    B. Check constraint

    C. Foreign key constraint

    D. Unique key constraint

16. Madeline is a database administrator who is optimizing the performance of a database. She notices that a query retrieves data from multiple tables using a nested subquery. She wants to improve the query's performance. What technique should Madeline use to make the query more efficient?

    A. Implement range control using referential integrity.

    B. Modify the query to use a join instead of a nested subquery.

    C. Add a check constraint to the affected columns.

    D. Apply a unique key constraint on the relevant columns.

17. Olivia is a database administrator responsible for ensuring the stability and performance of a critical database in the auction industry. She wants to evaluate the database's performance under extreme conditions to identify potential bottlenecks and weaknesses. What type of testing should Olivia perform?

    A. Regression testing

    B. Negative testing

    C. Stress testing

    D. Unit testing

18. Angela, a database administrator, is designing a stress test for her company's database. She wants to simulate a realistic high-stress condition to identify the database's maximum sustainable transaction volume and concurrent user capacity. Which of the following is crucial for Angela to ensure her stress test is accurate?

    A. Limit the test data to a small number of customers.

    B. Execute the test in an environment that does not resemble production.

    C. Generate large amounts of synthetic data for the test.

    D. Use invalid SQL queries for the test.

19. Samia, a database administrator, is optimizing the performance of her company's database. She wants to ensure that frequently executed queries retrieve all necessary data directly from an index without accessing the underlying table data. What concept should Samia focus on to improve query performance? Choose the best answer.

    A. Reducing the database's need to parse queries

    B. Ensuring data mapping consistency

    C. Implementing covered queries

    D. Enforcing data integrity rules

20. Ibrahim is a database administrator tasked with ensuring the database configuration's operational stability. He needs to verify the accuracy, consistency, and completeness of data stored in the database. Which aspect of database validation should Ibrahim focus on to achieve this goal?

    A. Data mapping

    B. Data values

    C. Query validation

    D. Index analysis

Chapter

5

Database Management and Maintenance

THE COMPTIA DATASYS+ EXAM TOPICS COVERED IN THIS CHAPTER INCLUDE:

✓ **Domain 3.0: Database Management and Maintenance**

- 3.1. Explain the Purpose of Monitoring and Reporting for Database Management and Performance
- 3.2. Explain Common Database Maintenance Processes
- 3.3 Given a Scenario, Produce Documentation and Use Relevant Tools
- 3.4 Given a Scenario, Implement Data Management tasks

As a data systems analyst, ensuring a database's efficiency, integrity, and security is paramount. This chapter focuses on the essential concepts and practices every IT professional should know to manage and maintain databases effectively. By understanding the purpose of monitoring, reporting, and maintenance, as well as being well-versed in the tools and techniques necessary for successful database management, you will be ready to handle a variety of real-world scenarios.

Throughout this chapter, we will explore various topics essential to database management. We will begin by delving into monitoring and reporting, examining the reasons behind these practices and their significance for database management and performance. This section explores system alerts/notifications, transaction log files, system log files, deadlock monitoring, and managing connections and sessions.

Next, we will introduce you to standard database maintenance processes, including query optimization, index optimization, patch management, database integrity checks, data corruption checks, periodic review of audit logs, performance tuning, load balancing, and change management.

Following maintenance, we will discuss the impact of high-quality documentation on database operations. We will explore specific artifacts, including data dictionaries, entity-relationship diagrams (ERDs), maintenance documentation, standard operating procedure (SOP) documentation, and the tools you can use to create them.

Lastly, we will delve into the practical side of database management, guiding you through various data management tasks in given scenarios. This section will provide insights on how to handle data management, data redundancy, and data sharing.

By the end of this chapter, you will have a solid understanding of the essential principles and practices involved in database management and maintenance. Armed with this knowledge, you will be better prepared to excel in the CompTIA DataSyst+ certification.

Monitoring and Reporting

In the realm of database management, monitoring and reporting are essential practices that contribute significantly to an operationally stable database. Database systems are complex, and there are many operational details to be concerned with. Understanding what to monitor and when to raise an alert is vital for efficient database operations.

The primary objective of monitoring and reporting is to maintain a consistent, high-quality user experience by ensuring the database performs well, as well as being reliable and secure. Collecting data from the operating system (OS) and the database is vital to monitoring resource utilization. A data systems analyst can use this data to proactively resolve issues, optimize performance, forecast future resource requirements, and validate database security.

Monitoring and reporting help with proactive issue resolution by detecting potential problems, such as slow queries, resource contention, or hardware failures—before they escalate into critical issues. Early detection and resolution are crucial for improving reliability.

By monitoring performance metrics, data systems analysts can identify potential bottlenecks and areas for improvement, then work to resolve them. Analysts can apply usage trends to make informed decisions regarding infrastructure upgrades and resource allocation, improving capacity-planning capabilities. In terms of security, analysts can use this data to identify unusual activity patterns and unauthorized access attempts.

Management by Exception

Management by exception is a strategy that focuses on identifying and addressing deviations from expected behavior instead of constantly raising alerts whenever an expected process occurs. Suppose you have a daily batch process that uses transactional data to populate a data warehouse. Instead of triggering a notification every time the batch process executes, you receive a message only if the process fails. This approach allows administrators to focus on tasks that ensure operational stability while minimizing the number of notifications. This approach is an ideal approach to preventing notification overload.

System Alerts and Notifications

System alerts are automated messages which notify administrators that action is required to keep a database operationally stable. You configure alerts to trigger when the system deviates from expected operational patterns. These messages help administrators quickly identify and address potential issues.

For example, an internal combustion vehicle has a fuel gauge on its dashboard. A driver can look at the fuel gauge and see the vehicle's fuel level at any time. When the fuel level falls below a certain threshold, a low-fuel warning light illuminates to alert the driver to the situation. Depending on the vehicle, a low-fuel notification message may accompany the warning light elsewhere on the dashboard, urging the driver to refuel.

Appropriate alert and notification thresholds are crucial when implementing a management-by-exception strategy. The goal is to help administrators identify deviations from the norm, such as abnormal growth in database size, unusually high resource consumption, or significant drops in throughput. Note that the alert-triggering threshold varies by system. For instance, you can set the central processing unit (CPU) alert threshold higher for a database with consistent, predictable use. Combine historical operational trends with changes in forecasted usage to determine the appropriate alert threshold for your database. Picking a suitable threshold is crucial to avoiding alert fatigue while ensuring that significant deviations get raised.

Many tools deliver alerts and facilitate monitoring, depending on organizational preferences and requirements. Similar to what you might find in vehicles, dashboards are visual displays that give an overview of key performance metrics at a glance. Dashboards aggregate data from operating systems, databases, and other sources, then present the information in an easy-to-read format. In most cases, text message (SMS) alerts and mobile phone push notifications are especially effective when immediate action is required.

Growth in Size/Storage Limits

Monitoring the growth of a database is crucial for capacity planning, as well as preventing storage-related issues. When identifying storage metrics to pay attention to, choose metrics and alert thresholds to help administrators take action and avoid impacting database operations. Capacity utilization, data growth rate, latency, read/write ratio, and storage tiering are among the crucial metrics to track.

Capacity utilization measures the percentage of total storage space currently in use. Monitoring capacity utilization helps administrators plan for future storage needs and ensure adequate storage is available for database growth.

Data growth rate is the rate at which data flows into the database over time. Tracking data growth helps administrators manage existing storage resources and plan capacity upgrades. Hosting location is one of the factors that influence data growth alerts. If you host your database locally, procuring additional storage hardware takes longer than allocating extra storage space in the cloud. If you can procure storage resources quickly, you might set an alert when the database size reaches 80 percent of the total storage capacity. However, use a lower threshold if it takes multiple weeks to obtain additional storage.

Latency measures the time it takes for a single I/O request to complete. Low latency is crucial for maintaining fast and responsive applications. Failing or overloaded disks and congestion on the storage area network can cause latency to increase. While relevant at the storage tier, latency also applies to network connections.

The *read/write ratio* is the proportion of read operations to write operations on the storage system. Monitoring this ratio helps administrators understand the workload patterns and optimize storage performance.

Storage tiering tracks database file distribution across storage tiers (e.g., SSDs, HDDs) based on performance needs and access frequency. Monitoring database file utilization across storage tiers helps administrators optimize cost and storage performance by allocating files to appropriate storage types.

Daily Usage

Tracking daily usage patterns helps administrators identify trends, anticipate resource needs, and ensure optimal performance during peak workloads. You want to track the number of active connections, queries, or transactions to establish a baseline of database activity and develop an understanding of system performance, user behavior, and potential areas for optimization. Standard daily usage metrics include the following:

- *Active Users*: The number of users actively interacting with the system, such as querying the database or using an application, within a given day. Create alerts when there is a significant deviation in active users.
- *Concurrent Connections*: The maximum number of simultaneous database connections. Configure the database to support more concurrent connections than the expected peak.
- *Error Rates*: The number of errors within a given day, including failed queries, transaction rollbacks, or system errors. Monitoring error rates can help administrators identify and resolve system performance and stability issues.
- *User Activity Patterns*: Analyzing user activity patterns, such as peak usage times or the most frequently accessed data, can help administrators optimize system performance and resource allocation based on actual usage patterns.

By monitoring these daily usage metrics, administrators can gain valuable insights into the system's performance, user behavior, and resource consumption. For example, you may want to configure an alert when concurrent users exceed 500, allowing administrators to alter configuration settings to accommodate the increased demand gracefully.

Throughput

Throughput is a performance metric measuring the amount of data flowing through a database within a specific timeframe (e.g., megabytes per second). Throughput reflects the efficiency of data transfer between the system components, such as the storage subsystem, memory, or network connections. Essential throughput metrics include the following:

- *Average Query Response Time*: The average time it takes for the database to return the results of a query. If the average query response time increases, it can signal an underlying performance bottleneck that needs resolution.
- *Transfer Volume*: The total amount of data transferred in and out of the database during a given time period. This metric helps monitor bandwidth utilization and is vital when planning for future capacity needs.

Suppose an order processing system fulfills 100 transactions per hour with an average response time of 800 milliseconds. For example, you could create an alert that triggers a notification when the average query response time exceeds 1.5 seconds for more than 5 minutes. This kind of degradation in response time might indicate an underlying bottleneck or configuration issue that needs to be resolved.

Resource Utilization

Monitoring the utilization of underlying hardware resources is essential to ensuring an operationally stable database. When considering utilization, it is vital to differentiate between resource utilization and saturation.

Resource utilization is the degree to which a system's resources, such as CPU, memory, disk, and network, are currently being used. Utilization is a percentage of the total resource capacity. Suppose a database has 96 GB of available memory. If the database uses 48 GB, its memory utilization is 50 percent.

Resource saturation occurs when a system's resources are fully utilized and can no longer handle additional workloads. When a resource is saturated, additional demands must wait, which creates a bottleneck on the underlying resource. For example, if CPU utilization is 100 percent, additional processes must wait for CPU time, causing the database system to exhibit a CPU bottleneck. This CPU bottleneck negatively impacts system performance.

While high resource utilization is not problematic, addressing the root cause of resource saturation is vital to ensure stable database performance. CPU, memory, disk, and network utilization are foundational OS performance resource categories to monitor. If any of these categories become saturated, you must resolve the underlying bottleneck to avoid ongoing database performance issues.

For instance, CPU saturation causes processing delays, leading to slow query performance and unhappy end users. Beyond overall utilization, including the load average and context-switching in your CPU monitoring approach is essential. The *load average* is the number of processes waiting in the CPU's queue. A good load average rule of thumb is that the load average shouldn't exceed the number of available CPU cores. *Context switches* occur when a CPU stops executing one task and starts processing another. Since this process takes time, frequent context switching indicates that the number of CPU cores is insufficient for the processing needs of the database.

Database performance degrades when there is insufficient memory. In addition to the available memory, monitoring paging activity and swap usage is essential to prevent memory saturation. *Paging* is when the database takes data that should be in memory and writes it to swap space on disk. *Swap space* is the portion of a disk designated as virtual memory. Since reading and writing from swap is slower than interacting with memory, paging negatively impacts performance. When a database experiences frequent paging, queries must retrieve data that should already be in memory from disk, resulting in poor query performance. During normal operations, it is not uncommon for databases to experience some paging, especially when handling diverse workloads. It is possible to mitigate the performance degradation associated with paging queries and processes using fast, SSD-based storage. However, additional RAM is typically a better solution when the database experiences consistently excessive paging.

On the storage side, a database can crash when the storage system becomes saturated. Several factors affect storage utilization, including the amount of data processed and other operational activities. For example, suppose a transactional database adds 2 GB worth of data daily. If the database has less than 60 GB of available storage, the database will run out of space within 30 days. Understanding data volume growth is vital to determining the appropriate threshold for a storage utilization alert.

Congestion, packet loss, and increased latency are possible symptoms of network saturation. Configure alerts that allow you to take action before saturation occurs. In addition to having network interfaces that support applications and user queries, large databases commonly connect to storage using a storage area network (SAN). Having alerts on overall utilization, amount of network traffic, changes in latency, and packet loss on all network interfaces that are part of the database infrastructure are essential.

Notifications

When crafting a notification strategy, incorporate a comprehensive understanding of database and OS needs. Regardless of resource category, starting with a conservative notification strategy is sound. The triggering limits for threshold and duration must incorporate the operational characteristics of the entire database system.

Using the CPU category as an example, OS tasks, security software, system monitoring software, backup tasks, and software patching activity contend with the database for available CPU. Taking a conservative approach, you can configure an alert to notify you when CPU utilization exceeds 75 percent for five consecutive minutes. The threshold of 75 percent allows for a 25 percent CPU reserve for unexpected activity spikes or OS maintenance activities. Setting the triggering duration to five minutes lets the database system occasionally use all the available CPU capacity. Operational context is vital for establishing appropriate alert and notification limits. As you develop an understanding of the entire database system's operational characteristics, you will adjust these limits over time.

Baseline Configuration/Trending

Establishing a resource utilization baseline is vital to defining the operational context for a database system. Without a baseline, it is challenging to determine whether current resource utilization is typical or if something unexpected is happening.

A baseline is also essential for performance benchmarking, providing a reference point for comparing system performance. For example, if a database typically uses 70 percent of CPU during peak load and suddenly it's consistently using 90 percent, it indicates that something has changed. The change could be an expected increase in data volume. Alternatively, the increase in CPU could indicate a problem, such as a missing index or a poorly performing set of queries.

A baseline is also helpful for capacity planning. You can accurately predict future resource needs by identifying system usage and performance trends. Suppose the data shows the database growing at 100 GB per month over several months. If that growth is linear and expected to continue, you can combine that with lead time estimates to ensure sufficient storage capacity to accommodate this growth. Figure 5.1 shows database utilization during peak demand and illustrates how a baseline impacts performance benchmarking and capacity planning.

FIGURE 5.1 Database CPU utilization

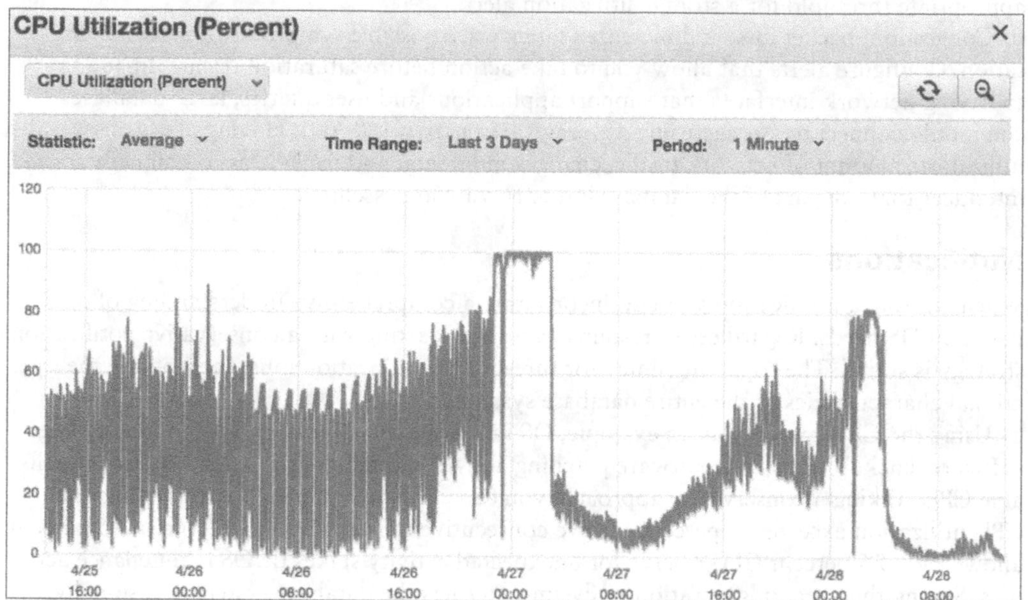

The baseline level for database CPU utilization in Figure 5.1 is between 4/25 at 16:00 through 4/26 just before 16:00. Under normal operations, the database uses between 2 percent and 60 percent CPU, with two spikes over 80 percent. The anticipated spike in demand begins at 16:00 on 4/26, continuing until CPU saturation occurs close to midnight on 4/27. Due to CPU saturation, the database could not meet the increase in demand.

To resolve the scaling and performance issues, administrators allocated additional CPU to the database server to resolve the CPU constraint.

The additional CPU capacity sufficiently handled the increase in demand, with a new peak at 80 percent CPU utilization before tapering off to normal operations. Adding the CPU utilization data from this demand spike to the trove of operational knowledge better equips data systems analysts to troubleshoot future operational issues proactively.

Baselines are also vital in understanding the impact of a change. Any change to a system, whether it's a hardware upgrade, software update, or change in system configuration, can affect performance. Having an established baseline allows you to measure the impact of those changes on database performance.

Monitoring Job Completion/Failure

Monitoring the completion and failure of various database jobs is a crucial aspect of maintaining the health and reliability of a database. Bulk load processes, batch extract processes, backups, automated data quality validation scripts, and routine index maintenance scripts are all examples of jobs that you must monitor. It is common to follow a management-by-exception approach when configuring job completion alerts by configuring notifications only when jobs fail.

When a job completes successfully, it is common to log details about the job, such as the start and end times, the duration, and a count of records loaded or manipulated. It is typical to log completion messages in a database or the organization's monitoring software of choice. Other valid job completion message destinations include email distribution lists and posts to the organization's collaboration and messaging platform. Once logged, administrators can review completion events at their leisure.

When a job fails, the monitoring system should generate a failure notification to minimize resolution time. In addition to a timestamp, failure notifications should include as much information as possible about the cause of the failure, such as error messages, job logs, and row counts. These details can help database administrators diagnose and resolve the issue as quickly as possible.

The ability to promptly detect and respond to job failures is vital. Undetected failures can lead to data loss, performance issues, or making incorrect business decisions. Figure 5.2 shows a database that receives nightly data loads from several separate source systems.

In Figure 5.2, the load from Source System C fails due to a corrupt record. Without the appropriate data from Source System C, people using the applications built on the database will make decisions using inaccurate information. Note that the notification message includes details as to why the load failed. An administrator can investigate line 4384 in the data file and resolve the situation by requesting a new source system feed or skipping the record.

FIGURE 5.2 Data load failure notification

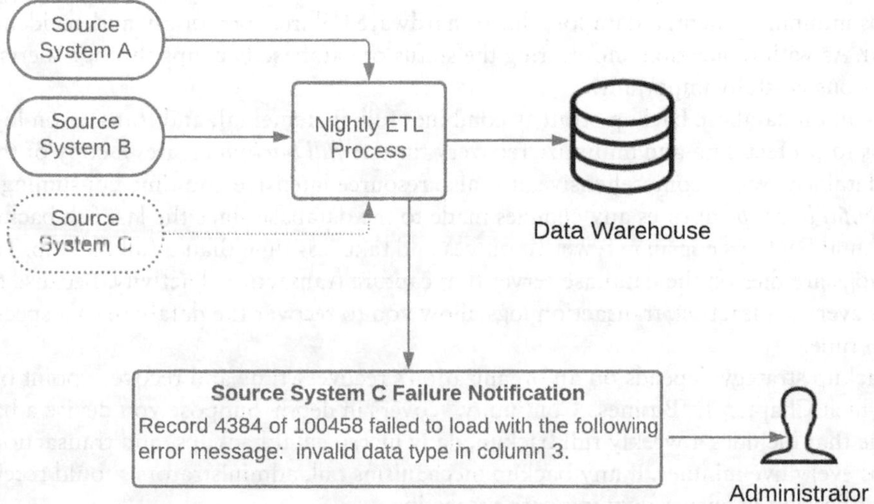

Replication

Replication is a common tactic to improve database availability in the event of a failure. Figure 5.3 illustrates the concept of database replication, where all changes made to a primary database get replicated in a secondary database.

FIGURE 5.3 Database replication

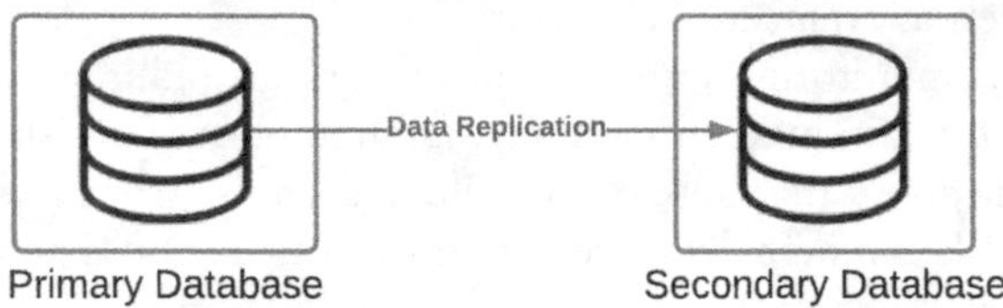

As with any complex automated process, issues can occur during replication. Suppose that during normal operations, the secondary database reflects the state of the primary database within one second. Due to increased load and resource utilization, imagine the replication increases to five minutes. This increase in replication lag is cause for concern, as you could lose five minutes of data changes if the primary database fails. As such, an increase in replication lag should minimally trigger an alert. If the lag continues to grow, a notification should accompany the alert. If replication entirely ceases to function, immediately send a failure notification to administrators.

Database Backups

Database backups are integral components of a comprehensive data protection strategy. Backups minimize potential data loss due to hardware failure, corruption, and accidental removal. As with replication, monitoring the status of database backups through alerts and notifications is vitally important.

A common database backup strategy combines full, incremental, and transaction log backups to protect data and minimize recovery time. A *full backup* creates a copy of the entire database. While comprehensive, it is also resource intensive and time-consuming. An *incremental backup* captures any changes made to the database since the last full backup. Incremental backups consume fewer resources and take less time than a full backup. Transaction logs are files on the database server that capture transactional activity. Because they capture every transaction, transaction logs allow you to recover the database to a specific point in time.

A backup strategy depends on an organization's recovery time and recovery point objectives, which Chapter 8, "Business Continuity," covers in depth. Suppose you devise a backup schedule that includes a weekly full backup, daily incremental backups, and transaction log backups every five minutes. If any backup mechanisms fail, administrators should receive an alert notification to ensure ongoing data protection.

It is essential to include backup duration and size when monitoring database backups. Suppose the baseline duration of a full backup is three hours. If the next full backup takes eight hours, that could indicate abnormal activity or a degradation in performance. Similarly, if a full backup is 700 GB when the baseline shows that 100 GB is typical, you need to understand the cause of this data growth to allow for accurate storage planning.

Log Files

Log files contain detailed information vital to understanding a database's stability and performance. Transaction logs and system logs are two primary categories of this essential information.

Transaction Logs

A *transaction log* is a chronological record of all changes made to the data in a database. Whenever you commit or roll back a transaction in the database, there is a corresponding entry in the transaction log. The rate at which the system generates transaction logs provides insight into the rate of change in the database. In a crash, you recover the database from the most recent backup, then apply changes from the transaction logs to account for new activity.

Transaction logs are also helpful when you need to audit changes in the database. For example, suppose someone temporarily falsifies information in the database and then reverts that change. Since the transaction log contains every transaction, you have a record of this potentially fraudulent activity.

There are times when it makes operational sense to disable transaction logging. Suppose you have a data warehouse where the only transactional activity comes from nightly source system bulk loads. If a load fails, a likely course of resolution is to get an updated file from the source system and rerun the load. Transaction logging consumes resources and storage space. Disabling transaction logging in this situation is an operationally viable option, as there is no other source of transactional activity. If the database crashes, you would restore from a backup and rerun the import jobs instead of applying the transaction logs.

System Logs

System logs are files stored on a server that record events and actions performed by software applications and the OS itself. System warnings and errors, software and OS versions, successful and attempted user logins, and system resource utilization data are all found in the various system logs on any operating system.

System logs assist with troubleshooting. For example, any production database must survive a "reboot test." To conduct a "reboot test," restart the database server. The expected result is that the database returns to an operationally viable state after the reboot. Suppose that during the last maintenance window, you install a new piece of software that causes a failure in the server's boot sequence. Examining the boot log on the server should help you identify the root cause of this failure.

System logs are also helpful when tuning a database for performance. While the specific log location depends on the OS, there are system logs that record resource usage or application events. Examining these logs is essential when resolving a memory, CPU, network, or storage subsystem bottleneck.

Additional Transaction Log Considerations

Disabling transaction logging is a viable way of ensuring the efficiency of bulk data loads. If you can truncate the target table and reload when a failure occurs, turning transaction logging off during the load makes sense. This approach consumes fewer resources, as you avoid the overhead of writing to the transaction log.

That said, turning off transaction logging sacrifices point-in-time recoverability. If you disable transaction logging during a bulk load, you will have no record of non-bulk-load-related transactions until you reenable transaction logging. Therefore, it is best to avoid disabling transaction logs for a database that supports transaction processing.

Deadlock Monitoring

A *deadlock* is a circular "standoff" where two or more transactions lock a resource the other needs and block each other indefinitely. Figure 5.4 illustrates a deadlock situation.

FIGURE 5.4 Deadlocked transactions

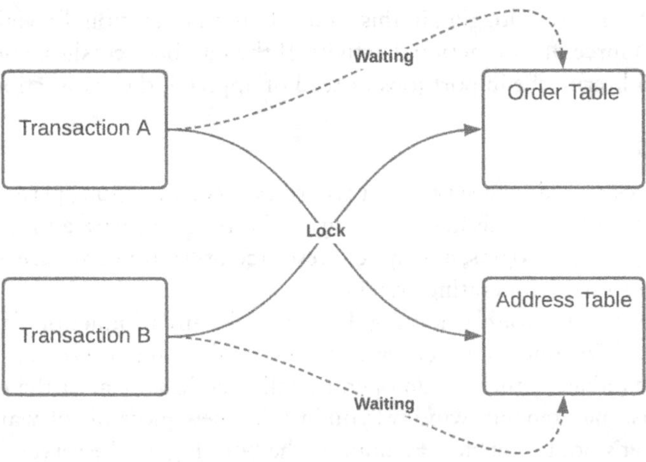

In Figure 5.4, Transaction A has a lock on the address table and is waiting to update the order table. Meanwhile, Transaction B has a lock on the order table and needs to update the address table. Transactions A and B are deadlocked since neither can proceed until the other releases its original lock.

Since deadlocks can severely impact database performance, databases have internal mechanisms to handle deadlocks. The most common way a database handles deadlocks is with a detection and resolution strategy. The database software regularly checks for deadlocks. When a deadlock occurs, the database automatically terminates and rolls back a blocking transaction. This action frees up the underlying resources, allowing the other transaction to proceed.

If you frequently observe deadlocks in the database, you might need to tune the application to prevent deadlocks from happening. One technique to avoid deadlocks is to start and end transactions explicitly. Another method is to minimize transaction size, reducing the number of tables necessary to complete a transaction. Since both approaches require code changes, you ideally want to detect and resolve deadlock situations during testing.

Connections and Sessions

Monitoring database connections and sessions is crucial to ensuring stable database operations. A *database connection* is a physical link between a client and a database server. Databases have a configurable limit on the total number of active connections. A *database session* is a set of transactions performed over a connection. In addition to processing queries, database sessions contain information about the user's connection. You can also set variables that last for the length of a session.

Concurrent connections are the number of simultaneous connections to the database. Monitoring the number of concurrent connections is fundamental to understanding the operational cadence of a database. Establishing a baseline number of connections helps inform whether the number of connections to the database increases, decreases, or remains stable. Each connection consumes a certain amount of network, CPU, and memory overhead. You want enough connections to let applications perform their functions without expending resources on idle connections.

Connection pooling is a common approach to maximize application functionality while minimizing idle connections. A connection pool reserves a configurable number of active connections in a group. Figure 5.5 illustrates how different applications can share a connection pool to interact with the database.

In Figure 5.5, five different applications need to access the database. However, not all five applications access the database simultaneously. Establishing a connection pool reduces database overhead, allowing the calling applications to use an open connection when needed. When using connection pooling, it is crucial to monitor the pool size to ensure enough connections meet demand. You also want to watch the connection wait time. If clients are waiting for a connection from the pool, it indicates that the pool size is too small. Adjusting the time period for reaping and refreshing dead connections is vital for ensuring that applications can reconnect to the database in case of failure.

FIGURE 5.5 Connection pooling

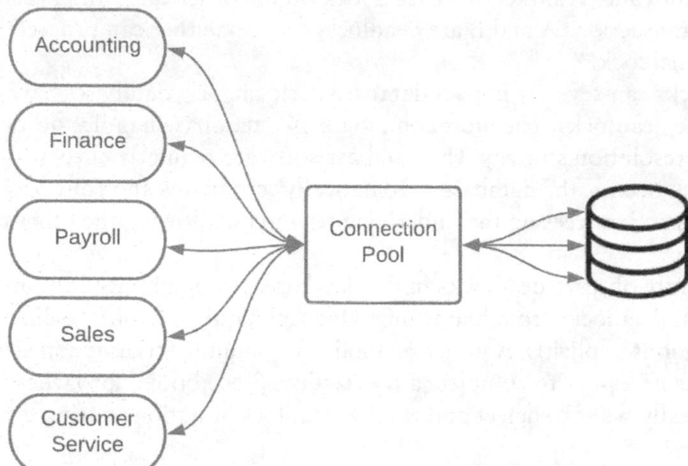

Additional connection metrics to monitor include attempted and failed connections. *Attempted connections* include all connection attempts, regardless of success. The number of attempted connections should settle into a pattern. For instance, you may see more connection attempts during business hours than early in the morning. An increase in connection attempts could signal business process changes that affect database usage. Alternatively, a sudden spike in connection attempts can indicate a denial-of-service attack.

Failed connections keep track of the number of unsuccessful connection attempts. The ratio between connection attempts and failed connections should remain constant. A spike in failed connections can be a symptom of underlying network issues or be another indicator of a denial-of-service attack.

Maintenance

Just as regular maintenance ensures the longevity of an automobile, ongoing database maintenance is essential for a healthy database. Properly maintaining a database helps ensure the database's stability, performance, and reliability. Database maintenance is not a one-time task, as the context in which a database operates, as well as its usage patterns and data volumes, continually evolve. Neglecting regular maintenance can lead to poor performance, data loss, and downtime, impacting business operations.

Database Stability

Like regularly changing an automobile's oil and essential fluids, several preemptive maintenance tasks help ensure a database's operational stability. Common database maintenance tasks that assist with stability include patch management, data integrity checks, data corruption checks, and periodic audits.

Patch Management

Like any other piece of software, databases evolve. New features, security vulnerabilities, and software bugs are all reasons why databases need patching. A systematic, organized approach to patch management is essential for ensuring consistency in development, testing, and production environments and helps assure the operational stability of the database.

Updates are enhancements to the database software. New features and performance improvements are typical reasons for database updates. For example, a vendor may add a valuable new SQL function or improve how the internal optimizer processes queries. Updating the database software lets you take advantage of the change in functionality.

Security patches address specific vulnerabilities in the database software that malicious users could potentially exploit. It is essential to consider the likelihood and impact of the underlying exposure when determining the appropriate time to apply a security patch. Suppose a user can take advantage of a bug to escalate database privileges with a simple SQL injection attack. Since SQL injection is a relatively well-known attack method, the likelihood of a malicious actor taking advantage of this type of vulnerability is high. The impact is similarly high, as privilege escalation can result in accessing sensitive data. When the likelihood and impact are high, promptly applying the appropriate security patch is best. If the likelihood or impact of a vulnerability is low, remediating the situation is less urgent.

Maintenance patches address software defects, memory leaks, and other issues in the database. Maintenance patches generally improve the database's stability. Maintenance patches are not typically time sensitive, giving you plenty of room to incorporate them into your broader change management processes.

Verifying that a patch works correctly in a non-production environment is a good idea. After verifying that the patch works and doesn't interfere with your database configuration or any client applications, you can schedule a time to apply the patch in production.

Database Integrity Checks

Database integrity checks ensure the correctness and consistency of data in a database. Classic integrity checks verify referential integrity, domain integrity, and entity integrity. *Referential integrity* validates relationships between tables. *Domain integrity* validates that column values conform to business rules and column definitions, and *entity integrity* ensures that tables have primary keys.

User-defined integrity is one of the most crucial types of integrity checks. *User-defined integrity* consists of business rules that are challenging to implement using basic database functionality. Instead, you usually enforce user-defined integrity with software rules. Suppose an application forces monthly password changes and prevents users from using any of their five most recently used passwords. Implementing the business rule governing password reuse is done with software, not native database functionality. As such, validating that no user is violating the password reuse business rule requires a custom integrity check.

Understanding table-locking techniques is essential when performing database integrity checks. One way table locks facilitate data integrity is by preventing users from reading data while a different transaction is modifying the data. *Shared locks* apply to read operations. A given row can have multiple simultaneous shared locks. *Exclusive locks* apply when a transaction inserts, updates, or deletes data. Existing at both the table and row level, exclusive locks ensure no other transaction can read or write the affected data until after the data change operation completes.

It is possible for a runaway query to get an exclusive lock that causes database performance to degrade. You can monitor lock wait times using internal database system tables. Note that these internal system tables are different for each type of relational database. If necessary, you can also identify hung transactions that are holding locks and terminate them.

Data Corruption Checks

Data corruption consists of errors or inconsistencies in data, rendering it partially or entirely unusable. Corruption can occur while reading, writing, storing, transmitting, or processing data. Power failures, hardware crashes, and inconsistent network performance contribute to data corruption. People can also cause data corruption by accidentally altering configuration settings or removing data files.

A checksum is a simple redundancy check for detecting data corruption. The process involves applying a checksum algorithm to an original data file that produces a single output called the *checksum*. It is common to use checksums when transmitting files between systems, as corruption exists if the checksum value of the original file doesn't match the checksum of the received file. For example, suppose you operate a data warehouse and receive a nightly load from a source system. If you validate that the checksums match before processing the file, you can be confident that you are processing what you received. However, if the checksums differ, you can avoid propagating corruption into the database by requesting a replacement file from the source system.

Database management systems typically have built-in tools to check for data corruption. These tools let you detect and repair corruption within database files. For example, the DBCC CHECKDB command in SQL Server checks the physical and logical integrity of all the objects in a database. Oracle offers DBVerify and DBMS_REPAIR to identify and repair corrupted data.

Duplicate checks validate that no two rows of data are logically identical. Suppose an airline customer uses a website to create a new loyalty account. If the customer accidentally submits the web data twice, it may create two redundant rows in the database, violating business rules. Checking for duplicates is typically done using custom scripts in addition to a database's built-in integrity constraints.

Range checks ensure that data falls within a specified range. For example, suppose you have a customer table that includes birth date as a column. It is unreasonable for a row to exist with a birth date value indicating that a person is 300 years old. Like duplicate checks, range checks typically require custom scripts to validate business logic.

Audits

Organizations are subject to numerous regulatory compliance obligations. Reviewing audit logs is a routine activity to validate security and compliance needs. By regularly reviewing audit logs, data systems professionals can ensure the security and integrity of their databases while ensuring compliance with relevant industry regulations. While you'll dive deeper into these topics in Chapter 6, "Governance, Security, and Compliance," let's explore how reviewing audit logs can help achieve these objectives.

Audit logs contain a record of who accessed the database, what they accessed, where the access came from, and when it happened. From a security standpoint, this information is crucial for identifying any unauthorized or suspicious activity. When reviewing audit logs, suppose you notice an increase in database update operations from a user who typically doesn't access the database. This suspicious deviation from the norm requires additional investigation, which could indicate a potential security breach. By regularly reviewing the audit logs, data systems professionals can identify such issues early and take appropriate action to mitigate damages.

Many industries have regulations requiring businesses to track who accesses certain types of restricted data. For example, in healthcare, the Health Insurance Portability and Accountability Act (HIPAA) mandates that any access to patient records be logged and regularly audited. Noncompliance can lead to hefty fines. External auditors may request access to audit logs to validate usage patterns. By periodically reviewing database audit logs, a business can ensure it stays compliant with these regulations.

In the event of an issue or outage, audit logs are invaluable for diagnosing and resolving the problem. For example, if a database unexpectedly crashes, the audit logs could show that a specific user ran a problematic query that caused the crash. Audit logs can also help identify patterns, such as repeated failed log-in attempts, indicating expired credentials, or potentially a brute-force attack.

Database Performance

Ensuring database performance is essential to meet user expectations while efficiently using resources. Query optimization, index management, performance tuning, and load balancing help ensure optimal database performance.

Query Optimization

Query optimization is a vital maintenance task that ensures a database runs as smoothly and efficiently as possible. Unoptimized queries consume significant system resources, causing contention that impacts the entire database. Optimized queries use the available hardware resources more efficiently, providing fast response times and meeting performance expectations. Properly optimized queries are crucial for databases with many concurrent users or large amounts of data. Since workloads evolve, query optimization is a recurring database maintenance task.

The first step is to identify the queries that need to be optimized. Internal database monitoring tools like *Oracle Enterprise Manager* and *Query Store for Microsoft SQL Server* help identify poorly performing queries. Typically, these queries consume a disproportionate share of the available hardware resources.

After selecting a query to optimize, you then need to understand what the query is doing. Queries might retrieve data from multiple views and tables or call numerous functions to create operational reports. Queries that support order processing activities create and modify data. Your goal is to develop an understanding of the underlying tables, columns, joins, and filtering conditions, which helps establish the context around poor performance.

Once you understand the query in context, you proceed by analyzing the execution plan. Recall from Chapter 2, "Database Fundamentals," that an execution plan is an internal road map that shows how the database will execute the query. The execution plan includes details about the order of operations, table joins, and index use.

Suppose an execution plan shows that a query performs full-table scans. Since a full-table scan sequentially reads every record in a table, this is an example of an uncovered query. Creating an index to cover the query and improve the performance is a viable approach to improving performance. An advantage to this approach is that you don't need to change the query's code to improve performance.

However, suppose the execution plan shows that the poorly performing query uses subselects instead of joins. Rewriting the query to use joins may be the best way to improve performance. You may also discover that the absence of bind variables is the root cause of the performance issue. Changing the code to use bind variables is the optimal way to resolve this issue. As both approaches require altering code, it is vital to have an efficient and reliable change management process to propagate the fix to production.

Sometimes you can resolve performance issues by adjusting database parameters. Suppose an application uses a database sequence number to generate synthetic primary key values. If the application performs thousands of inserts per second, the request rate for new sequence numbers may eclipse the database's ability to generate them. Fortunately, it is possible to pre-allocate and cache sequence values. You would need to increase the number of cached sequence values to remediate this bottleneck.

Index Optimization

Indexes can improve query performance and reduce the time it takes to retrieve data from a database. Recall from Chapter 4, "Database Deployment," that indexes physically contain the data from the columns they cover. Therefore, the more indexes a table has, the worse the write performance is for that table. Index optimization is the art of creating indexes that improve read performance without severely impacting write performance.

Choosing the right columns to index is essential. Covering your most frequently executed queries is an excellent place to start. Covering the query requires a multicolumn index for queries that retrieve data from multiple columns. However, columns with low selectivity increase index size while not significantly improving performance. For instance, a column for gender has fewer possible values than a column for last name. Including the gender column in an index would increase index size and may not improve performance.

Databases support a variety of index types. Table 5.1 provides a synopsis of some common types of indexes and their advantages and disadvantages.

TABLE 5.1 Common Database Index Types

Index Type	Advantages	Disadvantages
B-Tree	Balanced and sorted, allows for quick lookups and ordered access.	Becomes large and slow to update if the table has many columns or rows.
Bitmap	Efficient for columns with limited unique values.	Not suitable for columns with many unique values. Write performance can be suffer.
Hash	Ideal for fast lookups using the hash key.	Poor performance when matching on a partial key.
Clustered	Fast access for sequential data.	Write performance suffers for non-sequential data.
Nonclus-tered	A table can have more than one.	Write performance can suffer. Requires up-to-date index statistics.

Data composition and database usage characteristics influence the appropriate type of index to use.

Note that a database maintains index statistics that the optimizer uses to inform decisions about the best way to execute SQL queries. For tables with frequently changing data, you need to refresh index statistics periodically. If the statistics are not current, the optimizer may decide not to use the index, negatively impacting performance.

As data changes over time, the structure of database indexes becomes fragmented. This fragmentation can lead to inefficient data retrieval, which degrades query performance. Periodically rebuilding indexes resolves index fragmentation issues and is an essential index optimization task.

Monitoring usage is another component of the index optimization portfolio. Since indexes consume space and impact write performance, you only want to maintain actively used indexes. You can use database monitoring tools to identify infrequently used indexes and schedule their removal.

Performance Tuning

Query optimization and index optimization are crucial performance-tuning tasks. That said, you can manipulate numerous other performance-optimizing database settings to reduce bottlenecks and make the system as efficient as possible. Recall from Chapter 4 that horizontal and vertical scaling are viable options for improving performance. Table partitioning and memory tuning are database-specific options for optimizing performance.

Table partitioning is a technique that splits a single table into smaller, more manageable pieces, known as partitions. Each partition is stored independently, so a single table is logically divided across multiple storage devices. This independent storage characteristic improves performance when there is contention on a large table or for databases with heavy read/write transaction volumes. Four common approaches are range, list, hash, and composite partitioning.

- *Range partitioning*: With this approach, rows are partitioned based on a range of values in a column. For example, a sales table might be partitioned by sales date, with separate partitions for each year or month.
- *List partitioning*: List partitioning uses a set of discrete values to determine partition membership. For example, a customer table might be partitioned by country, with separate partitions for customers in Italy, France, Spain, the United Kingdom, and the United States.
- *Hash partitioning*: This approach spreads data randomly across partitions using a calculated hash key. An advantage of the hash approach is that it distributes data evenly across partitions. Suppose you need to analyze Italian customer data. With a list approach, only the Italy partition supports the query. With a hash approach, any partition with Italian customers is in play, improving read performance.
- *Composite partitioning*: Composite partitioning incorporates multiple partitioning techniques to optimize performance. Applying this technique to a very large sales table, you could use range partitioning to partition a sales table by year and hash partitioning to spread the data for each year across multiple sub-partitions.

Memory tuning is adjusting configuration parameters to optimize how a database system uses memory resources. A skilled administrator can tailor the amount of memory that supports queries, stored procedures, and transaction logging. You typically involve seasoned database administrators with years of experience to adjust memory settings.

As you consider performance-tuning techniques, it is essential to keep the purpose of the database in mind. You optimize analytical databases for bulk data loads and the read performance needed for querying massive data sets. However, transaction processing databases require a balance of read and write operations.

Transaction volumes also play a critical role in database performance. The higher the transaction volume, the more workload the database needs to handle. Incorporating performance tuning with stress testing in a test-tune-test approach is an ideal way to identify bottlenecks as transaction volumes increase.

In the initial test phase, you stress the database until you identify a bottleneck. In the tuning phase, you resolve the bottleneck by adjusting parameters or changing code in the database, application, or OS. In the second test phase, you verify that your changes resolve the bottleneck. An iterative approach lets you identify bottlenecks, fix them, and repeat the test-tune-test process until you attain your scalability objectives.

Load Balancing

Load balancing distributes client requests across a set of servers. As load balancing distributes transactions across multiple servers, it is a technique that enhances database availability and improves performance. Figure 5.6 shows how a load balancer sits between a client application and the nodes of a database cluster.

FIGURE 5.6 Load-balanced database

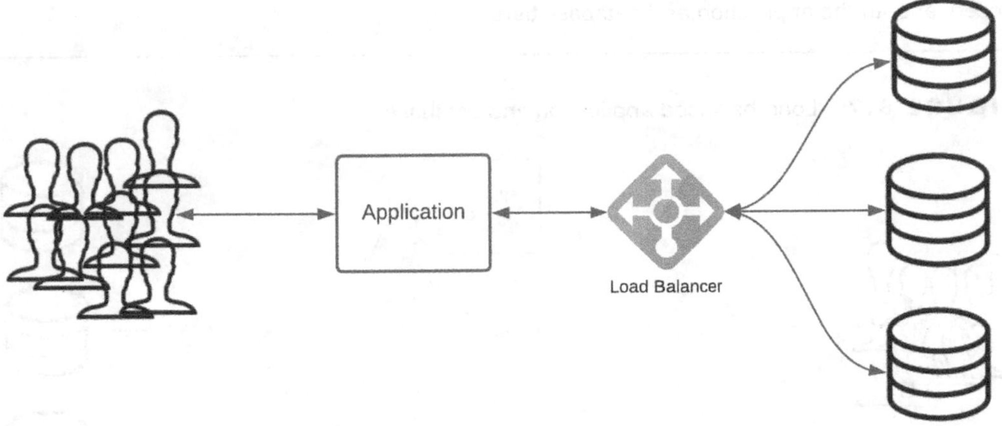

The load balancer's job is to send each incoming query to the appropriate database node. Round-robin, least connections, and resource-based are among the algorithms load balancers use to distribute queries.

Round-robin is the least sophisticated approach to load distribution. The Round-robin approach routes incoming requests evenly across the available database nodes in sequential order. The advantage of Round-robin lies in its simplicity, as it requires no context about the complexity of the query or the state of each database node.

With the *least connections* approach, a load balancer directs incoming queries to the server with the fewest active connections. Since it considers the number of active connections, the least connections approach is more sophisticated than round-robin.

The *resource-based* approach distributes queries based on the database servers' current resource utilization. For example, resource-based load balancing can distribute requests based on the servers' current CPU usage, memory usage, or other resource metrics. While establishing the current server context and making the appropriate routing decisions is more resource-intensive than round-robin, resource-based is a viable option for applications with a combination of short- and long-running queries.

Additional Load Balancing Considerations

Some applications centralize business logic in the database, while others put it in the application itself. Understanding potential bottlenecks across application components is essential when considering where to implement load balancing. If resource congestion occurs on the application server, putting a load balancer in front of the application gives you the option of horizontally scaling by adding additional application servers. If you are load balancing to improve availability, Figure 5.7 shows a configuration that uses load balancers at both the application and database tiers.

FIGURE 5.7 Load-balanced application and database

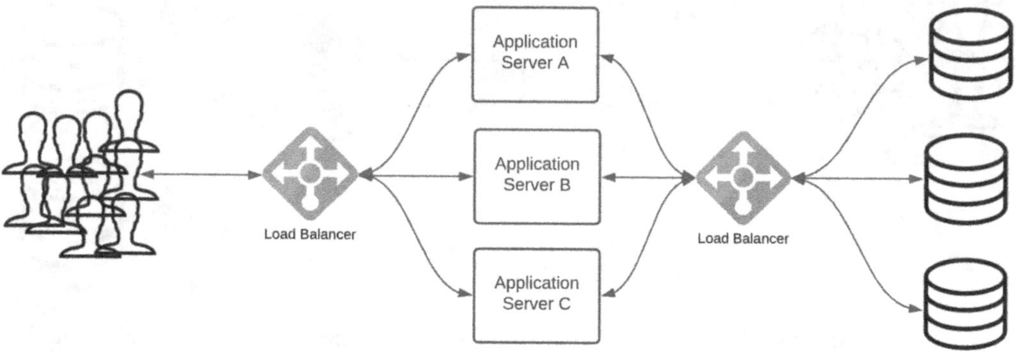

Database Reliability

It is vital to have organizational trust in a database. Database reliability is a crucial factor that influences the overall performance and usability of applications, impacts user experiences, and determines the operational efficiency of organizations.

Effective change management is essential to ensure database reliability. *Change management* is a structured approach to transitioning databases, applications, and people from a current state to a desired future state. Change management includes planning, implementing, and managing change to minimize disruption while maximizing reliability and acceptance of the change.

Managing change involves careful planning and execution of various aspects of database operations, including release schedules, capacity planning, system upgrades, vulnerability remediation, and database refreshes. Effective change management also includes a structured change approval process and communication plan.

Release Schedules

Consistent release schedules are essential to ensure database reliability. A release schedule commonly includes planning, deployment, testing, and validation phases.

The *planning phase* defines essential details about the release's size, scope, and timing. Determining the size and scope of a release is critical as they impact deployment time and the people involved in assuring its success. Aligning a database release with the organization's overall change calendar is essential, as any database change ultimately impacts the entire organization. For example, November and December are the most significant months in sales volume for online retailers. Planning a database release during these busy months doesn't make organizational sense. Therefore, you must include business and technical leaders to develop a release calendar that makes sense for everyone.

During the *deployment phase*, you implement the changes included in the release. Fixing data in production, modifying custom software, and updating database or OS software are among the changes made during the deployment phase.

The *testing phase* is when you test the changes included in the release. It is critical to consider the release's scope so that you allocate sufficient time to testing the changes. The amount of testing time aligns with the scope of the release: the smaller the scope, the shorter the time required to test. The scope of the release also determines who needs to be involved in the testing phase. For example, adding an index to cover a poorly performing query may only require technical validation, while a more complex feature enhancement needs to be tested by a business user.

Closely related to testing, the *validation phase* ensures that you are confident the change has the intended impact. The validation phase ultimately culminates in a "go/no-go" decision. You identify who has responsibility for this decision during the planning phase. If the release is a "go," the release is a success, and the changes now exist in the production environment. In a "no-go" situation, you must ensure you plan to revert the changes and get the database back to a known good state.

While not desirable, it's possible to have a partially successful release. For example, suppose most of the scope of the release is a success, but a minor feature doesn't work as intended. In that case, you can deploy the release to production and create a list of associated defects that needs resolution in a subsequent release.

Capacity Planning

Capacity planning determines future capacity needs based on current operations and is crucial to ensuring long-term database reliability. Estimating the future storage, computing resources, and network bandwidth needs are all capacity planning considerations. Incorporating capacity planning into your change management process is crucial, as new features, software upgrades, or user increases affect capacity requirements. For example, if a new feature requires significantly more memory, reflecting that need in the capacity plan ensures that database performance will not suffer.

Upgrades

Timely upgrades are vital to gain new features, remediate bugs, and avoid technical debt. Database software upgrades typically involve updating the database to a more recent version. Deprecating (removing) features, data type changes, and introducing new bugs are among the risks of any software update. Application upgrades also impact database reliability. For example, schema changes within a database can cause compatibility issues with existing SQL and stored procedures.

A key part of change management is managing the risks associated with changes, including upgrades. Executing a comprehensive regression test on the upgraded database in a non-production environment is crucial to mitigating upgrade risk. Another significant software-related risk is vendor support. As software ages, vendors drop support for older versions. From a change management standpoint, include upgrades in your release plan to ensure your production environment uses vendor-supported software.

Vulnerability Remediation

Security vulnerabilities can have an unanticipated impact on change management. Vendors issue periodic upgrades that include security-related fixes. When a new, time-sensitive security issue arises, vendors rush to create a software patch that addresses that vulnerability.

From a change management point of view, you must balance the risk and likelihood of exploitation when determining when to take a security patch. For example, you might consider incorporating the patch into your next planned release if a critical new vulnerability requires direct access to the database server, making it relatively difficult to exploit. However, you likely will apply the patch earlier if the vulnerability is easy to exploit.

Change Approval

Change approval processes are formal procedures describing how a governing body approves or rejects proposed changes to a database system. This governing body, frequently called the *change advisory board (CAB)*, typically includes stakeholders, technical experts, and occasionally business users. The CAB's primary responsibility is to assess the impacts of proposed changes.

Here's a high-level overview of a typical change approval process:

1. *Change request*: The process begins when a developer, administrator, or user proposes a change.
2. *Change evaluation*: The CAB evaluates the change using a set of predetermined criteria, including its potential impact, the resources required to implement it, the benefits it offers, and its associated risks.
3. *Change decision*: After evaluation, the CAB approves or rejects the proposed change. If it's approved, the change proceeds to the deployment phase. If rejected, the change is discarded or returned for further revisions and improvements.
4. *Change deployment*: If approved, the change is deployed, tested, and then migrated to the production environment.

5. *Change review*: After deployment, the change is reviewed during the release validation phase to ensure it was successful and met its objectives. If it did, the change is closed out. If it didn't, you need to either revert the change or make follow-on changes to accomplish the original objective.

A change approval process improves consistency and reduces the risk of implementing changes. It also provides a framework for communication and enhances accountability. From a change management perspective, a change approval process is essential for efficiently handling system modifications.

Database Refresh

A *database refresh* copies data from a source database to a destination database. Typically, database refreshes use a production database as the source for refreshing development and test environments. Database refreshes let you replicate production issues, test new features, and analyze data in a non-production environment.

Database refreshes may require downtime in the destination environment. As such, including a refresh schedule in your overall environmental change plan is essential. In addition, you need to consider data privacy and security concerns. Since more people have access to development and test environments, ensure you have procedures in your refresh process that obscure sensitive data.

Communication

A well-thought-out communication plan managed by dedicated personnel is an essential part of change management, as it ensures everyone understands why a change is happening, as well as how it will affect them and their role in the process. Clear and frequent communication aids in aligning stakeholders and mitigating surprises, and a comprehensive master release calendar provides an overall schedule to contextualize change.

It is essential to consider the intended audience when crafting communications. Internal stakeholders will likely be interested in the timing of database refreshes and application upgrades. External stakeholders like your database vendor may only be interested in the timing of major database version upgrades.

Regardless of the intended audience, a well-structured communication plan manages expectations by informing stakeholders about what to expect during the change. Expectations can include the overall timeline of the change and potential service disruptions.

Many channels for communicating change are available, including emails, newsletters, intranets, social networks, and messaging applications like Slack. Selecting a medium depends on the audience, the nature of the change, and the organizational culture. For example, using multiple redundant channels makes sense for a massive, multiday database upgrade that impacts the entire organization. Meanwhile, a minor change, like adding data to a reference table, may only require an email to the affected person.

Facilitating Operations

In a dynamic and complex database environment, well-structured, up-to-date documentation is essential to streamline operations and facilitate maintenance. Keeping documentation current takes significant effort and is not everyone's favorite task. However, accurate documentation is worth the effort as it facilitates troubleshooting, gives data systems professionals a playbook to follow when the unexpected occurs, and is required for some compliance-related requirements. The following sections delve deeper into document types, providing practical guidelines and examples to effectively manage database documentation and employ the appropriate tools in given scenarios.

Data Dictionaries

Recall from Chapter 4 that a data dictionary describes the structure of a database and defines the objects within the database. Whenever an internal database object changes, update the data dictionary to reflect that change so that developers and data analysts can rely on accurate definitions as they do their work. Figure 5.8 shows a data dictionary entry for a Customer table.

FIGURE 5.8 Customer table data dictionary entry

Table: Customer

Relationships	Name	Data Type	Length	Format	Nullable	Description	Source
Primary Key	cust_id	integer			No	Unique identifier for a customer	Values come from the cust_id_seq sequence number
	first_name	varchar	200		No	Customer's first name	Entered upon account creation
	last_name	varchar	200		No	Customer's last name	Entered upon account creation
	phone_num	integer	10		No	Customer's US phone number	Entered upon account creation
	email_addr	varchar	50		No	Customer's email address	Entered upon account creation
	last_update	timestamp			No	Last update date and timestamp for the row	Entered upon account creation and updated on account modification

Suppose a business wants to improve customer correspondence by offering a preferred contact method. To accomplish this business objective, you add a preferred_contact field to the Customer table to store the customer's preferred contact method. After altering the table's structure, you must ensure that the data dictionary reflects that change, as shown in Figure 5.9.

There are multiple available tools for maintaining data dictionaries. The simplest is to use a *word processor* like *Microsoft Word* or *Google Docs* and manually maintain data dictionary entries. While using a word processor is an easy, low-cost solution, it relies on a human to reflect database changes in the data dictionary, as the change must occur in two places: the database itself and the data dictionary.

FIGURE 5.9 Updated Customer table data dictionary entry

Table: Customer

Relationships	Name	Data Type	Length	Format	Nullable	Description	Source
Primary Key	cust_id	integer			No	Unique identifier for a customer	Values come from the cust_id_seq sequence number
	first_name	varchar	200		No	Customer's first name	Entered upon account creation
	last_name	varchar	200		No	Customer's last name	Entered upon account creation
	phone_num	integer	10		No	Customer's US phone number	Entered upon account creation
	email_addr	varchar	50		No	Customer's email address	Entered upon account creation
	preferred_contact	integer	1		Yes	Indicator to store customer's contact preference 1 == contact by phone 2 == contact by email	Entered upon account creation for new accounts and whenever an existing account is updated
	last_update	timestamp			No	Last update date and timestamp for the row	Entered upon account creation and updated on account modification

Another approach to data dictionary maintenance uses a data modeling tool like *DbSchema*, *Erwin Data Modeler*, *ER/Studio*, *MySQL Workbench*, or *Oracle SQL Developer Data Modeler*. Primarily used by database designers, *data modeling tools* are pieces of software that let you define, manage, and manipulate data models. These tools support forward engineering, generating DDL that you can use to create or update objects in your database. Data modeling software also supports reverse engineering by connecting to an existing database and generating a data dictionary from the database's internal metadata. The prospect of having a single source of truth for your data model is compelling, as any data model modification gets reflected in the database and supporting documentation.

If you decide to use a data modeling tool, you must commit to using it organizationally to make any data model change. For example, suppose one person makes a manual DDL change to the database. In that case, the definition in the data modeling tool, what exists in the database, and the description in the data dictionary won't match. Also, free data modeling tools may not directly integrate with your database platform, while paid tools are expensive.

Entity-Relationship Diagrams

Recall from Chapter 4 that an ERD illustrates database objects and how they connect. Extending the data dictionary example, suppose you need to adjust the Customer entity in your ERD to reflect the new preferred_contact field. Updating the ERD depends on your chosen tool.

Diagramming tools are software applications that let you maintain diagrams. Not limited to ERDs, you can use diagramming tools to create flowcharts, Unified Modeling Language (UML) diagrams, network diagrams, system architecture diagrams, and more. Well-known diagramming tools include *Microsoft Visio*, *Lucidchart*, and *Google Drawings*. Figure 5.10a shows a *Lucidchart* drawing of the original Customer table, while Figure 5.10b reflects the new preferred_contact field.

FIGURE 5.10a Original Customer entity

Customer		
PK	cust_id	integer
	first_name	varchar(200)
	last_name	varchar(200)
	phone_num	integer(10)
	email_addr	varchar(50)
	last_update	timestamp

FIGURE 5.10b Modified Customer entity

Customer		
PK	cust_id	integer
	first_name	varchar(200)
	last_name	varchar(200)
	phone_num	integer(10)
	email_addr	varchar(50)
	preferred_contact	integer(1)
	last_update	timestamp

Some diagramming tools let you generate DDL from your ERD. For example, Lucidchart can generate DDL for MySQL, PostgreSQL, SQL Server, and Oracle. Figure 5.11 illustrates generating Oracle-compatible DDL from Lucidchart, which results in a CREATE TABLE DDL statement that includes the new preferred_contact field.

Centralizing metadata definition is an advantage of investing in a data modeling tool. Figure 5.12 shows the dialog box used to modify the Customer table using *Oracle SQL Developer Data Modeler*.

Figure 5.12 also illustrates how leveraging a data modeling tool delivers the promise of maintaining a single source of truth for table metadata. To help keep the ERD and data dictionary current, the metadata in the database will contain the detailed description from the "Comments in RDBMS" tab. While the source of truth is the Oracle SQL Developer Data Modeler file, having comprehensive metadata in the database means you could use a different data modeling tool to reverse engineer an ERD and data dictionary from the database.

Figure 5.11 illustrates how table DDL from a diagramming tool uses the CREATE TABLE statement. While the CREATE TABLE approach works well when creating a new table, you should use an ALTER TABLE command for an existing table. Recall that a CREATE TABLE statement fails if a database object with the same name exists. To recreate the Customer table using the DDL from Figure 5.11, you must first drop the existing Customer table. Since dropping the Customer table destroys any existing customer data, this is not a good approach when the table you want to modify already contains data in production. Since the

ALTER TABLE command applies changes to an existing table, it is an ideal alternative for adding a column.

FIGURE 5.11 Generating DDL from an ERD in Lucidchart

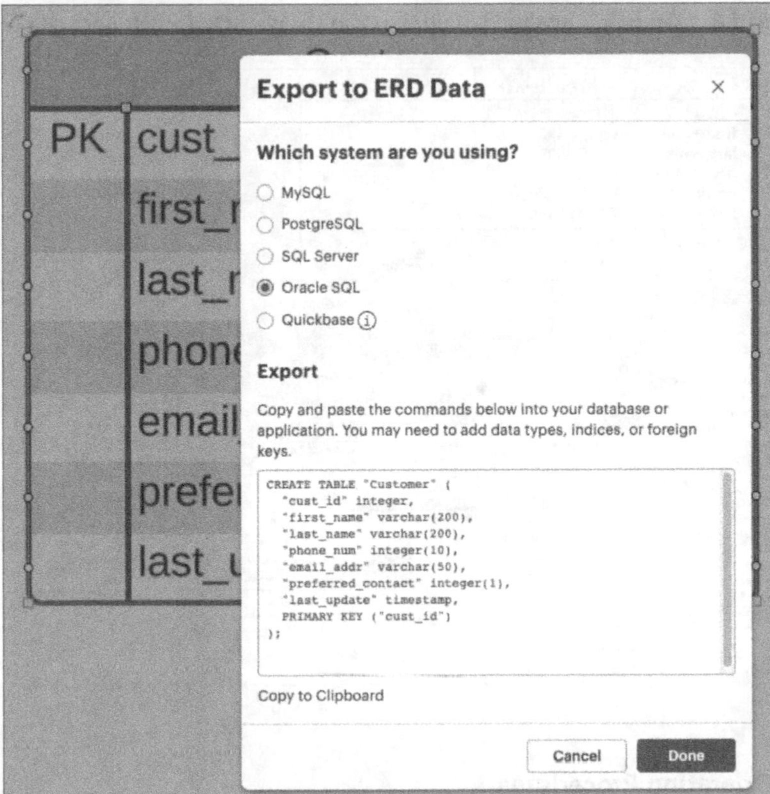

While diagramming tools can export ERDs into DDL scripts, data modeling tools have additional functionality that can generate differential DDL when integrated with a version control system. Figure 5.13 illustrates the ALTER TABLE DDL generated]by a data modeling tool for adding the preferred_contact field.

Note that the DDL in Figure 5.13 adds the new column and includes a column comment with the description from Figure 5.12. With the column comment in place, database users can get additional context about the column's purpose directly from the database.

Maintenance Documentation

Maintenance documentation is a critical aspect of database operations. While the data dictionaries and ERDs that describe the database schema are a component of maintenance documentation, it also includes standard operating procedures, system architecture information, and troubleshooting guides related to the database. Maintenance documentation's primary goal is ensuring that anyone interacting with the database understands how to operate, maintain, troubleshoot, and upgrade it properly.

FIGURE 5.12 Updating a table definition using Oracle SQL Developer Data Modeler

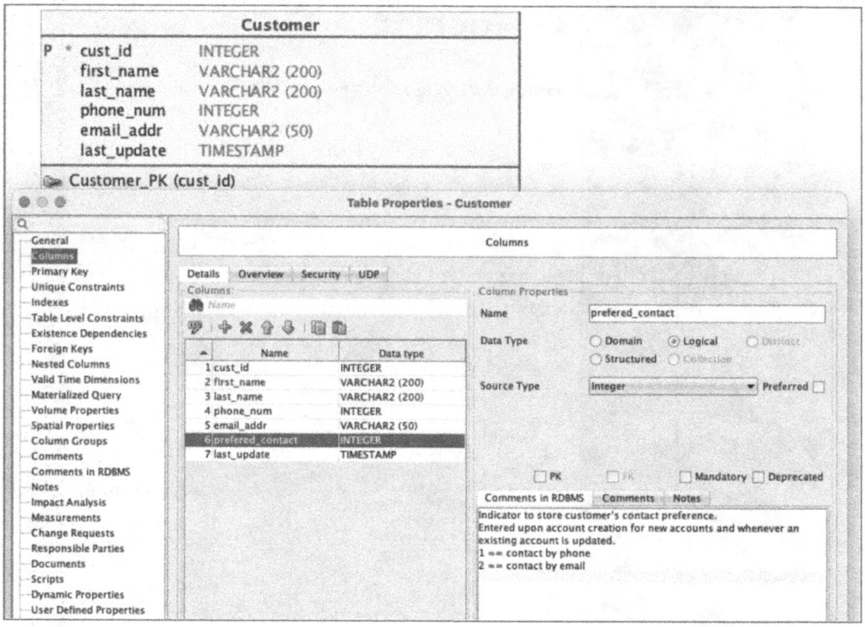

Standard Operating Procedures

SOPs are step-by-step instructions detailing how to perform routine database maintenance tasks. SOPs are particularly helpful when a new person joins the database team, as they help ensure stability by providing a reference for operational duties. SOPs help ensure operational consistency and aid in organizational and third-party compliance obligations.

Regularly updating SOPs to reflect changes in the database system or organizational policies is essential. Communicate these changes to all relevant team members to ensure consistent operations. In addition to normal database startup/shutdown procedures, the following are some subject areas covered by SOPs:

- *System Architecture*: This section describes the database, its infrastructure components, and what connects to it. Accompanied by detailed diagrams, the system architecture section describes the database platform's servers, storage, networking equipment, client applications, and other infrastructure components.

FIGURE 5.13 ALTER TABLE DDL from Oracle SQL Developer Data Modeler

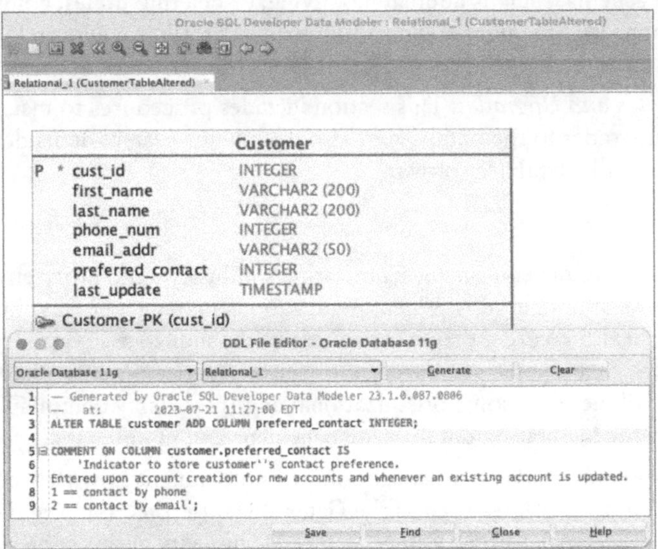

- *Data Backup and Restoration*: This SOP details when and how to perform data backups, where backups are stored, and the steps for restoring data.
- *Security Management*: This SOP includes user account creation, access level management, and credential management guidelines. Security management can also encompass data security and privacy considerations.
- *Data Quality*: Data Quality SOPs detail validating data feeds that flow into the database and steps that ensure data quality. For example, a duplicate resolution process helps to improve internal data quality.
- *Maintenance and Performance Tuning*: This subject area describes the frequency of and how to accomplish regularly scheduled tasks, such as index maintenance, query optimization, and checking for data corruption.
- *Troubleshooting*: This section adds operational context to the database by detailing anticipated performance irregularities and edge cases. It outlines steps for diagnosing and resolving the inevitable problems that arise.
- *Disaster Recovery Plan*: This SOP outlines the plan to recover the database in case of a disaster. It includes a playbook that details recovery and restart procedures and includes the roles and responsibilities of team members.
- *Incident Response Plan*: An Incident Response Plan (IRP) SOP defines the steps to follow when an incident occurs, such as a security breach or system failure. It would outline how to assess the situation, mitigate the damage, and resume normal operations.

- *Change Management*: This subject area documents procedures for making changes to the database schema, such as adding, modifying, or deleting tables, columns, or constraints. Change management documentation also describes where to log changes, as well as the CAB's membership, roles, and responsibilities.
- *System Updates and Upgrades*: This section includes procedures to install patches, updates, or upgrades to the database. It also documents system dependencies to validate after modifying the database software.

Compliance

Compliance obligations depend on an organization's industry, regulatory environment, and the data it processes and maintains. When organizations manage personal information, financial data, or health records, they must adhere to the industry, government, or third-party entities' laws, regulations, standards, and ethical practices. While Chapter 6 covers compliance in detail, here are some organizational and third-party compliance documentation requirements for facilitating database management and maintenance:

- *Data privacy and protection*: Organizations must document how they comply with applicable data privacy laws such as the General Data Protection Regulation (GDPR) or the California Consumer Privacy Act (CCPA). Documents in this subject area describe how data is collected, stored, processed, shared, and deleted. For example, GDPR gives European citizens the right to erasure, in which an individual can request proof of the removal of their data.
- *Record management*: This subject area defines data retention and deletion procedures that help organizations comply with relevant laws and industry regulations. For example, you need to describe how long you will keep financial records and how to destroy them at the appropriate time.
- *Vendor management*: If third-party vendors can access your database or handle data on your behalf, you need documentation on managing these relationships. Procedures for vetting vendors, managing contracts, monitoring vendor compliance, and addressing vendor data breaches are all examples of topics that need documentation.
- *Security compliance*: Documents related to security describe how the database aligns with industry security standards such as the Payment Card Industry Data Security Standard (PCI DSS). These documents typically include procedures for managing user access, data encryption, firewall configurations, virus scanning, intrusion detection, and incident response procedures.
- *Audit*: This SOP outlines the timing, frequency, and scope of audits to check for compliance with internal policies and external regulations. For example, the Sarbanes-Oxley Act (SOX) defines financial record-keeping and reporting practices for corporations in the United States. One item on a SOX compliance checklist asks an organization to document how it establishes safeguards to prevent data tampering. Suppose your organization needs to maintain SOX compliance. To address the data tampering checklist item, you could create an audit procedure that describes how to review access logs to accomplish that objective.

Documentation Tools

Maintaining comprehensive database documentation requires the use of a variety of tools. Choosing a tool depends on the use case, database complexity, and organizational culture. Tool options include word processors, spreadsheets, data modeling tools, and UML editors.

Word processors like Microsoft Word or Google Docs are essential when authoring SOPs. Word processors let you create sections, format text, maintain tables, and embed diagrams. These features are foundational for creating SOPs and compliance-related documentation. If you manage a small database with just a few tables, a word processor may be sufficient for maintaining the data dictionary.

Spreadsheets like Microsoft Excel or Google Sheets are also viable options for maintaining data dictionaries. Suppose you create a spreadsheet template with entries for database field name, data type, description, and constraints. You could create a spreadsheet tab for each table using that template. While spreadsheets are easy to work with and share, they do not generate DDL, which increases the probability that the definitions in your spreadsheet don't match what's in the database.

Diagramming tools and *data modeling tools* are excellent choices when creating ERDs. Both allow you to define table structures and export DDL. However, data modeling tools have additional features that make them attractive for maintaining complex database designs. Recall that data modeling tools can generate differential DDL, creating scripts that reflect changes to an existing model. In addition, modeling tools can reverse engineer ERDs and data dictionaries by connecting to a database and reading the metadata.

If your organization uses the *UML* for creating system diagrams, you will need a *UML diagramming tool* like *Lucidchart*, *Visio*, and *Visual Paradigm*. UML is a visual language for specifying, constructing, and documenting software systems artifacts. Traditionally used for object-oriented design, UML diagrams can be used to describe database structures and relationships.

For example, you can create a UML class diagram to show database tables as classes and the relationships between tables as associations. In UML, each class represents a database table, with the class name being the table name and the class attributes representing table columns. Similar to relationships in an ERD, class associations represent foreign key relationships between tables.

The ERD snippet in Figure 5.14a depicts a Customer table and a Customer_Address table. The UML diagram in Figure 5.14b illustrates these tables as UML classes and describes some of the more commonly used functions for each class.

Looking at the diagram, you can tell that the updateCustomer method requires the cust_id parameter. Similarly, you need to specify a cust_id to create an address, while updating an address requires the addr_id.

These UML diagrams can visually represent the database structure, making it easier for developers to understand and work with. As part of maintenance documentation, they can assist in the development of new features, debugging of issues, and general maintenance tasks. They also help ensure that all changes or enhancements to the database are carried out in a way that maintains the integrity and efficiency of the database structure.

FIGURE 5.14a Customer and Customer_Address ERD

Customer		
PK	cust_id	integer
	first_name	varchar(200)
	last_name	varchar(200)
	phone_num	integer(10)
	email_addr	varchar(50)
	preferred_contact	integer(1)
	last_update	timestamp

Customer_Address		
PK	addr_id	integer
	street_line_1	varchar(100)
	street_line_2	varchar(100)
	street_line_3	varchar(100)
	apt_suite	varchar(50)
	city	varchar(50)
	state_prov_code	varchar(2)
	postal_code	varchar(10)
	country_code	varchar(2)
FK	cust_id	integer

FIGURE 5.14b Customer and Customer_Address UML classes

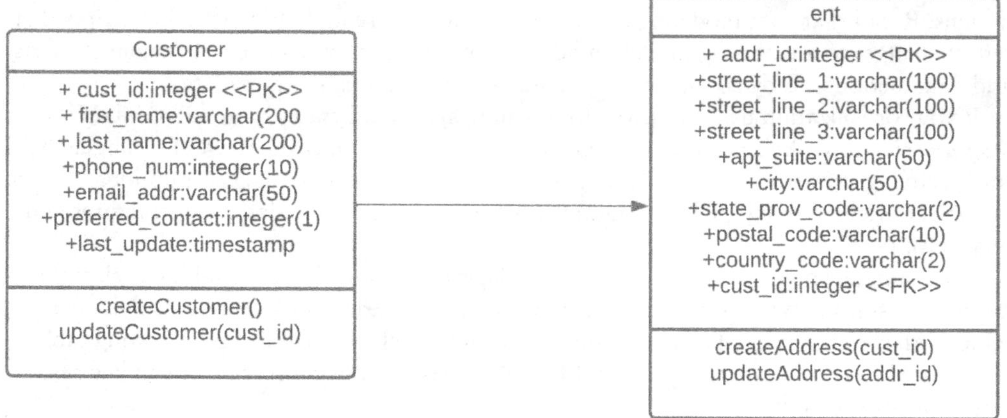

Data Management Tasks

Managing data is essential to fostering organizational confidence in the database and the applications it supports. Effective data management, strategic handling of data redundancy, and enabling data sharing are among the data management tasks that form the backbone of a robust database maintenance practice. By focusing on these aspects of database operations, organizations help improve data consistency, database efficiency, and overall reliability.

Data Management

Good data management ensures that the data in the database is accurate, relevant, and easily accessible, which in turn helps organizations make informed decisions. Let's explore some practical data management scenarios and how to address them.

Enhancing Tables to Support New Initiatives

Suppose you work for a retail company and use the Customer table from Figure 5.10b to maintain customer names, phone numbers, email addresses, and preferred contact methods. Your company wants to launch a new loyalty program to understand its customers better. With the launch of its loyalty program, the company needs to maintain the loyalty program numbers and associated reward point tallies for its customers.

To support this new business initiative, you must define the data elements required to support the new loyalty program. Discussing the requirements with the loyalty program business leader in your role as a data systems analyst, you determine that two new data elements are needed to support the loyalty program. Since the loyalty program number will only contain numbers, you define its associated data element as an integer. Similarly, since the loyalty point values are numbers, you define its data element as an integer.

With these new data elements defined, you can determine whether a new table is required. In this case, the loyalty program number and the number of points are customer attributes, so you decide to add them to the Customer table. Figure 5.15 shows an updated ERD with the new columns appended to the Customer table. The "UK" notation indicates that each customer's loyalty_pgm_id is unique.

FIGURE 5.15 Updated Customer table

Customer		
PK	cust_id	integer
	first_name	varchar(200)
	last_name	varchar(200)
	phone_num	integer(10)
	email_addr	varchar(50)
	preferred_contact	integer(1)
	last_update	timestamp
UK	loyalty_pgm_id	integer
	loyalty_points	integer

With these new data elements defined, you can determine whether a new table is required. In this case, the loyalty program number and the number of points are customer attributes, so you decide to add them to the Customer table. To append these new columns to the table, you create a DDL script consisting of ALTER TABLE statements as follows:

```
-- Append the loyalty program columns to the Customer table
ALTER TABLE customer ADD COLUMN loyalty_pgm_id INTEGER;
ALTER TABLE customer ADD COLUMN loyalty_points INTEGER;
-- Enforce uniqueness on the loyalty program column
ALTER TABLE customer ADD CONSTRAINT uc_loyalty_pgm_id UNIQUE(loyalty_pgm_id);

-- Add column comments to store descriptions in the database metadata
COMMENT ON COLUMN customer.loyalty_points IS 'Customer''s total loyalty
points.';
COMMENT ON COLUMN customer.loyalty_pgm_id IS 'Customer''s loyalty program
number.';
```

Note that the DDL first appends the new columns to the Customer table. The DDL further supports the new business requirement of avoiding duplicate loyalty program numbers by adding a unique constraint on the *loyalty_pgm_id* column. Adding comments to the new columns keeps the database metadata current. If you maintain the data dictionary independently from the ERD, you must update the Customer table definition. If you use a data modeling tool, you can regenerate the data dictionary to reflect the new columns.

Application modifications are necessary to support this new business requirement, as users want to see their loyalty point balances. Talking with application developers, you determine that the optimal way to retrieve loyalty point balances uses DML queries based on *loyalty_pgm_id*, similar to the following SQL Server example:

```
-- Retrieve a customer's loyalty point balance
-- First, set a bind variable, where <input_value> comes from the application
DECLARE loyalty_id = <input_value>

-- Second, execute the query
SELECT loyalty_points
FROM   customer
WHERE  loyalty_pgm_id = loyalty_id;
```

As a knowledgeable data systems analyst, you recognize that since the values of *loyalty_pgm_id* are unique, adding a unique index to that column will improve the query performance. The following SQL Server DDL illustrates this index creation:

```
-- Create a unique index on the customer.loyalty_pgm_id column
CREATE UNIQUE INDEX ui_cust_loyalty_id ON customer (loyalty_pgm_id);
```

Note that unique constraint behavior varies by the database engine you use. For example, when you create a unique key in Oracle or SQL Server, the database automatically creates an associated index. Verifying your database engine's behavior when working with unique constraints and indexes is essential to avoid creating duplicate indexes.

Creating Tables to Support New Initiatives

Based on customer feedback, business leaders create a new requirement to enable storing multiple phone numbers per customer. In discussions with business leaders, you learn that for each customer's phone number, it is necessary to maintain the number and the type of phone it represents. As a seasoned analyst, you determine the best way to accommodate this new requirement is to create two new tables: one for storing phone numbers and the other for maintaining phone types.

Since a phone number is related to a customer, you must connect the existing Customer table to the new Phone table. Figure 5.16 illustrates a viable design that accommodates maintaining multiple phones per customer.

FIGURE 5.16 New Phone and Phone_Type tables

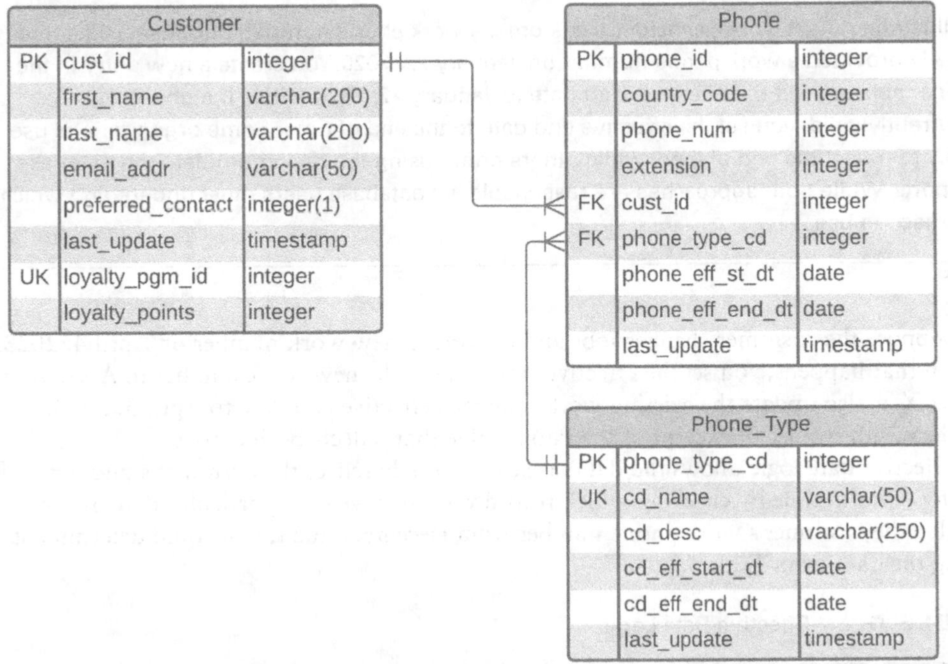

You need to use the CREATE TABLE command to create the new tables. Here's an example of the DDL to create the Phone_Type table in SQL Server:

```
-- Create the Phone_Type table
-- Note that since we are creating the table from scratch, the
-- indexes for the primary key and unique key are created
-- automatically

CREATE TABLE Phone_Type (
    phone_type_cd INTEGER PRIMARY KEY,
    cd_name VARCHAR(50) UNIQUE,
    cd_desc VARCHAR(250),
    cd_eff_start_dt DATE,
    cd_eff_end_dt DATE,
    last_update DATETIME
);
```

Effective Date Logic

Effective date logic is a common data management strategy to maintain an accurate history of data over time. Effective date logic typically uses two date columns, one for the effective start date and one for the effective end date. The effective start date column stores the date when a particular version of a record becomes effective. The effective end date column stores the date when a record ceases to be effective.

To illustrate how it works, consider a customer's work phone number. Suppose a customer initially provided a work phone number on January 22, 2020. You create a new entry in the Phone table and set the effective start date to January 22, 2020. Since the phone number is currently valid, you set the effective end date to the end of time. Some organizations use NULL to reflect the end of time, while others prefer using the maximum date the database supports. While both approaches are reasonable, all database users must understand which approach to use.

Suppose the customer changes jobs and provides a new work number on April 4, 2023. When that happens, you set the effective start date of the new work number to April 4, 2023. You also update the existing work number's effective end date to April 3, 2023. Table 5.2 illustrates an excerpt of the Phone table that reflects both entries.

Effective date logic allows the database to accurately reflect the customer's phone number at any point in time by checking which record was effective on a particular date. If you needed the customer's work phone number from December 2021, you could determine it using the data from Table 5.2.

TABLE 5.2 Effective Date Logic

Phone Number	Phone Type	Effective Start Date	Effective End Date
319.555.1212	Work	January 22, 2020	April 3, 2023
401.555.1232	Work	April 4, 2023	*NULL*

Both the new Phone and Phone_Type tables employ effective date logic. Since effective date logic can be confusing, describing its implementation in column comments/the data dictionary is imperative to promote organizational understanding.

You need a similar CREATE TABLE DDL statement to create the new Phone table. However, establishing the relationships between the Phone, Phone_Type, and Customer tables does not happen automatically. The following DDL illustrates how to create these data relationships in SQL Server:

```
-- Add a constraint to establish the phone-customer relationship
ALTER TABLE phone
   ADD CONSTRAINT FK_phone_cust_id FOREIGN KEY (cust_id)
      REFERENCES customer (cust_id);

-- Add a constraint to establish the phone-phone_type relationship
ALTER TABLE phone
   ADD CONSTRAINT FK_phone_phone_type_cd FOREIGN KEY (phone_type_cd)
      REFERENCES phone_type (phone_type_cd);
```

With the new table designs in place, you can proceed to determine how to propagate this change into your database. The first thing to realize is that if you have any existing customers, you must migrate their phone numbers from the Customer table into the new Phone table. Since storing the type of phone number is new, you also need to assign existing phone numbers to the appropriate phone type code.

Getting the phone type for customers' existing phone numbers is daunting. Contacting existing customers to associate their existing phone numbers with a phone type runs the risk of irritating them. An alternative approach is to create a new data set. You could set up a temporary phone type code for migration, then use a valid phone type the next time the customer interacts with the database. Table 5.3 shows an excerpt of the initial data for the Phone_Type table that supports this approach.

TABLE 5.3 Initial Phone_Type Data Values

Code	Name	Effective Start Date	Effective End Date
1	Home	1/1/2023	*NULL*
2	Work	1/1/2023	*NULL*
3	Mobile	1/1/2023	*NULL*
99	Migrated	1/1/2023	*NULL*

Using Views to Support Data Migration

Migrating data from one table to another can be complex. Suppose you want to implement the new Phone and Phone_Type tables and updated Customer table from the previous section. While modifying the table structures has an immediate effect, you likely want to allocate sufficient time for customers to provide the phone type for their existing phone numbers. One plausible timetable is as follows:

- *Months 1–3, Organic Update*: When interacting with the database, you prompt customers to validate their existing phone number and provide its phone type. Since most customers regularly interact with your organization, allowing three months for updates to happen organically offers sufficient time to collect this new attribute with minimal inconvenience.

- *Months 4–5, Prompted Update*: For the customers who still have a phone type of "Migrated," create an incentive for customers to update their information.
- *Month 6, Cleanup*: Decide what to do with the customers who haven't interacted with you for six months.

Suppose the manager responsible for tracking this data migration wants a dashboard to keep track of the number of outstanding customer records that need migration. Another requirement is a breakdown of customers by phone type. Instead of giving the manager direct access to the database tables, a better approach is to create a view that contains this information in the result set, similar to the following:

```
CREATE VIEW manager_phone_type AS
  SELECT     cd_name, count(*) as total
  FROM       phone_type pt
  INNER JOIN phone p
  ON         pt.phone_type_cd = p.phone_type_cd
  INNER JOIN customer c
  ON         c.cust_id = p.cust_id
  GROUP BY   cd_name;
```

While a regular view works well for this use case, you could use a materialized view for longer-running queries.

Suppose you still have some customers with a phone type of "Migrated" at the end of the six months. Since those customers are increasingly unlikely to engage with your business, you can determine whether or not it makes sense to continue having a "Migrated" phone type.

Discussing the issue with business leaders, you agree that it makes sense to rename the "Migrated" category to "Defunct." You also learn that your company wants to support an additional phone type of "School," and that these changes should go into effect on August 1, 2023. Table 5.4 shows the new definitions that reflect these new requirements.

TABLE 5.4 Initial Phone_Type Data Values

Code	Name	Effective Start Date	Effective End Date
1	Home	1/1/2023	*NULL*
2	Work	1/1/2023	*NULL*
3	Mobile	1/1/2023	*NULL*
4	School	8/1/2023	*NULL*
99	Defunct	1/1/2023	*NULL*

Note that this change represents modifying the definition of an existing, transient phone type code and creating a new definition. Naturally, you must follow your company's change request process to modify data in production.

Data Redundancy

Data redundancy refers to having duplicate data within the database. Duplicate data happens when you accidentally duplicate data representing the same transaction in a database. Data redundancy is typically the result of human error. Suppose you want to travel between New York and London and decide to shop for flights online. After selecting a convenient flight, you complete your purchase on a web page. Unintentionally, you double-click the purchase button. Instead of purchasing one ticket for your upcoming travels, you create two. The first is intentional, while the second is a duplicate.

Data systems analysts work diligently to prevent the creation of duplicate data. The optimal way to resolve duplicate data is to prevent it from happening. A common approach to preventing duplicate data is giving users a visual warning. If you've ever purchased something online, you likely have seen a web page with a warning message similar to "Please wait while your transaction is processing. Clicking Purchase Now again may result in a duplicate charge on your credit card."

Having multiple sources for the same data elements can also cause duplicate data. Consider a scenario where Enzo is a university student who starts working on campus during the fall of his first year. In Figure 5.17, Enzo supplies his home address to the Student System during enrollment. Later in the fall, Enzo's parents move, resulting in Enzo having a new home address. Months later, Enzo applies for a campus job with his new home address, which gets reflected in the Payroll System. Since both the Student and Payroll Systems feed the university's data warehouse, this causes Enzo to have duplicate home address data in the data warehouse.

FIGURE 5.17 Creating duplicate data

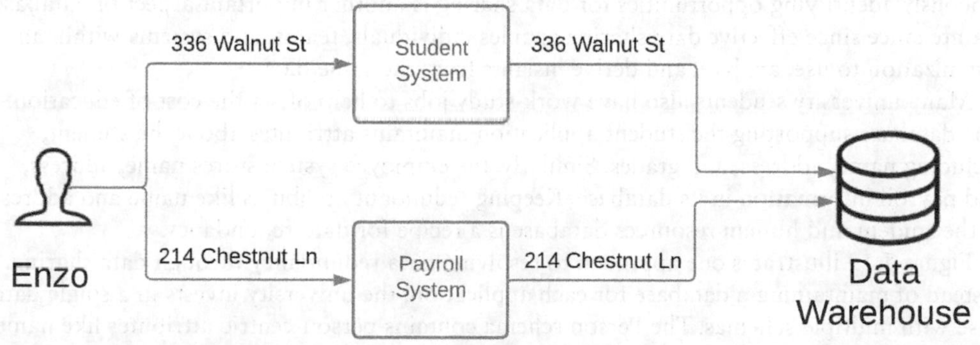

If the business processes that your database supports make duplicate data a potential occurrence, you need to have a duplicate resolution process. Figure 5.18 illustrates a duplicate resolution process that looks for students with multiple active home addresses; validates which address is correct; removes the invalid, duplicate record from the Data Warehouse database; and updates the Student System appropriately.

FIGURE 5.18 Duplicate resolution process

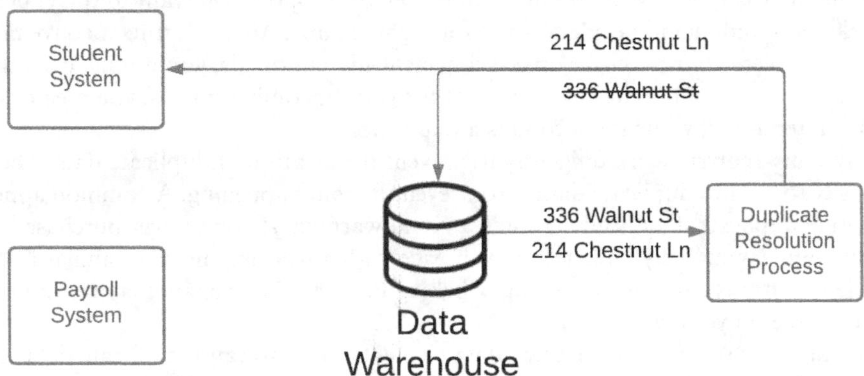

Mergers and acquisitions also contribute to data redundancy. When two companies merge, there's a high chance that their customer databases contain overlapping data. While implementing a duplicate resolution process to address data redundancy is time-consuming and complex, maintaining data integrity is worth the investment.

Data Sharing

Data sharing is the ability for multiple data consumers to access and manipulate data simultaneously. Identifying opportunities for data sharing is another important aspect of database maintenance since effective data sharing enables individuals, teams, and systems within an organization to use, analyze, and derive insights from the same data set.

Many university students also have work-study jobs to help offset the cost of education. The database supporting the student application maintains attributes about the student, including name, address, and grades. Similarly, the employee system stores name, address, and payroll information in its database. Keeping redundant attributes like name and address in the student and human resources database is a recipe for data redundancy.

Figure 5.19 illustrates one approach to resolving data redundancy through data sharing. Instead of maintaining a database for each application, the university invests in a single database with multiple schemas. The Person schema contains person-centric attributes like name and address in this scenario. Meanwhile, student-related grade data is in the Student schema, while the Employee schema contains employee-related data.

FIGURE 5.19 Data sharing with shared schemas

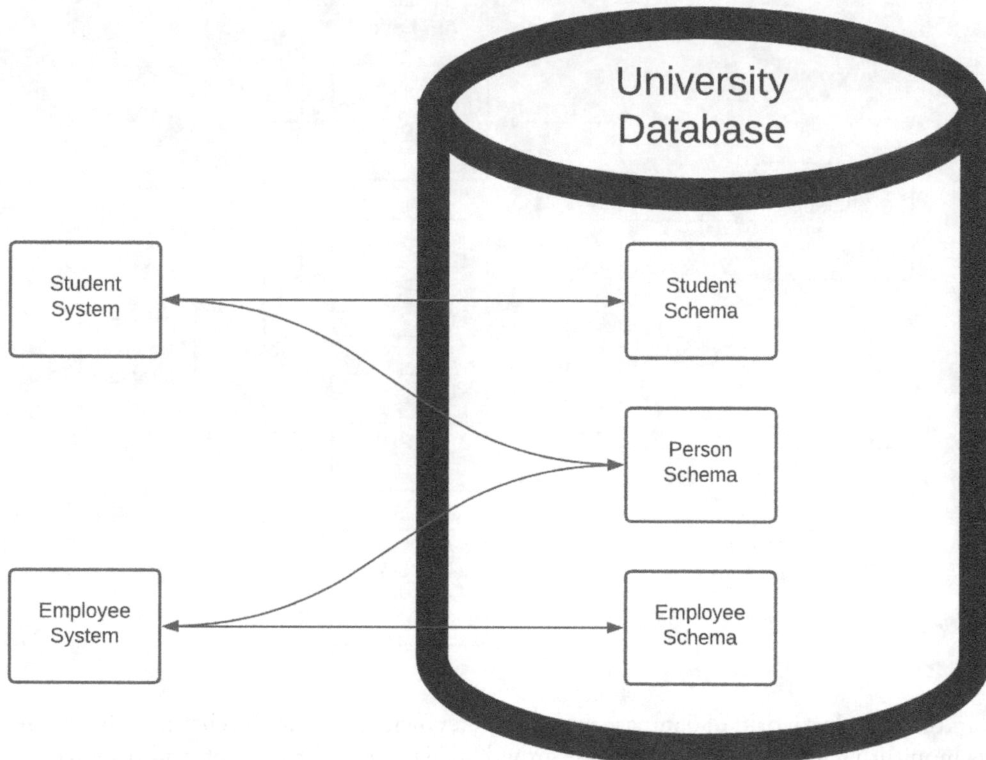

Another way to enable data sharing is to consolidate functionality into an API layer. In Figure 5.20, the Student and Employee systems do not have direct access to the database. Instead, both systems interact with the database using the APIs. In addition to enabling data sharing, this approach improves SQL consistency. Instead of multiple source systems independently retrieving person information, the SQL to get shared person attributes exists only in the Get_Person API.

Summary

Managing and maintaining a database are essential duties a data systems analyst must perform to ensure an efficient, stable, and secure database. To effectively perform their duties, data systems analysts must be able to create effective monitoring and alerting schemes, optimize database performance, create appropriate documentation, and perform routine data management tasks.

FIGURE 5.20 Data sharing with APIs

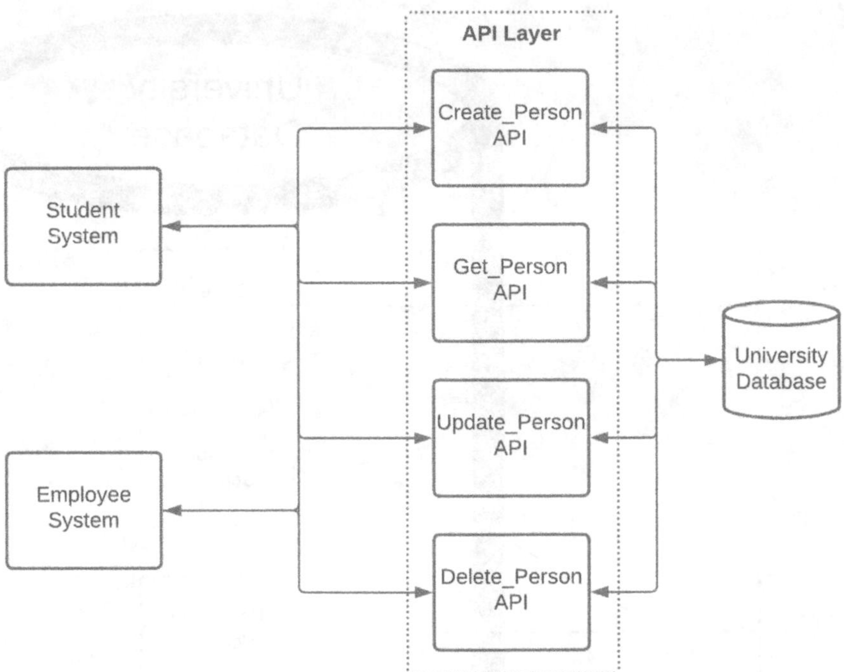

In the complex world of database management, efficient operation relies heavily on effective monitoring and reporting. Database growth, daily usage, throughput, and resource utilization are essential database characteristics to monitor. Establishing a baseline is vital to determine whether database behavior deviates from expected norms. Tracking activities such as batch jobs, data replication, and backups will give you confidence that your data protection processes are working as designed. Transaction and system logs facilitate troubleshooting and audit activities, while monitoring database deadlocks, connections, and sessions can help resolve performance issues.

Regular maintenance is necessary to stable database operations. Query and index optimization facilitate performance-tuning activities. Data integrity and corruption checks give you confidence that you are accurately maintaining the data entrusted to you. Applying maintenance patches lets you take advantage of feature enhancements and bug fixes, while security patches remediate vulnerabilities. Load balancing enables you to distribute load across multiple servers, reducing the risk of failure and improving availability.

Change management is essential to create organizational trust in your database. Creating release schedules helps an organization know when to expect change. Use current operations to inform your capacity planning activities. Regular upgrades help you gain new features, fix bugs, avoid technical debt, and ensure you are eligible for vendor support. While addressing security vulnerabilities is vital, balancing the risk and likelihood of exploitation is necessary when determining when to apply security patches.

A formal change approval process is an essential change management component. A governing body, typically called the CAB, assesses the impact of each proposed change. This process increases consistency, reduces risk, and enhances accountability.

Database refreshes are another change management component. Database refreshes typically copy production data to a non-production environment to help replicate production issues, test new features, and facilitate data analysis. It's important to consider data privacy and security during this process.

A well-structured communication plan is essential to management change. You need to ensure that all stakeholders understand the purpose and impact, as well as their roles, in the change process. The communication channels depend on the audience, the nature of the change, and the organizational culture.

Maintaining documentation is a crucial duty for data systems analysts. Up-to-date documentation can help with certain compliance obligations while troubleshooting guides and playbooks help colleagues resolve unexpected problems. Data dictionaries and ERDs provide additional details about tables and their columns for application developers and data analysts. SOPs detail routine database maintenance tasks. Creating this documentation involves a combination of tools, from word processors and spreadsheets to data modeling tools and UML editors.

Part of the daily life of a data systems analyst involves data management tasks. These tasks include assessing new requirements to determine where additional columns or new tables are required. If, during data definition, you decide that new tables are required, you must determine what data goes in them, where it comes from, and how the new tables relate to existing tables. Data management tasks regularly include creating or updating indexes, views, and materialized views. Occasionally, you may need to create a new data set to support a business initiative. While performing data management tasks, it is crucial to eliminate data redundancy and facilitate data sharing.

Exam Essentials

Explain the difference between resource utilization and saturation. Resource utilization measures the current usage level of resources such as CPU, memory, storage, and network bandwidth. Saturation is a state of maximum utilization where the resource can no longer handle additional work. A data systems analyst should maximize utilization while avoiding saturation.

Describe why establishing baseline performance data is crucial to database operations. Establishing baseline performance data creates a reference point for database behavior. Using this reference point, a data systems analyst can identify deviations, optimize resources, and inform future capacity needs.

Describe the query optimization process. The first step in the query optimization process is identifying poorly performing queries. After determining the query's purpose and impact on system resources, analyze the execution plan to understand the query's road map. Examine the execution plan for resource-consuming activities such as full table scans or subselects, and resolve the issues by rewriting the query, adjusting indexes, ensuring the use of bind variables, and adjusting other database parameters as necessary. After verifying that your change resolves the issue, use your established change management process to propagate the modified code/configuration settings into production.

Explain common database SOPs. SOPs are detailed step-by-step instructions for routine database maintenance tasks. They ensure stability, operational consistency, and compliance obligations. SOPs have a broad scope, covering system architecture, data backup and restoration, security management, data quality, maintenance and performance tuning, troubleshooting, disaster recovery, incident response, change management, and system updates and upgrades. Regularly updating and communicating SOPs is essential to reflect changes in the database system or organizational policies. SOPs provide a reference for operational duties and aid in maintaining a stable and compliant database environment.

Explain the difference between data redundancy and data sharing. Data redundancy refers to duplicate data within a database, leading to storage inefficiency and potential inconsistencies. Data sharing enables multiple users to access and manipulate the same data simultaneously. Having redundant data increases the risk of data duplication, while data sharing reduces that risk.

Review Questions

1. Dillon is a database administrator for an online retail company. His company requires hosting all its data locally, and due to procurement processes, obtaining additional storage hardware can take multiple weeks. The company has just launched a new product line, and he notices an unexpected surge in the data growth rate. Dillon wants to ensure the database operation stays stable by taking preventive action. The database grew from 50 percent to 70 percent of the total storage capacity in a week. Based on the information provided, which of the following should be Dillon's best course of action?
   - **A.** Set an alert threshold for the database size to 80 percent of the total storage capacity.
   - **B.** Ignore the surge since the storage utilization is within normal parameters.
   - **C.** Start the storage hardware procurement process and closely monitor the growth rate.
   - **D.** Set an alert threshold for the database size to 90 percent of the total storage capacity.
2. Vijay is a database administrator at a large manufacturing firm. He is responsible for maintaining the health and reliability of the organization's databases. After observing a sudden increase in CPU utilization during peak load, Vijay allocates additional CPU to the database server. The CPU utilization normalizes after this change. What is the importance of establishing a baseline configuration in this scenario? Choose the best answer.
   - **A.** It helps identify whether the change in CPU utilization was normal or due to an unexpected event.
   - **B.** It assists in forecasting the database's storage requirements for the next fiscal year.
   - **C.** It provides a reference point for comparing system performance before and after the change.
   - **D.** Vijay can log job completion details such as start and end times, duration, and record count.
3. Kelly is a database administrator trying to predict the future resource needs of her organization's database. After identifying system usage and performance trends, she notices that the database has grown by 100 GB monthly over several months. She expects this growth to continue linearly. Which of the following concepts is Kelly most likely utilizing for this purpose?
   - **A.** Database replication
   - **B.** Monitoring job completion
   - **C.** Baseline configuration/trending
   - **D.** Database backups
4. Giancarlo is a database administrator for a large company. His team routinely runs batch extract processes, backups, and data quality validation scripts. Giancarlo has set up a system that logs details about these jobs, such as start and end times, duration, and the number of records loaded or manipulated. However, Giancarlo only configures notifications to alert him when jobs fail, not when they complete successfully. What best describes the approach Giancarlo is using? Choose the best answer.
   - **A.** System logs
   - **B.** Database replication
   - **C.** Baseline configuration/trending
   - **D.** Management-by-exception

5. Michela is a database administrator at a healthcare company. To enhance the database's availability in case of failure, Michela has set up a secondary database where all the changes made to the primary database get replicated. What strategy is Michela using?
   - **A.** Baseline configuration/trending
   - **B.** Database backups
   - **C.** Database replication
   - **D.** Monitoring job completion/failure
6. Gianni works for a large petrochemical company and has observed a sudden increase in CPU utilization on his database server during peak load times. The database, which historically uses 70 percent of CPU during peak load, is now consistently using 90 percent. Gianni has established a baseline configuration for resource utilization. What could the change in CPU utilization indicate?
   - **A.** There is an expected increase in data volume.
   - **B.** There is a missing index in the database.
   - **C.** A set of queries is performing poorly.
   - **D.** All of the above.
7. Melody is troubleshooting unexpectedly high CPU utilization in her database. Examining the explain plan for one of the top queries, she sees it performs full table scans. What is the most likely maintenance task Melody needs to do next?
   - **A.** Patch management
   - **B.** Database integrity checks
   - **C.** Query optimization
   - **D.** Load balancing
8. Emily works for a pharmaceutical company and is making plans for an upcoming database release. She wants to ensure that the release is successful and minimizes disruption. Which of the following is essential for Emily to consider during the planning phase of the release?
   - **A.** Fixing data in the production environment
   - **B.** Determining the size and scope of the release
   - **C.** Testing the changes included in the release
   - **D.** Allocating sufficient time for database refresh
9. Germana is responsible for the capacity planning of her organization's database environment. Which of the following considerations should she take into account during capacity planning?
   - **A.** Implementing changes included in a database release
   - **B.** Estimating future storage, computing resources, and network bandwidth needs
   - **C.** Testing the changes to ensure their success
   - **D.** Assessing the impacts of proposed changes through the change advisory board (CAB)

10. Mahima is a data systems professional at an online retail business with a massive database handling thousands of daily transactions. She has noticed a slowdown in the database performance and suspects it might be due to an issue with a data issue. Which of the following best describes what Mahima should do to investigate and potentially resolve this issue?
    - **A.** Implement a new security patch to address potential vulnerabilities.
    - **B.** Check the system's audit logs to identify any suspicious activity.
    - **C.** Execute database integrity checks to ensure the correctness and consistency of data.
    - **D.** Schedule an immediate system update to improve overall performance.

11. Anitej is a data systems professional at a large healthcare company. Because of recent legislative changes, the company must comply with new data privacy laws. As part of this process, Anitej must update the database to accommodate a new feature allowing patients to request their data's removal. This new feature requires adding a data_removal_request field to an existing Patient table. Which of the following tools can Anitej use to generate the appropriate DDL and update the ERD for the database?
    - **A.** Microsoft Word
    - **B.** Google Sheets
    - **C.** Lucidchart
    - **D.** Oracle SQL Developer Data Modeler

12. Jane is a data systems analyst working for a startup company. The startup is small, with a modest database consisting of just a few tables. They don't have extensive resources to purchase advanced data modeling or diagramming tools, but they need to maintain a data dictionary for their database. Given these conditions, what tool would best suit Jane's needs for maintaining a data dictionary?
    - **A.** Oracle SQL Developer Data Modeler
    - **B.** DbSchema
    - **C.** Google Docs
    - **D.** Erwin

13. Meredith is a data systems analyst at a multinational company that employs the Unified Modeling Language (UML) for creating system diagrams, including visual representations of their database structures and relationships. She needs to update a UML class diagram to reflect the addition of five new database tables. Which of the following tools would be most appropriate for Meredith's task?
    - **A.** Microsoft Word
    - **B.** Google Sheets
    - **C.** DbSchema
    - **D.** Lucidchart

14. Alex is the newly hired database administrator at a small healthcare company and is reviewing the SOPs as part of his onboarding. In the context of Alex's healthcare company, which section of the SOPs should have the highest priority to align with the nature of the industry and regulatory requirements? Choose the best answer.
    - **A.** System Architecture
    - **B.** Security Management
    - **C.** Data Backup and Restoration
    - **D.** Performance Tuning

15. Laura works as a data systems analyst for an international financial corporation. She is responsible for working with a consulting firm to document how her company complies with industry standards and governmental regulations. Which of her company's SOPs should Laura review to ensure she doesn't miss something crucial? Choose the best option.
    - **A.** System Updates and Upgrades
    - **B.** Data Quality
    - **C.** Audit
    - **D.** Change Management

16. Sandra is a data systems analyst at a healthcare company. Recently, her company decided to start a patient wellness program that necessitates tracking new data elements like patient wellness program numbers and wellness point totals. Sandra has concluded that these data elements are patient attributes and must add them to the existing Patient table. She also realized the importance of enforcing uniqueness on the wellness program number to avoid duplicates. Which SQL statements should Sandra use to perform these tasks?
    - **A.** ALTER TABLE patient ADD COLUMN wellness_pgm_id INTEGER;

      ALTER TABLE patient ADD CONSTRAINT uc_wellness_pgm_id UNIQUE(wellness_pgm_id);
    - **B.** ALTER TABLE patient ADD wellness_pgm_id INTEGER;

      ALTER TABLE patient ADD CONSTRAINT UNIQUE(wellness_pgm_id);
    - **C.** ALTER TABLE patient ADD COLUMN wellness_pgm_id INTEGER;

      ALTER TABLE patient ADD CONSTRAINT wellness_pgm_id UNIQUE;
    - **D.** ALTER TABLE patient ADD wellness_pgm_id INTEGER;

      ALTER TABLE patient ADD CONSTRAINT uc_wellness_pgm_id UNIQUE;

17. Jackson is on the analytics team for an automotive company. One of the reports he is working on requires data from 18 tables. No matter how much he optimizes his query, running takes at least 8 minutes, which is too long for users to wait. Talking with business leaders, Jackson realizes that the information in the result set can be up to 30 minutes old without impacting business decisions. What should Jackson do to meet this requirement? Choose the best option.
    - **A.** Create an index.
    - **B.** Create a view.
    - **C.** Create a materialized view.
    - **D.** Remove data to reduce the number of joins.

18. Lisa is a data systems analyst working for an e-commerce company that recently merged with another similar company. As a result of the merger, the company has duplicate data in its customer database. Lisa needs to resolve this data redundancy and improve data sharing between different systems. Which approach should Lisa consider to resolve these issues effectively?

    A. She should delete all duplicated data manually without a standardized process.

    B. She should keep the databases separate and manage data redundancy individually for each database.

    C. She should implement a duplicate resolution process and consolidate functionality into an API layer.

    D. She should give users a visual warning about potential data duplication.

19. Miguel is a data analyst at a large university. To help offset the cost of education, many students at the university also have work-study jobs. Currently, the university maintains separate databases for student and employee information, causing data redundancy. Miguel needs to resolve this redundancy and improve data sharing. Which approach should Miguel adopt to tackle these issues?

    A. He should merge the two databases without considering the data schema.

    B. He should invest in a single database with multiple schemas and employ an API layer for data access and manipulation.

    C. He should manually update each student's data across both databases whenever changes occur.

    D. He should delete one of the databases and only maintain a single source of data.

20. Maddie is a data systems analyst for a motorcycle manufacturer. Product development is working on creating a new 1000 cc adventure touring motorcycle. The product owner wants to compare the features and specifications of existing motorcycles of similar displacement to better understand the competitive landscape. What can Maddie do to help product development? Choose the best answer.

    A. Modify data about her company's existing motorcycles.

    B. Create a view with details about her company's motorcycles.

    C. Create a new table to store information about the competition.

    D. Create a new data set using publicly available information about competitor's products.

Chapter 6

Governance, Security, and Compliance

THE COMPTIA DATASYS+ EXAM TOPICS COVERED IN THIS CHAPTER INCLUDE:

✓ **Domain 4.0: Data and Database Security**

- 4.1. Explain Data Security Concepts
- 4.2. Explain the Purpose of Governance and Regulatory Compliance
- 4.3. Given a Scenario, Implement Policies and Best Practices Related to Authentication and Authorization
- 4.4. Explain the Purpose of Database Infrastructure Security
- 4.5. Describe Types of Attacks and Their Effects on Data Systems

Data systems professionals have many responsibilities. Up until this point in the book, we've focused on the aspects of those responsibilities that build, maintain, and use the transactional and analytic data storage systems used in the modern organization. As we turn to the fourth domain of the DataSys+ exam, we look at the responsibilities that data professionals have to secure data and database systems.

We begin this chapter with a look at data governance practices that ensure the organization has data that is both useful and secure. We then move on to data security issues that protect the confidentiality and integrity of sensitive information, and we wrap up with a look at legal and regulatory compliance issues that ensure we stay on the right side of the law.

Data Governance

Data governance is the set of policies, procedures, and controls that an organization develops to safeguard its information while making it useful for transactional and analytic purposes. As the name implies, data governance is primarily a business function. Governments have a method for creating, interpreting, and enforcing laws. Part of this process ensures that these laws are known to the citizenry. For organizations, data governance is an umbrella term covering the creation, interpretation, and enforcement of data use.

Organizations develop numerous policies to govern their data. These policies promote data quality, specify the use of data attributes, and define access to different data domains. Additional governance policies identify how to secure data, comply with regulations, protect data privacy, and deal with data over time. Just as countries enforce laws, organizations implement procedural and technical controls to comply with data governance standards.

Strong executive support is vital to any data governance effort. An organization invests a significant amount of time and resources to define, develop, implement, and control access to data. For data governance to succeed, all levels of an organization must appreciate the importance of well-governed data. While technology is a critical component to facilitating adherence to policies, an information technology organization can't drive data governance efforts on its own. You need executive support across the organization for data governance efforts to succeed.

Data Governance Roles

It takes multiple people fulfilling a variety of roles for data governance to thrive. A crucial concept relating to data governance is data stewardship. Stewardship denotes looking after something, like an organization or property. *Data stewardship* is the act of developing the policies and procedures for looking after an organization's data quality, security, privacy, and regulatory compliance. The most vital role for effective data stewardship is that of the organizational data steward. An *organizational data steward*, or *data steward*, is the person responsible for data stewardship.

The data steward is responsible for leading an organization's data governance activities. As the link between the technical and nontechnical divisions within an organization, a data steward works with many people, from senior leaders to individual technologists. To establish policies, a data steward works with various data owners.

A *data owner* is a senior business leader with overall responsibility for a specific data domain. A *data domain*, or *data subject area*, comprises data about a particular operational division within an organization. Finance, human resources, and physical plant are all examples of operational divisions. Data owners work with the data steward to establish policies and procedures for their data domain.

In large, complex organizations, data owners may choose to delegate day-to-day governance activities to subject area data stewards. A *subject area data steward* works in the data owner's organization and understands the nuances that apply within that organizational unit. A subject area data steward works on behalf of their data owner to handle daily tasks. For example, processing access requests as people rotate in and out of roles is a responsibility a data owner may delegate to their subject area data steward. The need for subject area data stewards arises from the intricacies of different data domains. To implement data governance policies, data stewards work with data custodians.

A *data custodian* is a role given to someone who implements technical controls that execute data governance policies. Data custodians are frequently information technology employees who configure applications, dashboards, and databases. The data custodian carries out technical tasks on behalf of the data steward.

For example, unique laws govern an organization's finances, people, and physical plant. Figure 6.1 visualizes how an organizational data steward works both vertically and horizontally with the various data owners, subject area data stewards, and data custodians to actively steward, or take care of, the organization's data.

Access Requirements

One crucial component of data governance defines the access requirements for data. *Data access requirements* determine which people need access to what data. Access rights and privileges differ by data subject area and can be as granular as a single field. For example, managers need access to details about their employees, including their names and contact information. Since managers are responsible for providing feedback, they also need access to performance data. However, no manager has a compelling need to view their employees' Social Security numbers (SSN). While SSNs are necessary for payroll and tax purposes, malicious actors can also use them for identity theft.

When determining access requirements, it is essential to develop a data classification matrix. A *data classification matrix* defines categories, descriptions, and disclosure implications for data. Table 6.1 is an example of a data classification matrix. It is vital to consider data classification when considering access requirements to ensure proper data stewardship.

FIGURE 6.1 Organizational example

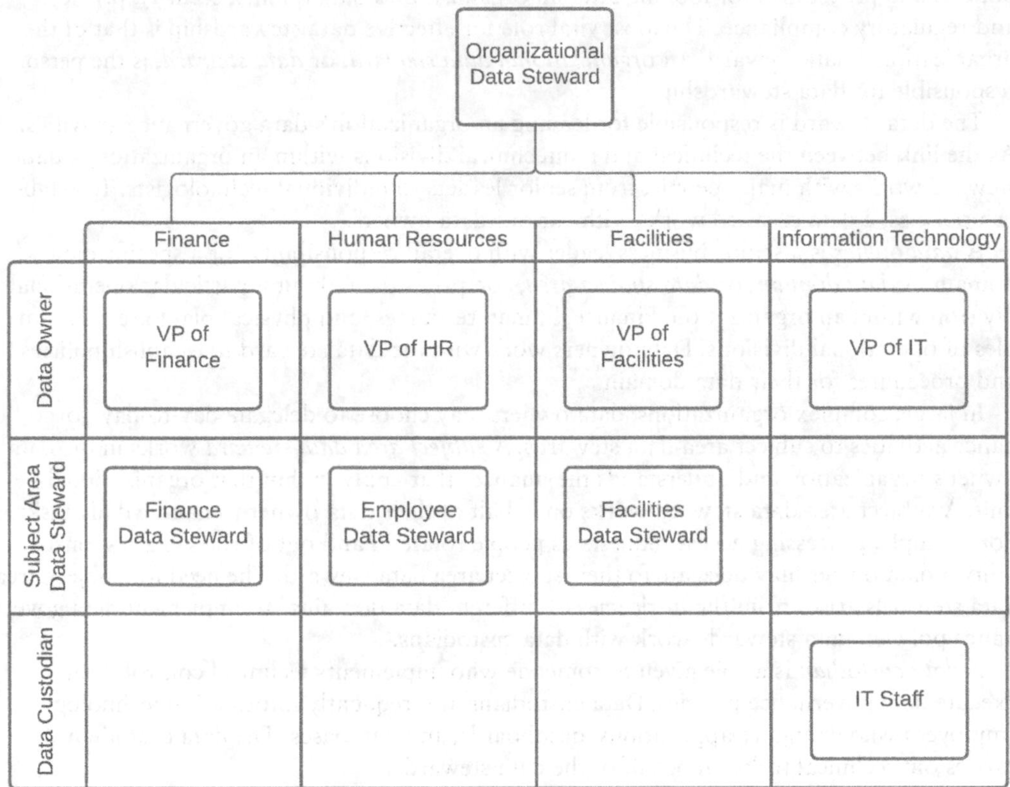

TABLE 6.1 Sample Data Classification Matrix

Classification Term	Classification Description
Public	Data intended for public consumption. For example, anything on a public-facing website meets this classification. No disclosure implications.
Internal	Data intended for use within an organization. For example, a comprehensive organization chart including names. Disclosure compromises an organization's reputation or operations, but not its privacy or confidentiality obligations.
Sensitive	Data intended for limited use within an organization. For example, a list of employees and their compensation. Disclosure implies a violation of privacy or confidentiality.
Highly Sensitive	Data intended for restricted use, typically due to compliance obligations. Examples include Social Security numbers and bank account numbers. Disclosure implies a legal obligation in the event of a data breach.

A data steward works with a data owner to establish broad classifications, with subject area data stewards to develop procedures for granting access to information, and with data custodians to ensure the appropriate technical controls are in place to protect information.

Access Permissions

It is a best practice to use role-based access to grant people permissions to access data. *Role-based access* means that instead of giving access to individual people, you grant access to the role they occupy. When you define roles, then assign people to those roles, it simplifies how you manage permissions.

For example, it is common for people to switch jobs within an organization, as it allows for developing new skills and a more comprehensive understanding of the overall business. Figure 6.2 illustrates a specific employee's jobs and how they change over time. In the first year, Ralph works in Finance. During his time in Finance, Ralph has access to data about the organization's finances.

FIGURE 6.2 Access roles over time

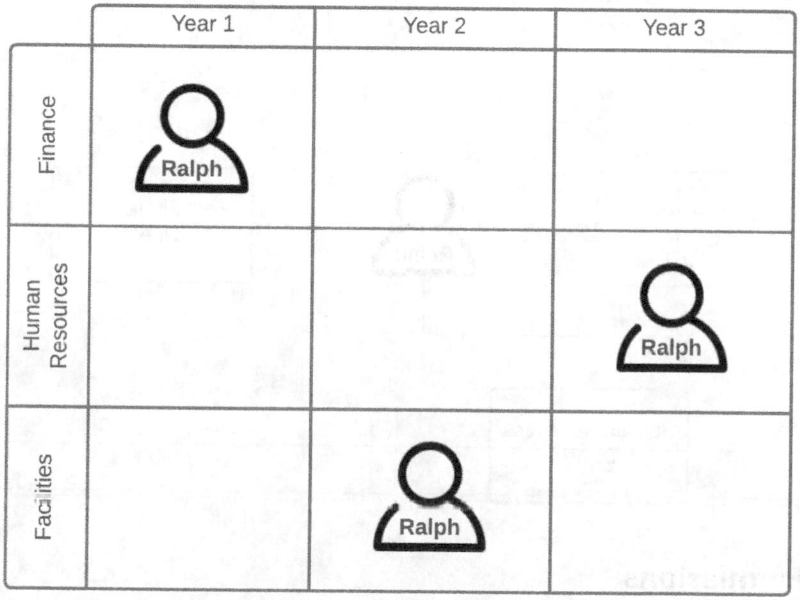

	Year 1	Year 2	Year 3
Finance	Ralph		
Human Resources			Ralph
Facilities		Ralph	

In the second year, Ralph takes a new position in Facilities. Ralph needs access to facilities-related data for his new position and doesn't need to retain access to the Finance system. A data custodian removes Ralph's finance role and assigns him a facilities role to reflect that change.

In the third year, Ralph takes a position in Human Resources. Ralph needs access to human resources data in this new job and no longer needs to see the facilities-related data. A data custodian implements the change to Ralph's access permissions.

A role-based access approach facilitates permissions maintenance and improves consistency. This approach also ensures that Ralph only has access to the data he needs to perform his current duties. Managing permissions with roles also pays dividends when auditing permissions for compliance.

The alternative to role-based access is *user-based access*, which assigns permissions directly to individuals. User-based access is a dangerous practice, as it increases operational complexity and the potential for mistakes. Suppose there are both online transaction processing (OLTP) and online analytical processing (OLAP) environments for each data subject area. Figure 6.3 illustrates what could happen at the end of Year 3 if the data custodian forgets to remove OLAP permissions at each role transition. In this scenario, Ralph winds up with too much access by the end of Year 3. This situation, where a user accumulates privileges as they move through different roles in an organization, is known as *privilege creep*.

FIGURE 6.3 Danger of user-based access

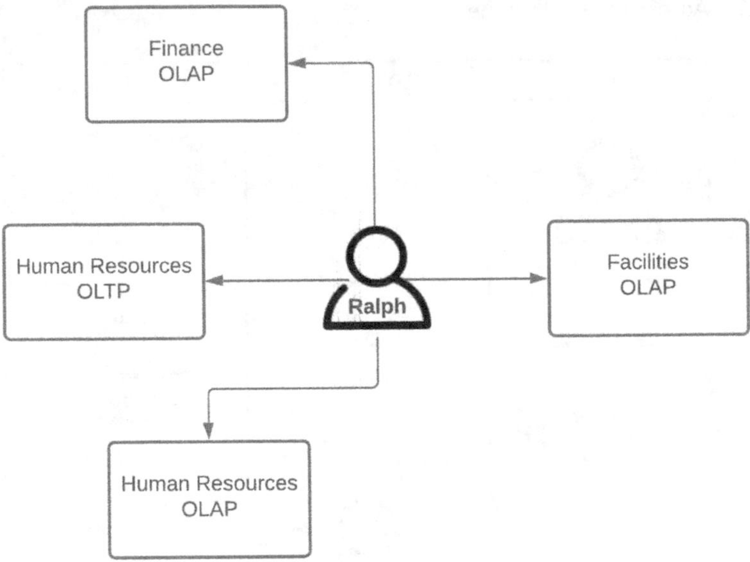

Group Permissions

It's best to start by visualizing people within an organization when creating data access roles. An organization chart documents the reporting structure within an organization. Looking at an organization chart, like the example in Figure 6.4, informs how you develop roles.

When developing a role-based access strategy, it is common to implement user group-based permissions, where each member of a role is assigned to a group for that role. Considering the sample organization chart from Figure 6.4, you can imagine vice presidents having broadly permissive access to data within their area of responsibility. Progressing down the organization chart reduces the scope of what someone in that role can access. Figure 6.5 illustrates how roles form naturally around groups of people.

FIGURE 6.4 Sample organization chart

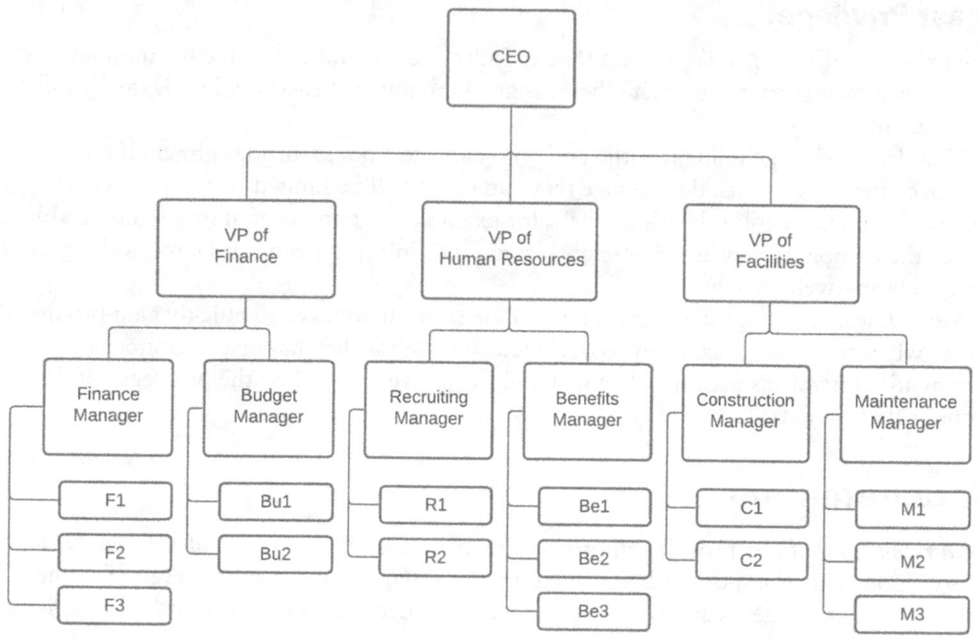

FIGURE 6.5 Sample user group-based roles

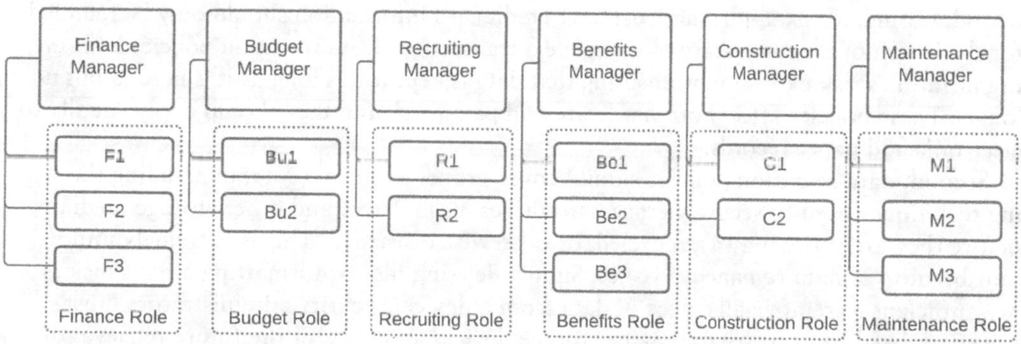

It's also important to recognize that while some roles correspond to the specific job an individual has, they also may correspond to other duties the user has within the organization. For example, a manager in the Finance department may be a member of a role for Finance team members, a role for managers throughout the organization, and a role for people working on a special project. They would then be placed into groups corresponding to each of these roles.

Least Privilege

The principle of *least privilege* states that an individual should only have the minimum set of privileges necessary to complete their assigned job duties. Least privilege is important for two reasons.

First, least privilege minimizes the potential damage from an insider attack. If an employee turns malicious, the damage they can cause will be limited by the privileges assigned to them by job role. It's unlikely, for example, that an accountant would be able to deface the company website because an accountant's job responsibilities have nothing to do with updating web content.

Second, least privilege limits the ability of an external attacker to quickly gain privileged access when compromising an employee's account. Unless they happen to compromise a system administrator's account, they will find themselves limited by the privileges of the account that they steal.

Data Retention

Data retention policies provide important guidance concerning the end-of-life process for information. This is important because information may retain sensitivity even after the organization no longer requires it. Data retention policies should address at least two important issues.

First, data retention policies should describe how long an organization will keep different data elements. This may include a minimum retention period, such as retaining all tax-related records for a seven-year period. It may also include a maximum retention period, stating, for example, that customer credit card information should only be retained for the length of time necessary to complete a transaction. Data retention policies limit an organization's risk exposure by ensuring that data is kept for as long as it is needed but no longer. These policies affect both hardware and personnel, and they should apply equally to electronic and paper records.

Second, data retention policies should cover proper disposal of data, including the wiping techniques used to securely erase hard drives, flash drives and other storage media before they are thrown away, recycled, or otherwise discarded. This is extremely important because of data remanence issues. Simply deleting files or formatting a hard disk is not sufficient to remove all traces of data from a device. Security administrators must use specialized tools to securely wipe storage devices and prevent the future retrieval of information believed to be deleted. These include software applications, such as Darik's Boot and Nuke, otherwise known as DBAN, and hardware tools, such as magnetic degaussers and device shredders.

Don't forget about paper records as well! While it's easy to get caught up in the technologies used to destroy electronic records, you still need a process for destroying sensitive paper records. Common techniques for destroying paper records include shredding, incinerating, and pulping.

Identity and Access Management

As data professionals, one of the most important things that we do is ensure that only authorized individuals gain access to information, systems, and databases under our protection. That's the role of *identity and access management (IAM)* programs.

Identification, Authentication, and Authorization

The access control process consists of three steps that you must understand. These steps are identification, authentication, and authorization.

During the first step of the process, *identification*, an individual makes a claim about their identity. The person trying to gain access doesn't present any proof at this point—they simply make an assertion. It's important to remember that the identification step is only a claim and the user could certainly be making a false claim!

Imagine a physical-world scenario in which you want to enter a secure office building where you have an appointment. During the identification step of the process, you might walk up to the security desk and say: "Hi, I'm Mike Chapple."

Proof comes into play during the second step of the process: *authentication*. During the authentication step, the individual proves their identity to the satisfaction of the access control system. In our office building example, the guard would likely wish to see my driver's license to confirm my identity.

Simply proving your identity isn't enough to gain access to a system, however. The access control system also needs to be satisfied that you are allowed to access the system. That's the third step of the access control process: *authorization*. In our office building example, the security guard might check a list of that day's appointments to see if it includes my name.

So far, we've discussed identification, authentication, and authorization in the context of gaining access to a building. Let's talk about how they work in the electronic world. When we log in to a system, we most often identify ourselves using a username, most likely composed of some combination of the letters from our names.

When we reach the authentication phase, we're commonly asked to enter a password. There are many other ways to authenticate, and we'll talk about those later in this chapter.

Finally, in the electronic world, authorization often takes the form of access control lists that itemize the specific file-system permissions granted to an individual user or group of users. Users proceed through the identification, authentication, and authorization processes when they request access to a resource.

Authentication Techniques

Computer systems offer many different authentication techniques that allow users to prove their identity. Let's take a look at three different authentication factors: something you know, something you are, and something you have.

Something You Know

Passwords are the most common example of a "something you know" authentication factor. The user remembers their password and enters it in a system during the authentication process.

Users should choose strong passwords consisting of as many characters as possible and combine characters from multiple classes, such as uppercase and lowercase letters, digits, and symbols.

Something You Are

The second authentication factor is something you are, otherwise known as *biometric* authentication. Biometrics measure one of your physical characteristics, such as a fingerprint, eye pattern, face, or voice. Using biometric authentication requires specialized readers, such as the retinal scanner shown in Figure 6.6(a) or the fingerprint reader shown in Figure 6.6(b).

FIGURE 6.6 Biometric authentication with a (a) retinal scanner (b) fingerprint scanner

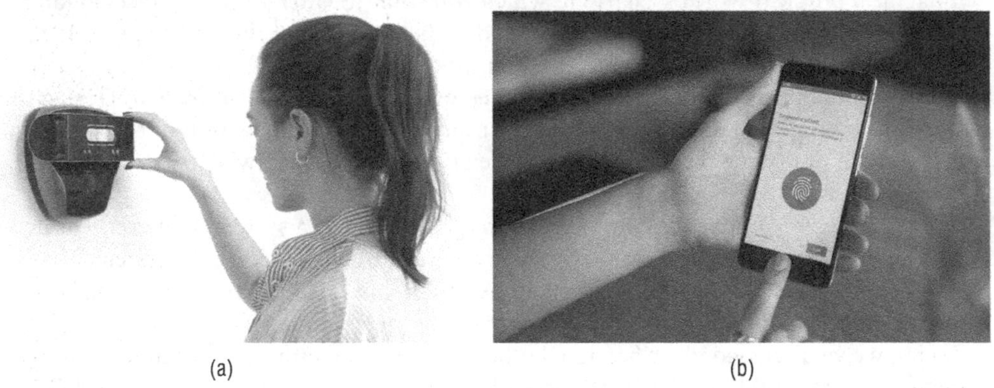

(a) (b)

Something You Have

The third authentication factor, something you have, requires the user to have physical possession of a device, such as a smartphone or authentication token key fob like the one shown in Figure 6.7.

Multifactor Authentication

When used alone, any one authentication factor provides some security for systems. However, they each have their own drawbacks. For example, an attacker might steal a user's password through a phishing attack. Once they have the password, they can then use that password to assume the user's identity. Other authentication factors aren't foolproof, either. If you use smart-card authentication to implement something you have, the user may lose the smart card. Someone coming across it may then impersonate the user.

FIGURE 6.7 Authentication token

The solution to this problem is to combine authentication techniques from multiple factors, such as combining something you know with something you have. This approach is known as *multifactor authentication (MFA)*.

Take the two techniques we just discussed: passwords and smart cards. When used alone, either one is subject to hackers either gaining knowledge of the password or stealing a smart card. However, if an authentication system requires both a password (something you know) and a smart card (something you have), it brings added security. If the hacker steals the password, they don't have the required smart card, and vice versa. It suddenly becomes much more difficult for the attacker to gain access to the account. Something you know and something you have are different factors, so this is an example of multifactor authentication.

We can combine other authentication factors as well. For example, a fingerprint reader (something you are) might also require the entry of a PIN (something you know).

When evaluating multifactor authentication, remember that the techniques must be *different* factors. An approach that combines a password with the answer to a security question is *not* multifactor authentication because both factors are something you know.

Password Policies

When you set a password policy for your organization, you have a number of technical controls available that allow you to set requirements for how users choose and maintain their passwords. Let's discuss a few of those mechanisms.

Password Length

The simplest and most common control on passwords is setting the *password length*. This is simply the minimum number of characters that must be included in a password. It's good practice to require that passwords be at least eight characters, but some organizations require even longer passwords. The longer a password, the harder it is to guess.

Password Complexity

Organizations may also set *password complexity* requirements. These requirements force users to include different types of characters in their passwords, such as uppercase and lowercase letters, digits, and special characters. Just as with password length, the more character types in a password, the harder it is to guess.

Password Expiration

Password expiration requirements force users to change their passwords periodically. For example, an organization might set a password expiration period of 180 days, forcing users to change their passwords every six months. These days, many organizations no longer have password expiration requirements, allowing users to keep the same password for as long as they'd like and only requiring that they change it if the password is compromised.

Password History

Password history requirements are designed to prevent users from reusing old passwords. Organizations with password history requirements configure their systems to remember the previous passwords used by each user and prevent them from reusing that password in the future. Password history controls allow the administrator to identify how many old passwords are remembered for each user.

Password Resets

Every organization should allow users to change their passwords quickly and easily. You want users to be able to privately select their own passwords and do so whenever they are concerned that their password may be compromised.

One point of caution is that organizations should carefully evaluate their password reset process for users who forget their passwords. If they're not designed well, these processes can provide an opportunity for attackers to gain access to a system by performing an unauthorized password reset

Password Reuse

IT teams should also strongly encourage users not to reuse the same password across multiple sites. This is difficult to enforce, but it does provide a strong measure of security. If a user reuses the same password on many different sites and one of those sites is compromised, an attacker might test that password on other sites, hoping that the password owner reuses the same password.

Password Managers

It's difficult for users to manage unique passwords for every site they visit. That's where password managers play a crucial role. These valuable tools are secure password vaults, often protected by biometric security mechanisms that create and store unique passwords. They then automatically fill those passwords into websites when the user visits them. That way users can have unique, strong passwords for every site they visit without having to remember them all.

Figure 6.8 shows an example of LastPass, a popular password manager, being used to create a new, strong password.

FIGURE 6.8 Creating a password in LastPass

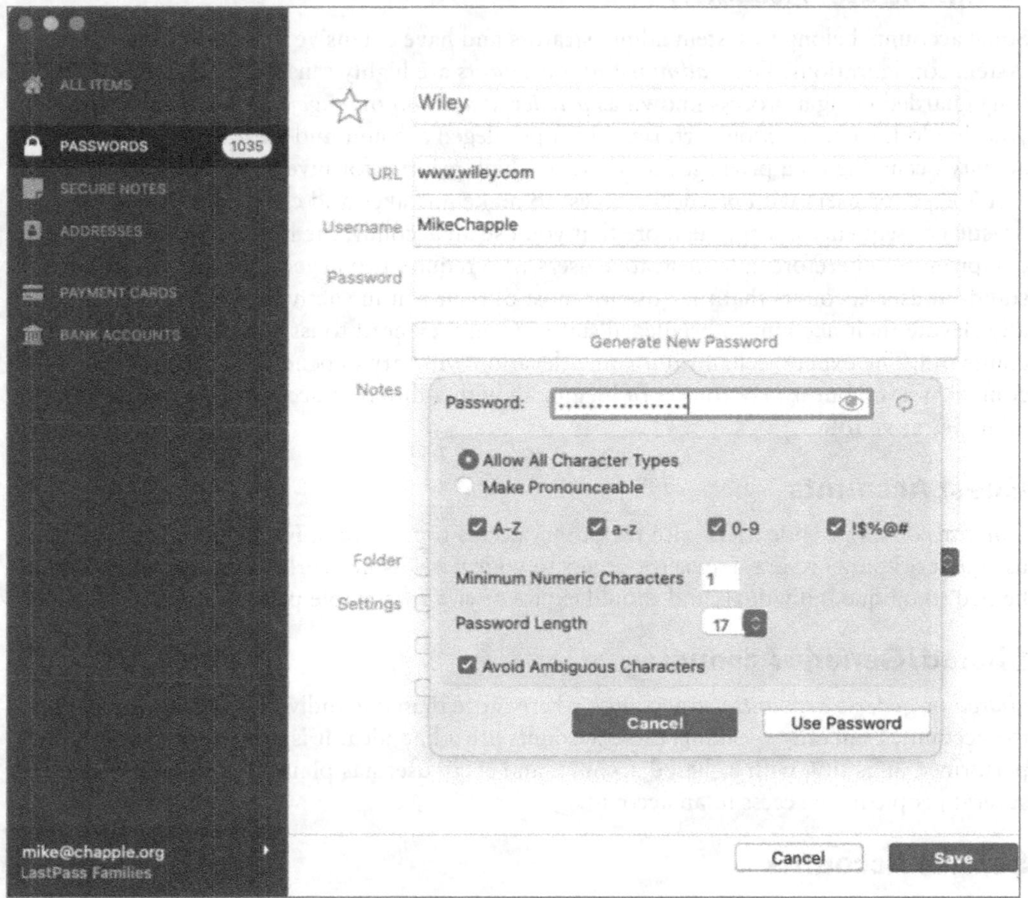

Account Types

Access control systems contain several different types of accounts, and each category requires different types of controls.

User Accounts

Most of the accounts that we manage are standard *user accounts*. They're assigned to an individual user and grant routine access to resources. Everyone from the receptionist to the CEO in an organization typically has a standard user account, even though those accounts may have dramatically different privileges. User accounts should be subject to routine monitoring for compromise and should follow a life-cycle management process for creation and removal.

Administrator Accounts

Some accounts belong to system administrators and have extensive privileges to modify system configurations. These *administrator accounts* are highly sensitive and should be carefully guarded using a process known as *privileged account management*. Generally speaking, you should log every action performed by a privileged account and treat any suspicious activity occurring on a privileged account as a high priority for investigation.

It's easy for users with privileged access to make mistakes and cause unintended but drastic consequences. Also, the more that you use an account, the higher the likelihood of compromise. Therefore, administrative users who require privileged access typically have standard user accounts that they use for most of their routine activity and then manually elevate their account to privileged status when they need to issue an administrative command. The exact mechanism for this elevation will vary depending on the access control system, but it may consist of logging in with a different account or assuming an administrative role.

Guest Accounts

Guest accounts provide users with temporary access to resources. For example, you might use guest accounts to grant a visitor access to your wireless network. Guest accounts should be tied to unique individuals and should expire after a reasonable period of time.

Shared/Generic Accounts

Shared or *generic accounts* are accounts where more than one individual has access to use the account. Generally speaking, these accounts are a bad idea. It is difficult to trace who performed an action with a shared account, and every user has plausible deniability when several people have access to an account.

Service Accounts

Service accounts are a special type of account used internally by a system to run a process or perform other actions. These accounts typically have privileged access and should be carefully controlled. You should configure service accounts so that they may not be used to log on to the system interactively, and their passwords should not be known by anyone.

Data Security

With data access requirements in place, you need to determine the technical controls for protecting data. In cryptography, *encryption* is the process of encoding data with a key so that only authorized parties can read it. Data encryption is one of the fundamental components of data protection, as the data is unusable without the key to decrypt it. An *encryption key* is a series of bits used during the encoding process to make data unreadable. Once encrypted, you can only access the data by decrypting it with a valid key. If you lose the encryption key, any data encrypted with that key becomes useless.

Protecting Data at Rest

To keep data secure, you must encrypt data at rest as well as data in transit. *Data at rest* is data that exists in permanent storage. The two most common locations for data at rest are databases and flat files. Databases have sophisticated access control mechanisms as part of the database software. Since databases centralize data and require a team of technologists to operate, they are comparatively easy to secure.

For example, both Oracle and Microsoft have *Transparent Data Encryption* (*TDE*) as part of their database offering. TDE ensures the database files and log files are encrypted. With TDE, even if an unauthorized party gains access to the database server, the database files themselves are encrypted.

The chance of someone picking up a database server and walking away with it is slight. However, it is much more challenging to secure flat files as you can put them on any device that stores electronic data. Desktop computers, laptops, tablets, mobile phones, and USB thumb drives are all examples of devices that store flat files. Since many of these devices are portable, there is a good chance that one will be lost or stolen. If the device is encrypted, your information is safe—if the encryption key isn't lost.

When you encrypt data at rest on a server (such as a database server) this is known as *server-side encryption*. When you encrypt data at rest on a laptop or other end user device, this is known as *client-side encryption*.

Data Discovery

One of the trickiest things about protecting information is often finding that information in the first place! Sensitive information has a way of creeping into the digital nooks and crannies of an organization, evading detection by security personnel. Many organizations use data discovery tools to search through repositories for signs of unsecured sensitive information.

Protecting Data in Transit

Data in transit is data that is actively moving between one location and another. During data transmission, you must encrypt the connection between the locations to ensure the data's security. When considering data in transit, you need to account for people interacting with computers and computers interacting with other computers.

Transmitting data over the Internet typically uses the Hypertext Transfer Protocol (HTTP). To ensure data security, use *Transport Layer Security* (*TLS*) as the cryptographic protocol for encrypting the connection. Adding TLS on top of HTTP results in *Hypertext Transfer Protocol Secure* (*HTTPS*), as seen in Figure 6.9.

FIGURE 6.9 Encrypted network connection

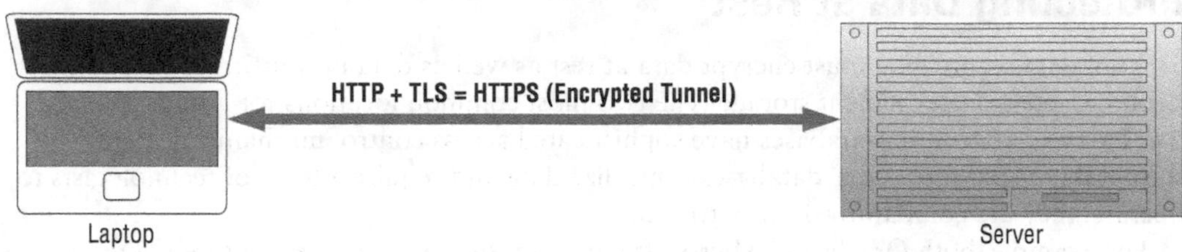

When a person navigates the Internet using a web browser, a padlock shows up in the address bar to indicate an encrypted HTTPS connection. Figure 6.10 illustrates the padlock in three common web browsers. As part of amplifying the security message in the context of data governance, part of your training should include reminders to look for the padlock when putting sensitive information into a browser. This indicates that in-transit encryption is taking place.

FIGURE 6.10 HTTPS padlock

Extract, transform and load (ETL) processes copy data between transactional and analytical systems. When copying files between the transactional and analytical servers, use the *Secure Copy Protocol* (*SCP*) or the *Secure File Transfer Protocol* (*SFTP*). As their names imply, both SCP and SFTP establish an encrypted tunnel to copy data, as shown in Figure 6.11.

Apart from encryption, you also need to consider whether or not there is a reason for sensitive data elements, like SSN, to exist in a nonproduction environment. *Data masking*, or *data obfuscation*, replaces sensitive information with a synthetic version. For example, you may use production data to populate your testing and training environments.

While testing or training, using a simulated instead of an actual SSN doesn't diminish the testing or training use case. To protect individual privacy and minimize organizational risk, you can implement a data masking strategy for sensitive information, as shown in Figure 6.12.

FIGURE 6.11 Encrypted ETL process

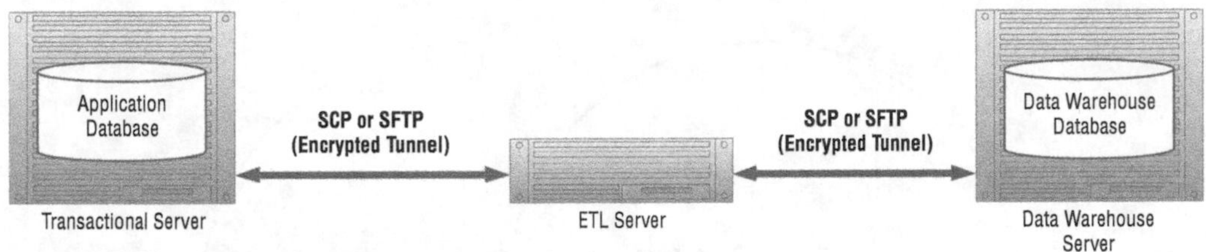

FIGURE 6.12 Data masking ETL process

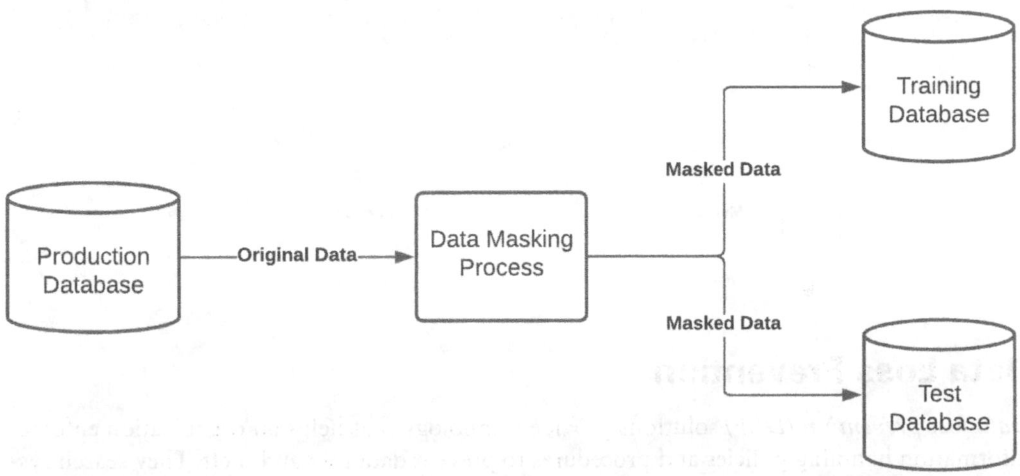

Depending on the use case, you also can de-identify sensitive data to improve security. *De-identifying data* is the process of removing identifiers that can compromise individual privacy. How you de-identify depends on your use case. One way of de-identifying data is to share only aggregated or summarized data. Another way is to remove variables from the data.

Re-identifying data happens when you take de-identified data sets and join them in a way that establishes the identity of individuals. For example, you can identify most Americans by combining their birth date, sex, and zip code. Figure 6.13 illustrates the danger of re-identification, as it shows two separate data sets which share three data elements: birth date, sex, and zip code. Although the medical data set is de-identified, you can re-identify individuals by combining the two data sets using the shared data elements. If the values for those three variables aren't essential to ongoing analysis, the most straightforward path to ensuring the de-identification of the data set is to remove the variables you don't need. It is especially vital to consider re-identification possibilities when sharing data with an external party.

FIGURE 6.13 Re-identification by combining data sets

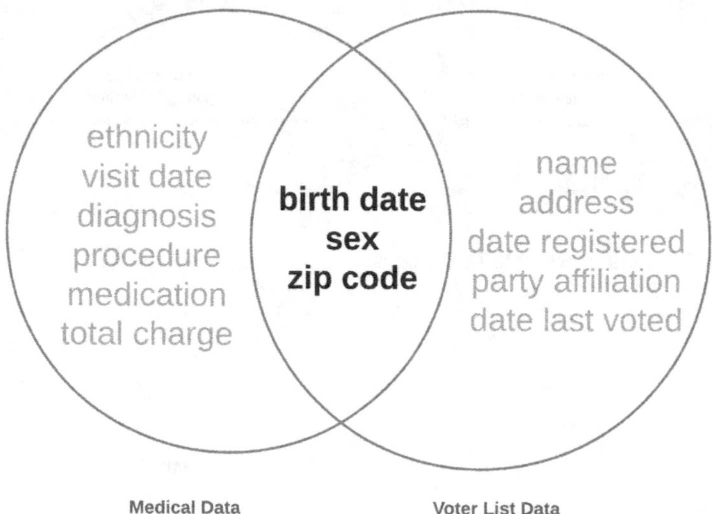

Data Loss Prevention

Data loss prevention (DLP) solutions provide technology that helps an organization enforce information handling policies and procedures to prevent data loss and theft. They search systems for stores of sensitive information that might be unsecured and monitor network traffic for potential attempts to remove sensitive information from the organization. They can act quickly to block the transmission before damage is done and alert administrators to the attempted breach.

DLP systems work in two different environments:

- **Host-based DLP** uses software agents installed on a single system that search the system for the presence of sensitive information. These searches often turn up Social Security numbers, credit card numbers, and other sensitive information in the most unlikely places! Detecting the presence of stored sensitive information allows security professionals to take prompt action to either remove it or secure it with encryption. Taking the time to secure or remove information now may pay handsome rewards down the road if the device is lost, stolen, or compromised.
- **Network-Based DLP** monitors outbound network traffic, watching for any transmissions that contain unencrypted sensitive information. They can then block those

transmissions, preventing the unsecured loss of sensitive information. DLP systems may simply block traffic that violates the organization's policy, or, in some cases, they may automatically apply encryption to the content. This automatic encryption is commonly used with DLP systems that focus on email.

DLP systems also have two mechanisms of action:

- **Pattern matching** watches for the telltale signs of sensitive information. For example, if the DLP system sees a number that is formatted like a credit card or Social Security number, it can automatically trigger on that. Similarly, the DLP system may contain a database of sensitive terms, such as "Top Secret" or "Business Confidential" and trigger when it sees those terms in a transmission.
- **Watermarking** approaches require that systems or administrators apply digital tags to sensitive documents and then the DLP system can monitor systems and networks for unencrypted content containing those tags.

Data Classification

Data classification is the process of analyzing data and organizing it into risk-based categories. Classifying data is appropriate for both structured and unstructured data. When classifying data, you put data elements into one of four classifications, similar to those in the data classification matrix found in Table 6.1. Note that the category names may differ. Instead of Public, Internal, Sensitive, and Highly Sensitive, you may come across Public, Internal-Only, Confidential, and Restricted. Regardless of the category names, it is vital to understand the attributes for each category so that you can make the appropriate category assignment.

Classifying data elements can feel like an overwhelming task. Fortunately, there are a variety of standards in place that simplify the classification process, enforce consistency, and protect privacy.

Personally Identifiable Information

Personally Identifiable Information (*PII*) is any data that can uniquely identify a person. In the United States, the *National Institute of Standards and Technology* (*NIST*) defines PII as follows:

> PII is any information about an individual maintained by an agency, including (1) any information that can be used to distinguish or trace an individual's identity, such as name, Social Security number, date and place of birth, mother's maiden name, or biometric records; and (2) any other information that is linked or linkable to an individual, such as medical, educational, financial, and employment information.

According to NIST, PII falls into two categories: linked and linkable. *Linked PII* is data that you can use to uniquely identify someone, including:

- Full name
- Social Security number

- Date and place of birth
- Driver's license number
- Passport number
- Credit card numbers
- Addresses
- Telephone numbers
- Email addresses
- Login credentials and passwords

NIST goes on to identify *linkable PII*, which is information that you can use in combination with other identifying information to identify, trace, or locate an individual. For example, suppose you have access to medical, educational, financial, or employment information. Data elements like country, state, city, zip code, gender, and race are all examples of linkable PII, as you can join that data to identify a person, as shown in Figure 6.13.

Protected Health Information

In the United States, the *Health Insurance Portability and Accountability Act* (*HIPAA*) is a comprehensive healthcare law that regulates the security and privacy of health data. HIPAA applies to two categories of information.

Under HIPAA, *Protected Health Information* (*PHI*) is the broad category of data elements identifying an individual's health information. This information can be about the individual's past, current, or future health status and covers providing healthcare, processing healthcare payments, or processing insurance claims. Alternatively, *Electronic Protected Health Information*, or *e-PHI*, is any PHI you store or transmit digitally.

Exam Tip

The CompTIA exam objectives use the acronym PHI to mean "personal health information." However, HIPAA and common usage define it as "protected health information." This difference doesn't alter the meaning or intent of the rules governing this information, so you should treat them both as meaning the same thing if you see either one on the exam.

While HIPAA is a broad regulation, under the *Privacy Rule* provision, it identifies eighteen data elements as PHI:

- Names
- All geographic identifiers smaller than a state, including street address, city, county, precinct, and zip code
- Dates other than year that relate to an individual, including birth date, admission date, date of treatment, etc.
- Telephone numbers

- Fax numbers
- Email addresses
- Social Security numbers
- Medical record numbers
- Health plan beneficiary numbers
- Account numbers
- Certificate or license numbers
- Vehicle identifiers and serial numbers, including license plate
- Device identifiers and serial numbers
- Web uniform resource locators (URLs)
- Internet protocol (IP) address numbers
- Biometric identifiers, including finger, retinal, voice, and facial prints
- Full-face photographs and any comparable images
- Any other unique identifying number, characteristic, or code, unless otherwise permitted by the Privacy Rule for reidentification

The rules around zip codes are slightly more complex. The first three digits of a zip code are not PHI. However, if all zip code combinations with the same first three digits contain fewer than 20,000 people according to the Bureau of Census, then the first three digits are PHI.

As you can tell by the list of data elements, PHI has a broad scope by design. However, there are two provisions in place if you need to share medical data without patient consent. The first is *Expert Determination*, where you use statistical and scientific principles or methods to make the risk of identifying an individual very small. The second is *Safe Harbor*, where you de-identify a data set by removing any PHI data elements.

Another aspect of HIPAA to be aware of is the *Security Rule*, which applies solely to e-PHI. While the Privacy Rule focuses on protecting patient privacy, the objective of the Security Rule is to ensure the confidentiality, integrity, and availability of e-PHI data. The Security Rule exists to ensure that digital records are in a secure location, that access is limited to authorized parties, and that systems and processes are in place to prevent unauthorized access or accidental disclosure.

The PHI provisions of HIPAA apply only to covered entities. A *covered entity* is an organization legally obligated under HIPAA to protect the privacy and security of health information. There are three different types of covered entities under HIPAA. They are:

- Healthcare providers (physicians, hospitals, clinics, etc.)
- Health insurance plans
- Healthcare information clearinghouses

Under HIPAA, several electronic transactions qualify as e-PHI. If a provider engages in any of these transactions in electronic form, they are a covered entity. These transactions include:

- Payment and remittance advice
- Claims status

- Eligibility
- Coordination of benefits
- Claims and encounter information
- Enrollment and disenrollment
- Referrals and authorizations
- Premium payment

Since this list has a broad scope, most medical facilities are considered covered entities.

HIPAA also extends beyond covered entities to business partners who handle PHI on the covered entity's behalf. HIPAA requires that covered entities enter into special agreements known as Business Associate Agreements with their partners. A *Business Associate Agreement* (*BAA*) requires that the business partner also complies with HIPAA provisions. For example, if you use cloud-based storage, the provider you use is a business partner under HIPAA.

It is vital to understand that information about an individual's health does not automatically imply that the data is governed by HIPAA, as there are three important exceptions to HIPAA. These exceptions include:

- Employment records
- Student educations that are covered by the Family Educational Rights and Privacy Act (FERPA)
- De-identified data

The laws surrounding PHI are complex. If you work in healthcare or with health-related data, you need to understand the Privacy Rule and Security Rule deeply. It is best to work with attorneys who specialize in the field if you have any doubts about PHI, processing, storing, and protecting e-PHI, or working with partners that require a BAA.

Payment Card Information

The *Payment Card Industry* (*PCI*) is a nongovernmental body that governs card-based financial payments. To protect the integrity of card-based financial transactions and to prevent fraud, leading financial service companies, including MasterCard, Visa, Discover, American Express, and the Japan Credit Bureau, created the *PCI Security Standards Council* (*PCI SSC*). The PCI SSC develops policies to govern the processing, transmission, and storage of electronic payments.

The *PCI Data Security Standard* (*PCI DSS*) is the industry's core information security standard. The following six principles encompass the objectives set out by the PCI DSS:

- Building and maintaining a secure network
- Protecting cardholder data
- Maintaining a vulnerability management program
- Implementing strong access controls
- Regularly monitoring and testing networks
- Maintaining an information security policy

While all of the PCI DSS objectives ensure the security of financial transactions, understanding what it means to protect cardholder data is vital from a data governance point of view. In terms of data classification, there are two primary categories according to PCI DSS. The first category is *Cardholder Data (CHD)*. Cardholder Data includes data from the front of a card, including the cardholder's name, primary account number, and expiration date. The service code, a three- or four-digit number encoded on the magnetic stripe, is also Cardholder Data.

The second category is *Sensitive Authentication Data (SAD)*. SAD includes complete track data from the magnetic stripe or embedded chip, Personal Identification Number (PIN), and the Card Verification Value (typically three digits on the back of a card).

The crucial thing to understand from a data governance perspective is that under PCI DSS, you can store Cardholder Data but cannot store Sensitive Authentication Data. Similar to PHI, complying with the PCI DSS is complex. If you need to process, transmit, or store electronic payment information, you must have a comprehensive understanding of PCI DSS. It is best to work with PCI DSS specialists if you have any doubts about complying with the PCI DSS objectives.

Regional Requirements

As you think through data governance, you must understand the impact of industry and governmental regulations on your organization. When thinking through regulatory and legal compliance obligations, there are four categories for you to consider. These categories include criminal law, civil law, administrative law, and private regulations.

The goal of *criminal law* is to discourage people from acting in a way that negatively impacts society. A legislative body creates criminal laws at the national, state, or local level. Legislative bodies include the United States Congress and state legislatures. There is a broad range of criminal offenses, including hacking, insider trading, espionage, robbery, and murder. One exclusive characteristic of criminal law is that punishment can include the deprivation of liberty, such as a jail sentence or probation.

The goal of *civil law* is to resolve disputes between individuals, organizations, and government agencies. Like criminal laws, a legislative body creates civil laws, which encompass almost anything not addressed by criminal law. For instance, civil law covers contractual disputes and liability claims. Instead of jail time, outcomes from civil lawsuits are typically monetary damages or orders by the court to perform or refrain from a specific action.

The goal of *administrative law* is to enable the effective operation of government by allowing government administrative agencies to propagate regulations. Administrative regulations frequently provide details missing from the criminal or civil law. For example, civil laws in the United States allow disabled individuals to receive government assistance. The Social Security Administration (SSA) is the administrative agency that implements social security and disability laws. In the United States, the Code of Federal Regulations (CFR) defines administrative law.

The goal of *private industry regulations* is to govern activities of individuals and organizations without the force of law. However, it is common for contracts to specify compliance with nongovernmental regulations. For example, if you process electronic payments, you will find language that ensures compliance with PCI DSS as part of the contract.

Especially for organizations that operate internationally, it is vital to understand the government with jurisdiction over your operations. Jurisdiction influences how and where to handle regulatory, administrative, civil, or criminal disputes. For example, the European Union has a law called the *General Data Protection Regulation* (*GDPR*). The goal of GDPR is to give individuals control over how their personal data is collected, stored, and used. GDPR is one of the strictest privacy and security laws in the world. If you have operations in Europe, GDPR applies. However, if you only operate within the United States, there is no legal obligation to comply with GDPR.

Remember that there are many different laws in many different jurisdictions around the world. As a data professional, you should be familiar with the global, national, and regional regulations that affect the data you store, process, and transmit.

Breach Reporting Requirements

Despite people's best efforts, data breaches do occur. From a data governance standpoint, it is essential to understand how to react to a breach. You also need to understand the reporting obligations to which you are legally or contractually bound. While there are many frameworks to handle breaches, they generally include the following steps:

- Verify the breach.
- Stop the breach.
- Assess the impact of the breach.
- Notify the impacted parties.
- Correct the cause of the breach.
- Conduct a comprehensive review.

Breach reporting requirements vary by data classification. As you can imagine, if an unsecured laptop containing public data gets lost or stolen, there is no obligation to report the event. However, if the breach involves PII, PHI, or payment data, you must escalate to the appropriate authority and notify impacted parties. Of particular note is the *Breach Notification Rule* for HIPAA, which provides a breach definition and notification requirements for individuals, the media, and the Secretary of Health and Human Services.

Within the United States, breach notifications are subject to state-level laws. Laws differ in the number of affected individuals that trigger a breach and the maximum number of days that can elapse before notifying people of the breach. On the other hand, there is greater consistency in the European Union, as the GDPR specifies a maximum seventy-two-hour limit for violation notifications. Understanding the classification of your data, the laws and regulations you are bound to, and the jurisdiction for litigation are all crucial to effective data governance.

Routine Auditing

As you've seen in this chapter, data systems professionals have a lot of serious responsibilities when it comes to data security and regulatory compliance. To stay on top of these responsibilities, data professionals design auditing practices that verify things are working properly. *Audits* apply tests to security controls and determine whether the control is working or whether some improvements are needed. In this section, we'll look at the ways that data professionals can perform data security auditing and code auditing.

Exam Tip

There are many different types of security audits that an organization might perform. That said, the CompTIA DataSys+ Exam objectives focus on four of them: two data security auditing practices and two code auditing practices. The data security audits are of expired accounts and connection requests, while the code audits are of SQL code and credential storage. For that reason, we also focus on those four types of auditing in this chapter. Make sure you're familiar with them when you take the exam!

Expired Accounts

Security administrators must pay careful attention to the permissions and use of end-user accounts to protect against and detect security incidents. This includes monitoring expired accounts to ensure that unused credentials are deactivated and that required accounts function properly. This is part of a broader account management practice.

Administrators should also monitor for inaccurate permissions assigned to accounts that either prevent a user from doing their work or violate the principle of least privilege. These permissions are often the result of privilege creep, a condition that occurs when users switch jobs and gain new permissions but never have their old permissions revoked.

To protect against inaccurate permissions, administrators should perform regular user account audits in cooperation with managers from around the organization. During each of these manual reviews, the administrators should pull a listing of all of the permissions assigned to each account and then review that listing with managers to ensure that it is appropriate for the user's role, making any necessary adjustments. Reviewers should pay careful attention to users who switched jobs since the last account review.

Connection Requests

Database connections come from a variety of sources. Power users and database administrators may have privileges to directly access the database. Applications around the organization may have read-only or read-write access to different tables to carry out their functions. Extract, transform, and load (ETL) jobs may export large amounts of data to populate a data warehouse. And intruders might try to connect to a database to steal or alter sensitive information.

Database administrators should routinely monitor database connection requests, watching for unusual activity. It's not reasonable to expect administrators to watch things 24/7, so automation can play an important role here. The goal is to identify unauthorized use of permissions either by someone other than the legitimate user accessing the account or by the user performing some illegitimate action. Protecting against unauthorized use of permissions is tricky because it can be hard to detect. This requires the use of *continuous account monitoring* systems that watch for suspicious activity and alert administrators to strange actions.

A continuous account monitoring system may flag violations of access policies, such as log-ons from strange geographic locations. For example, the system might flag:

- users connecting from two distant locations at the same time, such as a user connecting from both the home office and a remote location in Eastern Europe at the same time—cases like this are known as *impossible travel time logins* and should be treated as suspicious events.
- log-ons from unusual network locations, such as a user who always logs in from the HR network suddenly appearing on a guest network, and log-ons at unusual times of day, such as a mail clerk logging into the system in the middle of the night.
- deviations from normal behavior, such as users accessing database tables that they do not normally access.
- high volumes of activity that may represent bulk downloading of sensitive information.

The specific circumstances that merit attention will vary from organization to organization, but performing this type of behavior-based continuous account monitoring is an important security control.

SQL Code

As you've discovered throughout this book, SQL code is at the core of the work of data systems professionals. SQL is an incredibly powerful language that can create, retrieve, update, and delete data as well as alter the structure of the database itself. Users and administrators with access to issue SQL commands have immense power and, with this great power comes great responsibility.

Data systems professionals should conduct regular audits of SQL code to ensure that it is properly designed, appropriately permissioned, and functioning normally. These code audits can uncover security, operational, and performance issues.

Credential Storage Checks

Many databases and other IT systems grant access to users and services through the use of passwords, API keys, and other secrets. Managing these secrets is tricky, as they can be easily stolen if not properly secured. For this reason, credentials to sensitive systems should be stored in secure password repositories where they are accessed in real time when they are needed. These systems use technical mechanisms to avoid ever showing a password to a user, preserving the security of that password.

As data systems professionals perform code audits, they should watch for cases where developers have hard-coded passwords, API keys, or other secrets in their code. This practice exposes those secrets to everyone who reviews the code and jeopardizes the security of the system.

Summary

In this chapter, you learned about the data governance, data security, and regulatory compliance issues facing data systems professionals.

Data governance is a set of policies and procedures established by organizations to ensure the safety and use of their data for transactional and analytical purposes. Data stewardship is a key component of data governance, where an organizational data steward is responsible for leading the effort to maintain data quality, security, privacy, and regulatory compliance. Different roles, including data owners, subject area data stewards, and data custodians, work together to execute data governance policies and establish access requirements for data. The data steward works with data owners to develop a data classification matrix, which defines categories and descriptions for data, and with data custodians to implement technical controls for data protection.

Identity and access management (IAM) is a critical aspect of data security and ensures that only authorized individuals have access to information, systems and databases. The access control process consists of three steps: identification, authentication, and authorization. Identification is the claim of identity made by an individual, authentication is the process of proving the identity, and authorization is the process of ensuring that the individual is allowed to access the system. Computer systems offer various authentication techniques including something you know (passwords), something you are (biometric authentication), and something you have (authentication token). To ensure maximum security, multifactor authentication is often used by combining two or more authentication factors. In implementing a password policy, organizations should require strong passwords and consider setting a password expiration policy and limiting the number of password attempts.

Data systems professionals are responsible for protecting the security of information under their control. One of the primary means they use to achieve this goal is the use of encryption to protect both data at rest (stored on a system) and data in motion (being sent over a network). They must also ensure that organizations remain compliant with the local, national, and global laws and regulations affecting their businesses.

Exam Essentials

Understand the use of encryption to protect sensitive information. Encryption is the process of encoding data with a key so that only authorized parties can read it. Once encrypted, you can only access the data by decrypting it with a valid key. If you lose the encryption key, any data encrypted with that key becomes useless. To keep data secure, you must encrypt data at rest as well as data in transit. Data at rest is data that exists in permanent storage. Data in transit is data that is beign sent over a network.

Describe the four types of audits performed by data systems professionals. Expired account audits focus on monitoring and revoking unused credentials and ensuring accurate permissions. Connection request audits monitor for unusual activity and unauthorized use of permissions through continuous account monitoring systems. SQL code audits ensure the proper design, permissioning, and functionality of SQL code. Credential storage checks monitor for the safe storage of passwords and secrets to avoid exposure.

Explain the purpose of governance and regulatory compliance. Data systems professionals must ensure that their organization's information handling practices comply with local, national, and global laws and regulations. Personally identifiable information (PII) includes any information that uniquely identifies an individual person. PII is regulated by the GDPR in the European Union. Personal health information (PHI) includes medical records regulated by HIPAA in the United States. Credit and debit card data is regulated globally by PCI DSS.

Explain the major components of an identity and access management program. Identity and access management systems perform three major functions: identification, authentication, and authorization. Identification is the process of a user making a claim of identity, such as by providing a username. Authentication allows the user to prove their identity. Authentication may be done using something you know, something you have, or something you are. Multifactor authentication combines different authentication techniques to provide stronger security. Authorization ensures that authenticated users may only perform actions necessary to carry out their assigned responsibilities.

Review Questions

1. Victoria's organization has a disconnect between the human resources function and the information security function. As a result, employee transfers are not being properly handled. What is the greatest security risk resulting from this situation?
   - **A.** Privilege escalation
   - **B.** Separation of duties
   - **C.** Privilege creep
   - **D.** Two-person control
2. Which of these roles is assigned to an information technology professional who implements technical controls to further data governance objectives?
   - **A.** Data owner
   - **B.** Data custodian
   - **C.** Data janitor
   - **D.** Data steward
3. Eve is classifying data that is part of the interface between her organization and their health insurance provider. One of the fields in the data set is Social Security number. What data classification is most appropriate?
   - **A.** Public
   - **B.** Internal
   - **C.** Sensitive
   - **D.** Highly Sensitive
4. Silas works in communications and has been asked to classify the assets on the organization's externally-facing website. What data classification is most appropriate?
   - **A.** Public
   - **B.** Internal
   - **C.** Sensitive
   - **D.** Highly Sensitive
5. Clarence is developing a data access strategy for his organization which consists of 150 people across 5 groups, with 3 roles in each group. How many roles should Clarence expect to create to appropriately safeguard the data?
   - **A.** 3
   - **B.** 5
   - **C.** 15
   - **D.** 150

6. Zeke wants to protect his organization's data. What precautions should he take for cloud-based storage?
   A. Encryption at rest
   B. Encryption in transit
   C. Encryption at rest and in transit
   D. User-based encryption
7. Maxine is completing some new-hire paperwork using a form on the web. What should she do to ensure the connection is encrypted?
   A. Use HTTP.
   B. Use the Chrome browser.
   C. Check for HTTPS in the address bar.
   D. Check that the padlock icon is closed.
8. Zaid needs to share medical imagery data with a partner who is developing a machine learning model to identify cancer. What does Zaid need to do to ensure privacy? Choose the best answer.
   A. De-identify the data.
   B. Sort the data in random order.
   C. Encrypt the data.
   D. Aggregate the data.
9. Fred has two de-identified data sets. The first contains medical treatment data, and the other contains biographic information. The zip code, sex, and birth date exist in both data sets. Is personal privacy at risk? Choose the best answer.
   A. No, the data is de-identified.
   B. No, the data sets are separate.
   C. Yes, reidentification is possible using zip code, sex, and birth date.
   D. Yes, reidentification is possible because one of the data sets has biographic information.
10. Which of the following is not considered PII?
    A. Passport number
    B. Favorite food
    C. Address
    D. Credit card number
11. Which of the following is considered Sensitive Authentication Data by the PCI DSS?
    A. PIN
    B. Name
    C. Account number
    D. Expiration Date

12. Tom is building a multifactor authentication system that requires users to enter a passcode and then verifies that their face matches a photo stored in the system. What two factors is this system using?
    - A. Something you know and something you have
    - B. Somewhere you are and something you have
    - C. Something you have and something you are
    - D. Something you know and something you are
13. Gary is logging into a system and is providing his fingerprint to gain access. What step of the IAM process is he performing?
    - A. Identification
    - B. Authorization
    - C. Authentication
    - D. Accounting
14. Gwen recently discovered that sensitive API keys were located in a public code repository. What type of audit would detect this issue?
    - A. Expired account audit
    - B. Connection request audit
    - C. SQL code audit
    - D. Credential storage audit
15. Mike is worried that Social Security numbers are used throughout his organization, and he would like to discover cases where they were previously undetected. Which one of the following data loss prevention mechanisms would best meet his needs?
    - A. Host-based DLP
    - B. Network-based DLP
    - C. Pattern matching DLP
    - D. Watermarking DLP
16. Which of the following best describes the purpose of data masking in a data security framework?
    - A. To encrypt data for storage in a secure database
    - B. To prevent unauthorized access to sensitive data by making it unreadable
    - C. To make a copy of production data for use in non-production environments
    - D. To securely destroy data when it is no longer needed
17. Brian works for a company that handles the personal information of European Union residents. What law likely applies to this data?
    - A. GDPR
    - B. HIPAA
    - C. GLBA
    - D. PCI DSS

18. Andy is attempting to change his password and has created the following long password: p7djkqnr2LAD

    He receives an error message that he must use a symbol in his password. What password policy is he failing to meet?

    A. Password length
    B. Password history
    C. Password complexity
    D. Password reuse

19. You recently learned that a website belonging to one of your competitors was breached and you are concerned that users with accounts on both sites will have their passwords compromised on your site as well. Which one of the following password policies would best protect against this risk?

    A. Password reuse
    B. Password complexity
    C. Password length
    D. Password history

20. Renee is concerned that unauthorized applications may be retrieving information from her database. What type of audit would detect this issue?

    A. Expired account audit
    B. Connection request audit
    C. SQL code audit
    D. Credential storage audit

Chapter 7

Database Security

THE COMPTIA DATASYS+ EXAM TOPICS COVERED IN THIS CHAPTER INCLUDE:

✓ **Domain 4.0 Data and Database Security**

- 4.4. Explain the Purpose of Database Infrastructure Security
- 4.5. Describe Types of Attacks and Their Effects on Data Systems

Data systems professionals work hand in hand with cybersecurity professionals to protect the confidentiality, integrity, and availability of the data and systems under their care. Effectively carrying out this shared responsibility requires a strong understanding of the security issues affecting data systems. In this chapter, we explore database infrastructure security as well as the different types of attacks commonly waged against data systems. Technologists with a strong understanding of the threat environment will find themselves well prepared to defend their systems against those threats.

Database Infrastructure Security

Protecting databases against attack requires controls that work in two dimensions. First, database professionals must coordinate with physical security teams to ensure that databases are housed in secure locations. Second, they must coordinate with cybersecurity experts to build a set of logical security controls that adequately protect data and systems from technical attacks.

Physical Security

While technology professionals often focus on technical controls, one of the most important lines of defense for an organization is the set of physical controls that it puts in place. Physical access to systems, facilities, and networks is one of the best ways to circumvent technical controls, whether by directly accessing a machine, stealing drives or devices, or plugging into a trusted network to bypass layers of network security control keeping it safe from the outside world.

Site Security

The first step in preventing physical access is by implementing a site security plan. Site security looks at the entire facility or facilities used by an organization and implements a security plan based on the threats and risks that are relevant to each specific location. That means that facilities used by an organization in different locations will typically have different site security plans and controls in place.

Some organizations use *industrial camouflage* to help protect them. A common example is the nondescript location that companies pick for their call centers. Rather than making the call center a visible location for angry customers to seek out, many are largely unmarked and otherwise innocuous. While security through obscurity is not a legitimate technical control, in the physical world, being less likely to be noticed can be helpful in preventing many intrusions that might not otherwise happen.

Many facilities use fencing as a first line of defense. *Fences* act as both a deterrent by making it look challenging to access a facility, as well as providing an actual physical defense. Highly secure facilities will use multiple lines of fences, with barbed wire or razor wire at the top, and other techniques to increase the security provided by the fence. Fence materials, the height of the fence, the placement and design of entrances, as well as a variety of other factors are all taken into consideration for security fencing.

Lighting plays a part in exterior and interior security. Bright lighting that does not leave shadowed or dark areas is used to discourage intruders and to help staff feel safer. Automated lighting can also help to indicate where staff are active, allowing security guards and other staff members to know where occupants are.

Physical Access Control

Inside a facility, physical security is deployed in layers designed to allow authorized individuals access to an area while denying access to unauthorized individuals. Organizations use many different technologies to achieve this goal.

Badges

Badges can play a number of roles in physical security. In addition to being used for entry access via magnetic stripe and radio frequency (RFID) access systems, badges often include a picture and other information that can quickly allow personnel and guards to determine whether the person is who they say they are, what areas or access they should have, and whether they are an employee or guest. This also makes badges a target for social engineering attacks by attackers who want to acquire, copy, or falsify a badge as part of their attempts to get past security. Badges are often used with *proximity readers*, which use RFID to query a badge without requiring it to be inserted or swiped through a magnetic stripe reader.

Alarms

Alarms and alarm systems are used to detect and alert about issues, including unauthorized access, environmental problems, and fires. Alarm systems may be local or remotely monitored and can vary significantly in complexity and capabilities. Much like alerts from computer-based systems, alarms that alert too often or with greater frequency are likely to be ignored, disabled, or worked around by staff. In fact, some penetration testers will even find ways to cause alarms to go off repeatedly so that when they conduct a penetration test and the alarm goes off, staff will not be surprised and won't investigate the alarm that the penetration tester actually caused!

Signage

Signage may not immediately seem like a security control, but effective signage can serve a number of purposes. It can remind authorized personnel that they are in a secure area and that others who are not authorized should not be permitted to enter and should be reported if they are seen. It can also serve as a deterrent control such as signs that read "authorized personnel only." Much like many other deterrent controls, signs act to prevent those who might casually violate the rules the sign shows, not those actively seeking to bypass the security controls an organization has in place.

It's a good idea to include a contact telephone number on any signs so that people know who to call in the event of a suspected security breach.

Access Control Vestibules

Some organizations use *access control vestibules* as a means to ensure that only authorized individuals gain access to secure areas and that attackers do not use piggybacking attacks to enter places they shouldn't be. A mantrap is a pair of doors that both require some form of authorized access to open. The first door opens after authorization and then closes, and only after it is closed can the person who wants to enter provide their authorization to open the second door. This means a person following behind (piggybacking) will be noticed—and presumably will be asked to leave or will be reported.

Locks

Locks are one of the most common physical security controls you will encounter. A variety of lock types are commonly deployed, ranging from traditional physical locks that use a key, push buttons, or other code entry mechanisms to locks that use biometric identifiers like fingerprints, or electronic mechanisms connected to computer systems with card readers or passcodes associated with them. Locks can be used to secure spaces, devices, or to limit access to those who can unlock them. Cable locks are a common solution to ensure that devices like computers or other hardware are not removed from a location.

Biometrics

In addition to standard locks, physical facilities may also be protected with biometric access controls. As we discussed in Chapter 6, "Governance, Security, and Compliance," these biometric controls measure some physical aspect of an individual's body to confirm their identity. Biometric security controls used in a physical setting may include eye scans, fingerprint readers, hand geometry scanners, or any other mechanism that uniquely identifies a person. Biometric access controls ("something you are") are often used in conjunction with a personal identification number ("something you know") or identification card ("something you have") to achieve multifactor authentication for facility access.

Environmental Protection

Environmental controls ensure that data center facilities are physically suitable for housing sensitive electronic equipment and are prepared for physical disasters, such as fires. Data systems professionals should ensure that their systems are housed in facilities with appropriate controls to ensure the ongoing availability of their databases.

Fire Suppression

Fire suppression systems are an important part of safety systems that help with resilience by reducing the potential for disastrous fires. One of the most common types of fire suppression system is sprinkler systems. There are four major types.

- **Wet sprinkler** systems have water in them all the time.
- **Dry sprinklers** remain empty until needed.
- **Pre-action sprinklers** fill when a potential fire is detected and then release at specific sprinkler heads as they are activated by heat.
- **Deluge sprinklers** remain empty with open sprinkler heads until they are activated and then quickly cover a large area.

Water-based sprinkler systems are not the only type of fire suppression system in common use. Gaseous agents which displace oxygen, reduce heat, or help prevent the ability of oxygen and materials to combust are used, often in areas where water might not be a viable or safe option such as data centers, vaults, and art museums. Chemical agents, including both wet and dry agents, are used as well, with examples including foam-dispensing systems used in airport hangars and dry-chemical fire extinguishers used in homes and other places.

Cooling

Electronic equipment generates a significant amount of heat and, if a data center does not have appropriate cooling equipment, the facility can become extremely hot. Excessive heat can dramatically reduce the expected life of servers and other electronic equipment, so data center facility managers invest heavily in maintaining a temperature friendly to that equipment. This investment requires massive cooling systems, such as the one shown in Figure 7.1 on a data center roof.

FIGURE 7.1 Cooling equipment on a data center roof

The current standards for data center cooling come from the American Society of Heating, Refrigeration, and Air Conditioning Engineers (ASHRAE). ASHRAE experts now recommend what's called the *expanded environmental envelope* that permits maintaining data centers at a temperature in the range between 64.4–80.6 degrees Fahrenheit.

Data centers design facilities around the use of *hot aisles* and *cold aisles*. This approach allows data centers to more efficiently house servers and other devices that generate large amounts of heat and require cool air intake. A hot aisle/cold aisle design places air intakes and exhausts on alternating aisles to ensure proper airflow, allowing data center designers to know where to provide cool air and where exhaust needs to be handled.

Humidity

Temperature isn't the only concern in managing the data center environment. Facilities' staff must also carefully manage the humidity in the data center. If the humidity in the room is too high, condensation forms, and water is definitely not the friend of electronic equipment! If the humidity falls too low, static electricity builds up, which can be just as damaging.

Environmental specialists measure data center humidity using the dew point and recommend maintaining the facility at a dew point somewhere between 41.9–50.0 degrees Fahrenheit. That's the sweet spot that keeps both condensation and static electricity away.

You can calculate the dew point using tools such as the online calculator available at `www.calculator.net/dew-point-calculator.html`.

Of course, we need to do more than monitor the temperature and humidity environment in our data centers. *Heating, ventilation, and air conditioning (HVAC)* systems allow us to control temperature and humidity, keeping them within acceptable ranges.

Surveillance Systems

Secure data centers also provide the ability to monitor and record the activity of people inside the facility. This includes the use of security guards, cameras, and other sensors.

Guards

Security guards are used in areas where human interaction is either necessary or helpful. Guards can make decisions that technical control systems cannot. They can also provide both detection and response capabilities. Guards are commonly placed in reception areas and are deployed to roam around facilities, as well as being stationed in security monitoring centers with access to cameras and other sensors.

Visitor logs are a common control used in conjunction with security guards. A guard can validate an individual's identity, ensure that they only enter the areas they are supposed to be in, and that they have signed a visitor log and that their signature matches a signature on file or on their ID card. While each of these can be faked, an alert security guard can significantly increase the security of a facility.

Security guards also bring their own challenges, as humans can be fallible, and social engineering attempts can persuade guards to violate policies or even to provide attackers with assistance. Guards are also relatively expensive, requiring ongoing pay, while technical security controls are typically installed and maintained at lower costs. This means that guards are a solution that is only deployed where there is a specific need for their capabilities in most organizations.

Cameras and Sensors

Camera systems are a common form of physical security control, allowing security practitioners and others to observe what is happening in real time and to capture video footage of areas for future use when conducting investigations or for other reasons. Cameras come in a broad range of types including black and white, infrared, and color cameras with each type suited to different scenarios. In addition to the type of camera, the resolution of the camera, whether it is equipped with zoom lenses, or a pan/tilt/zoom (PTZ) capability are all factors in how well it works for its intended purpose and how much it will cost. There are three main attributes of camera systems.

- **Motion recognition cameras** activate when motion occurs. These are particularly useful in areas where motion is relatively infrequent and can help to conserve storage space. Motion recognition cameras will normally have a buffer that will be retrieved when motion is recognized so that they will retain a few seconds of video before the motion started so that you can see all of what occurred.
- **Object detection cameras** and similar technologies can detect specific objects or have areas that they watch for changes. These can be useful to ensure that an object is not moved or can detect specific types of objects like a gun or a laptop.
- **Facial recognition systems** not only capture video but can help to recognize individuals.

Cameras are not the only type of sensor system that organizations and individuals will deploy. Common sensor systems include motion, noise, moisture, and temperature detection sensors. Motion and noise sensors are used as security sensors, as well as to turn on or off environment control systems based on occupancy. Temperature and moisture sensors help to maintain data center environments and other areas that require careful control of the environment, in addition to other monitoring purposes.

Logical Security

Networks also play a crucial role in an organization's cybersecurity program. Endpoints, servers, and other devices all rely on the network to communicate with one another. Networks are often trusted to carry sensitive information within an organization. Cybersecurity professionals use a variety of controls to ensure the security of their networks.

Network Segmentation

Well-designed networks group systems into network segments based on their security level. This approach limits the risk that a compromised system on one network segment will be able to affect a system on a different network segment. It also makes it more difficult for a malicious insider to cause the organization damage.

Firewalls

Network *firewalls* serve as the security guards of a network, analyzing all attempts to connect to systems on a network and determining whether the request should be allowed or denied according to the organization's security policy. They also play an important role in network segmentation.

Firewalls often sit at the network perimeter, in between an organization's routers and the Internet. From this network location, they can easily see all inbound and outbound connections. Traffic on the internal network may flow between trusted systems unimpeded, but anything crossing the perimeter to or from the Internet must be evaluated by the firewall.

Typical border firewalls have three network interfaces because they connect three different security zones together, as shown in Figure 7.2.

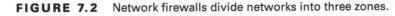

FIGURE 7.2 Network firewalls divide networks into three zones.

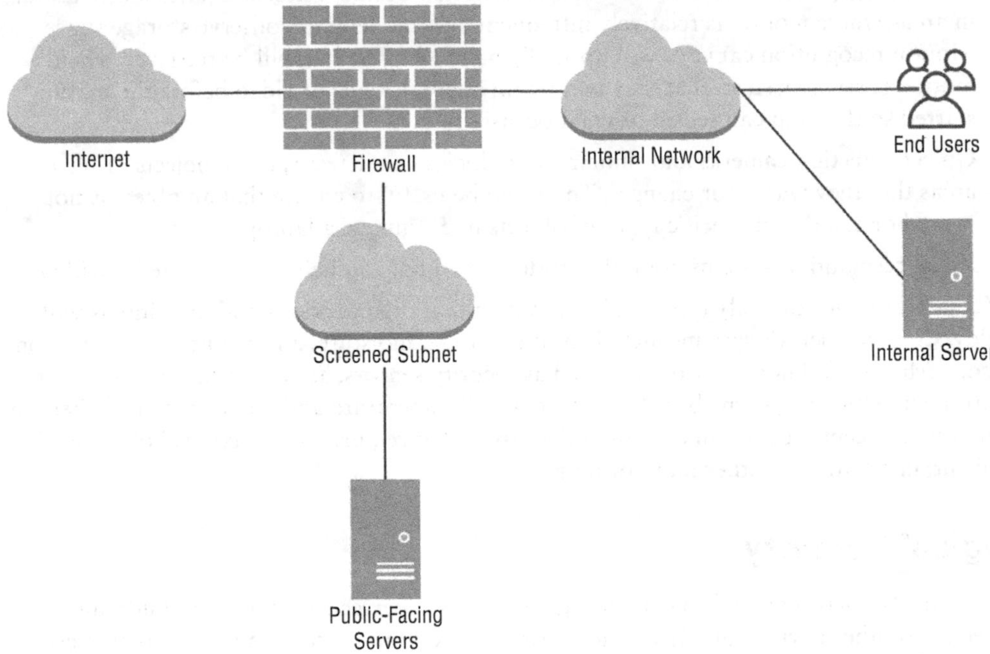

One interface connects to the Internet or another untrusted network. This is the interface between the protected networks and the outside world. Generally speaking, firewalls allow many different kinds of connections out to this network when initiated by a system on more trusted networks, but they block most inbound connection attempts, allowing only those that meet the organization's security policy.

A second interface connects to the organization's *intranet*. This is the internal network where most systems reside. This intranet zone may be further subdivided into segments for endpoint systems, wireless networks, guest networks, data center networks, and other business needs. The firewall may be configured to control access between those subnets, or the organization may use additional firewalls to segment those networks.

The third interface connects to the *screened subnet*. This is a network where you can place systems that must accept connections from the outside world, such as a mail or web server. Those systems are placed in a separate security zone because they have a higher risk of compromise. If an attacker compromises a screened subnet system, the firewall still blocks them from breaching the intranet. This approach is also known as a *screened subnet*.

Previously, network designs using this philosophy often created an implicit trust in systems based on their network security zone. This approach is now going out of style in favor of a security philosophy known as *zero trust*. Under the zero-trust approach, systems do not gain privileges based solely on their network location.

Exam Tip

Databases are almost always found on the internal network. There is rarely a need for a system outside the organization to directly connect to the database, so they should not be placed on a DMZ network.

Virtual LANs

Virtual LANs (*VLANs*) are an important network security control. VLANs allow you to logically group together related systems, regardless of where they normally exist on the network.

When you create diagrams of your desired network layouts, you typically place different functional groups in different network locations. Users in the accounting department, for example, all share a network that is separate from users in the sales department and those in the IT department.

If your building and floor layout matched those network diagrams exactly, you'd be all set. More often than not, though, you usually wind up in a situation where users from different departments are mingled together, and departments are spread across buildings. That's where virtual LANs come into play. You can use them to connect people who are on different parts of the network to one another, while also separating them from other users who might be geographically close.

Virtual LANs extend the broadcast domain, which means that users on the same VLAN will be able to directly contact one another as if they were connected to the same switch. All of this happens at layer two of the network stack, without involving routers or firewalls.

Network Device Security

Networks carry all types of data over distances short and far. Whether it's a transatlantic videoconference or an email across the room, many different networks carry the 1s and 0s that make communications work. Routers and switches are the core building blocks of these networks and require special security attention.

Switches create networks, but they are limited to creating local networks. Routers play a higher-level role, connecting networks together by serving as a central aggregation point for network traffic heading to or from a large network. The router serves as the air traffic controller of the network, making decisions about the best paths for traffic to follow as it travels to its final destination. Routers also perform some security functions, using access control lists to limit the traffic that may enter or leave a network based on the organization's security policies. This type of filtering using access control lists does not pay attention to connection state and is known as *stateless inspection*.

Switches

Network engineers use *switches* to connect devices to networks. They are simple-looking devices that contain a large number of network ports. Switches may be very small, with 8 or fewer ports, or they can be quite large, with 500 or more ports.

Switches are normally hidden away inside wiring closets and other secure locations. Each switch port is connected to one end of a network cable. Those cables then disappear into special pipes known as conduits for distribution around a building.

When the cable reaches the final destination, it usually terminates in a neat-looking wall faceplate. This provides a way for users and technicians to connect and disconnect computers from the network easily without damaging the cables inside the wall or having unsightly unused wires lying about the room.

Some devices directly connect to switch ports through the use of wired networks. Many other devices don't use wires but instead depend on radio-based wireless networks. These networks are created by wireless access points (WAPs). These WAPs contain radios that send and receive network signals to mobile devices. The WAP itself has a wired connection back to the switch, allowing the wireless devices to connect to the rest of the network.

Switch Physical Security

One of the most important security tasks for switches is maintaining physical security of the device. Unlike routers, which are normally centrally located in secure data centers or network rooms, switches are generally spread all over the place, providing connectivity at the edge of the network in every building and floor throughout an organization. From a security perspective, this can be a nightmare because it is critical to keep those switches locked away where nobody can physically access them without authorization. The reason for this is simple: if someone gains access to your switch, they can take control of that portion of the network.

Port Security

Port security protects against attackers disconnecting an authorized device from the wired network and replacing it with a rogue device that may eavesdrop on other users or attempt to access secure network resources. Port security works by limiting the hardware media access control (MAC) addresses that may be used on a particular switch port and requiring administrator intervention to change out a device. Port security works in two modes:

- In *static* mode, the administrator manually configures each switchport with the allowable MAC addresses. This is very time-consuming, but this MAC filtering approach is the most secure way to implement port security.
- In *dynamic*, or "sticky" mode, the administrator enables port security and then tells the switch to memorize the first MAC address that it sees on any given port and then restrict access to that MAC address. This makes configuration much faster but can be risky if you have unused but active switch ports.

Routers

Routers play a higher-level role, connecting networks together by serving as a central aggregation point for network traffic heading to or from a large network. The router makes decisions about the best paths for traffic to follow as it travels to its final destination. The router plays a role on the network that is similar to the way an air traffic controller organizes planes in the sky, sending them to their correct destination.

Routers also play an important role in network security. They are often located both physically and logically between the firewall and another network. Because they see traffic before network firewalls, they can perform filtering that reduces the load on the network firewall. Routers aren't great at performing complex filtering, but network administrators can configure them to perform basic screening of network traffic. Routers share some common functionality with firewalls, but they are definitely not a substitute for firewall technology. Firewalls differ from routers in a number of ways.

- Firewalls are purpose-specific devices and are much more efficient at performing complex filtering than routers.
- Firewalls have advanced rule capabilities. They allow you to create rules that are conditional upon the time of day, users involved, and other criteria.
- Firewalls offer more advanced security functionality. They can incorporate threat intelligence, perform application inspection, and integrate with intrusion prevention systems to provide enhanced protection to a network.

Firewalls do offer advanced security protection, but administrators may still choose to place some access control lists at the router level to filter traffic before it reaches the firewall to reduce the burden on downstream devices.

Routers also allow you to configure *quality of service (QoS)* controls that provide guaranteed bandwidth to high-priority applications. For example, you might prioritize database traffic over routine file transfers.

Database Attacks

Databases often contain very sensitive information and, therefore, become significant targets for attackers seeking to find that valuable data. Data systems professionals must understand the various attacks used against databases to build robust defenses against them.

SQL Injection

Injection attacks occur when an attacker is able to send commands through a web server to a backend system, bypassing normal security controls and fooling the backend system into believing that the request came from the web server. The most common form of this attack is the *SQL injection attack*, which exploits web applications to send unauthorized commands to a backend database server.

Web applications often receive input from users and use it to compose a database query that provides results that are sent back to a user. For example, consider the search function on an e-commerce site. If a user enters **orange tiger pillows** into the search box, the web server needs to know what products in the catalog might match this search term. It might send a request to the backend database server that looks something like this:

```
SELECT ItemName, ItemDescription, ItemPrice
FROM Products
WHERE ItemName LIKE '%orange%' AND
ItemName LIKE '%tiger%' AND
ItemName LIKE '%pillow%'
```

This command retrieves a list of items that can be included in the results returned to the end user. In a SQL injection attack, the attacker might send a very unusual-looking request to the web server, perhaps searching for the following:

```
orange tiger pillow'; SELECT CustomerName, CreditCardNumber FROM Orders; --
```

If the web server simply passes this request along to the database server, it would do this (with a little reformatting for ease of viewing):

```
SELECT ItemName, ItemDescription, ItemPrice
FROM Products
WHERE ItemName LIKE '%orange%' AND
ItemName LIKE '%tiger%' AND
ItemName LIKE '%pillow';
SELECT CustomerName, CreditCardNumber
FROM Orders;
--%'
```

This command, if successful, would run two SQL queries (separated by the semicolon). The first would retrieve the product information, and the second would retrieve a listing of customer names and credit card numbers.

Blind SQL Injection

In the basic SQL injection attack, the attacker is able to provide input to the web application and then monitor the output of that application to see the result. While that is the ideal situation for an attacker, many web applications with SQL injection flaws do not provide the attacker with a means to directly view the results of the attack. However, that does not mean the attack is impossible; it simply makes it more difficult. Attackers use a technique called *blind SQL injection* to conduct an attack even when they don't have the ability to view the results directly. We'll discuss two forms of blind SQL injection: content-based and timing-based.

Blind Content-Based SQL Injection

In a content-based blind SQL injection attack, the perpetrator sends input to the web application that tests whether the application is interpreting injected code before attempting to carry out an attack. For example, consider a web application that asks a user to enter an account number. A simple version of this web page might look like the one shown in Figure 7.3.

FIGURE 7.3 Account number input page

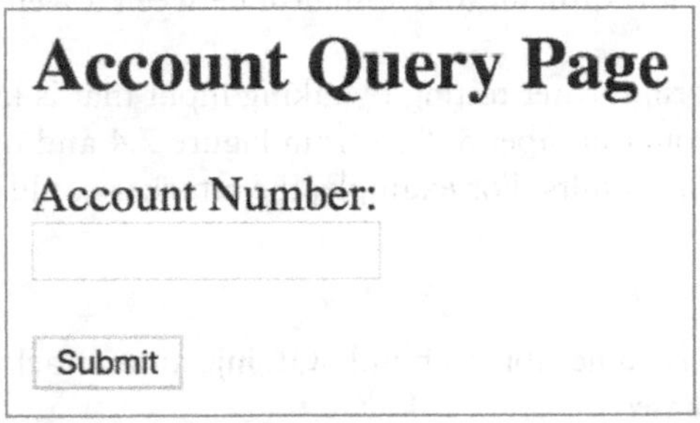

When a user enters an account number into that page, they would next see a listing of the information associated with that account, as shown in Figure 7.4.

FIGURE 7.4 Account information page

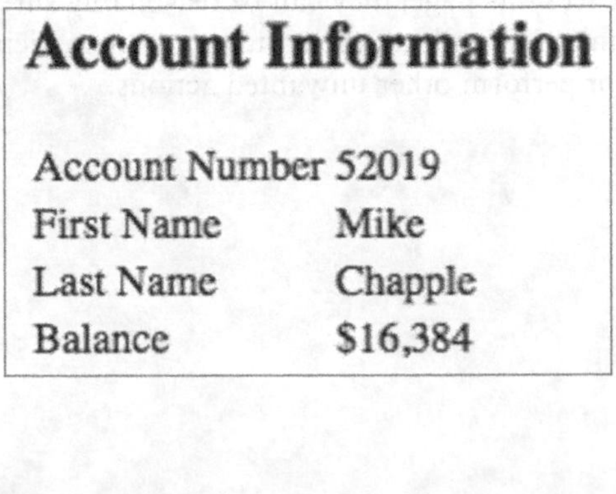

The SQL query supporting this application might be something similar to this:

```
SELECT FirstName, LastName, Balance
FROM Accounts
WHERE AccountNumber = '$account'
```

where the `$account` field is populated from the input field in Figure 7.3. In this scenario, an attacker could test for a standard SQL injection vulnerability by placing the following input in the account number field:

```
52019' OR 1=1;--
```

If successful, this would result in the following query being sent to the database:

```
SELECT FirstName, LastName, Balance
FROM Accounts
WHERE AccountNumber = '52019' OR 1=1
```

This query would match all results. However, the design of the web application may ignore any query results beyond the first row. If this is the case, the query would display the same results as shown in Figure 7.4. While the attacker may not be able to see the results of the query, that does not mean the attack was unsuccessful. However, with such a limited view into the application, it is difficult to distinguish between a well-defended application and a successful attack.

The attacker can perform further testing by taking input that is known to produce results, such as providing the account number 52019 from Figure 7.4 and using SQL that modifies that query to return *no* results. For example, the attacker could provide this input to the field:

```
52019' AND 1=2;--
```

If the web application is vulnerable to blind SQL injection attacks, it would send the following query to the database:

```
SELECT FirstName, LastName, Balance
FROM Accounts
WHERE AccountNumber = '52019' AND 1=2
```

This query, of course, never returns any results, because one is never equal to two! Therefore, the web application would return a page with no results, such as the one shown in Figure 7.5. If the attacker sees this page, they can be reasonably sure that the application is vulnerable to blind SQL injection and can then attempt more malicious queries that alter the contents of the database or perform other unwanted actions.

FIGURE 7.5 Account information page after blind SQL injection

Account Information
Account Number
First Name
Last Name
Balance

Blind Timing-Based SQL Injection

In addition to using the content returned by an application to assess susceptibility to blind SQL injection attacks, penetration testers may use the amount of time required to process a query as a channel for retrieving information from a database.

These attacks depend upon delay mechanisms provided by different database platforms. For example, Microsoft SQL Server's Transact-SQL allows a user to specify a command such as this:

```
WAITFOR DELAY '00:00:15'
```

This would instruct the database to wait 15 seconds before performing the next action. An attacker seeking to verify whether an application is vulnerable to time-based attacks might provide the following input to the account ID field:

```
52019'; WAITFOR DELAY '00:00:15'; --
```

An application that immediately returns the result shown in Figure 7.4 is probably not vulnerable to timing-based attacks. However, if the application returns the result after a 15-second delay, it is likely vulnerable.

This might seem like a strange attack, but it can actually be used to extract information from the database. For example, imagine that the accounts database table used in the previous example contains an unencrypted field named "password." An attacker could use a timing-based attack to discover the password by checking it letter by letter.

The SQL to perform a timing-based attack is a little complex, and you won't need to know it for the exam. Instead, here's some pseudocode that illustrates how the attack works conceptually:

```
For each character in the password
   For each letter in the alphabet
    If the current character is equal to the current letter, wait 15 seconds
    before returning results
```

In this manner, an attacker can cycle through all of the possible password combinations to ferret out the password character by character. This may seem very tedious, but hacker tools automate blind timing-based attacks, making them quite straightforward.

Protecting Against SQL Injection

Cybersecurity professionals and application developers have several tools at their disposal to help protect against injection vulnerabilities. The most important of these is *input validation*. Applications that allow user input should perform validation of that input to reduce the likelihood that it contains an attack.

The most effective form of input validation uses an *input allow list*, in which the developer describes the exact type of input that is expected from the user and then verifies that the input matches that specification before passing the input to other processes or servers. For example, if an input form prompts a user to enter their age, input white-listing could verify that the user supplied an integer value within the range 0–120. The application would then reject any values outside that range.

When performing input validation, it is very important to ensure that validation occurs on the server rather than within the client's browser. Browser-based validation is useful for providing users with feedback on their input, but it should never be relied upon as a security control. Later in this chapter, you'll learn how easily hackers and penetration testers can bypass browser-based input validation.

It is often difficult to perform input allow-listing because of the nature of many fields that allow user input. For example, imagine a classified ad application that allows users to input the description of a product that they wish to list for sale. It would be very difficult to write logical rules that describe all valid submissions to that field that would also prevent the insertion of malicious code. In this case, developers might use *input deny listing* to control user input. With this approach, developers do not try to explicitly describe acceptable input but instead describe potentially malicious input that must be blocked. For example, developers might restrict the use of HTML tags or SQL commands in user input. When performing input validation, developers must be mindful of the types of legitimate input that may appear in a field. For example, completely disallowing the use of a single quote (') may be useful in protecting against SQL injection attacks, but it may also make it difficult to enter last names that include apostrophes, such as O'Reilly.

Parameter Pollution

Input validation techniques are the go-to standard for protecting against injection attacks. However, it's important to understand that attackers have historically discovered ways to bypass almost every form of security control. *Parameter pollution* is one technique that attackers have successfully used to defeat input validation controls.

Parameter pollution works by sending a web application more than one value for the same input variable. For example, a web application might have a variable named `account` that is specified in a URL like this:

```
www.mycompany.com/status.php?account=12345
```

An attacker might try to exploit this application by injecting SQL code into the application.

```
www.mycompany.com/status.php?account=12345' OR 1=1;--
```

However, this string looks quite suspicious to a web application firewall and would likely be blocked. An attacker seeking to obscure the attack and bypass content filtering mechanisms might instead send a command with two different values for `account`.

```
www.mycompany.com/status.php?account=12345&account=12345' OR 1=1;--
```

This approach relies on the premise that the web platform won't handle this URL properly. It might perform input validation on only the first argument but then execute the second argument, allowing the injection attack to slip through the filtering technology.

Parameter pollution attacks depend upon defects in web platforms that don't handle multiple copies of the same parameter properly. These vulnerabilities have been around for a while, and most modern platforms are defended against them, but successful parameter pollution attacks still occur today due to unpatched systems or insecure custom code.

Web Application Firewalls

Web application firewalls (WAFs) also play an important role in protecting web applications against attack. While developers should always rely upon input validation as their primary defense against injection attacks, the reality is that applications still sometimes contain injection flaws. This can occur when developer testing is insufficient or when vendors do not promptly supply patches to vulnerable applications.

WAFs function similarly to network firewalls, but they work with application traffic. A WAF sits in front of a web server, as shown in Figure 7.6, and receives all network traffic headed to that server. It then scrutinizes the input headed to the application, performing input validation (allow-listing and/or deny-listing) before passing the input to the web server. This prevents malicious traffic from ever reaching the web server and acts as an important component of a layered defense against web application vulnerabilities.

FIGURE 7.6 A WAF

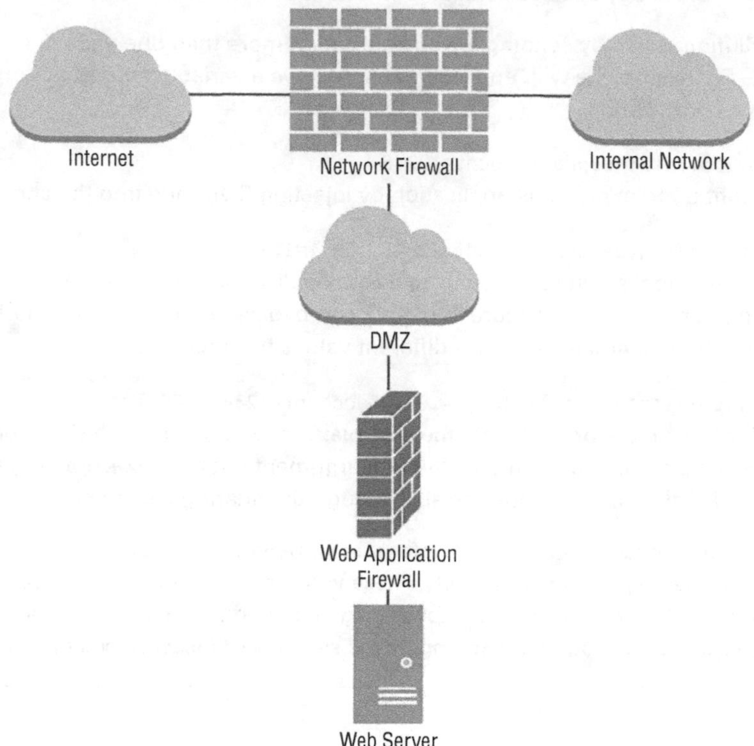

Denial of Service

Most of the attack techniques used by hackers focus on undermining the confidentiality or integrity of data. One of the common goals of attackers is to steal sensitive information, such as credit card numbers or Social Security numbers, or alter information in an unauthorized fashion, such as increasing bank account balances or defacing a website.

Some attacks, however, focus on disrupting the legitimate use of a system. We call these attacks *denial-of-service (DoS)* attacks. These attacks make a system or resource unavailable to legitimate users by sending thousands or millions of requests to a network, server, or application, overwhelming it and making it unable to answer any requests. It is difficult to distinguish well-executed DoS attack requests from legitimate traffic.

There are two significant issues with this basic DoS approach from the attacker's perspective.

- *DoS attacks require large amounts of bandwidth.* Sending lots of requests that tie up the server requires a large network connection. It becomes a case of who has the bigger network connection.
- *DoS attacks are easy to block.* Once the victim recognizes they are under attack, they can simply block the IP addresses of the attackers.

Distributed denial-of-service (DDoS) attacks overcome these limitations by using botnets to overwhelm their target. The attack requests come from many different network locations, so it is difficult to distinguish them from legitimate requests.

DDoS attacks are a serious threat to system administrators because these attacks can quickly overwhelm a network with illegitimate traffic. Defending against them requires security professionals to understand them well and implement blocking technology on the network that identifies and weeds out suspected attack traffic before it reaches servers. This is often done with the cooperation of Internet service providers (ISPs) and third-party DDoS protection services.

On-Path Attacks

An *on-path attack* occurs when an attacker causes traffic that should be sent to its intended recipient to be relayed through a system or device the attacker controls. Once the attacker has traffic flowing through that system they can eavesdrop or even alter the communications as they wish. Figure 7.7 shows how traffic flow is altered from normal after an on-path attack has succeeded.

FIGURE 7.7 On-path attack

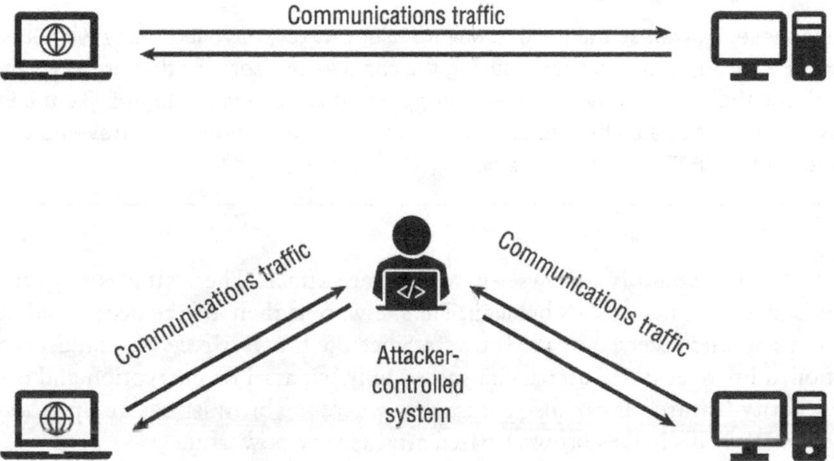

An on-path attack can be used to conduct *SSL stripping*, an attack that in modern implementations actually removes TLS encryption to read the contents of traffic that is intended to be sent to a trusted endpoint. A typical SSL stripping attack occurs in three phases.

1. A user sends an HTTP request for a web page.
2. The server responds with a redirect to the HTTPS version of the page.
3. The user sends an HTTPS request for the page they were redirected to, and the website loads.

An SSL stripping attack uses an on-path attack when the HTTP request occurs, redirecting the rest of the communications through a system that an attacker controls, allowing the communication to be read or possibly modified. While SSL stripping attacks can be conducted on any network, one of the most common implementations is via an open wireless network where the attacker can control the wireless infrastructure, and thus modify traffic that passes through their wireless access point and network connection.

Stopping SSL Stripping and HTTPS On-Path Attacks

Protecting against SSL stripping attacks can be done in a number of ways, including configuring systems to expect certificates for sites to be issued by a known certificate authority, thus preventing certificates for alternate sites or self-signed certificates from working. Redirects to secure websites are also a popular target for attackers, since unencrypted requests for the HTTP version of a site could be redirected to a site of the attacker's choosing to allow for an on-path attack. The HTTP Strict Transport Security, or HSTS security policy mechanism, is intended to prevent attacks like these that rely on protocol downgrades and cookie-jacking by forcing browsers to only connect via HTTPS using TLS. Unfortunately, HSTS only works after a user has visited the site at least once, allowing attackers to continue to leverage MiTM attacks.

Attacks like these, as well as the need to ensure user privacy, have led many websites to require HTTPS throughout the site, reducing the chances of users visiting an HTTP site that introduces the opportunity for an SSL stripping attack. Browser plugins like the EFF's HTTPS Everywhere can also help to ensure that requests that might have traveled via HTTP are instead sent via HTTPS automatically.

A final on-path variant is a browser-based on-path attack. These attacks rely on malware that is inserted into a user's browser. The malware is then able to access and modify information sent and received by the browser. Since the browser receives and decrypts information, a browser-based attack can successfully bypass TLS encryption and other browser security features. It can also access sites where the browser has an open session or saved credentials. This makes browser-based attacks very powerful.

Malware

Malware, or malicious software, is code created by attackers in an effort to undermine security controls. While malware often affects end-user devices, database servers and other data center platforms are vulnerable to these same attacks.

Viruses

Viruses are malicious code objects that spread from system to system after some human action. They might be transported on removable media or spread via email attachments, for example. They carry a malicious payload that carries out the virus author's intent, such as stealing data or disrupting system activity.

Trojan Horses

Trojan horses pretend to be legitimate pieces of software that a user might want to download and install. When the user runs the program, it does perform as expected; however, the Trojan horse also carries a malicious, hidden payload that performs some unwanted action behind the scenes.

Rootkits

The root account is a special super-user account on a system that provides unrestricted access to system resources. It's normally reserved for system administrators, but it's also the ultimate goal of many hackers.

Rootkits are a type of malware that originally were designed for privilege escalation. A hacker would gain access to a normal user account on a system, and then use the rootkit to "gain root," or escalate the normal user access to unrestricted super-user access. Use of the term *rootkit* has changed over the years, however. It is now used to describe software techniques designed to hide other software on a system.

Spyware

Spyware is malware that gathers information without the user's knowledge or consent. It then reports that information back to the malware author, who can use it for any type of purpose, which might be identity theft or access to financial accounts—or even in some cases, espionage. Spyware uses many different techniques.

Keyloggers, or keystroke loggers, are a type of spyware that captures every key a user presses so that they can report everything back to the malware author. Or they might monitor for visits to certain websites and capture the usernames and passwords used to access banks or other sensitive sites.

Ransomware

Ransomware blocks a user's legitimate use of a computer or data until a ransom is paid. The most common way of doing this is encrypting files with a secret key and then selling that key for ransom.

The big question when a ransomware infection occurs is whether you should pay. Your first response might be to say, no, you don't want to pay the malware author. But it's a very difficult question when they're your files that have been encrypted and are no longer accessible. A 2021 survey showed that more than 40 percent of those infected with ransomware actually did pay the ransom, and an analysis of Bitcoin payments for an earlier piece of ransomware called CryptoLocker shows that malware authors have received more than $27 million to date.

Crypto-miners

Crypto-miners are a form of malware that takes over the computing capacity of a user's system and uses that capacity to mine cryptocurrencies, such as Bitcoin, generating revenue for the malware author.

Exam Tip

It's easy to confuse ransomware and crypto-miners because both employ cryptography. Ransomware uses cryptography to encrypt files and demand a ransom from a user. Crypto-miners steal computing capacity from a user's system and use it to mine cryptocurrency. If you get confused, remember that the beginning of the name is what the attacker hopes to get. In ransomware, the attacker hopes to get a ransom, whereas crypto-miners hope to mine cryptocurrency.

Antivirus/Antimalware

You can use the same tools to protect against many different types of malware threats. Modern *antivirus/antimalware* software protects against viruses, worms, Trojan horses, and spyware. Figure 7.8 shows an example of the Windows Security antimalware package provided by Microsoft as part of the Windows operating system.

FIGURE 7.8 Windows Defender Antimalware package

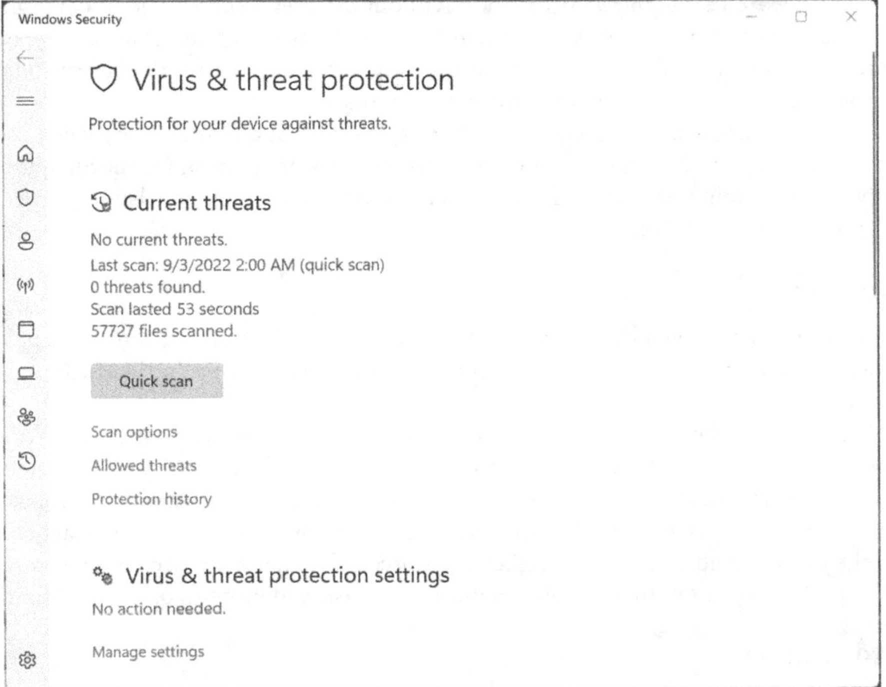

Antivirus software uses two mechanisms to protect systems against malicious software.

- *Signature detection* uses databases of known malware patterns and scans the files and memory of a system for any data matching the pattern of known malicious software. If it finds suspect contents, it can then remove the content from the system or quarantine it for further analysis. When you're using signature detection, it is critical that you frequently update the virus definition file to ensure that you have current signatures for newly discovered malware.
- *Behavior detection* takes a different approach. Instead of using patterns of known malicious activity, these systems attempt to model normal activity and then report when they discover anomalies—activity that deviates from that normal pattern.

Behavioral detection techniques are found in advanced malware protection tools known as *endpoint detection and response (EDR)* solutions. These advanced tools go beyond basic signature detection and perform deep instrumentation of endpoints. They analyze memory and processor usage, Registry entries, network communications, and other system behavior characteristics. They offer advanced real-time protection against malware and other security threats by using agents installed on endpoint devices to watch for signs of malicious activity and trigger automated responses to defend systems from attack.

In addition, EDR tools often have the capability of performing *sand-boxing*. When a system receives a suspicious executable, the advanced malware protection system sends that executable off to a malware sandbox before allowing it to run on the protected system. In that sandbox, the malware protection solution runs the executable and watches its behavior, checking for suspicious activities. If the malware behaves in a manner that resembles an attack, it is not allowed to execute on the protected endpoint.

Phishing

Phishing attacks target sensitive information like passwords, usernames, or credit card information. While most phishing is done via email, there are many related attacks that can be categorized as types of phishing:

- *Vishing*, or voice phishing, is social engineering over the phone system.
- *SMS-phishing*, or smishing, is phishing via SMS messages.
- *Whaling* targets high-profile or important members of an organization, like the CEO or senior vice presidents.
- *Spearphishing* is aimed at specific individuals rather than a broader group.

Regardless of the method or technology used, phishing attempts are aimed at persuading targeted individuals that the message they are receiving is true and real and that they should respond. In many cases, phishing messages are sent to very large populations, since a single mistake is all that is really necessary for the attack to succeed.

User Education

Successful phishing attacks depend on the insecure behavior of individuals. An intentional or accidental misstep by a single user can completely undermine many security controls, exposing an organization to unacceptable levels of risk. Security training programs that include user education regarding common threats help protect organizations against these risks. In particular, they help educate users about how they can avoid falling victim to malware and phishing attacks.

Security education programs include two important components:

- *Security training* provides users with the detailed information they need to protect the organization's security. These may use a variety of delivery techniques, but the bottom-line goal is to impart knowledge. Security training demands time and attention from students.
- *Security awareness* is meant to remind employees about the security lessons they've already learned. Unlike security training, it doesn't require a commitment of time to sit down and learn new material. Instead, it uses posters, videos, email messages, and similar techniques to keep security top-of-mind for those who've already learned the core lessons.

Organizations may use a variety of methods to deliver security training. This may include traditional classroom instruction, providing dedicated information security course material, or it might insert security content into existing programs, such as a new employee orientation program delivered by Human Resources. Students might also use online computer-based training providers to learn about information security or attend classes offered by vendors. Whatever methods an organization uses, the goal is to impart security knowledge that employees can put into practice on the job.

Exam Tip

User education regarding common threats is the best defense in preventing malware.

Anti-phishing Simulation

Anti-phishing simulation programs add an interesting twist. Instead of simply providing security awareness training, the company PhishMe allows you to measure the success of your training efforts by actually conducting simulated phishing attacks. Users receive fake phishing campaigns in their inboxes and, if they respond, they're directed to training materials that warn them of the dangers of phishing and help prevent them from falling victim to a real attack. Backend reporting helps security professionals gauge the effectiveness of their security education efforts by measuring the percentage of users who fall victim to the simulated attack.

Password Attacks

While malware and phishing attacks are often used to acquire passwords or access, there are other ways to attack passwords as well. Everything from trying password after password in a brute-force attack to technical attacks that leverage precomputed password hashes in lookup systems to check acquired password hashes against a known database can help attackers crack passwords.

There are four common attacks used against passwords.

- *Brute-force attacks*, which simply iterate through passwords until they find one that works. Actual brute force methods can be more complex that just using a list of passwords, and often involve word lists which use common passwords, words specifically picked as likely to be used by the target, as well as modification rules to help account for complexity rules. Regardless of how elegant or well thought out their input is, brute force in the end is simply a process that involves trying over and over until it succeeds.
- *Password spraying* attacks are a form of brute-force attack that attempts to use a single password or a small set of passwords against many accounts. This can be particularly effective if you know that a target uses a specific default password or a set of passwords. For example, if you were going to attack a sports team's fan website, common chants for the fans, names of well-known players, and other common terms that were related to the team might be good candidates for a password spraying attack.
- *Dictionary attacks* are yet another form of brute-force attack that uses a list of words for their attempts. Commonly available brute force dictionaries exist, and tools like John the Ripper, a popular open-source password cracking tool have built-in lists of common passwords.
- *Credential-stuffing* attacks depend upon the fact that many users reuse the same passwords from one site to another. The attackers steal a set of usernames and passwords from a website and then use those same username/password combinations to attempt to login to other sites. If a user has the same username and password on the two sites, the attacker gains access to the second account.

Summary

Physical security plays a crucial role in database security by preventing unauthorized access to systems, facilities, and networks, thereby protecting against circumvention of technical controls. Physical security measures include site security, physical access control, badges, alarms, signage, access control vestibules, locks, and biometrics. These measures are implemented through various techniques like fencing, lighting, and door systems, and are designed to allow authorized access while denying access to unauthorized individuals. Physical security is an essential aspect of database security and must be given the same level of attention and resources as technical controls.

Logical security is an important aspect of ensuring the safety and confidentiality of data stored in databases. Firewalls act as security guards, analyzing all connections to systems on a network and allowing or denying them based on the organization's security policy. Virtual LANs allow for logical grouping of related systems and separating them from other users. Routers and switches, the core building blocks of networks, also require special security attention, with routers using access control lists to limit traffic entering or leaving a network and switches connecting devices to networks. Port security helps to prevent unauthorized access to network devices by limiting the number of devices that can connect to a switch port and specifying which MAC addresses are allowed to connect.

Data systems professionals also need to understand different types of attacks against databases so that they can build robust defenses against those attacks. These include SQL injection, where an attacker sends unauthorized commands to a backend database server through a web server; DoS attacks, which focus on disrupting the legitimate use of a system by overwhelming it with thousands or millions of requests; on-path attacks, which occur when an attacker causes traffic to be relayed through a system they control, leading to eavesdropping or altering of communications; brute-force attacks, which rely on trying many passwords or keys in the hope of eventually guessing correctly; phishing, where an attacker tricks a user into revealing sensitive information; and malware, such as viruses, which is code created by attackers to undermine security controls.

Exam Essentials

Know that physical security controls are a first line of defense. Keeping your site secure involves techniques like using industrial camouflage as well as security controls like fences, lighting, alarms, signage, bollards, mantraps, cameras, and other sensors. Ensuring that only permitted staff are allowed in using locks, badges, and guards helps prevent unauthorized visitors. Fire suppression and other environment controls keep systems and devices safe from risks caused by natural or human disasters like fires, floods, or other issues.

Explain how logical security controls protect data systems. Firewalls serve as the first line of defense for networked systems, preventing unauthorized connections to databases and other secure servers. Firewalls create a perimeter network and protect everything inside that perimeter from attack. Network engineers may also use port security controls to limit the systems that may physically connect to switches on the internal network.

Describe how injection vulnerabilities allow attackers to interact with backend systems. SQL injection vulnerabilities are the most common example, allowing an attacker to exploit a dynamic web application to gain access to the underlying database. The best defense against injection vulnerabilities is to perform rigorous input validation on any user-supplied input.

Understand the concepts of DoS and DDoS Attacks. DoS attacks target the availability aspect of the CIA triad and aim to make a system or resource unavailable to legitimate users by overwhelming it with numerous requests. Unlike other types of attacks, DoS attacks focus on disrupting the legitimate use of a system. However, the drawback of basic DoS attacks is that they require a large amount of bandwidth and can easily be blocked. DDoS attacks overcome these limitations by using botnets to overwhelm the target, making it difficult to distinguish attack requests from legitimate requests. DDoS attacks pose a serious threat to system administrators, and defending against them requires understanding the attack techniques and implementing blocking technology to identify and weed out suspected attack traffic.

Understand the concept of on-path attacks and their variants. An on-path attack is a type of attack where an attacker causes traffic that should be sent to its intended recipient to be redirected through a system or device under their control. This enables the attacker to eavesdrop or modify the communications. One of the most well-known on-path attack variants is the SSL stripping attack, in which an attacker removes the TLS encryption from communications to read the contents. Another on-path attack variant is the man-in-the-browser (MitB) attack, in which malware inserted in a user's browser is used to access and modify information sent and received by the browser.

Describe the different types of malware and how they work to undermine the security of systems. Viruses are malicious code objects that spread from one system to another and carry out the intentions of the attacker, such as stealing data or disrupting system activity. Trojan horses appear to be legitimate software but also carry a hidden malicious payload that performs unwanted actions. Rootkits target the special super-user account on a system to gain unrestricted access to system resources. Spyware gathers information without the user's knowledge and reports it back to the attacker for purposes such as identity theft or espionage. Ransomware uses encryption to block access to a system or data until a ransom is paid.

Understand the risk posed to data systems security by phishing attacks and their variants. Phishing attacks target sensitive information like passwords, usernames, or credit card information by tricking the targeted individual into believing that the message they received is true and real. There are various forms of phishing such as vishing (voice phishing via the phone system), smishing (phishing via SMS messages), whaling (aimed at high-profile individuals in an organization), and spearphishing (aimed at specific individuals).

Review Questions

1. Helen would like to configure her organization's switches so that they do not allow systems connected to a switch to spoof MAC addresses. Which one of the following features would be helpful in this configuration?
   A. Loop protection
   B. Port security
   C. Flood guard
   D. Traffic encryption

2. Madhuri wants to implement a camera system but is concerned about the amount of storage space that the video recordings will require. What technology can help with this?
   A. Infrared cameras
   B. Facial recognition
   C. Motion detection
   D. PTZ

3. What factor is a major reason why organizations do not use security guards?
   A. Reliability
   B. Training
   C. Cost
   D. Social engineering

4. Which one of the following approaches, when feasible, is the most effective way to defeat injection attacks?
   A. Browser-based input validation
   B. Input allow-listing
   C. Input deny-listing
   D. Signature detection

5. Examine the following network diagram. What is the most appropriate location for a web application firewall (WAF) on this network?

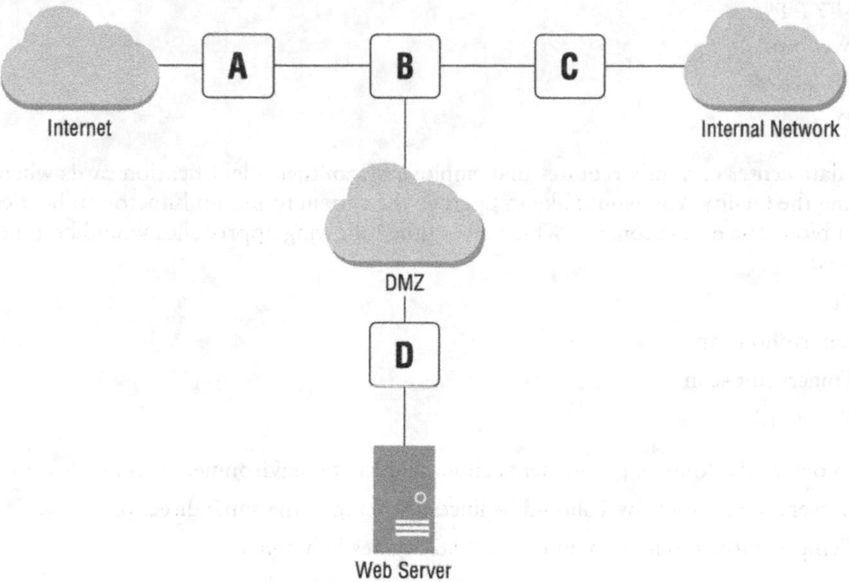

A. Location A
B. Location B
C. Location C
D. Location D

6. Joe is examining the logs for his web server and discovers that a user sent input to a web application that contained the string `WAITFOR`. What type of attack was the user likely attempting?

A. Timing-based SQL injection
B. HTML injection
C. Cross-site scripting
D. Content-based SQL injection

7. Which one of the following network zones is usually the most appropriate location for a database server?

A. Internal network
B. DMZ
C. Internet
D. Screened subnet

8. What type of fire-suppression system dispenses water using only the specific sprinkler heads that are activated by a fire?
   - A. Dry pipe
   - B. Wet pipe
   - C. Pre-action
   - D. Deluge
9. Your data center currently requires that employees scan their identification cards when entering the facility. You would like to upgrade the system to use multifactor authentication with a biometric access control. Which one of the following approaches would best meet this need?
   - A. PIN
   - B. Smartphone app
   - C. Fingerprint scan
   - D. Password
10. Which one of the following statements about data center environmental controls is incorrect?
    - A. Servers in different rows should be lined up facing in the same direction.
    - B. Temperatures should remain below 80.6 degrees Fahrenheit.
    - C. Temperatures should remain above 64.4 degrees Fahrenheit.
    - D. An appropriate dew point would be 45.5 degrees Fahrenheit.
11. Vivian is investigating a website outage that brought down her company's e-commerce platform for several hours. During her investigation, she noticed that the logs are full of millions of connection attempts from systems around the world, but those attempts were never completed. What type of attack likely took place?
    - A. Cross-site scripting
    - B. DDoS
    - C. DoS
    - D. Cross-site request forgery
12. In the image shown here, what type of attack is Mal waging against Alice?

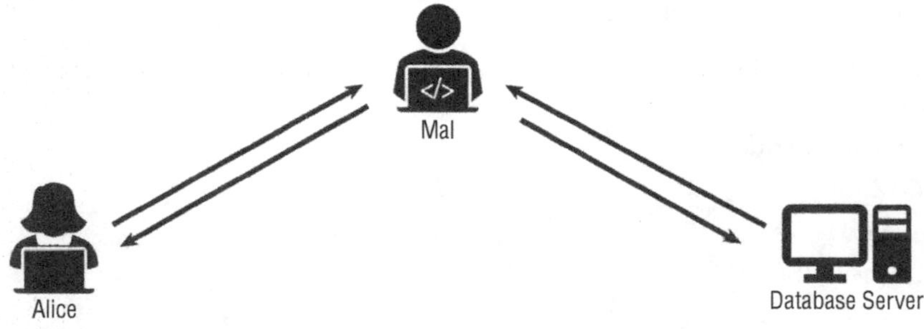

A. On-path attack

B. Social engineering attack

C. Brute-force attack

D. SQL injection attack

13. Fran received a call from her company's help-desk supervisor telling her that customers were receiving email messages informing them of a special promotion available for a limited time. Upon investigating these messages, Fran learned that they were sent by an attacker who somehow gained possession of her organization's customer list. What term best describes this attack?

A. Spearphishing

B. Phishing

C. Whaling

D. SQL injection

14. T. J. is inspecting a system where the user reported a strange error message and the inability to access files. He sees the window shown here. What type of malware should T. J. suspect?

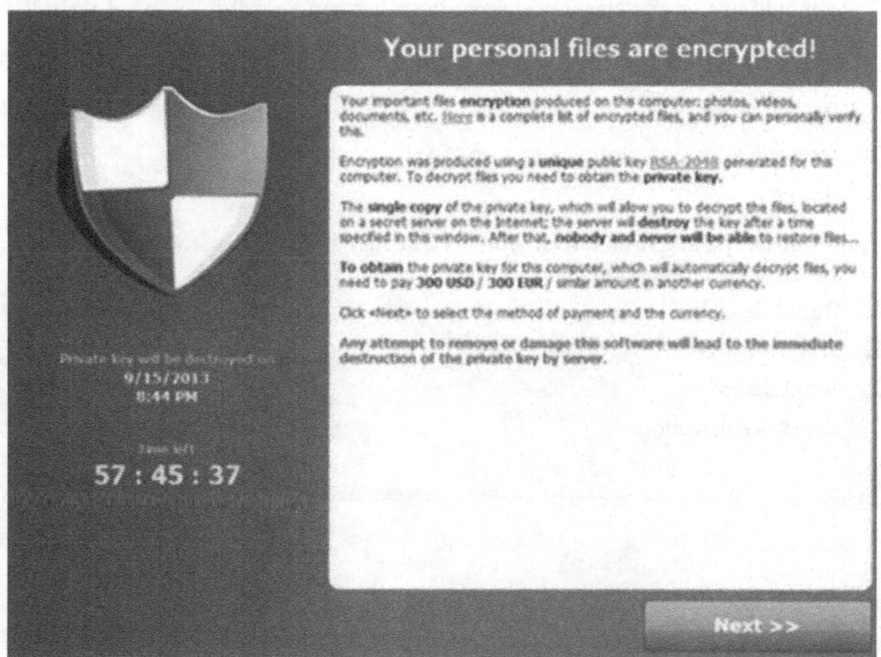

A. Virus

B. Worm

C. Trojan horse

D. Ransomware

15. Kim is the system administrator for a small business network that is experiencing security problems. She is in the office in the evening working on the problem, and nobody else is there. As she is watching, she can see that systems on the other side of the office that were previously behaving normally are now exhibiting signs of infection one after the other. What type of malware is Kim likely dealing with?

   A. Virus

   B. Worm

   C. Trojan horse

   D. Logic bomb

16. What technology is commonly used to logically group related systems on a network regardless of their physical location?

   A. Firewalls

   B. VLANs

   C. Port security

   D. Biometrics

17. Darcy would like to implement port security on her network. Which one of the following network devices can implement this control?

   A. Switch

   B. Router

   C. Firewall

   D. Bridge

18. Ryan is installing antivirus software on his database server. The software is designed to watch for known signs of common malware. What technique is he using?

   A. Rapid detection

   B. Behavior detection

   C. Blind detection

   D. Signature detection

19. Carl is a help-desk technician and received a call from an executive who received a suspicious email message. The content of the email is shown here. What type of attack most likely took place?

Claim Your Tax Refund Online

We identified an error in the calculation of your tax from the last payment, amounting to $ 419.95. In order for us to return the excess payment, you need to create a e-Refund account after which the funds will be credited to your specified bank account.

Please click "Get Started" below to claim your refund:

Get Started

We are here to ensure the correct tax is paid at the right time, whether this relates to payment of taxes received by the department or entitlement to benefits paid.

A. Phishing
B. Whaling
C. Vishing
D. Spearphishing

20. Dorian is investigating an attack where the attacker has large lists of usernames and passwords stolen during attacks against large websites. They then attempted to use those lists to log into systems belonging to Dorian's organization. What type of attack took place?

A. Password-spraying
B. Dictionary attack
C. Brute-force attack
D. Credential-stuffing

Chapter 8 Business Continuity

THE COMPTIA DATASYS+ EXAM TOPICS COVERED IN THIS CHAPTER INCLUDE:

✓ **Domain 5.0: Business Continuity**

- 5.1. Explain the Importance of Disaster Recovery and Relevant Techniques
- 5.2. Explain Backup and Restore Best Practices and Processes

Despite our best intentions, disasters of one form or another eventually strike every organization. Whether it's a natural disaster such as a hurricane, earthquake, or pandemic, or a human-made calamity such as a building fire, burst water pipe, or cybersecurity incident, every organization will encounter events that threaten their operations or even their very existence.

Resilient organizations have plans and procedures in place to help mitigate the effects a disaster has on their continuing operations and to speed the return to normal operations. Disaster recovery (DR) planning implements controls that prevent disruptions and facilitate the restoration of service as quickly as possible after a disruption occurs. The DR plan guides the actions of emergency-response personnel until the end goal is reached—which is to see the business restored to full operating capacity in its primary operations facilities.

The Nature of Disaster

Disaster recovery planning brings order to the chaos that surrounds the interruption of an organization's normal activities. By its very nature, a *disaster recovery plan (DRP)* is designed to cover situations where tensions are already high and cooler heads may not naturally prevail. Picture the circumstances in which you might find it necessary to implement DRP measures—a hurricane destroys your main operations facility; a fire devastates your main processing center; terrorist activity closes off access to a major metropolitan area. Any event that stops, prevents, or interrupts an organization's ability to perform its work tasks (or threatens to do so) is considered a disaster. The moment that information technology (IT) becomes unable to support mission-critical processes is the moment DRP kicks in to manage the restoration and recovery procedures.

A disaster recovery plan should be set up so that it can almost run on autopilot. The DRP should also be designed to reduce decision-making activities during a disaster as much as possible. Essential personnel should be well trained in their duties and responsibilities in the wake of a disaster and also know the steps they need to take to get the organization up and running as soon as possible. We'll begin by analyzing some of the possible disasters that might strike your organization and the particular threats that they pose.

To plan for natural and unnatural disasters in the workplace, you must first understand their various forms, as explained in the following sections.

Natural Disasters

Natural disasters reflect the occasional fury of our habitat—violent occurrences that result from changes in the earth's surface or atmosphere that are beyond human control. In some cases, such as hurricanes, scientists have developed sophisticated predictive models that provide ample warning before a disaster strikes. Others, such as earthquakes, can cause devastation at a moment's notice. A disaster recovery plan should provide mechanisms for responding to both types of disasters, either with a gradual buildup of response forces or as an immediate reaction to a rapidly emerging crisis.

Earthquakes

Earthquakes are caused by the shifting of seismic plates and can occur almost anywhere in the world without warning. However, they are far more likely to occur along known fault lines that exist in many areas of the world. A well-known example is the San Andreas Fault, which poses a significant risk to portions of the western United States. If you live in a region along a fault line where earthquakes are likely, your DRP should address the procedures your business will implement should a seismic event interrupt your normal activities.

The United States Geological Survey (USGS) publishes earthquake hazard information for locations in the United States. A summary map of the risk appears in Figure 8.1. You can consult the USGS to determine more specific earthquake risk information for areas where your organization has physical facilities.

FIGURE 8.1 US earthquake risk map

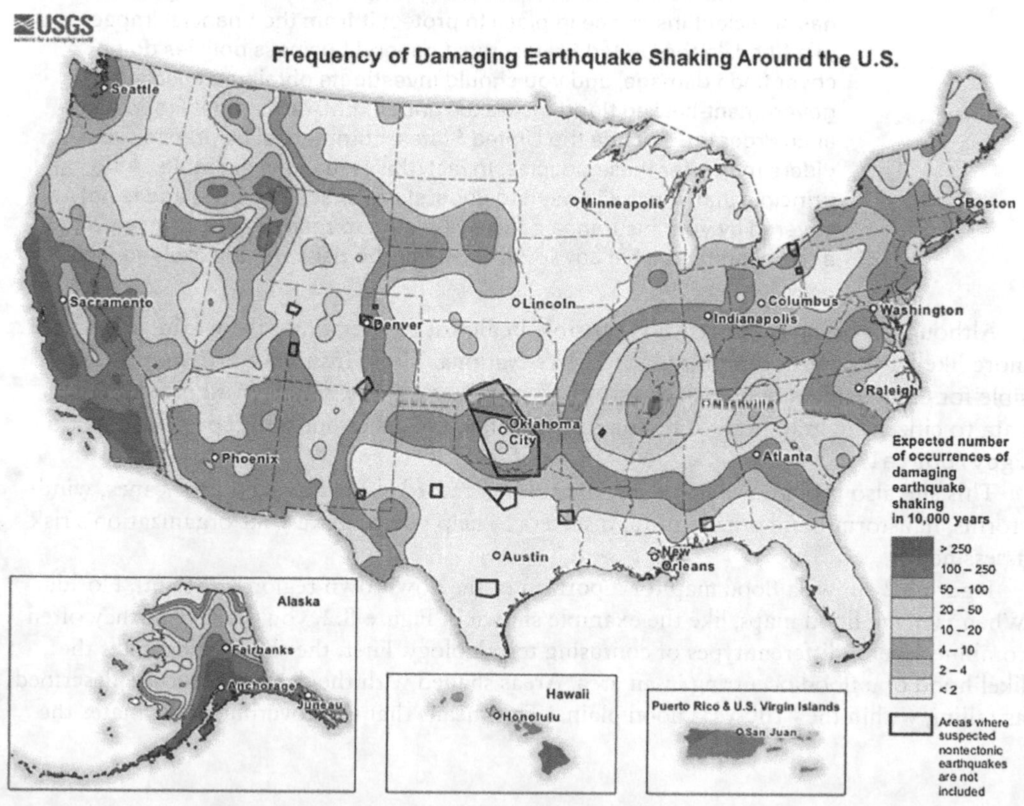

Source: USGS

Floods

Flooding can occur almost anywhere in the world at any time of the year. Some flooding results from the gradual accumulation of rainwater in rivers, lakes, and other bodies of water that then overflow their banks and flood the community. Other floods, known as *flash floods*, strike when a sudden severe storm dumps more rainwater on an area than the ground can absorb in a short period of time. Floods can also occur when dams are breached. Large waves caused by seismic activity, or *tsunamis*, combine the awesome power and weight of water with flooding, as we saw during the 2011 tsunami in Japan. This tsunami amply demonstrated the enormous destructive capabilities of water and the havoc it can wreak on various businesses and economies when it triggered an unprecedented nuclear disaster at Fukushima.

According to government statistics, flooding is responsible for approximately $8 billion (that's billion with a *b*!) in damage to businesses and homes each year in the United States. It's important that your DRP make appropriate response plans for the eventuality that a flood may strike your facilities.

When you evaluate a firm's risk of damage from flooding to develop business continuity and disaster recovery plans, it's also a good idea to check with responsible individuals and ensure that your organization has sufficient insurance in place to protect it from the financial impact of a flood. In the United States, most general business policies do not cover flood damage, and you should investigate obtaining specialized government-backed flood insurance under FEMA's National Flood Insurance Program. Outside the United States, commercial insurance providers may offer these policies. In fact, this is just one example of the principle that you really need to understand exactly what is, and is not, covered by your insurance policies. Be sure to read the fine print carefully and understand what coverage exists for the risks you are likely to face.

Although flooding is theoretically possible in almost any region of the world, it is much more likely to occur in certain areas. FEMA's National Flood Insurance Program is responsible for completing a flood risk assessment for the entire United States and providing this data to citizens in graphical form. You can view flood maps online at `http://msc.fema.gov/portal`.

This site also provides valuable information on recorded earthquakes, hurricanes, windstorms, hailstorms, and other natural disasters to help you prepare your organization's risk assessment.

Figure 8.2 shows a flood map for a portion of the downtown region of Miami, Florida. When viewing flood maps, like the example shown in Figure 8.2, you'll find that they often combine several different types of confusing terminology. First, the shading indicates the likelihood of a flood occurring in an area. Areas shaded with the darkest color are described as falling within the "100-year flood plain." This means that the government estimates the chance of flooding in that area are 1 in 100, or 1.0 percent. Those shaded more lightly lie within the "500-year flood plain," meaning that there is a 1 in 500, or 0.2 percent, annual risk of flood.

FIGURE 8.2 Flood hazard map for Miami–Dade County, Florida

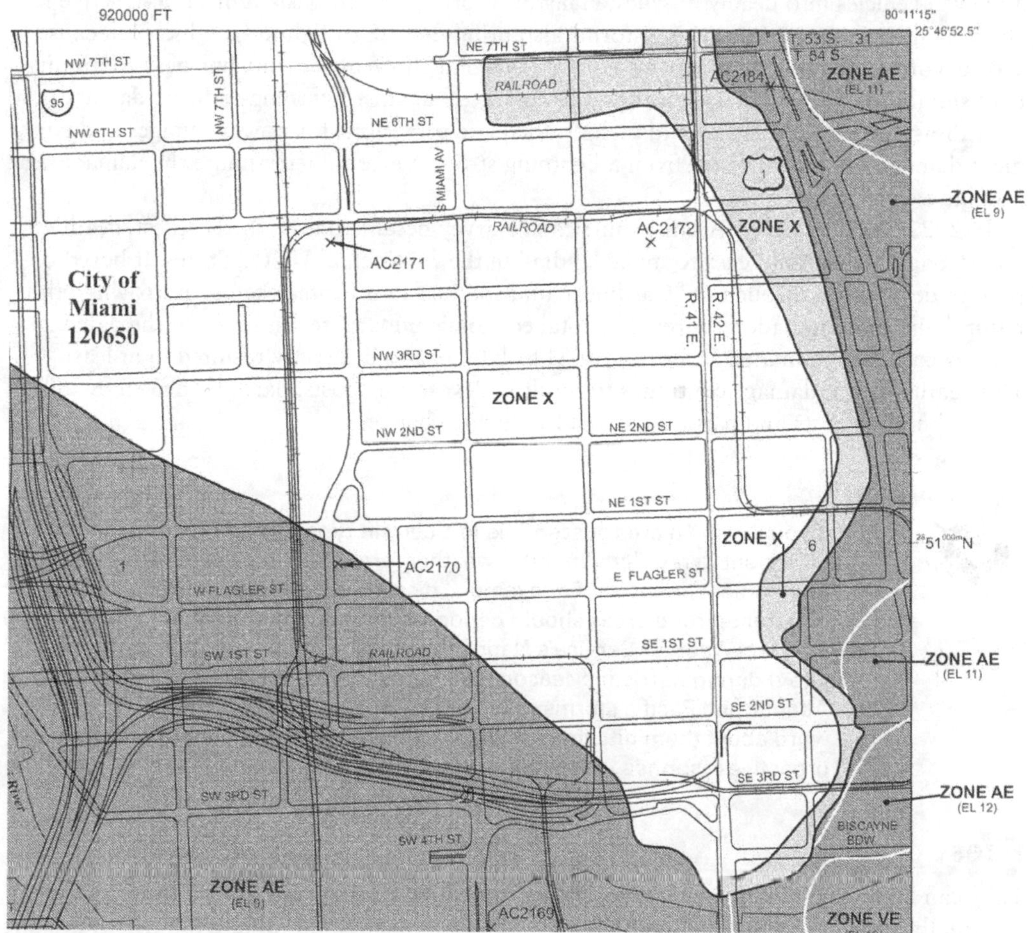

These maps also contain information about the impact of a flood, measured in terms of the depth of flooding expected during a flooding event. Those are described as zones having many different letter codes, which you will not need to memorize for the exam.

For a more detailed tutorial on reading flood maps and current map information, visit `www.fema.gov/sites/default/files/2020-07/how-to-read-flood-insurance-rate-map-tutorial.txt`.

Storms

Storms come in many forms and pose diverse risks to a business. Prolonged periods of intense rainfall bring the risk of flash flooding described in the previous section. Hurricanes and tornadoes come with the threat of winds exceeding 100 miles per hour that undermine the structural integrity of buildings and turn everyday objects such as trees, lawn furniture, and even vehicles into deadly missiles. Hailstorms bring a rapid onslaught of destructive ice chunks falling from the sky. Many storms also bring the risk of lightning, which can cause severe damage to sensitive electronic components. For this reason, your business continuity plan should detail appropriate mechanisms to protect against lightning-induced damage, and your disaster recovery plan should include adequate provisions for power outages and equipment damage that might result from a lightning strike. Never underestimate the damage that a single storm can do.

In 2022, the Category 4 Atlantic hurricane Harvey became one of the costliest, deadliest, and strongest hurricanes ever to make landfall in the continental United States. It bored a path of destruction through the Caribbean and southeastern United States, destroying both natural and human-made features. The total economic impact stemming from the damage Harvey caused is estimated at more than $113 billion, and it directly resulted in at least 160 deaths. Storm damage continues to result in devastating costs, partially driven by inflation in building costs and partially driven by climate change.

If you live in an area susceptible to a certain type of severe storm, it's important to regularly monitor weather forecasts from responsible government agencies. For example, disaster recovery specialists in hurricane-prone areas should periodically check the website of the National Weather Service's National Hurricane Center (`www.nhc.noaa.gov`) during hurricane season. This website allows you to monitor Atlantic and Pacific storms that may pose a risk to your region before word about them hits the local news. This lets you begin a gradual and proactive response to the storm before time runs out.

Fires

Fires can start for a variety of reasons, both natural and human-made, but both forms can be equally devastating. During the BCP/DRP process, you should evaluate the risk of fire and implement at least basic measures to mitigate that risk and prepare the business for recovery from a catastrophic fire in a critical facility.

Some regions of the world are susceptible to wildfires during the warm season. These fires, once started, spread in somewhat predictable patterns, and fire experts working with meteorologists can produce relatively accurate forecasts of a wildfire's potential path. It is important, of course, to remember that wildfires can behave unpredictably and require constant vigilance. In 2018, the Camp Fire in California destroyed the town of Paradise within 4 hours of ignition.

The damage caused by forest fires continues to increase, driven by climate change and other factors. In 2020, the state of California experienced more than 9,600 fires burning over 4.3 million acres of the state. To put that in context, 4 percent of the land area of the state of California burned in a single year.

As with many other types of large-scale natural disasters, you can obtain valuable information about impending threats on the web. In the United States, the National Interagency Fire Center posts daily fire updates and forecasts on its website: `www.nifc.gov/fireInfo/nfn.htm`. Other countries have similar warning systems in place.

Pandemics

Pandemics pose significant health and safety risks to society and have the potential to disrupt business operations in a manner unlike many other disasters. Rather than causing physical damage, pandemics threaten the safety of individuals and prevent them from gathering in large numbers, shutting down offices and other facilities.

The COVID-19 coronavirus pandemic that began in 2020 was the most severe example to occur in the past century, but numerous other smaller outbreaks have occurred, including the SARS outbreak, avian flu, and swine flu. Although major outbreaks like COVID-19 may be infrequent, the severity of this risk requires careful planning, including building contingency plans for how businesses will operate in a pandemic-response mode and what types of insurance may or may not provide coverage in response to a pandemic.

Other Natural Events

Some regions of the world are prone to localized types of natural disasters. During the DRP process, your assessment team should analyze all of your organization's operating locations and gauge the impact that such events might have on your business. For example, many parts of the world are subject to volcanic eruptions. If you conduct operations in an area in close proximity to an active or dormant volcano, your DRP should probably address this eventuality. Other localized natural occurrences include monsoons in Asia, tsunamis in the South Pacific, avalanches in mountainous regions, and mudslides in the western United States.

If your business is geographically diverse, it is prudent to include local emergency-response experts on your planning team. At the very least, make use of local resources such as government emergency preparedness teams, civil defense organizations, and insurance claim offices to help guide your efforts. These organizations possess a wealth of knowledge and are usually more than happy to help you prepare your organization for the unexpected—after all, every organization that successfully weathers a natural disaster is one less organization that requires a portion of their valuable recovery resources after disaster strikes.

Human-Made Disasters

Our advanced civilization has become increasingly dependent on complex interactions between technological, logistical, and natural systems. The same complex interactions that make our sophisticated society possible also present a number of potential vulnerabilities from both intentional and unintentional *human-made disasters*. In the following sections, we'll examine a few of the more common disasters to help you analyze your organization's vulnerabilities when preparing a business continuity plan and disaster recovery plan.

Fires

Earlier in the chapter, we explained how some regions of the world are susceptible to wildfires during the warm season, and these types of fires can be described as natural disasters. Many smaller-scale fires result from human action—be it carelessness, faulty electrical wiring, improper fire protection practices, arson, or other reasons. Studies from the Insurance Information Institute indicate that there are at least 1,000 building fires in the United States *every day*. If such a fire strikes your organization, do you have the proper preventive measures in place to quickly contain it? If the fire destroys your facilities, how quickly does your disaster recovery plan allow you to resume operations elsewhere?

Acts of Terrorism

Since the terrorist attacks on September 11, 2001, businesses are increasingly concerned about risks posed by terrorist threats. These attacks caused many small businesses to fail because they did not have business continuity/disaster recovery plans in place that were adequate to ensure their continued viability. Many larger businesses also experienced significant losses that caused severe long-term damage. The Insurance Information Institute issued a study one year after the attacks that estimated the total damage from the attacks in New York City at $40 billion (yes, that's with a *b* again!).

General business insurance may not properly cover an organization against acts of terrorism. In years past, most policies either covered acts of terrorism or didn't mention them explicitly. After suffering catastrophic terrorism-related losses, many insurance companies responded by amending policies to exclude losses from terrorist activity. Policy riders and endorsements are sometimes available but often at extremely high cost. If your business continuity or disaster recovery plan includes insurance as a means of financial recovery (as it probably should!), you'd be well advised to check your policies and contact your insurance professionals to ensure that you're still covered.

Power Outages

Even the most basic disaster recovery plan contains provisions to deal with the threat of a short power outage. Critical business systems are often protected by uninterruptible power supply (UPS) devices to keep them running at least long enough to shut down or to get emergency generators up and working. Even so, could your organization keep operating during a sustained power outage?

After Hurricane Ian made landfall in 2022, millions of people in Cuba and Florida lost power. Similar power outages occurred in 2020 in response to the California wildfires. Does your business continuity plan include provisions to keep your business viable during a prolonged period without power? If so, what is your planning horizon? Do you need enough fuel and other supplies to last for 48 hours? Seven days? Does your disaster recovery plan make ample preparations for the timely restoration of power even if the commercial power grid remains unavailable? All of these decisions should be made based on the requirements in your business continuity and disaster recovery plans.

Check your UPSs regularly! These critical devices are often overlooked until they become necessary. Many UPSs contain self-testing mechanisms that report problems automatically, but it's still a good idea to subject them to regular testing. Also, be sure to audit the number and type of devices plugged into each UPS. It's amazing how many people think it's OK to add "just one more system" to a UPS, but they wouldn't want to be surprised if the device can't handle the load during a real power outage! UPS systems and backup generators are discussed more thoroughly later in this chapter.

Today's technology-driven organizations depend increasingly on electric power, so your BCP/DRP team should consider provisioning alternative power sources that can run business systems for an extended period of time. An adequate backup generator could make a huge difference when the survival of your business is at stake.

Network, Utility, and Infrastructure Failures

When planners consider the impact that utility outages may have on their organizations, they naturally think first about the impact of a power outage. However, keep other utilities in mind, too. Do any of your critical business systems rely on water, sewers, natural gas, or other utilities? Also consider regional infrastructure such as highways, airports, and railroads. Any of these systems can suffer failures that might not be related to weather or other conditions described in this chapter. Many businesses depend on one or more of these infrastructure elements to move people or materials. Their failure can paralyze your business's ability to continue functioning.

You must also think about your Internet connectivity as a utility service. Do you have sufficient redundancy in your connectivity options to survive or recover quickly from a disaster? If you have redundant providers, do they have any single points of failure? For example, do they both enter your building in a single fiber conduit that could be severed? If there are no alternative fiber ingress points, can you supplement a fiber connection with wireless connectivity? Do your alternate processing sites have sufficient network capacity to carry the full burden of operations in the event of a disaster?

If you quickly answered no to the question whether you have critical business systems that rely on water, sewers, natural gas, or other utilities, think again. Do you consider people a critical business system? If a major storm knocks out the water supply to your facilities and you need to keep those facilities up and running, can you supply your employees with enough drinking water to meet their needs?

What about your fire protection systems? If any of them are water-based, is there a holding tank system in place that contains ample water to extinguish a serious building fire if the public water system is unavailable? Fires often cause serious damage in areas ravaged by storms, earthquakes, and other disasters that might also interrupt the delivery of water.

Hardware/Software Failures

Like it or not, computer systems fail. Hardware components simply wear out and refuse to continue performing, or they suffer physical damage. Software systems contain bugs or fall prey to improper or unexpected inputs. For this reason, DR teams must provide adequate redundancy in their systems. If zero downtime is a mandatory requirement, one solution is to use fully redundant failover servers in separate locations attached to separate communications links and infrastructures (also designed to operate in a failover mode). If one server is damaged or destroyed, the other will instantly take over the processing load.

Because of financial constraints, it isn't always feasible to maintain fully redundant systems. In those circumstances, the DR team should address how replacement parts can be quickly obtained and installed. As many parts as possible should be kept in a local parts inventory for quick replacement; this is especially true for hard-to-find parts that must otherwise be shipped in. After all, how many organizations could do without telephones for three days while a critical private branch exchange (PBX) component is en route from an overseas location to be installed on-site?

Strikes/Picketing

When designing your business continuity and disaster recovery plans, don't forget about the importance of the human factor in emergency planning. One form of human-made disaster that is often overlooked is the possibility of a strike or other labor crisis. If a large number of your employees walk out at the same time, what impact would that have on your business? How long would you be able to sustain operations without the regular full-time employees that staff a certain area? Your DR teams should address these concerns and provide alternative plans should a labor crisis occur. Labor issues normally fall outside the purview of cybersecurity teams, offering a great example of an issue that should be included in a disaster recovery plan but requires input and leadership from other business functions, such as human resources and operations.

Theft/Vandalism

Earlier, we talked about the threat that terrorist activities pose to an organization. Theft and vandalism represent the same kind of threat on a much smaller scale. In most cases, however, there's a far greater chance that your organization will be affected by theft or vandalism than by a terrorist attack. The theft or destruction of a critical infrastructure component, such as scrappers stealing copper wires or vandals destroying sensors, can negatively impact critical business functions.

Insurance provides some financial protection against these events (subject to deductibles and limitations of coverage) but acts of this kind can cause serious damage to your business, on both a short-term and a long-term basis. Your business continuity and disaster recovery plans should include adequate preventive measures to control the frequency of these occurrences as well as contingency plans to mitigate the effects theft and vandalism have on ongoing operations.

Cybersecurity Incidents

When we conduct business continuity planning and disaster recovery planning, we often first think of physical disasters that might damage our equipment, facilities, and data. It's also important to consider the risk posed by cybersecurity incidents. Cybersecurity incidents that disrupt business activity or threaten to do so may cause an organization to invoke business continuity and disaster recovery plans. For this reason, the teams conducting DR efforts should carefully coordinate with cybersecurity incident response teams and ensure that the plans are tightly integrated.

Disaster Recovery Planning

The goal of disaster recovery planning is to step in when disaster disrupts the organization's business activities, provide temporary operating capabilities, and support a speedy transition back to normal operations.

> **Exam Tip**
>
> The CompTIA DataSys+ Exam objectives specifically address "transition/failback to normal operations" as the end goal of the disaster recovery plan. Remember this when you take the exam—the work of disaster recovery is not complete when you have temporary capabilities restored. The DR effort continues until you've returned to your normal operational state.

Prioritizing Disaster Recovery Efforts

As you begin your DR work, you will undoubtedly need to prioritize your efforts to focus on the most important areas first. Depending on your line of business, certain activities are essential to your day-to-day operations when disaster strikes. You should create a comprehensive list of critical business functions and rank them in order of importance. Although this task may seem somewhat daunting, it's not as hard as it looks.

These critical business functions will vary from organization to organization, based on each organization's mission. They are the activities that, if disrupted, would jeopardize the organization's ability to achieve its goals. For example, an online retailer would treat the ability to sell products from their website and fulfill those orders promptly as critical business functions.

A great way to divide the workload of this process among the team members is to assign each participant responsibility for drawing up a prioritized list that covers the business functions for which their department is responsible. When the entire team convenes, team members can use those prioritized lists to create a master prioritized list for the organization as a whole. One caution with this approach—if your team is not truly representative of the organization, you may miss critical priorities. Be sure to gather input from all parts of the organization, especially from any areas not represented on the team.

This process helps identify business priorities from a qualitative point of view. It's best if you can combine both qualitative and quantitative efforts to get a full picture of your organization's critical dependencies. Let's look at four key metrics.

Asset Values

To begin the quantitative assessment, the team should develop a list of organization assets and then assign an *asset value (AV)* in monetary terms to each asset. Teams creating this list may draw on other existing documentation within the organization, such as accounting information, insurance policies, and configuration management systems.

Maximum Tolerable Downtime

The second quantitative measure that the team must develop is the *maximum tolerable downtime (MTD)*. The MTD is the maximum length of time a business function can tolerate a disruption before suffering irreparable harm. The MTD provides valuable information when you're performing DR planning. The organization's list of critical business functions plays a crucial role in this process. The MTD for critical business functions should be lower than the MTD for activities not identified as critical. Returning to the example of an online retailer, the MTD for the website selling products may be only a few minutes, whereas the MTD for their internal email system might be measured in hours.

Recovery Time Objective

The *recovery time objective (RTO)* for each business function is the amount of time in which you think you can feasibly recover the function in the event of a disruption. This value is closely related to the MTD. Once you have defined your recovery objectives, you can design and plan the procedures necessary to accomplish the recovery tasks.

As you conduct your work, ensure that your RTOs are less than your MTDs, resulting in a situation in which a function should never be unavailable beyond the maximum tolerable downtime.

While the RTO and MTD measure the time to recover operations and the impact of that recovery time on operations, organizations must also pay attention to the potential data loss that might occur during an availability incident. Depending on the way that information is collected, stored, and processed, some data loss may take place.

Recovery Point Objective

The *recovery point objective (RPO)* is the data loss equivalent to the time-focused RTO. The RPO defines the point in time before the incident where the organization should be able to recover data from a critical business process. For example, an organization might perform database transaction log backups every 15 minutes. In that case, the RPO would be 15 minutes, meaning that the organization may lose up to 15 minutes' worth of data after an incident. If an incident takes place at 8:30 a.m., the last transaction log backup must have occurred sometime between 8:15 a.m. and 8:30 a.m. Depending on the precise timing of the incident and the backup, the organization may have irretrievably lost between 0 and 15 minutes of data.

Disaster Recovery Documentation

Once you've established your business unit priorities and have a good idea of the appropriate alternative recovery sites for your organization, it's time to put pen to paper and begin drafting a true disaster recovery plan. Don't expect to sit down and write the full plan in one sitting. It's likely that the DRP team will go through many draft documents before reaching a final written document that satisfies the operational needs of critical business units and falls within the resource, time, and expense constraints of the disaster recovery budget and available personnel.

In the following sections, we explore some important items to include in your disaster recovery plan.

Disaster Recovery Manual

Organizations should maintain a disaster recovery manual that contains all of the documentation required to support your DR plan. The contents will depend on the size of your organization and the number of people involved in the DRP effort. You may want to include the following:

- Executive summary providing a high-level overview of the plan
- Department-specific plans
- Technical guides for IT personnel responsible for implementing and maintaining critical backup systems
- Checklists for individuals on the disaster recovery team
- Full copies of the plan for critical disaster recovery team members

Using custom-tailored documents becomes especially important when a disaster occurs or is imminent. Personnel who need to refresh themselves on the disaster recovery procedures that affect various parts of the organization will be able to refer to their department-specific plans. Critical disaster recovery team members will have checklists to help guide their actions amid the chaotic atmosphere of a disaster. IT personnel will have technical guides helping them get the alternate sites up and running. Finally, managers and public relations personnel will have a simple document that walks them through a high-level view of the coordinated symphony that is an active disaster recovery effort without requiring interpretation from team members busy with tasks directly related to that effort.

Visit the Professional Practices library at https://drii.org/resources/professionalpractices/EN to examine a collection of documents that explain how to work through and document your planning processes for BCP and disaster recovery. Other good standard documents in this area include the BCI Good Practice Guideline (GPG) (www.thebci.org/training-qualifications/good-practice-guidelines.html), ISO 27001 (www.iso.org/standard/27001), and NIST SP 800-34, "Contingency Planning Guide for Federal Information Systems" (csrc.nist.gov/publications/detail/sp/800-34/rev-1/final).

System Security Plan

In Chapter 6, "Governance, Security, and Compliance," and Chapter 7, "Database Security," you learned about the importance of implementing strong cybersecurity controls to protect your systems and data. Those protections (or equivalent protections) should remain in place when you activate your organization's disaster recovery plan. The DR plan should include a *system security plan* that outlines the ways that security controls may need to be enhanced or modified during disaster operations.

Continuity of Operations Plan

Business continuity efforts are a collection of activities designed to keep a business running in the face of adversity. This may come in the form of a small-scale incident, such as a single system failure, or a catastrophic incident, such as an earthquake or tornado. Business continuity plans may also be activated by man-made disasters, such as a terrorist attack or hacker intrusion.

The focus of business continuity is keeping operations running and, because of this, business continuity planning is sometimes referred to as continuity of operations planning and may be documented in a *continuity of operations plan (COOP)*.

When an organization begins a business continuity effort, it's easy for the planners to quickly become overwhelmed by the many possible scenarios and controls that the project might consider. For this reason, the team developing a business continuity plan should take time up front to carefully define their scope.

- Which business activities will be covered by the plan?
- What types of systems will it cover?
- What types of controls will it consider?

The answers to these questions will help make critical prioritization decisions down the road.

Business Continuity Planning vs. Disaster Recovery Planning

Students often become confused about the difference between business continuity planning (BCP) and disaster recovery planning (DRP). They might try to sequence them in a particular order or draw firm lines between the two activities. The reality of the situation is that these lines are blurry in real life and don't lend themselves to neat and clean categorization.

The distinction between the two is one of perspective. Both activities help prepare an organization for a disaster. They intend to keep operations running continuously, when possible, and recover functions as quickly as possible if a disruption occurs. The perspective difference is that business continuity activities are typically strategically focused and center themselves on business processes and operations. Disaster recovery plans tend to be more tactical and describe technical activities such as recovery sites, backups, and fault tolerance.

In any event, don't get hung up on the difference between the two. We've yet to see an exam question force anyone to draw a solid line between the two activities. It's much more important that you understand the processes and technologies involved in these two related disciplines.

Continuity planners use a tool known as a *business impact analysis (BIA)* to help make these decisions. The BIA is a risk assessment that follows one of the quantitative or qualitative processes that we discussed earlier in this course. It begins by identifying the organization's mission-essential functions and then tracing those backwards to identify the critical IT systems that support those processes. Once planners have identified the affected IT systems, they then identify the potential risks to those systems and conduct a risk assessment.

The output of a BIA is a prioritized listing of risks that might disrupt the organization's business. Planners can then use this information to help select controls that mitigate the risks facing the organization within acceptable expense limits. For example, you might develop the list of risks shown in Table 8.1. Notice that the risks in this scenario are listed in descending order of expected loss.

TABLE 8.1 Business Impact Analysis

Risk	Annualized Loss Expectancy
Hurricane damage to data center	$145,000
Fire in data center	$18,000
Power outage	$12,000
Theft of equipment	$3,400

It makes sense to place the highest priority on addressing the risk at the top of the list—hurricane damage to the data center—but the organization must then make decisions about control implementation that factor in cost. For example, if a $50,000 flood prevention system would reduce the risk of hurricane damage to the data center by 50 percent, purchasing the system is clearly a good decision because it has an expected payback period of less than one year.

In a cloud-centric environment, business continuity planning becomes a collaboration between the cloud service provider and the customer. For example, the risk of a hurricane damaging a data center may be mitigated by building a flood prevention system, but it also may be mitigated by the customer choosing to replicate services across the cloud provider's different data centers, availability zones, and geographic regions.

Build Documentation

During a disaster, database administrators and other technology professionals will often need to build systems on the fly. If you include system *build documentation* in your disaster recovery plan, that information may prove invaluable to those technologists during the heat of a crisis.

Build documentation should provide step-by-step instructions for configuring and deploying critical systems, including software, hardware, and network components. By having detailed documentation readily available, IT staff can quickly and efficiently rebuild critical systems to their pre-disaster state, which is essential for minimizing downtime and restoring business operations. The documentation can also help ensure consistency and accuracy across the different technology components, reducing the risk of errors or omissions that could compromise the recovery effort.

Disaster Recovery Technology

Disaster recovery can be tedious work. Fortunately, there are quite a few technologies focused on making the job easier. Let's examine some of the important technologies for disaster recovery.

System Resilience, High Availability, and Fault Tolerance

System resilience refers to the ability of a system to maintain an acceptable level of service during an adverse event. This could be a hardware fault managed by fault-tolerant components, or it could be an attack managed by other controls, such as effective intrusion-prevention systems. In some contexts, it refers to the ability of a system to return to a previous state after an adverse event. For example, if a primary server in a failover cluster fails, fault tolerance ensures that the system fails over to another server. System resilience implies that the cluster can fail back to the original server after the original server is repaired.

Fault tolerance is the ability of a system to suffer a fault but continue to operate. Fault tolerance is achieved by adding redundant components, such as additional disks within a properly configured redundant array of inexpensive disks (RAID) array, or additional servers within a failover clustered configuration.

High availability is the use of redundant technology components to allow a system to quickly recover from a failure after experiencing a brief disruption. High availability is often achieved through the use of load-balancing and failover servers.

Technology professionals measure the objective and effectiveness of these controls by the percentage of the time that a system is available. For example, a fairly low availability threshold would be to specify that a system must be available 99.9 percent of the time (or "three nines" of availability). This means that the system may only experience 0.1 percent of downtime during whatever period is measured. If you apply this metric to a 30-day month of system operation, 99.9 percent availability would require less than 44 minutes of downtime. If you move to a 99.999 percent (or "five nines") requirement, the system would only be permitted 26 seconds of downtime per month.

Of course, the stronger your availability requirement, the more difficult it will be to meet. Achieving higher availability targets on a consistent basis requires the use of high availability, fault tolerance, and system resilience controls.

Protecting Hard Drives

A common way that fault tolerance and system resilience is added for computers is with a RAID array. A RAID array includes two or more disks, and most RAID configurations will continue to operate even after one of the disks fails. Some of the common RAID configurations are as follows:

RAID 0 This is also called *striping*. It uses two or more disks and improves the disk subsystem performance, but it does not provide fault tolerance.

RAID 1 This is also called *mirroring*. It uses two disks that both hold the same data. If one disk fails, the other disk includes the data so that a system can continue to operate after a single disk fails. Depending on the hardware used and which drive fails, the system may be able to continue to operate without intervention, or the system may need to be manually configured to use the drive that didn't fail.

RAID 5 This is also called *striping with parity*. It uses three or more disks with the equivalent of one disk holding parity information. This parity information allows the reconstruction of data through mathematical calculations if a single disk is lost. If any single disk fails, the RAID array will continue to operate, though it will be slower.

RAID 6 This offers an alternative approach to disk striping with parity. It functions in the same manner as RAID 5 but stores parity information on two disks, protecting against the failure of two separate disks but requiring a minimum of four disks to implement.

RAID 1RAID 10 This is also known as RAID 1+0 or a *stripe of mirrors* and is configured as two or more mirrors (RAID 1) with each mirror configured in a striped (RAID 0) configuration. It uses at least four disks but can support more as long as an even number of disks are added. It will continue to operate even if multiple disks fail, as long as at least one drive in each mirror continues to function. For example, if it had three mirrored sets (called M1, M2, and M3 for this example) it would have a total of six disks. If one drive in M1, one in M2, and one in M3 all failed, the array would continue to operate. However, if two drives in any of the mirrors failed, such as both drives in M1, the entire array would fail.

Fault tolerance is not the same as a backup. Occasionally, management may balk at the cost of backup tapes and point to the RAID, saying that the data is already backed up. However, if a catastrophic hardware failure destroys a RAID array, all the data is lost unless a backup exists. Similarly, if an accidental deletion or corruption destroys data, it cannot be restored if a backup doesn't exist.

Both software- and hardware-based RAID solutions are available. Software-based systems require the operating system to manage the disks in the array and can reduce overall system performance. They are relatively inexpensive since they don't require any additional hardware other than the additional disk(s). Hardware RAID systems are generally more efficient and reliable. Although a hardware RAID is more expensive, the benefits typically outweigh the costs when used to increase availability of a critical component.

Hardware-based RAID arrays typically include spare drives that can be logically added to the array. For example, a hardware-based RAID 5 could include five disks, with three disks in a RAID 5 array and two spare disks. If one disk fails, the hardware senses the failure and logically swaps out the faulty drive with a good spare. Additionally, most hardware-based arrays support hot-swapping, allowing technicians to replace failed disks without powering down the system. A cold-swappable RAID requires the system to be powered down to replace a faulty drive.

Protecting Servers

Fault tolerance can be added for critical servers with failover clusters. A failover cluster includes two or more servers, and if one of the servers fails, another server in the cluster can take over its load in an automatic process called *failover*. Failover clusters can include multiple servers (not just two), and they can also provide fault tolerance for multiple services or applications.

As an example of a failover cluster, consider Figure 8.3. It shows multiple components put together to provide reliable web access for a heavily accessed website that uses a database. DB1 and DB2 are two database servers configured in a failover cluster. At any given time, only one server will function as the active database server, and the second server will be inactive. For example, if DB1 is the active server it will perform all the database services for the website. DB2 monitors DB1 to ensure it is operational, and if DB2 senses a failure in DB1, it will cause the cluster to automatically fail over to DB2.

In Figure 8.3, you can see that both DB1 and DB2 have access to the data in the database. This data is stored on a RAID array providing fault tolerance for the disks.

Additionally, the three web servers are configured in a network load-balancing cluster. The load balancer can be hardware- or software-based, and it balances the client load across the three servers. It makes it easy to add additional web servers to handle increased load while also balancing the load among all the servers. If any of the servers fail, the load balancer can sense the failure and stop sending traffic to that server. Although network load balancing is primarily used to increase the scalability of a system so that it can handle more traffic, it also provides a measure of fault tolerance.

FIGURE 8.3 Failover cluster with network load balancing

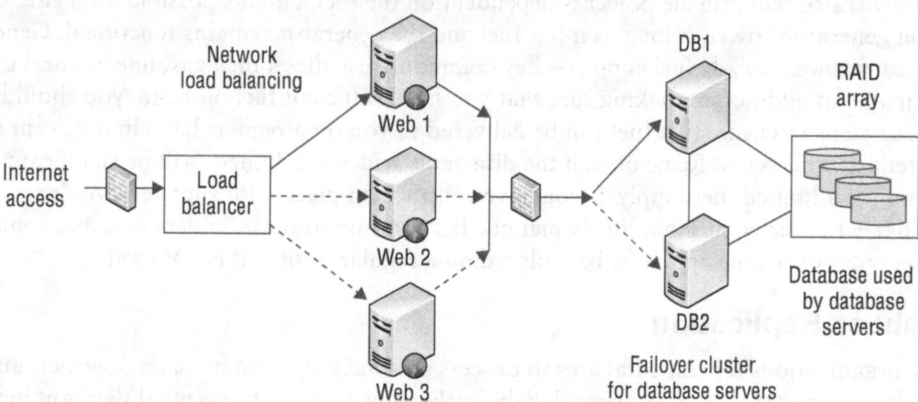

If you're running your servers in the cloud, you may be able to take advantage of fault tolerance services offered by your cloud provider. For example, many IaaS providers offer load-balancing services that automatically scale resources on an as-needed basis. These services also incorporate health checking that can automatically restart servers that are not functioning properly.

Similarly, when designing cloud environments, be sure to consider the availability of data centers in different regions of the world. If you are already load-balancing multiple servers, you may be able to place those servers in different geographic regions and availability zones within those regions to add resiliency in addition to scalability.

Failover clusters are not the only method of fault tolerance for servers. Some systems provide automatic fault tolerance for servers, allowing a server to fail without losing access to the provided service. For example, in a Microsoft domain with two or more domain controllers, each domain controller will regularly replicate Active Directory data with the others so that all the domain controllers have the same data. If one fails, computers within the domain can still find the other domain controller(s), and the network can continue to operate. Similarly, many database server products include methods to replicate database content with other servers so that all servers have the same content.

Protecting Power Sources

Fault tolerance can be added for power sources with an *uninterruptible power supply*, a generator, or both. In general, a UPS provides battery-supplied power for a short period of time, between 5 and 30 minutes, and a generator provides long-term power. The goal of a UPS is to provide power long enough to complete a logical shutdown of a system or until a generator is powered on and providing stable power.

Generators provide power to systems during long-term power outages. The length of time that a generator will provide power is dependent on the fuel, and it's possible for a site to stay on generator power as long as it has fuel and the generator remains functional. Generators also require a steady fuel supply—they commonly use diesel fuel, gasoline, natural gas, or propane. In addition to making sure that you have sufficient fuel on hand, you should also take steps to ensure that fuel can be delivered to you on a regular basis in the event of an extended emergency. Remember, if the disaster is widespread, there will be significant demand for a limited fuel supply. If you have contracts in place with suppliers, you're much more likely to receive fuel in a timely manner. It's also important to understand that some fuel degrades over time and must be replaced on a regular basis if it is not used.

Database Replication

Many organizations rely on databases to process and track operations, sales, logistics, and other activities vital to their continued viability. For this reason, it's essential that you include database recovery techniques in your disaster recovery plans. It's a wise idea to have a database specialist on the DR team who can provide input as to the technical feasibility of various ideas. After all, you shouldn't allocate several hours to restore a database backup when it's impossible to complete a restoration in less than half a day!

In the following sections, we'll cover the three main techniques used to create off-site copies of database content: database dumping, log shipping, and remote mirroring. Each one has specific benefits and drawbacks, so you'll need to analyze your organization's computing requirements and available resources to select the option best suited to your firm and within the boundaries of your RPO. Selecting solutions that lose data beyond your RPO pose unwarranted risk, while selecting those that are more aggressive than your RPO may incur unnecessary costs.

Database Dumping

In a *database dumping* scenario, database backups are moved to a remote site using bulk transfers. The remote location may be a dedicated alternative recovery site or simply an off-site location managed within the company or by a contractor for the purpose of maintaining backup data.

If you use database dumping, remember that there may be a significant delay between the time you declare a disaster and the time your database is ready for operation with current data. If you decide to activate a recovery site, technicians will need to retrieve the appropriate backups from the archive and apply them to the soon-to-be production servers at the recovery site.

As with any type of backup scenario, be certain to periodically test your database dumping setup. A great method for testing backup solutions is to give disaster recovery personnel a "surprise test," asking them to restore data from a certain day to an alternative location.

It's important to know that database dumping introduces the potential for significant data loss. In the event of a disaster, you will only be able to recover information as of the time of the last dump operation.

Log Shipping

With *log shipping*, data transfers are performed in a more expeditious manner. Data transfers still occur in a bulk transfer mode, but they occur on a more frequent basis, usually once every hour and sometimes more frequently. Unlike database dumping scenarios, where entire database backup files are transferred, log shipping setups transfer copies of the database transaction logs containing the transactions that occurred since the previous bulk transfer.

Remote Mirroring

Remote mirroring is the most advanced database backup solution. Not surprisingly, it's also the most expensive! Remote mirroring goes beyond the technology used by database dumping and log shipping; with remote mirroring, a live database server is maintained at the backup site with real-time current data. The remote server receives copies of the database modifications at the same time they are applied to the production server at the primary site. Therefore, the mirrored server is ready to take over an operational role at a moment's notice.

Remote mirroring is a popular database backup strategy for organizations seeking to reduce their recovery time. However, when weighing the feasibility of a remote mirroring solution, be sure to take into account the infrastructure and personnel costs required to support the mirrored server, as well as the processing overhead that will be added to each database transaction on the mirrored server. Also, don't forget that the remote location and server will require the same level of security controls to protect any sensitive data they contain.

Cloud-based database platforms may include redundancy capabilities as a built-in feature. If you operate databases in the cloud, consider investigating these options to simplify your disaster recovery planning efforts, but be sure to understand the limitations of the specific service you consider!

Disaster Recovery Plan Testing

Every disaster recovery plan must be tested on a periodic basis to ensure that the plan's provisions are viable and that it meets an organization's changing needs. The types of tests that you conduct will depend on the types of recovery facilities available to you, the culture of your organization, and the availability of disaster recovery team members. The five main test types—checklist tests, structured walk-throughs, simulation tests, parallel tests, and full-interruption tests—are discussed in the remaining sections of this chapter.

For more information on this topic, consult NIST Special Publication 800-84, "Guide to Test, Training, and Exercise Programs for IT Plans and Capabilities Recommendations," available at `https://csrc.nist.gov/publications/detail/sp/800-84/final`.

Read-Through Test

The *read-through test* is one of the simplest tests to conduct, but it's also one of the most critical. In this test, you distribute copies of disaster recovery plans to the members of the disaster recovery team for review. This lets you accomplish three goals simultaneously:

- It ensures that key personnel are aware of their responsibilities and have that knowledge refreshed periodically.
- It provides individuals with an opportunity to review the plans for obsolete information and update any items that require modification because of changes within the organization.
- In large organizations, it helps identify situations in which key personnel have left the company and nobody bothered to reassign their disaster recovery responsibilities. This is also a good reason why disaster recovery responsibilities should be included in job descriptions.

Structured Walk-Through

A *structured walk-through* takes testing one step further. In this type of test, often referred to as a *tabletop exercise*, members of the disaster recovery team gather in a large conference room and role-play a disaster scenario. Usually, the exact scenario is known only to the test moderator, who presents the details to the team at the meeting. The team members then refer to their copies of the disaster recovery plan and discuss the appropriate responses to that particular type of disaster.

Walk-throughs may vary in their scope and intent. Some exercises may include taking physical actions or at least considering their impact on the exercise. For example, a walk-through might require that everyone leave the building and go to a remote location to participate in the exercise, simulating the scenario that might occur in an actual disaster.

Simulation Test

Simulation tests are similar to structured walk-throughs. In simulation tests, disaster recovery team members are presented with a scenario and asked to develop an appropriate response. Unlike with the tests previously discussed, some of these response measures are then tested. This may involve the interruption of noncritical business activities and the use of some operational personnel.

Parallel Test

Parallel tests represent the next level in testing and involve relocating personnel to the alternate recovery site and implementing site activation procedures. The employees relocated to the site perform their disaster recovery responsibilities just as they would for an actual disaster. The only difference is that operations at the main facility are not interrupted. That site retains full responsibility for conducting the day-to-day business of the organization.

Full-Interruption Test

Full-interruption tests operate like parallel tests, but they involve actually shutting down operations at the primary site and shifting them to the recovery site. These tests involve a significant risk, as they require the operational shutdown of the primary site and transfer to the recovery site, followed by the reverse process to restore operations at the primary site. For this reason, full-interruption tests are extremely difficult to arrange, and you often encounter resistance from management.

Lessons Learned

At the conclusion of any disaster recovery operation or other security incident, the organization should conduct a *lessons learned* session. The lessons learned process is designed to provide everyone involved with the incident response effort an opportunity to reflect on their individual role in the incident and the team's response overall. It is an opportunity to improve the processes and technologies used in incident response to better respond to future security crises.

The most common way to conduct lessons learned is to gather everyone in the same room, or connect them via videoconference or telephone, and ask a trained facilitator to lead a lessons learned session. Ideally, this facilitator should have played no role in the incident response, leaving him or her with no preconceived notions about the response. The facilitator should be a neutral party who simply helps guide the conversation.

Time is of the essence with the lessons learned session because, as time passes, details quickly become fuzzy and memories are lost. The more quickly you conduct a lessons learned session, the more likely it is that you will receive valuable feedback that can help guide future responses.

In SP 800-61, NIST offers a series of questions to use in the lessons learned process. They include the following:

- Exactly what happened and at what times?
- How well did staff and management perform in dealing with the incident?
- Were documented procedures followed?
- Were the procedures adequate?
- Were any steps or actions taken that might have inhibited the recovery?
- What would the staff and management do differently the next time a similar incident occurs?
- How could information sharing with other organizations have been improved?
- What corrective actions can prevent similar incidents in the future?
- What precursors or indicators should be watched for in the future to detect similar incidents?
- What additional tools or resources are needed to detect, analyze and mitigate future incidents?

The responses to these questions, if given honestly, will provide valuable insight into the state of the organization's incident response program. They can help provide a roadmap of future improvements designed to bolster disaster recovery. The facilitator should work with the team leader to document the lessons learned in a report that includes suggested process improvement actions.

Plan Maintenance

Remember that a disaster recovery plan is a living document. As your organization's needs change, you must adapt the disaster recovery plan to meet those changed needs to follow suit. You will discover many necessary modifications by using a well-organized and coordinated testing plan. Minor changes may often be made through a series of telephone conversations or emails, whereas major changes may require one or more meetings of the full disaster recovery team.

A disaster recovery planner should refer to the organization's business continuity plan as a template for its recovery efforts. This and all the supportive material may need to comply with applicable regulations and reflect current business needs. Business processes such as payroll and order generation should contain specified metrics mapped to related IT systems and infrastructure.

Most organizations apply formal change management processes so that whenever the IT infrastructure changes, all relevant documentation is updated and checked to reflect such changes. Regularly scheduled fire drills and dry runs to ensure that all elements of the DRP are used properly to keep staff trained present a perfect opportunity to integrate changes into regular maintenance and change management procedures. Design, implement, and document changes each time you go through these processes and exercises. Know where everything is and keep each element of the DRP working properly. In case of emergency, use your recovery plan. Finally, make sure the staff stays trained to keep their skills sharp—for existing support personnel—and use simulated exercises to bring new people up to speed quickly.

Backup and Restore

Backups play an important role in the disaster recovery plan. They are copies of data stored on tape, disk, the cloud, or other media as a last-ditch recovery option. If a natural or human-made disaster causes data loss, administrators may turn to backups to recover lost data.

Your disaster recovery plan should fully address the backup strategy pursued by your organization. Indeed, this is one of the most important elements of any business continuity plan and disaster recovery plan.

Many system administrators are already familiar with various types of backups, so you'll benefit by bringing one or more individuals with specific technical expertise in this area onto the BCP/DRP team to provide expert guidance. There are three main types of backups:

Full Backups As the name implies, *full backups* store a complete copy of the data contained on the protected device. Full backups duplicate every file on the system regardless of the setting of the archive bit. Once a full backup is complete, the archive bit on every file is reset, turned off, or set to 0.

Incremental Backups *Incremental backups* store only those files that have been modified since the time of the most recent full or incremental backup. Only files that have the archive bit turned on, enabled, or set to 1 are duplicated. Once an incremental backup is complete, the archive bit on all duplicated files is reset, turned off, or set to 0.

Differential Backups *Differential backups* store all files that have been modified since the time of the most recent full backup. Only files that have the archive bit turned on, enabled, or set to 1 are duplicated. However, unlike full and incremental backups, the differential backup process does not change the archive bit.

Some operating systems do not actually use an archive bit to achieve this goal and instead analyze file system timestamps. This difference in implementation doesn't affect the types of data stored by each backup type.

The most important difference between incremental and differential backups is the time needed to restore data in the event of an emergency. If you use a combination of full and differential backups, you will need to restore only two backups—the most recent full backup and the most recent differential backup. On the other hand, if your strategy combines full backups with incremental backups, you will need to restore the most recent full backup as well as all incremental backups performed since that full backup. The trade-off is the time required to *create* the backups—differential backups don't take as long to restore, but they take longer to create than incremental ones.

The storage of the backup media is equally critical. It may be convenient to store backup media in or near the primary operations center to easily fulfill user requests for backup data, but you'll definitely need to keep copies of the media in at least one off-site location to provide redundancy should your primary operating location be suddenly destroyed. One common strategy used by many organizations is to store backups in a cloud service that is itself geographically redundant. This allows the organization to retrieve the backups from any location after a disaster. Note that using geographically diverse sites may introduce new regulatory requirements when the information resides in different jurisdictions.

Using Backups

In the case of system failure, many companies use one of two common methods to restore data from backups. In the first situation, they run a full backup on Monday night and then run differential backups every other night of the week. If a failure occurs Saturday morning, they restore Monday's full backup and then restore only Friday's differential backup. In the second situation, they run a full backup on Monday night and run incremental backups every other night of the week. If a failure occurs Saturday morning, they restore Monday's full backup and then restore each incremental backup in original chronological order (that is, Wednesday's, then Friday's, and so on).

Most organizations adopt a backup strategy that utilizes more than one of the three backup types along with a media rotation scheme. Both allow backup administrators access to a sufficiently large range of backups to complete user requests and provide fault tolerance while minimizing the amount of money that must be spent on backup media. A common strategy is to perform full backups over the weekend and incremental or differential backups on a nightly basis. The specific method of backup and all of the particulars of the backup procedure are dependent on your organization's fault-tolerance requirements, as defined by your RPO values. If you are unable to survive minor amounts of data loss, your ability to tolerate faults is low. However, if hours or days of data can be lost without serious consequence, your tolerance of faults is high. You should design your backup solution accordingly.

The Oft-Neglected Backup

Backups are probably the least practiced and most neglected preventive measure known to protect against computing disasters. A comprehensive backup of all operating system and personal data on workstations happens less frequently than for servers or mission-critical machines, but they all serve an equal and necessary purpose.

Damon, an information professional, learned this the hard way when he lost months of work following a natural disaster that wiped out the first floor at an information brokering firm. He never used the backup facilities built into his operating system or any of the shared provisions established by his administrator, Carol.

Carol has been there and done that, so she knows a thing or two about backup solutions. She has established incremental backups on her production servers and differential backups on her development servers, and she's never had an issue restoring lost data.

The toughest obstacle to a solid backup strategy is human nature, so a simple, transparent, and comprehensive strategy is the most practical. Differential backups require only two container files (the latest full backup and the latest differential) and can be scheduled for periodic updates at some specified interval. That's why Carol elects to implement this approach and feels ready to restore from her backups any time she's called on to do so.

Disk-to-Disk Backup

Over the past decade, disk storage has become increasingly inexpensive. With drive capacities now measured in terabytes, tape and optical media can't cope with data volume requirements anymore. Many enterprises now use disk-to-disk (D2D) backup solutions for some portion of their disaster recovery strategy.

Many backup technologies are designed around the tape paradigm. *Virtual tape libraries (VTL)* support the use of disks with this model by using software to make disk storage appear as tapes to backup software.

One important note: Organizations seeking to adopt an entirely disk-to-disk approach must remember to maintain geographical diversity. Some of those disks have to be located off-site. Many organizations solve this problem by hiring managed service providers to manage remote backup locations.

As transfer and storage costs come down, cloud-based backup solutions are becoming very cost effective. You may wish to consider using such a service as an alternative to physically transporting backup tapes to a remote location.

Scheduling and Automating Backups

Backup and restoration activities can be bulky and slow. Such data movement can significantly affect the performance of a network, especially during regular production hours. Thus, backups should be scheduled during the low peak periods (for example, at night).

The amount of backup data increases over time. This causes the backup (and restoration) processes to take longer each time you perform a backup. Each backup also consumes more space on the backup media. Thus, you need to build sufficient capacity to handle a reasonable amount of growth over a reasonable amount of time into your backup solution. What is reasonable depends on your environment and budget.

One of the best ways to ensure backups are performed as needed is to automate the entire process. Put technology in place that automatically schedules and triggers backups to run when needed.

With periodic backups (that is, backups that are run every 24 hours), there is always the potential for data loss up to the length of the period. Murphy's law dictates that a server never crashes immediately after a successful backup. Instead, it is always just before the next backup begins. To avoid the problem with periods, you may deploy some form of real-time continuous backup, such as RAID, clustering, or server mirroring.

Only include necessary information in backups. For example, it might not be important to store operating system files in routine backups. Do you really need hundreds of copies of the operating system? The answer to this question should be influenced by your recovery objectives. If your RTO dictates a rapid recovery capability, the storage cost of maintaining many copies of the operating system may be justified by the fact that it makes restoring the entire system from a stored image quite fast. If you can tolerate a longer recovery time, you might be able to reduce your storage costs by eliminating the backup of redundant files.

You may apply a similar approach to the number of backup copies that you maintain. Most restoration operations use recent copies of the backup, so you may choose to keep only a couple of weeks' worth of backup copies readily available. You might keep a full year of backups on less expensive archive media, which requires more time to restore, and then you might purge backups after they are a year old. This process is known as creating a *backup retention policy*, which specifies the purge and archive cycles appropriate for your organization.

Testing Backups

We discussed the importance of testing your disaster recovery plan earlier in this chapter. Backups should play an important role in those tests. You should periodically attempt to fully recover systems and data from backup to ensure that everything is functioning properly and that you have the backups you need to restore operations.

Organizations often rely on the fact that their backup software reports a successful backup and fail to attempt recovery until it's too late to detect a problem. This is one of the biggest causes of backup failures.

You can also use *hashing* to verify that your backups are properly maintained. This is especially important when transferring backups to off-site locations. Backup software uses mathematical functions to compute a unique hash value for each backup file. You may then compute the hash values of each copy of that file to ensure that the copies are identical and were not altered accidentally. As long as the hash values computed for each copy are identical, you can be confident that the files themselves contain the same data.

Summary

A disaster recovery plan is critical to a comprehensive information security program. DRPs serve as a valuable complement to business continuity plans and ensure that the proper technical controls are in place to keep the business functioning and to restore service after a disruption.

An organization's disaster recovery plan is one of the most important documents under the purview of security professionals. It should provide guidance to the personnel responsible for ensuring the continuity of operations in the face of disaster. The DRP provides an orderly sequence of events designed to activate alternate processing sites while simultaneously restoring the primary site to operational status. Once you've successfully developed your DRP, you must train personnel on its use, ensure that you maintain accurate documentation, and conduct periodic tests to keep the plan fresh in the minds of responders.

You also learned about the ways that organizations back up and restore data in support of their disaster recovery plans. This includes the ability to create and restore full, incremental, and differential backups. Backup strategies should describe how backups are created, tested, and stored and document a retention policy for archiving and purging backups, as appropriate.

Exam Essentials

Describe the common elements of disaster recovery plan documentation. The disaster recovery plan should be documented in a detailed manual that provides sufficient detail to support the efforts of team members during a disaster. It should also include related documentation, such as the system security plan, continuity of operations plan, and build documentation.

Explain the different technologies used to provide high availability and fault tolerance. Fault tolerance is achieved by adding redundant components, such as additional disks, within a properly configured redundant array of inexpensive disks (RAID) array or additional servers within a failover clustered configuration. High availability is often achieved through the use of load balancing and failover servers.

Explain the different technologies used to support disaster recovery plans. Database dumping moves backups of the database to a remote site in a bulk transfer operation. Log shipping provides more frequent updates, moving only changed data stored in transaction logs. Database mirroring uses real-time updates to maintain a live copy of the production database at a remote location.

Understand the concepts of MTD, RTO, and RPO. The maximum tolerable downtime is the maximum length of time a business function can tolerate a disruption before suffering irreparable harm. The recovery time objective for each business function is the amount of time in which you think you can feasibly recover the function in the event of a disruption. Ensure that your RTOs are less than your MTDs, resulting in a situation in which a function should never be unavailable beyond the maximum tolerable downtime. The recovery point objective defines the point in time before the incident where the organization should be able to recover data from a critical business process.

Explain the different types of backups. Full backups store a complete copy of the data contained on the protected device. Incremental backups store only those files that have been modified since the time of the most recent full or incremental backup. Differential backups store all files that have been modified since the time of the most recent full backup.

Know the five types of disaster recovery plan tests and the impact each has on normal business operations. The five types of disaster recovery plan tests are read-through tests, structured walk-throughs, simulation tests, parallel tests, and full-interruption tests. Checklist tests are purely paperwork exercises, whereas structured walk-throughs involve a project team meeting. Neither has an impact on business operations. Simulation tests may shut down noncritical business units. Parallel tests involve relocating personnel but do not affect day-to-day operations. Full-interruption tests involve shutting down primary systems and shifting responsibility to the recovery facility.

Review Questions

1. James is working with his organization's leadership to help them understand the role that disaster recovery plays in their cybersecurity strategy. The leaders are confused about the differences between disaster recovery and business continuity. What is the end goal of disaster recovery planning?
   - **A.** Preventing business interruption
   - **B.** Setting up temporary business operations
   - **C.** Restoring normal business activity
   - **D.** Minimizing the impact of a disaster
2. Kevin is attempting to determine an appropriate backup frequency for his organization's database server and wants to ensure that any data loss is within the organization's risk appetite. Which one of the following security process metrics would best assist him with this task?
   - **A.** RTO
   - **B.** MTD
   - **C.** RPO
   - **D.** MTBF
3. Brian's organization recently suffered a disaster and wants to improve their disaster recovery program based upon their experience. Which one of the following activities will best assist with this task?
   - **A.** Training programs
   - **B.** Awareness efforts
   - **C.** Impact analysis review
   - **D.** Lessons learned
4. Brad is helping to design a disaster recovery strategy for his organization and is analyzing possible storage locations for backup data. He is not certain where the organization will recover operations in the event of a disaster and would like to choose an option that allows them the flexibility to easily retrieve data from any DR site. Which one of the following storage locations provides the best option for Brad?
   - **A.** Primary data center
   - **B.** Field office
   - **C.** Cloud computing
   - **D.** IT manager's home
5. Randi is designing a disaster recovery mechanism for her organization's critical business databases. She selects a strategy where an exact, up-to-date copy of the database is maintained at an alternative location. What term describes this approach?
   - **A.** Transaction logging
   - **B.** Log shipping
   - **C.** Database dumping
   - **D.** Remote mirroring

6. Ingrid is concerned that one of her organization's data centers has been experiencing a series of momentary power outages. Which one of the following controls would best preserve their operating status?
   A. Generator
   B. Dual power supplies
   C. UPS
   D. Redundant network links

7. Harry is conducting a disaster recovery test. He moved a group of personnel to the alternate recovery site where they are mimicking the operations of the primary site but do not have operational responsibility. What type of disaster recovery test is he performing?
   A. Checklist test
   B. Structured walk-through
   C. Simulation test
   D. Parallel test

8. Vince would like to perform a backup that will copy only those files that have been modified since the most recent full backup. What type of backup should he perform?
   A. Full backup
   B. Incremental backup
   C. Transaction log backup
   D. Differential backup

9. What combination of backup strategies provides the fastest backup restoration time?
   A. Full backups and differential backups
   B. Partial backups and incremental backups
   C. Full backups and incremental backups
   D. Incremental backups and differential backups

10. What type of disaster recovery plan test fully evaluates operations at the backup facility but does not shift primary operations responsibility from the main site?
    A. Structured walk-through
    B. Parallel test
    C. Full-interruption test
    D. Simulation test

11. Gavin is conducting a test of his organization's disaster recovery plan and reached the phase of the test where they shut down the primary data center. What type of test is he running?
    A. Parallel test
    B. Simulation
    C. Walk-through
    D. Full interruption

12. What database backup technology applies database transactions in real time at both primary and alternate sites?
    A. Remote mirroring
    B. Database dumping
    C. Log shipping
    D. Fault tolerance

13. Barbara configures a system to perform full backups on Sundays and differential backups on Mondays through Saturdays. The system fails on Thursday. What backups must be applied?
    A. Sunday only
    B. Sunday, Monday, Tuesday, and Wednesday
    C. Sunday and Wednesday only
    D. Sunday, Monday, and Wednesday only

14. David gathered his organization's disaster recovery team on a videoconference and asked them to consider how they would respond if the area suffered an earthquake and they were unable to return to their primary facility. What type of testing is he conducting?
    A. Full-interruption test
    B. Parallel test
    C. Simulation test
    D. Structured walk-through

15. Kayleigh's organization recently suffered a disaster that disrupted their transactional database systems. She is working to stand up a temporary cloud database to support business activity. At what point is the DR effort complete?
    A. When the original database is back up and running again
    B. When the temporary database is built
    C. When data is restored to the temporary database
    D. When the temporary database is supporting business operations

16. Ricky is conducting the quantitative portion of his organization's business impact analysis. Which one of the following concerns is *least* suitable for quantitative measurement during this assessment?
    A. Loss of a plant
    B. Damage to a vehicle
    C. Negative publicity
    D. Power outage

17. Adam is reviewing the fault tolerance controls used by his organization and realizes that they currently have a single point of failure in the disks used to support a critical server. Which one of the following controls can provide fault tolerance for these disks?
    A. Load balancing
    B. RAID
    C. Clustering
    D. HA pairs

18. Bryn runs a corporate website and currently uses a single server, which is capable of handling the site's entire load. She is concerned, however, that an outage on that server could cause the organization to exceed its RTO. What action could she take that would best protect against this risk?

    A. Install dual power supplies in the server

    B. Replace the server's hard drives with RAID arrays

    C. Deploy multiple servers behind a load balancer

    D. Perform regular backups of the server

19. Which one of the following plans would normally contain details on an organization's backup procedures?

    A. Systems security plan

    B. Continuity of operations plan

    C. Build documentation

    D. Disaster recovery plan

20. What technology may be used to perform disk-to-disk backups with systems designed to work only with tapes?

    A. Journaling

    B. D2D

    C. VLAN

    D. VTL

Appendix Answers to Review Questions

Chapter 2: Database Fundamentals

1. C. Key-value databases are ideal for storing audio, image, and video data. Document databases store data in a JSON-like structure. Graph databases excel at exploring the relationships between data. With data stored in columns instead of rows, column-oriented databases are well-suited for aggregations in a data warehouse.

2. B. Cassandra is a column-oriented database, MongoDB is a document database, DynamoDB is a key-value database, and Neo4j is a graph database.

3. C. Primary Keys uniquely identify individual rows within a table and do not directly help associate data between separate tables. Tuples contain specific data about a single data subject within a table. Relations are structures containing a collection of attributes about a data subject. Foreign Keys create a link between two tables by adding an attribute to one table that references the primary key of another table.

4. A. Tuples contain specific data about a single data subject within a table. Relations are structures containing a collection of attributes about a data subject. Foreign Keys create a link between two tables by adding an attribute to one table that references the primary key of another table. Primary Keys uniquely identify individual rows within a table.

5. B. Access is Windows only, and SQL Server is primarily for the Windows operating system. Aurora is a cloud-only database offering. PostgreSQL runs on Linux and supports thousands of concurrent connections.

6. D. Access is Windows only, and SQL Server is primarily for the Windows operating system. While PostgreSQL runs on Linux and can run in the cloud, Aurora is a cloud-only database offering.

7. D. Key-value databases store data as a collection of keys and their corresponding values, a simplistic approach to storing data. Document databases extend the key-value concept by adding restrictions on the stored values, and column-oriented databases use an index to identify data in groups of related columns. A recommendation engine requires analyzing relationships between users and items, exactly where graph databases excel.

8. D. Column-oriented databases are optimal for handling columnar data, and graph databases excel at handling connected data. While a key-value database could work, a document database is ideal for storing semi-structured data.

9. C. MySQL and SQLite are relational databases, and MongoDB is a document database. Of the options, only Cassandra supports a column-oriented design.

10. B. A relational database with linear data format is ideal for tabular data, and a relational database with nonlinear data format and a NoSQL database with linear data format are not recommended approaches. As JSON objects are nonlinear, a NoSQL database is the best option.

11. B. ORM frameworks don't have a direct impact on the size of the database and do not inherently improve security. While ORM frameworks can help make the code more portable and adaptable to different database platforms, their primary purpose is to provide an

abstraction layer that allows developers to work with data using object-oriented programming languages.

12. B. Graph databases are specifically designed for handling highly interconnected datasets and would be the best choice in this scenario. Both relational and flat-file databases are better for linear data, and spreadsheets are not databases. Of the listed options, NoSQL databases are best suited to handling nonlinear data.

13. B. Relational databases are more suited for linear data, key-value databases store data as key-value pairs, and column-oriented databases store data as columns instead of rows.

14. C. JSON is a file format used for representing structured data, XML represents data in a tree-like structure of nested objects and elements, and BSON (Binary JSON) is a binary serialization format used for storing JSON documents. CSVs are simple, easy to create, read, and write, and are a popular choice for storing and exchanging data.

15. D. CSVs are simple, comma-separated files, ill-suited to storing complex data. DOCX is an Open Office XML document specific for word processing. While JSON is a viable choice, it may not be as easily readable as XML, particularly when working with more complex data structures. The tags within an XML document facilitate readability.

16. C. CSVs are simple, comma-separated files, ill-suited to storing and transmitting structured data. TSVs are similar to CSVs, using tabs instead of commas as the separator. While XML is a viable choice, JSON is more efficient.

17. A. Nonlinear data formats are ideal for hierarchical or nested structures, graph data formats map in the form of nodes and relationships, and tree data formats represent data in a hierarchical structure, similar to a nonlinear data format. As Christa is working with linear data, she should choose a linear data format.

18. A. Database optimization involves improving the performance of a database system, and load balancing distributes network traffic across multiple resources. APIs allow different software components to interact with each other. UX focuses on enhancing the experience users have with an application.

19. B. Functional, procedural, and logic programming all encapsulate logic into subcomponents. Object-oriented programming differs by focusing programming on data objects instead of procedural flow.

20. C. LINQ is an ORM for .NET, ActiveRecord is built into Ruby on Rails, and Django is an ORM for Python. Hibernate is an ORM for Java.

Chapter 3: SQL and Scripting

1. C. Since Eve is modifying existing information, she needs to use the UPDATE command. SELECT retrieves data, INSERT creates new data, and DELETE removes existing data.

2. B. A client-side approach is ruled out because patching database software is a network-sensitive task. Batch is a scripting language for Windows servers that would not work in a Linux environment, leaving option B as the most viable choice.

3. A. Option B combines DDL with DML statements incorrectly, while the DML SQL flavor in options C and D are incorrect. Monica is performing DDL tasks, in which she creates a table and then alters it.

4. D. Data Definition Language (DDL) creates, alters, or removes database objects, Data Control Language (DCL) controls access and permissions to database objects, and a transaction control language (TCL) manages transactions within a database system. Data Manipulation Language (DML) performs Create, Read, Update, and Delete (CRUD) operations on data within a database.

5. D. Option A doesn't have a WHERE clause and retrieves the information for all employees. Option B matches employees in the HR department, not the IT department. Option C retrieves the correct data but doesn't combine the salary and bonus information. Option D correctly retrieves the appropriate columns, joins the table, and filters on the proper department.

6. B. The original SQL query has a missing equal sign (=) in the ON clause of the INNER JOIN, which results in a syntax error. Option B corrects the error by including the equal sign in the ON clause, making the join condition complete and accurate. Option A still results in an error, option C changes the filter but doesn't address the join error, and option D doesn't address the join error.

7. C. Option A does not use a GROUP BY clause, option B only groups the rows by *country*, and option D omits the *country* and *product_category* columns in the SELECT clause.

   Option C correctly uses the GROUP BY clause to group the rows by *country* and *product_category* and then calculates the sum of the revenue column within each group. The result set will display the total revenue for each product category in each country.

8. A. A LEFT JOIN returns every row from the Customer table, even if there is no matching address information in the Address table; a RIGHT JOIN returns every row from the Address table, even if there is no matching customer information in the Customer table; and a FULL JOIN combines the results of both LEFT JOIN and RIGHT JOIN, returning all rows from both tables. An INNER JOIN is appropriate because Xavier must retrieve rows for customers with a work address.

9. B. An INNER JOIN returns only the rows where customers have addresses. A RIGHT JOIN returns every row from the Address table, even if there is no matching customer data in the Customer table, and a FULL JOIN combines the results of both LEFT JOIN and RIGHT JOIN, returning all rows from both tables. Andy needs to use a LEFT JOIN to retrieve every row from the Customer table, even if there is no matching address information in the Address table.

10. D. Stored procedures and functions do not automatically execute when an event occurs. A before-update trigger takes action before the intended data modification. An after-update trigger is the right choice for this scenario, as it executes automatically after a data modification.

11. B. A server-side script consumes resources on the database server, while extract, transform, load (ETL) and extract, load, transform (ELT) scripts typically migrate data between databases. Client-side scripts consume resources on the client machine, sending instructions to the database server only over a network connection.

12. A. A client-side script is vulnerable to network problems, while extract, transform, load (ETL) and extract, load, transform (ELT) scripts typically migrate data between databases. A server-side script is well-suited for administrative tasks like applying security patches to database software.

13. C. JavaScript, Python, and Bash are general-purpose programming languages without native SQL Server support. T-SQL runs within Microsoft SQL Server, allowing for flow control and exception handling.

14. D. T-SQL is Microsoft's proprietary extension of SQL, and PL/SQL is Oracle's language for developing stored procedures. While Bash is useful for everyday administrative tasks on the server, Python is more versatile, with numerous packages that facilitate text manipulation.

15. B. Java is a general-purpose programming language not designed explicitly for Windows administration, Batch scripts are primitive, and VBScript is a scripting language that predates PowerShell. PowerShell is a powerful and flexible scripting language designed specifically for Windows environments, making it an ideal choice for Tracey's administrative tasks on a Windows Server.

16. D. PowerShell is designed primarily for Windows, and Batch scripts work only on Windows. While you can use Python for automation, it is not native in all Linux environments. Bash is a widely used shell and scripting language for Unix-like operating systems, including Linux.

17. A. File Transfer Protocol (FTP) is a protocol for transferring files between computers, and application programming interfaces (APIs) are interfaces between systems. While extract, load, and transform (ELT) is a valid approach, it puts more load on the database and doesn't take advantage of her team's existing skills. ETL is the best approach for Elinor, as she can leverage her team's Python skills for the complex transformation work.

18. C. While stored procedures and functions encapsulate business logic, they require invocation. A view is a virtual table that presents the result set of a SELECT statement. A trigger is the most appropriate object for this use case, as it executes SQL automatically when a specific event occurs.

19. B. A stored procedure is ideal for this scenario, as it uses a precompiled set of SQL statements stored within the database and implements complex flow control logic with a single invocation. Functions are too limited in scope, and while triggers are useful for enforcing business rules, they don't provide the same flow control and reusability as stored procedures. A view is a virtual table presenting the result set of a SELECT statement and is inappropriate for this use case.

20. A. Using the BEGIN TRANSACTION command, Allison starts a new transaction and ensures that a series of SQL statements execute as a single atomic unit. If any statement within the transaction fails, the entire transaction will revert to its original state, maintaining data consistency. COMMIT saves the changes made by the statements in a transaction, ROLLBACK reverts any changes made during the current transaction, and SAVEPOINT creates a marker within the current transaction in case you don't want to revert all changes during a rollback.

Chapter 4: Database Deployment

1. A. Executive management are important data users, but they primarily use reporting tools to track operational performance and inform strategic decisions. They do not typically interact directly with the database and might not provide detailed input on specific design aspects.

   Regulators are concerned with compliance and regulatory aspects of the database, such as HIPAA or PCI DSS. Although important, their focus is not primarily on informing the database design but ensuring that it meets industry or government regulations.

   Legal teams review the database for compliance with legal requirements or litigation preparation. They are not directly involved in designing the database but might provide input on aspects related to legal compliance.

   End users are the ones who directly input or retrieve data from the database, making them essential stakeholders in gathering requirements to ensure the database meets their needs and expectations.

2. D. Data analysts use the database to perform complex queries, generate reports, and carry out other data-related tasks. While they are important stakeholders, they do not manage the servers where the database runs.

   Application developers write applications that interact with the database using programming languages like JavaScript, Java, and C#. While they contribute to the project, they do not directly manage the server infrastructure for the database.

   Database developers write SQL to create tables, views, stored procedures, and other database objects, so they might be involved in maintaining or upgrading the database. However, they do not directly operate the database servers.

   System administrators are responsible for operating the virtual or physical servers where the database runs. They handle tasks such as sizing servers, allocating and configuring disk space, and operating system upgrades and maintenance, making them essential stakeholders in gathering requirements for database design.

3. B. Data capture requirements are relevant when collecting, validating, and cleaning data, ensuring accuracy and completeness. While important, data capture is separate from determining the appropriate storage type for a database.

   Data processing techniques are essential when considering data aggregation, calculations, and transformations within the database. Although data processing is an important aspect of database management, it does not directly help determine the storage type for the database.

   Data security classifications help ensure the security and privacy of data stored in the database by grouping individual data elements into categories. While data security is a critical aspect of database management, it does not directly determine the appropriate storage type for a database.

   When determining the appropriate storage type for a database, Giacomo should consider the volume (how much data is stored) and the velocity (how quickly data changes). This analysis helps inform the size of the database and how much storage capacity it will need.

Depending on the results of this analysis, the company may choose to use solid-state drives (SSDs), hard disk drives (HDDs), or a combination of both for their storage needs.

4. C. A transactional database would provide real-time data access but is not ideal for historical reporting and analytical needs.

   Implementing a data warehouse would not provide real-time data access for medical staff, as data warehouses primarily store historical data and support analytical activities. Although a data warehouse can facilitate reports and business intelligence, it is not suitable for real-time transaction processing.

   Implementing a single use case database would not meet the requirements of providing real-time access to patient information for medical staff and historical reporting for the organization's management. When designing a database system with both transactional and analytical requirements, planning for a transactional database to support operational use cases and an analytical database for reporting purposes is best. The transactional database can handle real-time data access for medical staff, while the analytical database, such as a data warehouse, can facilitate historical reporting for the organization's management.

5. D. Data capture is a use-case category focusing on collecting, validating, and cleaning data for accuracy and completeness. While important, data capture does not directly address the company's requirements for analyzing historical sales data and predicting future trends.

   Data storage is a use case category that impacts the type of storage needed, informed by size and speed requirements. Although data storage is essential in designing the database, it does not directly address the company's requirements for analyzing historical sales data and predicting future trends.

   Data retrieval is a use-case category that focuses on how users access the data they need from the database. While data retrieval is essential in designing the database, it does not directly address the company's requirements for analyzing historical sales data and predicting future trends.

   The data analysis use-case category focuses on using data from the database to develop insights for making data informed decisions. Coleman can ensure that the e-commerce company's database supports data mining, predictive modeling, and trend analysis by focusing on data analysis. Data scientists are typically the primary constituents in this use-case category.

6. B. Infrastructure as a service (IaaS) is incorrect because, while it abstracts away physical hardware, engineers are still needed to build, operate, and maintain servers. IaaS offers less abstraction and less ease of administration compared to PaaS.

   Software as a service (SaaS) is incorrect because it delivers functioning software applications over the Internet, and the hardware, database version, and application software are opaque to the user. SaaS is unsuitable for Diane's organization's custom database infrastructure needs.

   On-premises data center is incorrect because Diane's organization wants to move its database to the cloud to ensure scalability and performance. An on-premises data center would not provide the flexibility and ease of management that cloud-based solutions offer.

Platform as a service (PaaS) is a cloud-computing tier that provides a platform for users to develop, deploy, and manage applications without worrying about the underlying infrastructure. It goes further than IaaS by abstracting the management of virtual servers and database software. PaaS providers offer various database-management tools and services, reducing the effort to administer, operate, monitor, backup, and recover the database. PaaS is the ideal choice for Diane's organization to maintain performance and scalability in a growing environment.

7. A. Platform as a service (PaaS) is not the correct answer because, although it also outsources the physical infrastructure, it abstracts the management of virtual servers and database software. As a result, Jenna would have less control and flexibility than IaaS.

   Software as a service (SaaS) is not the correct answer because it provides fully functioning software applications over the Internet, with hardware and database versions being opaque to the user. Jenna would have no control over the server configuration in a SaaS environment.

   On-premises environment is not the correct answer because it requires Jenna's organization to manage the physical infrastructure, including data centers, servers, and other hardware. This option doesn't fulfill her goal of outsourcing the physical infrastructure.

   Infrastructure as a service (IaaS) is the correct answer because it gives Jenna the flexibility and control she desires over server configuration while outsourcing the physical infrastructure. With IaaS, Jenna can customize virtual servers to meet the needs of her organization.

8. C. Physical schema design occurs after conceptual data modeling and logical design. It involves a detailed, low-level representation of the database structure, including technical details necessary for physical implementation.

   Logical schema design is also a later step in the design process, following conceptual data modeling. The goal of logical schema design is to refine the data model, identify the attributes of each entity, and normalize the structure of the entities.

   Implementing access controls is a way of implementing business requirements.

   Conceptual data modeling is the correct answer because it is the first step in the design process. It is a high-level representation of an organization's data that defines the relationships between entities without including implementation details. Conceptual data modeling aims to document an organization's business requirements and facilitate communication and collaboration between stakeholders, such as business analysts, developers, and end users.

9. B. First normal form (1NF) is incorrect because it only ensures that every row in a table is unique and every column contains a unique value. It does not specifically address the dependency of nonprimary key values on the primary key.

   Third normal form (3NF) is incorrect because it builds upon 2NF by adding a rule stating all columns must depend on only the primary key.

   Prime normal form (PNF) is a fictitious normal form.

   Second normal form (2NF) is the correct answer because it ensures that all nonprimary key values must depend on the entire primary key. 2NF picks up where 1NF leaves off, with each row being unique, and applies an additional rule to achieve the desired structure. This normal form helps eliminate redundancy and reduce the possibility of data anomalies.

10. B. A data dictionary provides valuable metadata about database objects' structure, definition, and relationships. However, it does not visually represent the database structure and the relationships between entities.

A business requirements document (BRD) outlines a project's high-level business objectives and requirements.

A functional requirements document (FRD) describes the functional requirements for a database, such as use cases, user roles, input and output requirements, and data processing rules.

An entity-relationship diagram (ERD) is a visual artifact representing entities and their relationships within a database. ERDs help administrators, developers, and analysts understand the database structure and the connections between entities.

11. B. Configuring the database server to use a static IP address does not enhance security, as a static IP provides a fixed address to the database server.

Disabling the firewall on the database server to allow unrestricted access does not distinguish between authorized and unauthorized database clients.

Placing the database and web application servers on the same public network exposes both servers to potential intruders, allowing them to attack the database server directly.

Placing the database server in a private network and implementing a perimeter network (also known as a demilitarized zone, or DMZ) is the best approach as it provides an additional layer of security by separating the database server from the public Internet.

12. B. Domain Name System (DNS) translates human-readable domain names into their corresponding Internet Protocol (IP) addresses. A database schema refers to the structure of the database and its data structures, not the security of network connections or the prevention of unauthorized access. A Dynamic Host Configuration Protocol (DHCP) server assigns dynamic IP addresses to clients and does not monitor or control network traffic.

A firewall is a security device that monitors and controls incoming and outgoing network traffic based on predetermined security rules. By properly setting up firewall configurations, Housni can control and monitor the traffic between clients and the database server, allowing only legitimate requests and blocking potential threats.

13. C. The default port for Oracle is 1521, the default for PostgreSQL is 5432, and the default for Db2 is 50000. 1433 is the default port for Microsoft SQL Server.

14. A. The Update, Delete, and Foreign Key Rules do not pertain to inserting new records. The Insert Rule says that when you insert a new record into a table with a foreign key, the foreign key value must match an existing primary key value in the related table.

15. D. A primary key constraint enforces uniqueness on the column(s) that make up the primary key, and its main purpose is to identify individual rows. A check constraint limits the range of values and does not prevent duplicate data in a column. A foreign key constraint enforces a relationship between two tables, ensuring referential integrity. A unique key constraint ensures that each value in a specific column is unique, effectively preventing duplicate data in that column.

16. B. Implementing range control using referential integrity limits the values in a column to a specific range, ensuring that the data remains consistent. Check constraints enforce domain restrictions on a column, such as limiting the range of values. A unique key constraint ensures that each value in a specific column is unique, preventing duplicate data in that column instead of improving the performance of a query retrieving data from multiple tables. Modifying the query to use a join instead of a nested subquery is generally more efficient than using a nested subquery. By using a join, Madeline can improve the performance of the query that retrieves data from multiple tables.

17. C. Regression testing re-executes existing tests to ensure that changes do not have unintended negative consequences. Negative testing provides invalid, unexpected, or incorrect inputs to ensure the database can handle such aberrant situations gracefully. Unit testing tests individual components or functions in isolation to ensure they perform as expected. Stress testing evaluates a database's performance, stability, and reliability under extreme conditions. By intentionally exceeding the target operating capacity of the database, Olivia can identify the system's breaking point and address potential bottlenecks and weaknesses.

18. C. Limiting the test data to a small number of customers can lead to inaccurate results due to caching data in RAM. Test environments should closely mimic the production environment to provide a more accurate understanding of how the production system will perform. Using invalid SQL queries falls under the scope of negative testing. Generating large amounts of synthetic data ensures that stress testing accurately reflects real-world scenarios.

19. C. Reducing the database's need to parse queries relates to using bind variables instead of hard-coded parameters in SQL queries. While it improves query consistency and performance, it does not address Samia's goal of retrieving all necessary data directly from an index.

    Ensuring data mapping consistency involves mapping data correctly when integrating multiple systems or migrating data from an existing database to a new one. Enforcing data integrity rules involves testing the enforcement of data integrity rules and constraints, such as primary keys, foreign keys, unique constraints, and check constraints.

    A covered query retrieves the required data directly from an index without accessing the base table data.

20. B. Data mapping consistently maps data elements to similar data types as data flows between the database and the systems it interacts with. Query validation tests the correctness and performance of SQL queries, stored procedures, and views within the database and connected applications. Index analysis focuses on analyzing and optimizing database indexes to improve query performance. Validating data values involves ensuring the accuracy, consistency, and completeness of data stored in the database.

Chapter 5: Database Management and Maintenance

1. C. Setting an alert threshold at 80 or 90 percent are incorrect because setting the threshold to 80 or 90 percent might not provide enough lead time to procure and install additional storage hardware. Ignoring the surge is also incorrect because, although 70 percent utilization might be within normal parameters, the unexpected surge in data suggests that the database could quickly reach its capacity, potentially leading to operational issues. Starting the procurement process and closely monitoring the growth rate is the most prudent course of action since the database grew rapidly in only a week.

2. A. While baselines help with forecasting storage requirements, the original scenario does not mention storage. The question does not mention batch processing inferred in logging job completion details. While providing a reference point is true, identifying whether the CPU change was normal or unexpected describes the real value in having a baseline so Vijay can compare the spike against past database behavior.

3. C. Database replication is incorrect because database replication concerns availability and redundancy rather than capacity planning or predicting future resource needs. Monitoring job completion is incorrect as it describes tracking the success or failure of database jobs, which doesn't involve predicting future resource needs or identifying usage trends. Database backups is incorrect because backups aren't the source of this growth.

   Kelly is using baseline configuration and trending to identify and predict storage consumption, making baseline configuration/trending the correct choice. Observing database growth at 100 GB/month helps her plan for future storage capacity needs effectively.

4. D. Database replication is incorrect since database replication improves database availability. Baseline configuration/trending is incorrect as it establishes a standard level of resource utilization to compare against future utilization. While Giancarlo is logging job details, system logs is not the best answer. This scenario describes a management-by-exception approach, as Giancarlo is crafting notifications only in a failure situation.

5. C. Baseline configuration/trending is incorrect as it establishes a standard level of resource utilization to compare against future utilization. Monitoring job completion/failure is incorrect, as monitoring job completion/failure involves checking the status of various database jobs and setting alerts for when jobs fail. While database backups are vital to data protection, database backups is incorrect since backups are offline copies of the database. In the scenario, Michela is creating a live copy of the database, which describes replication, making database replication the best option.

6. D. The change in CPU utilization could indicate any or all of the options provided. An expected increase in data volume could lead to higher CPU utilization. A missing index in the database could also result in higher CPU utilization as the database would need to scan more data. Similarly, a poorly performing set of queries could cause an increase in CPU utilization. Therefore, any of these changes could be responsible for increased CPU utilization.

7. C. Database integrity checks is incorrect as explain plans have nothing to do with validating data integrity. Load balancing is incorrect because load balancing involves distributing work across multiple servers. While a patch could impact how the optimizer executes a query, query optimization best describes what Melody needs to do next.

8. B. While fixing data in the production environment is important, it is not directly related to a release's planning phase, making fixing data in the production environment incorrect. Not all database releases require a database refresh, making allocating time for a database refresh incorrect. While testing the changes included in the release helps minimize downtime, determining the size and scope of the release during planning helps determine how to implement the change and impacts what needs testing, making size and scope the best option.

9. B. Germana needs to estimate the future storage, computing resources, and network bandwidth needs during capacity planning based on the organization's current operations, making estimating future needs the best choice. While a database release can impact capacity requirements, identifying its impact on capacity requirements is done during planning, making implementing changes incorrect. Testing changes is incorrect, as it relates to validating functionality, not capacity planning. While changes need CAB approval, it is not directly related to capacity planning.

10. C. The correct answer is executing database integrity checks. If Mahima suspects a data problem, she should first run database integrity checks. These checks verify referential, domain, and entity integrity, ensuring that relationships between tables are valid, column values conform to business rules and column definitions, and tables have primary keys. Nothing in the scenario implies a security vulnerability, making implementing a security patch incorrect. Checking audit logs would be useful if Mahima suspected a security breach or unauthorized access. Scheduling a system update may impact overall performance but does not address a specific data issue.

11. D. The correct answer is option D, Oracle SQL Developer Data Modeler, which Anitej can use to update an ERD and generate differential DDL. Microsoft Word and Google Schees are incorrect because Word and Sheets are not diagramming tools. While Anitej can maintain an ERD and generate DDL using Lucidchart, Lucidchart cannot generate differential DDL Oracle SQL Developer Data Modeler.

12. C. Of the options listed, Google Docs would be the most appropriate tool for maintaining a small data dictionary. Oracle SQL Developer Data Modeler, DbSchema, and Erwin are best suited for maintaining ERDs.

13. D. Lucidchart is a diagramming tool that supports Unified Modeling Language (UML) diagrams, making it the best choice for Meredith's needs. Microsoft Word is a word processor, Google Sheets is a spreadsheet tool, and DbSchema is a data modeling tool, none of which directly support modeling in UML.

14. B. In the healthcare industry, protecting sensitive patient data is a top priority due to laws such as the Health Insurance Portability and Accountability Act (HIPAA) in the United States. Therefore, the correct answer is option B. While understanding the system architecture is important for a new database administrator, other priorities take precedence in the context of regulatory requirements, making system architecture incorrect. Data protection is vital for any business, but less important than Security Management, making data backup and restoration incorrect. Performance tuning is incorrect, as performance has nothing to do with regulatory requirements.

15. C. Auditing procedures are critical in documenting compliance, making it the best answer. Although System Updates and Upgrades are crucial to keeping a database current, these activities don't directly address regulatory considerations data quality is incorrect, as data quality is only partially related to compliance. Not all change management procedures are crucial to compliance, making change management incorrect.

16. A. The correct answer is A. The ALTER TABLE command adds a new column to an existing table, and the ADD CONSTRAINT command applies the unique constraint. Option B is incorrect because it lacks the COLUMN keyword when attempting to add a new column, and the UNIQUE keyword is incorrect—the column name should be inside the parentheses. Option C is incorrect as the UNIQUE constraint is not correctly defined. The unique constraint name is missing after the ADD CONSTRAINT keyword, and the column name should be inside the parentheses after UNIQUE. Option D is incorrect because it lacks the COLUMN keyword when attempting to add a new column.

17. C. Configuring a materialized view that refreshes every 30 minutes would satisfy Jackson's need, making option C the best choice. Jackson has already optimized his query, making creating an index an invalid choice. A standard view wouldn't address the performance issue. Removing data could not be done without approval, making reducing the number of joins incorrect.

18. C. The correct answer is C. Lisa should implement a duplicate resolution process to identify and remove duplicate records from the customer database. Consolidating functionality into an API layer will help improve data sharing and SQL consistency across multiple systems. Manually deleting duplicated data is incorrect because manually deleting duplicates isn't scalable or reliable. Keeping separate databases is incorrect, as keeping databases separate without a plan to manage redundancy doesn't address the problem. Giving users a visual warning is incorrect because giving users a visual warning does not address the underlying data duplication.

19. B. By investing in a single database with multiple schemas, Miguel can better manage and reduce data redundancy. This approach allows for a shared schema with common attributes like name and address, leaving student- and employee-specific elements in their own schemas. An API layer ensures consistent and controlled access to the data across different systems, thereby improving data sharing and SQL consistency. Merging databases is incorrect because merging the two databases without considering the schema design leads to additional data inconsistency and could worsen redundancy. Manually updating data is incorrect because manually updating each student's data across both databases is tedious, time consuming, inefficient, and prone to error. Deleting a database is incorrect because deleting one of the databases doesn't solve the problem, since the university still needs to maintain student- and employee-specific data.

20. D. Modifying data or creating a view for the existing motorcycles are incorrect as the product owner is looking for information about the competition. While she may need a new table to store the information she needs to gather, creating a new data set using publicly available information best describes how Maddie can help collect the information product management wants.

Chapter 6: Governance, Security, and Compliance

1. C. Privilege creep occurs when an employee transfers within the organization and does not have their old privileges revoked. Privilege creep may occur when transfers are not properly processed and, if left unchecked, violates the principle of least privilege.

2. B. A data owner is a senior leader over a functional unit, a data steward is responsible for looking after an organization's data, and a data janitor is not a valid role.

3. D. Public applies to data intended for public consumption, internal applies to data for use within an organization, sensitive applies to data that is for limited use within an organization, and highly sensitive data is reserved for restricted use.

4. A. Public applies to data intended for public consumption, internal applies to data for use within an organization, sensitive applies to data that is for limited use within an organization, and highly sensitive data is reserved for restricted use.

5. C. With role-based access, Clarence should create a data access role that allows each person in a group to perform their job function. Five groups with three roles per group comes out at fifteen roles.

6. C. To keep his organizational data secure, Zeke needs to encrypt his data at rest as well as during transmission.

7. D. Maxine wants to ensure she is using HTTPS, which will appear in the browser's address bar at the beginning of the URL.

8. A. While aggregation is an option, it's not viable for individual images. While the data need to be encrypted, especially in transit, it is more important to de-identify. The sort order does not matter.

9. C. The point of this question is that it is possible, using zip code, sex, and birth date, to re-identify individuals making personal privacy at risk.

10. B. Passport number, credit card number, and address are all considered PII.

11. A. Name, account number, and expiration date are all classified as Cardholder Data under PCI DSS. Personal identification numbers (PINs) fall under the more restrictive category of Sensitive Authentication Data.

12. D. A passcode is an example of a knowledge-based authentication technique, or "something you know."

    Facial recognition technology is an example of a biometric authentication technique, or "something you are."

13. C. Gary is proving his identity with his fingerprint, a biometric mechanism. Steps that prove your identity are examples of authentication techniques.

14. D. A credential storage audit focuses on the security of stored sensitive information, such as passwords and API keys. In this scenario, Gwen discovered that sensitive API keys were located in a public code repository.

15. C. Mike should use pattern matching to meet this need. Pattern matching does not depend upon knowing where sensitive data is stored in advance and is ideal for detecting previously undetected cases of sensitive information storage. Watermarking is only useful when you are able to identify sensitive documents in advance. The trick to answering this question correctly is realizing that it is asking about the mechanism of action and not the environment (network-based or host-based).

16. B. Data masking is a technique used to protect sensitive information by obscuring it. Data masking does not use encryption but instead substitutes nonsensitive values to take the place of sensitive ones. Data masking does not copy or destroy data.

17. A. The European Union's General Data Protection Regulation (GDPR) applies to the personally identifiable information of European Union residents. The Health Insurance Portability and Accountability Act (HIPAA) applies to protected health information (PHI) in the United States. The Gramm Leach Bliley Act (GLBA) applies to personal financial information in the United States. PCI DSS is a private regulation, not a law, and it only applies to credit and debit card data, which is not mentioned in this scenario.

18. C. This is an example of a password complexity requirement. The message is requiring that Andy use a symbol in his password, and password complexity requirements require the use of different character types.

    There is no indication that Andy is attempting to reuse an old password that would violate a password history requirement or use a password from another site that would violate a password reuse requirement. There is also no indication that his password is too short and does not meet the password length requirements.

19. A. The primary risk here is that some of your customers are using the same password on your competitor's site and your site. If the breach compromised passwords, the attacker would be able to use credentials from the other site to access accounts on your site. A password reuse policy would protect against this risk.

    Password length and complexity requirements ensure that users create strong passwords, but the strength of the password is not in question here. If the attacker is able to obtain the passwords from another site, it does not matter how strong they are.

    Password history requirements may be of some use in this situation because they would prevent a user from reusing the compromised password at a later date, but that is not the primary threat here. The major risk is that an account will be compromised now because it shares a password with an account on the compromised site.

20. B. A connection request audit is the best fit for Renee's concern because it focuses on tracking and reviewing the incoming requests made to the database. By conducting a connection request audit, Renee can determine if any unauthorized applications have been accessing her database and gather information to help secure it.

Chapter 7: Database Security

1. B. Port security restricts the number of unique MAC addresses that may originate from a single switch port. It is commonly used to prevent someone from unplugging an authorized device from the network and connecting an unauthorized device but may also be used to prevent existing devices from spoofing MAC addresses of other devices.

2. C. Motion-detecting cameras can be used to help conserve storage space for video by only recording when motion is detected. In low-usage spaces like data centers, this means recording will only occur occasionally. In more heavily used areas, the impact on total space used will be smaller but can still be meaningful, particularly after business hours. Infrared cameras, facial recognition, and the ability to pan, tilt, and zoom (PTZ) a camera are important features but do not help to conserve storage space.

3. C. Security guards can be one of the costliest physical security controls over time, making the cost of guards one of the most important deciding factors guiding when and where they will be employed. Reliability, training, and the potential for social engineering are all possible issues with security guards, but they are not the major driver in the decision process.

4. B. Input allow-listing approaches define the specific input type or range that users may provide. When developers can write clear business rules defining allowable user input, allow-listing is definitely the most effective way to prevent injection attacks.

5. D. Web application firewalls must be placed in front of web servers. This requirement rules out location C as an option. The next consideration is placing the WAF so that it can filter all traffic headed for the web server but sees a minimum amount of extraneous traffic. This makes location D the best option for placing a WAF.

6. A. The use of the SQL `WAITFOR` command is a signature characteristic of a timing-based SQL injection attack.

7. A. Database servers should be accessible only to internal systems and users, so they belong on the internal network. Database servers should not be accessible to the general public and, therefore, they should not be placed in a DMZ. Screened subnet is simply another name for the DMZ. The Internet zone is completely unprotected by the firewall and is, therefore, also not appropriate for a database server.

8. C. Pre-action systems fill when a potential fire is detected and then release at specific sprinkler heads as they are activated by heat. Dry pipe, wet pipe, and deluge systems all release water from all sprinkler heads when the system is activated.

9. C. Fingerprint scans are an example of biometric authentication ("something you are") and would complement the use of an identification card (a "something you have" factor) to provide multifactor authentication. Using a PIN or password ("something you know") would also provide multifactor authentication but they are not biometric. Using a smartphone app would not provide multifactor authentication because, like the ID card, it is also an example of "something you have."

10. A. Data centers design facilities around the use of hot aisles and cold aisles. This approach allows data centers to more efficiently house servers and other devices that generate large amounts of heat and require cool air intake. A hot aisle/cold aisle design places air intakes and exhausts on alternating aisles to ensure proper airflow, allowing data center designers to know where to provide cool air and where exhaust needs to be handled. The temperature and dew-point values provided in other answer choices all fit within the acceptable ranges provided by ASHRAE (temperature between 64.4–80.6 degrees Fahrenheit and dew point between 41.9–50.0 degrees Fahrenheit).

11. B. This is a clear example of a distributed denial-of-service (DDoS) attack. The half-open connections indicate the use of a denial-of-service attack. The fact that the requests came from all over the world makes it clear that it is more than a standard denial-of-service attack. There is no indication that there was a web application flaw, such as cross-site request forgery or cross-site scripting.

12. A. In this figure, Mal is intercepting the traffic that Alice is sending to the database server and passing it along to the database. This is an example of an on-path attack.

13. A. Answering this question correctly is a little confusing because there are two possible correct answers. This is a common occurrence on CompTIA exams. This is definitely a phishing attack, because it is soliciting sensitive information from customers over email. However, it is better described as a spearphishing attack because it was not sent blindly to many recipients but rather targeted at individuals who are actually customers of the company. It is not a whaling attack because it did not target a high-value individual. It is not an SQL injection attack because no attempt was made to access a database. When answering exam questions, keep an eye out for cases where two answers might be correct and then choose the one that is the BEST answer.

14. D. Messages similar to the one shown in the figure are indicative of a ransomware attack. The attacker encrypts files on a user's hard drive and then demands a ransom, normally paid in Bitcoin, for the decryption key required to restore access to the original content.

15. B. Worms have built-in propagation mechanisms that do not require user interaction, such as scanning for systems containing known vulnerabilities and then exploiting those vulnerabilities to gain access. Viruses and Trojan horses typically require user interaction to spread. Logic bombs do not spread from system to system but lie in wait until certain conditions are met, triggering the delivery of their payload.

16. B. Virtual LANs (VLANs) allow you to logically group together related systems, regardless of where they normally exist on the network. Firewalls are used to restrict the traffic that may enter and leave a network. Port security is used to limit the devices that may physically connect to a network. Biometrics are used to control access to systems and facilities.

17. A. Port security is a switch-based control that is used to limit the devices that may connect to a physical switch port based upon their MAC address.

18. D. Signature detection uses databases of known malware patterns and scans the files and memory of a system for any data matching the pattern of known malicious software. Behavior detection takes a different approach. Instead of using patterns of known malicious

activity, these systems attempt to model normal activity and then report when they discover anomalies—activity that deviates from that normal pattern. Blind detection and rapid detection are not malware detection techniques.

19. A. This is a straightforward phishing attack. The message is generic and not targeted at a specific user, as you would find in a spearphishing attack. Although the user is an executive, there is no indication that the message was specifically sent to this user because of his status as an executive, so it is not likely a whaling attack. The attack was sent over email, not the telephone, so it is not an example of vishing.

20. D. This is an example of a credential-stuffing attack where the attacker stole a set of usernames and passwords from a website and then used those same username/password combinations to attempt to log into other sites. Brute-force attacks simply try to guess a user's password by trying all possible combinations. Dictionary attacks refine brute-force attacks by using words found in a master dictionary to inform guesses. Password-spraying attacks are a form of brute-force attack that attempts to use a single password or a small set of passwords against many accounts.

Chapter 8: Business Continuity

1. C. Once a disaster interrupts the business operations, the goal of DRP is to restore regular business activity as quickly as possible. Thus, disaster recovery planning picks up where business continuity planning leaves off. Preventing business interruption is the goal of business continuity, not disaster recovery programs. While disaster recovery programs are involved in setting up temporary operations and minimizing the impact of disasters, this is not their end goal.

2. C. The recovery point objective (RPO) specifies the maximum amount of data that may be lost during a disaster and should be used to guide backup strategies. The maximum tolerable downtime (MTD) and recovery time objective (RTO) are related to the duration of an outage, rather than the amount of data lost. The mean time between failures (MTBF) is related to the frequency of failure events.

3. D. The lessons learned session captures discoveries made during the disaster recovery process and facilitates continuous improvement. It may identify deficiencies in training and awareness or the impact analysis.

4. C. Cloud computing services provide an excellent location for backup storage because they are accessible from any location. The primary data center is a poor choice, as it may be damaged during a disaster. A field office is reasonable, but it is in a specific location and is not as flexible as a cloud-based approach. The IT manager's home is a poor choice, as the IT manager may leave the organization or may not have appropriate environmental and physical security controls in place.

5. D. When you use remote mirroring, an exact copy of the database is maintained at an alternative location. You keep the remote copy up-to-date by executing all transactions on both the primary and remote site at the same time. Database dumping follows a similar process of storing all data at the remote location, but it does not do so in real time. Transaction logging and log shipping send logs, rather than full data replicas, to the remote location.

6. C. An uninterruptible power supply (UPS) provides a battery-backed source of power that is capable of preserving operations in the event of brief power outages. Generators take a significant amount of time to start and are more suitable for longer-term outages. Dual power supplies protect against power supply failures and not power outages. Redundant network links are a network continuity control and do not provide power.

7. D. The parallel test involves relocating personnel to the alternate recovery site and implementing site activation procedures. Checklist tests, structured walk-throughs, and simulations are all test types that do not involve actually activating the alternate site.

8. D. Differential backups copy all files modified since the most recent full backup. Incremental backups copy all files that have been modified since the most recent full or incremental backup. Full backups copy all files. Transaction log backups copy database transactions, rather than files.

9. A. Any backup strategy must include full backups at some point in the process. If a combination of full and differential backups is used, a maximum of two backups must be restored. If a combination of full and incremental backups is chosen, the number of required restorations may be large.

10. B. Parallel tests involve moving personnel to the recovery site and gearing up operations, but responsibility for conducting day-to-day operations of the business remains at the primary operations center.

11. D. Full-interruption tests are the only type of test where the primary data center is shut down. Parallel tests also activate the alternate processing facility but do not shift operational responsibility away from the primary data center. Simulations and walk-throughs do not activate the alternate site.

12. A. Remote mirroring technology maintains mirrored images of servers at both the primary and alternate sites. Database dumping copies full data to a backup site but does not do so in real time. Log shipping copies only transaction log entries to the remote site. Fault tolerance is a mechanism to increase the resilience of technology systems against failures.

13. C. With differential backups, Barbara must first restore the most recent full backup and then apply the most recent differential backup.

14. C. Simulation tests are similar to structured walk-throughs. In simulation tests, disaster recovery team members are presented with a scenario and asked to develop an appropriate response. That is the case in David's earthquake exercise. There is no activation of any alternate facility, as would take place in a full-interruption or parallel test.

15. A. The end goal of a disaster recovery effort is to transition back to normal operations. Kayleigh's work is not complete when the temporary database is up and running. The effort continues until the organization returns to a permanent state.

16. C. It is difficult to put a dollar figure on the business lost because of negative publicity. Therefore, this type of concern is better evaluated through a qualitative analysis. The other items listed here are all more easily quantifiable.

17. B. Redundant arrays of inexpensive disks (RAID) are a fault tolerance control that allow an organization's storage service to withstand the loss of one or more individual disks. Load balancing, clustering, and HA pairs are all fault-tolerance services designed for server compute capacity, not storage.

18. C. All of these are good practices that could help improve the quality of service that Bryn provides from her website. Installing dual power supplies or deploying RAID arrays could reduce the likelihood of a server failure, but these measures only protect against a single risk each. Deploying multiple servers behind a load balancer is the best option because it protects against any type of risk that would cause a server failure. Backups are an important control for recovering operations after a disaster and different backup strategies could indeed alter the RTO, but it is even better if Bryn can design a web architecture that lowers the risk of the outage occurring in the first place.

19. D. Disaster recovery plans tend to be tactical and describe technical activities such as recovery sites, backups, and fault tolerance. Business continuity activities are typically more strategically focused and center themselves on business processes and operations. The systems security plan focuses on the security controls that should be put in place during a disaster, and build documentation contains details on how to build new systems.

20. D. Virtual tape libraries (VTL) are used to make disk-based storage appear as tape libraries to backup software expecting tapes. This is used to support disk-to-disk (D2D) backups, but D2D technology alone does not provide this functionality. Journaling is a backup technique used to write changes to a transaction log that is backed up. Virtual Local Area Networks (VLANs) are used to perform network segmentation and are not a backup technology.

Index

A

B

C

D

E

F

G

H

I

J

K

L

M

N

O

P

Q

R

S

T

U

V

W

Online Test Bank

To help you study for your CompTIA DataSys+ certification exam, register to gain one year of FREE access after activation to the online interactive test bank—included with your purchase of this book! All of the practice questions in this book are included in the online test bank so you can study in a timed and graded setting.

Register and Access the Online Test Bank

To register your book and get access to the online test bank, follow these steps:

1. Go to `www.wiley.com/go/sybextestprep`. You'll see the "**How to Register Your Book for Online Access**" instructions.
2. Click "here to register" and then select your book from the list.
3. Complete the required registration information, including answering the security verification to prove book ownership. You will be emailed a pin code.
4. Follow the directions in the email or go to `www.wiley.com/go/sybextestprep`.
5. Find your book on that page and click the "Register or Login" link with it. Then enter the pin code you received and click the "Activate PIN" button.
6. On the Create an Account or Login page, enter your username and password, and click Login or, if you don't have an account already, create a new account.
7. At this point, you should be in the test bank site with your new test bank listed at the top of the page. If you do not see it there, please refresh the page or log out and log back in.